# OCR
**National** Level 3

# Business

Karen Hough
Jackie Tye
Nick Colburn

Approved publication
**OCR**
RECOGNISING ACHIEVEMENT

**www.heinemann.co.uk**
✓ Free online support
✓ Useful weblinks
✓ 24 hour online ordering

**01865 888058**

**Heinemann**
*Inspiring generations*

Heinemann Educational Publishers
Halley Court, Jordan Hill, Oxford OX2 8EJ
Part of Harcourt Education

Heinemann is the registered trademark of
Harcourt Education Limited

© Karen Hough, Jackie Tye, Nick Colburn 2006

First published 2006

10 09 08 07 06
10 9 8 7 6 5 4 3 2 1

British Library Cataloguing in Publication Data is available
from the British Library on request.

10-digit ISBN: 0 435 44980 X
13-digit ISBN: 978 0 435 44980 3

Typeset and illustrated by Saxon Graphics Ltd, Derby

Original illustrations © Harcourt Education Limited, 2006

Cover design by Peter Stratton

Printed in the UK at Bath Press

Websites
Please note that the examples of websites suggested in this book were up to date at the time of writing. It is essential for tutors to preview each site before using it to ensure that the URL is still accurate and the content is appropriate. We suggest that tutors bookmark useful sites and consider enabling students to access them through the school or college intranet.

# Contents

## Acknowledgements

The author and publisher would like to thank the following for permission to reproduce copyright material:

AOL (UK) Ltd.
BARB (British Audience Research Board)
*Businesslink.gov.uk*
Corby Borough Council (*corby.gov.uk*)
Department of Trade and Industry
*Direct.gov.uk*
Equal Opportunities Commission (*eoc.org.uk*)
Federation of Small Businesses
*Kelkoo.co.uk*
Liverpool Victoris
Lloyds TSB Group plc
*Meeting.co.uk*
Nationwide
Office of National Statistics
*Play.com*
*The News*, Portsmouth
Travelodge
Vodafone
Yahoo! Inc.
*Young Entrepreneurs Revisited* by Gerard Darby

Microsoft product screen shot(s) reprinted with permission from Microsoft Corporation.

Crown copyright material is reproduced under Class License No. C01W0000141 with the permission of the Controller of HMSO and the Queen's Printer in Scotland.

Every effort has been made to contact copyright holders of material reproduced in this book. We would be glad to hear from any unacknowledged sources at the first opportunity. Any omissions will be rectified in subsequent printings if notice is given to the publishers.

The author and publisher would like to thank the following for permission to reproduce photographs:

Alamy Images, pages 59, 242, 251, 263
Corbis, page 317
Corbis/ Andrew Fox, page 161
Corbis/ Franz-Marc Frei, page 145
Corbis/ Helen King, page 298
Corbis/ Mark Bolton, page 104
Corbis/ Muriel Dovic, page 181
Corbis/ Owen Franken, page 375
Corbis/ Reuters, pages 1, 216
Corbis/ Stock Photos/Zefa, page 295
Gareth Boden, page 8
Getty Images, page 45
Getty Images (Editorial), page 15
Getty Images/ Imagebank, pages 62, 176, 192, 209, 315, 350, 362
Getty Images/ Photodisc, pages 81, 89, 149, 199, 355
Getty Images/ Stone, page 335
Getty Images/ Taxi, pages 110, 131, 137, 343
Maria Joannou, pages 48, 211, 225, 227, 236, 243, 279, 283
Rex Features/ Alex Segre, pages 67, 267
Rex Features/ Brian Smith, page 254
Rex Features/ BYB, page 34
Rex Features/ Clive Dixon, page 304
Rex Features/ David Hartley, page 26
Rex Features/ Jonathan Banks, page 231
Rex Features/ Nicholas Bailey, page 232
Rex Features/ Per Lindgren, page 240
Will Burgess/Reuters/Corbis, page 37

# Introduction

This book has been written to help you achieve your OCR Level 3 National Certificate in Business.

In order to achieve the qualification you are required to:

- pass six units to gain the certificate
- pass twelve units to gain the diploma
- pass eighteen units to gain the extended diploma.

Units are achieved through the preparation of assignments. Four of the assignments are mandatory – this means they are compulsory. The other units are chosen from the option units. All units are weighted equally and each contributes a sixth, twelfth or eighteenth to your overall qualification.

In order to pass an assignment you will need to produce evidence that is proof that you have met the requirements of the unit.

Evidence could be:

- completed assignments or projects
- products of real work that you have completed during work experience
- statements from witnesses
- records made by your assessor when observing you carrying out your work.

Evidence could be anything that proves:

- what you can do
- how well you can do it
- the level of knowledge that you have in relation to what you do
- the level of understanding you have about what you do, how you do it and why you do it.

The mandatory units in this book are:

Unit 1:     Investigating business
Unit 2:     Customer service
Unit 3:     Business communications
Unit 4:     Finance for business

The option units are:

Unit 5:     Marketing for business
Unit 12:    Skills and the entrepreneur
Unit 17:    Recruitment and selection
Unit 21:    Practical administration

All units are broken down in exactly the same way. Every unit is introduced with a learning outcome. The learning outcome section describes what you will achieve while completing the unit.

Assessment objectives describe what you are required to do in order to achieve the learning outcome. You must achieve every assessment objective in the unit.

Assessment objectives are further broken down into knowledge, understanding and skills. This section provides further clarification of the type of evidence required in order to achieve the assessment objective.

Your assignments will be marked against clearly laid-out grading descriptions.

You are able to achieve a pass (1 point), merit (2 points) or distinction (3 points) for each unit. You must achieve all units in order to pass the six unit qualification. However, there is compensation for the twelve and eighteen unit award. In order to calculate your overall grade you will need the following points:

National Certificate in Business (6 units)

- Pass – 6 points
- Merit – 10 points
- Distinction – 14 points

National Diploma in Business (12 units)

- Pass – 12 points
- Merit – 20 points
- Distinction – 28 points

National Extended Diploma in Business

- Pass – 18 points
- Merit – 30 points
- Distinction – 42 points

The layout of the book has been designed to enable you to work through each unit easily. Each unit is laid out in assessment objective order. All the knowledge, skills and understanding have also been clearly explained. Each section contains exercises to help you understand the theory being covered. You will also find portfolio tips to help you with your assignments.

Remember that if you find some of the information confusing or overwhelming at the beginning of the course you should seek help from your course tutor.

We hope that you find the book interesting, enjoyable and that it fully supports you through your studies.

Nick Colburn
Karen Hough
Jackie Tye

# Investigating business

## Getting started

In your daily life you come into contact with many different types of business ranging from newsagents to banks and supermarkets to bus companies. This unit investigates the different types of business organisation that exist.

To complete this unit successfully you will need to produce portfolio evidence, which includes an investigation into a business organisation, and carry out a presentation. You will need to address the eight assessment objectives in the specification. In this unit you will look at the aims of business and the different forms of business ownership. You will investigate in detail how a business is structured and why organisations may change over time. You will also look at the various groups which have an interest in the activities of a business, known as stakeholders, and you will consider the various factors which influence where the business is located and why a business may wish to relocate. You will examine the competitive environment in which the business operates, identify trends in an industrial sector and look at how the business maintains its competitive position. You should apply the information in this unit to your chosen businesses.

### This unit will cover

- AO1 Investigate three contrasting businesses and describe their aims and objectives and current forms of ownership.
- AO2 Explain why one of the selected businesses might wish to change its form of ownership in the future.

- AO3 Investigate the internal structure and functional areas of a selected business and explain how its internal structure and functional areas have changed over time.

- AO4 Explain the roles of both internal and external stakeholders in the selected business and show how their objectives and expectations have changed over time.

- AO5 Investigate and explain the reasons for the location of the selected business and explain why the selected business might wish to relocate in the future.

- AO6 Explain the competitive environment in which the business operates and any legislative constraints affecting its ability to compete in the future.

- AO7 Illustrate the growth or decline of the industrial sector associated with the business selected, in comparison with other industrial sectors.

- AO8 Carry out a presentation to explain how the business maintains its competitive position and propose appropriate strategies to improve this level of competitiveness in the future.

# AO1 Investigate three contrasting businesses and describe their aims and objectives and current forms of ownership

Businesses vary considerably in terms of what they are trying to achieve and in terms of their form or ownership. We will now investigate these areas.

## Aims

Aims are the long-term goals of a business organisation. Businesses may have a number of aims which will influence the way in which they behave. Corporate aims help to build commitment within the business and give employees an understanding of what the business is about. Some businesses develop **mission statements** which state the long-term aims of the business.

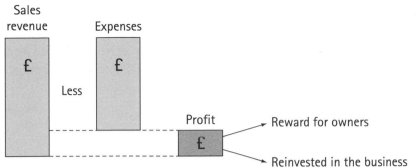

**Figure 1.1** *The role of profit in business*

## Financial

The owners of a business, sometimes called **entrepreneurs**, risk their capital in a business and profit is their reward for risk-taking. If a business is to grow it will need to earn **profit**. Some of the profit can be put back or reinvested into the business to buy new equipment or vehicles, expand the premises or take on additional staff. In the long run the business must generate a profit if it is to survive and grow.

## Ethical

Businesses may also have other important aims. Some businesses take a strong **ethical stance** on issues such as the environment or fair trade. Café Direct is the UK's largest fair trade hot drinks company and one of its key aims is to provide reasonable incomes for the coffee and tea growers who supply the business.

## Market centred

Businesses such as Coca Cola, McDonalds and Tesco have **market-centred** aims such as maintaining market leadership. The Kraft food group, which owns brands such as Kenco, Maxwell House, Dairylea and Terrys, states 'Our brands are among the leaders in the UK market and many are household names.' Maintaining this position will be a key objective for the business (www.kraftfoods.co.uk).

### Real business

All private sector businesses have the key aim of making a **profit**. If the **sales revenue** coming in from selling a product or service is greater than the total costs involved in making or supplying it, then business has made a profit.

## ACTIVITY

In pairs or small groups decide what you think are the aims of the following organisations:
1   your college or school
2   Cadburys
3   a new car valeting service set up locally
4   Greenpeace
5   Chelsea Football Club.

## Customer centred

Some businesses put a strong emphasis on putting the customer's needs first and their aims are therefore said to be **customer centred**. The aims of such a business will be to provide high levels of customer satisfaction with products and services.

# Objectives

Objectives are the goals which, if achieved, will enable the business to achieve its longer term aims. If managers and the workforce understand and are committed to their objectives, then the business is much more likely to be successful.

Objectives may be **financial**, e.g. to achieve a 20 per cent return on capital, or **market-based**, e.g. market growth. **Market share** may be of crucial interest to many businesses. Market share is the proportion of the total market sales that are made by one company, brand or product. Market share can be calculated by the formula:

$$\frac{\text{Sales of brand X}}{\text{Total market sales}} \times 100 = \text{Percentage market share}$$

**QUESTIONS**

'Glitz' brand nail polish achieved sales of £12m in a market estimated to be worth £240m. Calculate the market share for 'Glitz'.

The firm or brand that has the biggest market share is known as the **market leader**. If a market is growing then all of the businesses in that market may see their sales rise.

However, if a firm is able to increase its market share, it shows that it is winning customers from its competitors so many businesses have increasing market share as one of their key objectives.

Businesses such as pharmaceutical and electronics companies have a strong emphasis on **research and development (R&D)**, developing new products and technologies. If these companies do not constantly strive to develop new products their profitability will fall as they are overtaken by more innovative rivals.

## SMART objectives

Whatever the objectives that a business sets itself, it is important that they are SMART:

S – Specific
M – Measurable
A – Attainable
R – Realistic
T – Timed

**Real business**

Tesco is the market leader in the UK supermarket business. In April 2005 Tesco announced annual profits of £2.03bn. Over this period, Tesco achieved sales of £29.5bn, well ahead of rivals Asda and Sainsbury. One of Tesco's key aims is to maintain its market leadership.

## Specific

The target must be clear and unambiguous so that all staff involved know exactly what they are trying to achieve. Managers will have to communicate objectives to their staff and gain their commitment. Demanding that staff simply 'work harder' is not a SMART objective whereas aiming to reduce the number of defective products by 5 per cent is a more specific target.

## Measurable

The objectives should be measurable so that it is possible to see whether the objective has been achieved. This is fairly straightforward in areas such as sales where a measurable target might be to increase sales by 3 per cent. However, if the business is aiming to improve product or service quality then it will need to develop ways of measuring improvements. It may need to record the amount of waste or monitor the number of complaints being received about products so that improvements can be measured.

## Attainable

The targets set must be attainable or achievable given the financial and human resources of the business. Attainable is seen by many as being the same as **realistic,** so some business writers prefer to use **agreed** when talking about SMART targets. A target is much more likely to be hit by workers if it has been discussed with them and they have agreed that it is a realistic target.

## Realistic

Realistic means that employees must believe that the target can be achieved. The business must take into account its size, expertise and financial resources when setting targets. It would be totally unrealistic for a new soft drinks manufacturer to set an objective of becoming the best-selling soft drinks company in the UK given the market strength of Coca Cola and Pepsi. If employees feel that targets are not realistic then they are unlikely to be motivated to achieve them. For example, if a car salesman is told to increase his monthly sales figure by 50 per cent when new car sales are falling nationally, he may feel that the target is unfair and unrealistic and he may become de-motivated in his work.

## Timed

The objective must be set within an appropriate time frame. When do we wish this objective to be achieved? Is it within the next month or the next year? A time scale will help staff to prioritise and focus on objectives. If students are given three months to complete an assignment at college, then many will not regard it as a priority and will not start working on it immediately. Similarly, an employee is likely to be less motivated to achieve a longer-term objective, e.g. within the next five years, than a short-term one, e.g. within the next month.

## ACTIVITY

A sales manager has been given the target of increasing sales by at least 5 per cent. The current value of sales is £200,000 per month. What is the new monthly sales target?

## ACTIVITY

For the completion of your Unit 1 assignment write a SMART target for a manager responsible for the launch of a new body spray for men.

# Forms of ownership

Businesses in the UK range from small, one-person businesses, such as a self-employed plumber, to large organisations, such as supermarkets and oil companies. When setting up in business for the first time the owners will have to decide upon the legal structure of their business based upon their aims, the amount of money they have to invest and how much risk they wish to take. Over time, the business may grow and its aims may change. The owners may then decide to change the legal structure of the business to adapt to the new circumstances. The main forms of business ownership are:

- sole trader
- partnership
- private limited company
- public limited company
- franchise
- worker co-operative
- building and friendly societies
- charities.

## Sole trader

Sole traders, or sole proprietors, are the simplest form of business organisation in the UK. There are very few legal formalities in most cases, though a licence may be required to run a business such as a pub or a taxi firm. The owner may employ workers to work in the business but there is only one legal owner. This means that the owner has a great deal of freedom in how they run the business and they are able to make all their own decisions and keep all of the profits. However, they are likely to have a heavy workload as they will have to deal with customers and suppliers, do their own accounts and all of the many other things involved in running their own business. Taking holidays can be difficult and a long period of illness may mean that no income is earned. Sole proprietors have **unlimited liability**, meaning that if the business fails the owner may have to sell off their own assets, such as their house, to pay off debts of the business. This can make being a sole proprietor a stressful occupation if the business is not going well. Typical sole traders might be small newsagents, hairdressers, decorators and window cleaners.

## GLOSSARY

**Unlimited liability**: where the business is unable to pay its debts, the owners may have to sell off their own possessions, e.g. their house, to pay their creditors (people who are owed money by the business).

## CASE STUDY

*'When I'm cleaning windows...'*

George Crosby set up his own window cleaning business following the closure of a local factory where he had been employed for 11 years. George was a relatively unskilled worker and spent several months unemployed before deciding to run his own business.

1 Outline three advantages of George running his own business.
2 Outline three drawbacks of George being self-employed.

## Partnerships

A **partnership** is a business owned by between two and twenty partners. Partnerships are common in professions such as solicitors, accountants and doctors. They are easy to set up but it is usually sensible to draw up a **partnership agreement**, or **Deed of Partnership**, which sets out how profits will be shared, how much salary each will earn and what will happen if a partner wishes to leave. This can help to resolve any disputes in the future between partners. **Silent**, or **sleeping**, **partners** invest money in the business but take no part in the running of it.

### Advantages of partnerships

- Taking on new partners is a way of bringing new capital into the business.
- A new partner may bring fresh ideas and enthusiasm into the business.
- The workload can be shared among the partners.
- Partners may be able to specialise in the area in which they have skills and experience.

### Drawbacks of partnerships

- In an ordinary partnership all of the partners have **unlimited liability** and they are all liable for the debts of the business so it is important that they trust each other and know what is going on in the business.
- There may be disagreements between the partners which can make decision-making a slow and difficult process.
- The retirement or death of one of the partners can cause serious problems. The retiring partner or the family of the deceased partner will probably want their share of the assets and the remaining partners will have to find the money to buy them out.

## CASE STUDY

*Hard as Nails*

On leaving college, Natasha, Thea and Rochelle decide to open their own nail bar. Thea and Rochelle will each work full-time but Natasha will only work three days as she will be working in her mother's beauty salon for the rest of the week. Natasha's mother is willing to invest in the business but will not work in it.

The business is to be organised as a partnership and each partner will contribute the following amounts of capital:

| | |
|---|---|
| Natasha | £1,000 |
| Natasha's mother | £2,000 |
| Thea | £2,000 |
| Rochelle | £1,000 |

1  Why might disagreements arise between the partners?
2  Working in pairs or small groups, draw up a partnership agreement for this business. You should consider issues such as:
   - how profits/losses will be shared
   - how major decisions will be reached
   - what will happen if one of the partners wishes to leave the partnership.

---

## GLOSSARY

**Limited liability:** where shareholders only risk the money that they have invested in the business. Their own assets are not at risk if the business fails.

## Private limited companies

Private limited companies (Ltds) are businesses owned by **shareholders** who have bought shares in the company. They enjoy the advantage of **limited liability**. This means that if the business fails, the shareholders only lose the money invested in the business and their own personal assets, such as their home, are not at risk. This makes people more willing to invest their money in the business as the risk is reduced but shares cannot be sold on the Stock Exchange. There are more legal formalities involved in setting up this type of business and two important documents that are required are outlined below.

- **Memorandum of association.** This gives the outline of the company with information such as its name, registered address, its aims and the amount of authorised capital. In some ways it is like the birth certificate of a company, giving the business its legal identity.

- **Articles of association.** This document gives details of the number of directors, how meetings are conducted, voting rights and other information about the company's ownership and structure.

The business must comply with various Companies Acts and the company's accounts must be independently audited annually. Profits are subject to corporation tax rather than income tax. The company has its own legal identity, meaning that it can sue and be sued and it will still exist even if one or more of the shareholders dies.

The shareholders elect a **board of directors** to run the company and if the business is profitable the shareholders may receive a **dividend**. Ordinary shares carry voting rights and the more shares a shareholder owns, the more votes they have. If one shareholder has over 50 per cent of the shares they effectively control the business. Selling new shares is a way of raising more capital to expand the business. However, in a Ltd shares cannot be sold to the general public and so the shares are not traded on the Stock Exchange. If shareholders wish to sell shares they can only do so with the consent of the other shareholders. In a small Ltd there may only be a small number of shareholders and quite often the directors and the shareholders are the same people.

Private limited companies range from small-scale businesses with only two shareholders to firms as large as the Virgin Group. The majority, however, tend to be small or medium-sized businesses such as local building firms, printers etc. Most football clubs outside the Premiership are Ltds.

## ACTIVITY

Imagine that you have been asked to give advice to a group of individuals who are all interested in setting up their own businesses. In pairs or small groups prepare and give a five minute presentation outlining the advantages and disadvantages of sole proprietors, partnerships and private limited companies as forms of ownership.

### Real business

*A dividend is a share of the company's profit. Dividends are not guaranteed and if the business suffers a loss there will be no dividend payment for shareholders. Tesco announced record profits of £1.96bn for the year ending 26 February 2005. Shareholders received a dividend of 7.56p per share.*

## Public limited companies

Public limited companies (plcs), such Barclays plc and Vodafone plc, are the giants of the business world. Their shares can be bought and sold on the stock market and the business is able to raise millions of pounds of capital by selling shares to the public. When a plc sells shares on the stock market for the first time, this is known as a **flotation**. They must sell at least £50,000 of shares. Plcs are expensive to set up, however, as there are far more legal formalities than for any of the other types of organisation above, and it is not realistic to float on the stock market unless the business wishes to raise several million pounds. Plcs have to abide by the Companies Acts, Stock Exchange rules and publish their accounts.

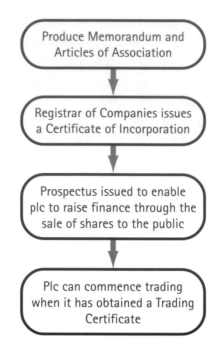

**Figure 1.2** *The stages in setting up a public company*

It is not possible to keep the affairs of a plc secret as accounts are published and anyone can purchase shares in the business. There is also a risk that a plc may be taken over by an organisation or individual buying over 50 per cent of the voting shares in the company. This is known as a **takeover**. If the share price of a plc falls they will become vulnerable to such a takeover because a potential buyer is able to buy the shares cheaply.

## The divorce between ownership and control

The phrase 'divorce between ownership and control' means that in larger businesses, the owners do not run and control the business. A limited liability company is owned by shareholders but the decisions about how it is run are made by the directors. In a small, family-run private limited company, it is likely that there will be only a few shareholders and they will also be the directors. However, in a large plc, such as HSBC plc, there will be millions of shares issued and possibly thousands of shareholders. Most shareholders will own only a small number of shares and so they have little influence over how the business is run. Most do not attend the Annual General Meeting (AGM) and they do not vote. In these circumstances, the owners (shareholders) are separated (divorced) from the day-to-day control of the business.

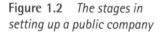

## ACTIVITY

Select a number of companies from the share pages of a newspaper such as the *Financial Times* or the *Daily Telegraph* and track their share prices over the course of a number of weeks. You may wish to plot their prices on a graph and comment upon the movements in the share prices.

## ACTIVITY

Create and complete Table 1.1, showing some of the key features of different types of business organisations.

| BUSINESS | OWNERS | LIABILITY | SOURCES OF FINANCE DISTRIBUTION OF PROFITS | OTHER FEATURES, E.G. LEGAL FORMALITIES, ADVANTAGES/DRAWBACKS |
|---|---|---|---|---|
| Sole trader | | | | |
| Partnership | | | | |
| Private limited company | | | | |
| Public limited company | | | | |

**Table 1.1** *Comparing various types of business organisation*

# Franchise

A franchise is not so much another form of ownership but a legal agreement which enables an entrepreneur to become part of an existing business. The best known type of franchise is the **business format franchise**. The potential entrepreneur (**franchisee**) buys a licence to trade under an existing business name from the parent company (the **franchisor**). Some familiar high street names such as Body Shop and Pizza Hut operate in this format.

## Advantages of franchises

- The franchisee benefits from buying into an established business and they usually receive training and support from the franchisor. The result is that a franchisee is far more likely to be successful than if they started up their own business from scratch.

- The franchisor benefits because it can be a way of expanding the business without the need for large sums of capital and they usually receive a percentage of the profits earned by the franchisee known as **royalties** as well as the licence fee.

- The franchisee is likely to be far more motivated than a manager as they have invested their own money in the business and will be keen to succeed.

## Drawbacks of franchises

- A large amount of capital is usually required to buy into a successful franchise such as McDonalds though less well known brand names will be cheaper.

- The franchisee also has to purchase all their stock from the franchisor, generating more revenue for the franchisor.

## Did you know?

*The first McDonalds was opened in 1955 by Ray Kroc in Des Plaines, Illinois, USA. McDonalds is now the largest fast food restaurant chain in the world with over 30,000 restaurants in 119 countries. Over 70 per cent of restaurants are run by independent entrepreneurs, making McDonalds the world's largest franchising company.*

- The franchisee is usually required to follow quite strict guidelines so they will not enjoy the same amount of independence as if they had set up their own business.

### QUESTIONS

1 What might be the advantages to an entrepreneur of buying into a well-established franchise business such as McDonalds?
2 What are the drawbacks of this compared to setting up a new fast food business?
3 Why might McDonalds wish to encourage franchisees to buy into the business?
4 If an entrepreneur was considering buying into a franchise, what type of information might they require before making a financial commitment?

## Worker co-operatives

Worker co-operatives are a quite rare type of business in the UK and often arise when a business is threatened with closure. The workforce raise money to buy the company from the current owners to protect their jobs. The workers then become the owners of the business and so make all the decisions regarding how the business is run. The workers are likely to be well motivated because they have invested their own capital in the business and want the business to succeed but they may lack the necessary management skills.

## CASE STUDY

### Edinburgh Bicycle Co-operative

The Edinburgh Bicycle Co-operative was set up in 1977 as a worker co-operative. It was initially set up to repair and sell cycles but it now also manufactures its own range of bikes as well as selling cycle clothing and accessories. The business has been very successful and it has grown by taking over retail outlets in Aberdeen and Newcastle. All full-time employees become owners known as 'members' after a two year probationary period and they elect a management committee to run the business. There are currently 33 members who are able to vote and all members are eligible to stand for the committee.

1 Why might you expect the workers at Edinburgh Bicycle Co-operative to be better motivated than the workers in a typical retail outlet such as Halfords?
2 What problems might arise from workers running the business?

## Building and friendly societies

Building societies are limited liability organisations which are owned by the membership. When an investor opens an account with a building society they usually become a 'member' of the society. Building societies are **mutual societies**, meaning that any profits earned by the society are kept within the business for the benefit of the members. There are no outside shareholders to receive dividends. Over the last ten years, a number of building societies, such as the Halifax, have converted into banks operated as public limited companies. However, some such as Nationwide have chosen to remain as mutual building societies.

> 'We're different because we're a building society. We're run for the benefit of our members, unlike banks who put their shareholders first. In fact, we have returned around £4 billion to our members since 1996 through better deals on all the products and services we offer.'
> *Source: Nationwide marketing material, April 2005*

**Friendly societies** are another type of mutual society. They tend to be found in financial services providing savings and life assurance services for their members. Liverpool Victoria, the UK's largest friendly society, states:

> 'As a mutual society our members own us. That means we have no shareholders taking a share of the profits and we can be 100% committed to getting the best returns for you.'
> *Source: Liverpool Victoria marketing material*

**QUESTIONS**
Why might a customer prefer to save with or borrow from a mutual society rather than a with a business operating as a plc?

## Charities

There are thousands of charitable trusts registered with the Charity Commissioners in the UK. A charity is not run with the purpose of making a profit but it is run to promote a particular cause or help people. A charitable trust can be set up for one of four purposes:

1 for the relief of poverty, e.g. Child Poverty Action Group, Oxfam
2 for the advancement of education, e.g. most private schools in the UK have charitable status
3 for the advancement of religion, e.g. the Church of England
4 for other purposes, such as to promote animal welfare or to campaign on environmental issues, e.g. Friends of the Earth.

Some charities, such as the RSPCA (Royal Society for the Prevention of Cruelty to Animals), are large-scale organisations with millions of pounds of income. They will employ a large number of staff and run highly professional marketing campaigns. Charities such as these need funds to cover their expenses and they are run on business lines. Others are small scale and rely entirely on voluntary workers. Whatever the size of a charity,

**ACTIVITY**

Identify five charities that are known to you, one of which is local. What is the purpose of each of these charities and how do they attract funding and support?

it will need to raise money to promote its cause and it will need to keep accurate records. The Charity Commissioners have the power to investigate allegations of misuse of funds or types of impropriety.

## Portfolio tip

*It may be useful to start your assignment by giving a clear statement of the main aims and objectives of your chosen businesses. You could include a mission statement if there is one. You should comment upon the legal structure of your chosen businesses and examine why the owners opted for this particular type of legal structure.*

## AO2 Explain why one of the selected businesses might wish to change its form of ownership in the future

Some of the UK's largest businesses started out many years ago as small-scale enterprises. They have grown over the years to become familiar household names. By contrast, others have shrunk in size as a result of competition or changes in patterns of demand. This section of work examines some of the reasons why businesses may change their form of ownership.

## Growth or decline of the business

The most common form of business ownership in the UK is sole proprietorship. However, as a business grows it will need to seek out new sources of capital and it may need to change its legal structure. A sole proprietor may decide to take on a partner to introduce more capital into the business but he or she will sacrifice their sole control over the business. If the business continues to grow, it may convert to a limited liability company owned by a number of shareholders. The largest businesses are public limited companies with thousands of shareholders. It may also be the case that the business changes its format as a result of it shrinking in size.

## Change of management

Sometimes two or more businesses will voluntarily choose to merge together to form a stronger, more profitable business. Sometimes the change of management may be forced when one business takes over another. Such a takeover might lead to a change in the legal format of the business.

## CASE STUDY

### MUFC USA

In May 2005 the American multi-millionaire Malcolm Glazer made a successful takeover bid for Manchester United Football Club, which at the time was operating as a public limited company (plc). Mr Glazer and his family already owned 28.1 per cent of the club's shares and his offer of £3 per share valued the club at approximately £800m.

With Mr Glazer's shareholding exceeding 75 per cent, he was able to convert the club to a private limited liability company and de-list from the Stock Exchange.

1 What rights do shareholders in limited liability companies have?
2 Why might Mr Glazer prefer to operate Manchester United as a private limited company rather than as a plc?

## Change of liability

Limited liability is an important legal protection for shareholders as they only risk losing the amount of money that they have invested in the business and not their own personal assets. The owners of a partnership may decide to convert the business to a private limited company to give themselves the legal protection of limited liability.

## Obtaining finance

One reason for a change in the legal structure of a business is to raise finance. A partnership will be able to raise more capital than a sole proprietorship and a public limited company (plc) will be able to raise considerably more capital than a private limited company (Ltd). Floating on the stock market will enable a plc to raise millions of pounds through the sale of shares to the public as well as raising the profile of the business.

### Real business

*In January 2005 Britvic, the soft drinks group that owns brands such as Tango and Robinsons, announced that it was delaying its planned £800m flotation on the stock market. There were concerns that last summer's poor sales figures might depress its stock market valuation.*

## Portfolio tip

*The specification makes it clear that you must explain why* **one** *of your chosen businesses might wish to change its form of ownership in the future.*

**AO3 Investigate the internal structure and functional areas of a selected business and explain how its internal structure and functional areas have changed over time**

We will now look at how businesses organise and manage themselves internally.

## Organisational structures

### Organisation charts

It is possible to use diagrams called organisation charts to visually represent the relationships that exist between different employees in the organisation. We will now examine some of the terminology associated with organisation charts.

### Hierarchical structures

Large organisations such as banks are usually organised as **hierarchies**, that is, they have a number of layers of management. When an organisation chart is drawn it usually resembles a pyramid with a small number of senior managers at the top and a larger number of workers lower down. This gives rise to a promotion ladder as staff can see how they can work their way up the hierarchy gaining more authority and responsibility as they go up the organisation. Staff know their position in the hierarchy and their position and job title may give them power and status within the organisation. However, these organisations may be bureaucratic with many separate departments and management layers and with slow decision making.

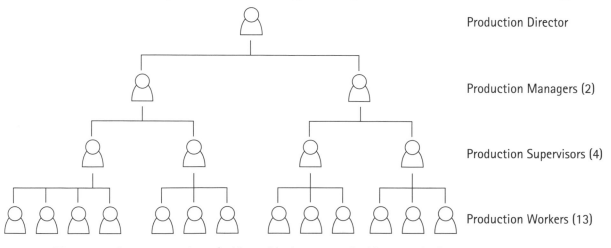

Figure 1.3 *Diagrammatic representation of a hierarchical structure. In this example there are four different levels in the hierarchy*

# Flat structure

In a flat structure there are fewer levels of management. This can encourage a team approach as many of the staff are on the same level or grade but fewer promotion opportunities exist as there are a limited number of managerial grades. It is often claimed that decision-making is quicker but spans of control tend to be larger, making close supervision more difficult. A flat structure is likely to be more successful in small organisations or where staff are well-motivated, skilled, experienced and are capable of working with minimal supervision.

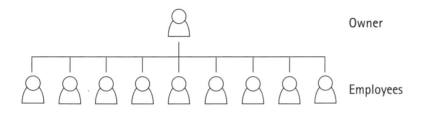

**Figure 1.4**   *Diagrammatic representation of a flat structure. There are only two levels of authority in this chart and larger spans of control*

## CASE STUDY

### The Virgin Group

To many outsiders Virgin's management style seems unusual. Virgin is a group of companies with global presence and employing thousands of workers but it has no high-profile head office, virtually no management hierarchy and minimal bureaucracy. Virgin's management may seem very casual but it is agile and fast on its feet. Managers are encouraged to be innovative and creative. The company does not believe in bureaucracy or cumbersome committees, so important business decisions can generally be made quickly.

**What are some of the benefits of this structure in a fast-moving retail market?**

# Matrix management

In most large businesses, workers tend to be organised along **functional** lines so they usually work in departments alongside colleagues doing similar work. For example, an accounts clerk will usually be working in the finance department alongside other finance assistants. However, a business may decide to put together a team drawn from different areas of the business to work on a specific new project. This is known as **matrix management**. The advantage is that this team will have a range of skills and experience that they can bring to bear on a particular project. The team members will not have their usual line manager as their boss while they are working on the project but will, instead, be managed by the team leader.

## CASE STUDY

### See-Thru Lenses Ltd (Part 1)

See-Thru Lenses Ltd manufactures contact lenses at its plant on the outskirts of Southampton. The business is organised into four departments: production, finance, marketing and distribution. The company has developed a new disposable contact lens and the directors have decided to opt for matrix management and set up a team to organise the launch of the new product, led by the marketing manager.

1 Outline the roles that staff from each of the departments might play in ensuring a successful launch.
2 What are the advantages of using a matrix management approach in this situation?

## The entrepreneurial model

In a small business it is quite possible for the owner to deal directly with all of his or her employees face to face and important information can be quickly exchanged. This is sometimes called the entrepreneurial model. However, this is only possible in relatively small organisations where the owner/manager knows all of the staff and is able to meet with them on a regular basis. In a larger organisation, it is likely that an individual boss would suffer from 'information overload' if they tried to manage every single aspect of the business

## *Functional areas*

Large organisations tend to be **functionally** organised with workers belonging to a department or section in the company according to the function or job that they perform in the business, e.g. marketing, finance, human resources and so on. **Line managers** are responsible for getting work done in their section and the line manager has direct authority over employees in their section.

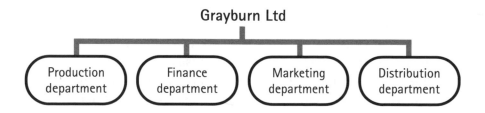

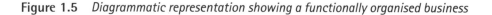

**Figure 1.5** *Diagrammatic representation showing a functionally organised business*

**QUESTIONS**

In which department would the following probably work?

(a) a cost accountant (b) a sales person (c) a recruitment officer (d) a production line worker (e) a market researcher (f) a delivery van driver (g) a credit controller (h) a warehouse supervisor.

## Chain of command

The **chain of command** is the channel by which decisions and instructions work their way down the hierarchy from the senior managers to the shop-floor workers. Superiors (managers) have **authority** over their subordinates, that is, they are able to ask them to carry out tasks but the manager remains **responsible** for seeing that work is carried out.

## Span of control

The **span of control** refers to the number of subordinates that a manager has direct authority over. It will be difficult to closely supervise a large number of employees if they are carrying out complex tasks so in this situation the span of control will probably be small. However, if employees are carrying out a simple, routine task then a manager's span of control can be larger. As we have seen, spans of control tend to be larger in flat organisational structures.

## Authority and responsibility

**Authority** is having the power to make decisions, e.g. a bank manager may have authority to grant loans of up to £100,000 but beyond this figure he or she may have to refer the decision to a more senior manager. **Responsibility** involves being 'accountable' for a part of the business. A manager may be expected to justify the performance of his or her section to a more senior manager. An employee should only be held accountable for things that they have control over. **Delegation** occurs when a manager grants a subordinate authority to carry out certain tasks. Managers usually have a range of responsibilities and cannot carry out every task themselves. When tasks are delegated, the manager still retains overall responsibility. For example, the principal of a college is responsible for everything that goes on, from academic results to health and safety, but he or she will delegate certain responsibilities to vice-principals, heads of department, premises staff and so on.

Delegation allows subordinates to gain more responsibility and can make their job more interesting and challenging. However, the subordinate must have sufficient training and experience to take on the task and feel that they are trusted by their manager.

## *Line, staff and functional authority*

### Line authority

A **line management** system will operate in a department or section with a clear chain of command. For example, the section manager in a supermarket has line authority over a supervisor in that section and the supervisor has authority over the shop-floor employees.

### Staff authority

A manager will have line authority over the workers in his or her department. However, it is quite likely that on some issues another specialist department, e.g. IT, will have input. This is known as a **staff** function. Under a line management system, if the marketing department wanted a new marketing assistant then the marketing manager might produce a job description, advertise the post and select candidates. However, in a large organisation these functions might be performed for all departments by the personnel, or human resources, section. In some cases there can be conflict between line and staff managers. The line manager may feel that she knows best what type of employee is needed but human resource specialists are likely to have a more thorough knowledge of employment laws and be more experienced at carrying out selection interviews.

### QUESTIONS

Are there any staff functions within your chosen organisation or is everything organised on strictly functional lines?

## *Centralisation and decentralisation*

Some businesses are highly **centralised** with all the key decisions being made centrally at head office and then being communicated down the organisation. The advantage of this system is that the important decisions are made by the most experienced managers (directors) in the business. It also ensures that there are common standards and procedures being followed throughout the organisation. This is particularly important if the business has a strong brand image to protect or if it has a distinctive company culture. However, some ambitious managers may feel frustrated by their lack of authority and it is difficult for them to gain much decision-making experience if all decisions are made by senior managers.

**Decentralised** organisations allow more junior managers and the managers of individual stores or plants to have much more authority to make decisions. Some managers may enjoy this freedom and responsibility but it will mean that different procedures and standards may develop in different parts of the organisation and customers may face different levels of service in different parts of the business.

## CASE STUDY

### See-Thru Lenses Ltd (Part 2)

See-Thru Lenses Ltd is led by a managing director and has four main departments: marketing, production, finance and distribution. Each department is headed up by the relevant director. Within the finance department is the finance manager who manages four finance clerks. The production department has a works manager who manages two production supervisors who in turn each manage 12 production line staff. The production department also has a product development manager who manages a team of three product development researchers and reports directly to the production director. The marketing department has a marketing manager who manages the head of market research and a team of five sales staff. The head of market research manages a team of three market researchers. The distribution manager has two supervisors, one supervises the five staff who work in the warehouse and loading bay and the other supervises the seven van drivers.

1 **Draw the organisational chart for See-Thru Lenses Ltd.**
2 **What is the span of control of the product development manager?**
3 **Explain how a decision to change marketing strategy might move down the chain of command.**

# Changes in organisational structures

Over time, businesses may need to adapt and change their organisational structures to fit new circumstances. Such changes may be aimed at improving efficiency or because of growth or shrinkage of the business. A change in ownership will often result in restructuring as will the outsourcing of some of the business's traditional functions.

## The need to increase efficiency

Many organisations in recent years have implemented a **delayering** process. This means removing layers of hierarchy to create a flatter, more efficient structure. For instance, in June 2004 Barclays Bank announced that 800 management jobs were to be cut as part of a plan aimed at improving customer service in the retail banking division. The firm is able to reduce its costs by having fewer layers of management, communication and decision-making may be quicker and junior staff may find that they have more responsible jobs as they take on some of the supervisory and managerial work. However, delayering may damage morale as jobs are lost and it may just increase the workload of the remaining staff.

## The growth or shrinkage of the business

In a small business, the entrepreneur may know all of his staff individually and be able to run the business in a relatively informal way. However, as a business grows it will take on more specialist staff and it is likely that a hierarchy will develop and the business will begin to structure itself into different functional areas. It may also be the case that the business adapts in response to falling demand for its products or services. In these circumstances a business may aim to reduce its costs by carrying out a restructuring process.

## CASE STUDY

### Clydesdale Bank

In May 2005 Clydesdale Bank announced that it was closing 60 of its 217 branches. The Glasgow-based bank is aiming to shed 750 jobs as part of a plan to cut costs by £117m. Many of the smaller branches were now not economically viable as fewer people visit their branch but use ATMs and telephone and internet banking instead.

1  How does the closure of branches reduce the bank's costs?
2  Analyse the costs associated with shedding 750 staff?

### GLOSSARY

**ATM:**
Abbreviation for automated teller machine.

## Takeover or merger

Takeovers and mergers involve the joining together of two or more separate businesses to form a new, larger business. Following such a move, it is quite likely that a significant amount of reorganisation will be required.

## Outsourcing of business functions

Outsourcing means buying in services or materials rather than providing it in-house. The usual reason for this is to reduce the firm's costs. Many businesses no longer employ their own cleaners and catering staff. Instead they have contracted these functions out, meaning that they have specialist firms to come in to provide these services on a separate contract. British Airways, for example, no longer makes its own in-flight meals but has contracted out this function.

### QUESTIONS

Your college will employ its own lecturers and administrative staff. However, who are the catering and cleaning staff employed by?

### Portfolio tip

*You will need to either produce or obtain an organisational chart for your chosen business to illustrate its structure and analyse how its structure and organisation have changed over time.*

## CASE STUDY

### Morrisons' takeover of Safeway

----------------------------------------------------------------

Morrisons became the fourth largest supermarket group in March 2004 when it bought Safeway for £3bn. However, its profits have suffered, partly as a result of the cost of converting the Safeway stores to the Morrisons format. The company's profitability has also remained 'heavily impacted by the temporary dual running costs of distribution, administration and IT functions' and Morrisons said that these duplicate costs would 'remain higher and take longer to eliminate' than previously thought.

1  Give examples of some of the changes that will need to occur at the combined Morrisons/Safeway group.
2  What problems may be faced in bringing together the Morrisons and Safeway chains?

## AO4  Explain the roles of both internal and external stakeholders in the selected business and show how their objectives and expectations have changed over time

When business owners set up their businesses they do so primarily to make a profit. However, other groups and individuals in the business may have different interests. The term stakeholder refers to any individual or group who has an interest in how the business is run or who is affected by its activities. Some of these individuals and groups are shown in the diagram below.

**Figure 1.6**  *Typical stakeholders in a business*

# Internal stakeholders

Stakeholders can be divided up into internal stakeholders and external stakeholders. **Internal stakeholders** are those individuals or groups within the organisation.

## Owners

The owner, partners or **shareholders** of the business have invested their money and want the business to be profitable. They will expect the business to be run efficiently and that managers will be committed to increasing revenues and controlling the firm's costs. Wages and salaries are often important costs for businesses so there is the potential for conflict between the interests of the owners and the employees.

## Managers

Managers are a particular type of employee. They are employed on contracts and paid wages or salaries like other employees. However, they are expected to act in the interests of the owners and manage the business as efficiently as possible. This may, at times, bring them into conflict with other employees over issues such as pay, working conditions, shift patterns etc.

## Employees

The employees are another important group who have an interest in the business. They will rely upon the business to provide them with a regular wage or salary. They will hope for job security, safe working conditions and perhaps training and the chance of promotion. They need the business to be successful but, equally, they will hope to see their wage or salary rising. Managers, on the other hand, may be expected to hold down staff wage costs to improve the profitability of the business, so there is the potential for conflict.

# External stakeholders

**External stakeholders** are those individuals or groups outside the business who are affected by its activities.

## Customers

Customers will expect products and services to be safe and reliable and that replacement parts and servicing facilities will be available for a reasonable time. They will also expect that the price charged appears fair, given the quality of the product, and that any complaints will be dealt with quickly and fairly.

## Suppliers

Firms that supply the business with raw materials, components, packaging or services will expect to be paid promptly. They may also rely upon regular orders to ensure the success of their own business. Marks & Spencer plc were heavily criticised when they decided to end links with some of their British suppliers and use cheaper foreign clothing manufacturers in North Africa and Eastern Europe. A number of UK clothing manufacturers relied heavily on Marks & Spencer orders and faced severe problems.

## Government

Some organisations, such as NHS hospitals and further education colleges, are funded by government, so the government has a direct stakeholding role in the organisation. It also has a direct interest in receiving corporation tax from successful businesses, which will also create jobs. However, its wide-ranging responsibilities towards employment and the environment mean that it may have an indirect interest in many UK businesses.

## Local communities

Some businesses have a considerable impact on their local communities. Sometimes the impact is positive, for example a business may be one of the few sources of employment in an area of high unemployment and generate positive publicity for the area. However, a business may also be a source of pollution, noise and traffic congestion in the local area and local communities have the right to express their views on the behaviour of business. Pressure groups in society may press a business to change its behaviour if they feel that it is having a negative impact on the environment or particular individuals and groups.

## ACTIVITY

Below is a list of some possible stakeholders in your college or school. For each group explain what their interest is in the school or college or how they may be affected by its activities. (This might change over a period of time.):

- students
- lecturers / teachers
- local businesses
- governors
- the government
- local residents.

## Portfolio tip

*Who are the key stakeholders in your chosen business? Are there any conflicts or tensions between the different stakeholders and have their aims changed over time?*

## CASE STUDY

*MG Rover*

In April 2005 thousands of MG Rover employees were laid off at Longbridge in the West Midlands, when the UK car manufacturer went into administration. Suppliers of components in the Midlands and South Wales were also forced to lay off workers. MG Rover employs about 6,000 workers but an additional 15,000–20,000 jobs are supported by business from the firm. The government has set up a task force to advise how best to support MG

Rover suppliers as well as Longbridge workers and the local community.

Meanwhile, there has been criticism of the four businessmen who set up Phoenix Venture Holdings, the parent company that owns MG Rover. The men are understood to have made over £30m from the company over five years while the car-maker has lost millions of pounds and has a deficit on the workers' pension fund of £67m. Workers were understandably angry that Phoenix Venture Holdings was able to draw money out of MG Rover while the company's financial position deteriorated.

1  Explain the impact on the various stakeholders mentioned in the article that MG Rover's closure will have.
2  Outline some of the conflicts of interest that can exist between stakeholders.
3  What is the government's interest in this situation?

# AO5 Investigate and explain the reasons for the location of the selected business and explain why the selected business might wish to relocate in the future

Businesses are constantly having to respond to changing circumstances. New competition may arrive in the market or customer tastes may change. A business will need to be aware of these trends and may need to assess, from time to time, whether it is appropriate to stay in its current location. This section looks at some of the factors that may be relevant when a business is deciding where to locate.

The following are some of the factors which may be relevant to the location decision:

# Access to raw materials

A new business or a relocating business will want to be confident that it will have easy access to all the materials that it needs in production. Businesses such as coal mines and oil refineries have to be located on or near the source of raw materials, so mines are located on coalfields and refineries tend to be located at particular coastal sites such as Fawley and Milford Haven, where oil is brought ashore. Vegetables and fruit can be heavy and costly to transport, so many canning or freezing plants are located close to the growing areas. For example, sugar beet is a bulky root vegetable and there are sugar refining businesses located in East Anglia, close to the growing areas to reduce transport costs.

# Distribution costs

If the finished product of a manufacturing firm is heavy or bulky then this pushes up transport costs. In these cases, a business may choose to locate close to its final customers to reduce distribution costs as much as possible.

# Access to markets

For many businesses nearness to the customer is of great importance. There is a limit to how far customers will travel to buy fish and chips even if they are of excellent quality. For the same reason a department store will usually be situated in a reasonable sized town or city. Marks & Spencer will only consider locating a new store in an area of relatively high population density.

Over the last 30 years a number of foreign companies such as Samsung and Nissan have located in the UK to gain access to the European market. Non-EU (European Union) businesses face a tariff barrier when selling their goods into the EU. However, if a non-European business locates within the EU, employs EU workers and uses some EU components then it will gain access to the lucrative European market.

# Communications and ICT

For some businesses, such as hypermarkets and distribution companies, good transport links are essential. However, for information technology based businesses, geographical location may be relatively unimportant so long as the business has Internet access.

# Scaling up or scaling down

An established business may consider relocating to meet changing circumstances. A successful, expanding business may feel that it has outgrown its current site and needs to move to a larger location.

Conversely, if a business is in decline or experiencing falling sales as a result of recession, it may wish to move to smaller premises. This might give the business the opportunity to cut its fixed costs such as rent. This type of cost-cutting is known as **retrenchment**.

## Land cost

A new business may decide to locate where land prices are cheap. Out of town locations are cheaper than city-centre sites and so they are popular for new retail developments, such as Cribbs Causeway on the outskirts of Bristol. Land prices in the south east of England tend to be higher than elsewhere and this can deter certain developments, with foreign businesses in particular opting for cheaper sites elsewhere, with South Wales and the north east of England being popular.

## Labour cost and skills available

The average wage offered by businesses varies significantly in different parts of the country, as is shown in Table 1.2. For some firms, wages are a key cost so a business may decide to locate in an area of relatively low wages. These areas tend also to be areas of above average unemployment as workers are keen to find work and are prepared to accept lower wages.

## ACTIVITY

| REGION | AVERAGE GROSS WEEKLY EARNINGS (£) OF FULL-TIME EMPLOYEES |
|---|---|
| North East | 388 |
| North West | 399 |
| Yorks & Humberside | 412 |
| East Midlands | 420 |
| West Midlands | 410 |
| East | 485 |
| London | 566 |
| South East | 510 |
| South West | 441 |
| Wales | 410 |
| Scotland | 426 |
| Northern Ireland | 393 |

Source: Labour Force Survey – Office of National Statistics (2005) www.statistics.gov.uk

**Table 1.2** *Wage differences in the UK by region (Winter 2004/05)*

1  Rank the 12 UK economic regions based on average earnings.
2  Which two regions have the highest average wages?
3  Which two regions have the lowest wages?
4  How might this information be helpful to a new business deciding where
   to locate a manufacturing plant requiring 400 workers?

In some cases the **quality** of the local labour force, that is, the skills and experience of workers, may be more important than the cost. A shortage of computer analysts or bricklayers in London or the South East will force up wages and businesses will have no choice but to offer higher wages if they are to recruit and retain workers.

University towns can be a useful source of well-educated and trained workers. Significant numbers of hi-tech and research businesses are located on business parks on the outskirts of Cambridge and Oxford. A pool of skilled labour grows up in an area where particular industries are concentrated encouraging more new businesses to locate there.

## Government and EU influence

Because certain parts of the country, e.g. Northern Ireland, suffer from high unemployment the government uses regional policy to encourage businesses to locate in areas of high unemployment. The areas are classified by the government as Assisted Areas (see Figure 1.7) and businesses may be able to obtain government grants if they create jobs in these areas.

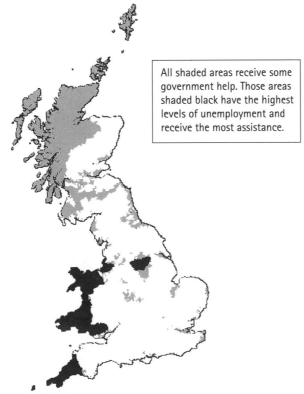

All shaded areas receive some government help. Those areas shaded black have the highest levels of unemployment and receive the most assistance.

**Figure 1.7**  *Map of Assisted Areas in Great Britain.*
Source: www.dti.gov.uk

A number of foreign companies, including Nissan and Samsung, have over the last thirty years received millions of pounds from the UK government to locate in areas of high unemployment. The government also designates some small areas of particularly high unemployment as Enterprise Zones. They tend to be run down inner-city areas or towns that have suffered from the closure of one large employer. Firms wishing to locate in these areas and create jobs may be eligible for a significant amount of government assistance. The European Union (EU) also has a Regional Fund which helps to support projects that create jobs and improve the infrastructure of the more economically deprived parts of the EU.

## International location

A multinational business is able to take a wide range of factors into account when deciding where to locate a new plant. Government incentives may be available and so, for instance, a Taiwanese company which wishes to locate in the EU will be able to assess competing financial incentives offered by a number of EU countries, all anxious to create new jobs in their economies.

More recently, many UK businesses, including Marks & Spencer, have set up call centres in India to take advantage of lower wage rates and the large number of English-speaking graduates who are available. Increased trade and the movement of jobs from one economy to another is part of a process known as **globalisation**.

## CASE STUDY

*Samsung quits Teesside*

--------------------------------------------------------------------------------

In January 2004 the Korean electronics giant announced plans to close its plant near Billingham, Teesside, with the loss of over 400 jobs. The company planned to switch production to Spain and Eastern Europe to cut production costs. This will be a serious blow to employment in the area and comes only ten years after the company had established itself in the area. Samsung had received £58m in government grants and loans to encourage it to locate on Teesside.

**What problems does this illustrate about offering foreign businesses incentives to locate in areas of high unemployment?**

## Historical reasons

A business will sometimes stay in a location long after the original reasons for locating there have gone. This is known as **industrial inertia**. Once established in an area a business may be reluctant to relocate given all the expense and upheaval that this involves. The area around Stoke-on-Trent is known as the Potteries. This is because during the 18th and 19th centuries a large number of pottery businesses set up in the area because of the availability of suitable fireclay. However, despite the fact that production methods have changed, earthenware and chinaware businesses such as Waterford Wedgwood and Royal Doulton still operate in the area.

**QUESTIONS**

1 List 5 factors a business may take into account when deciding where to locate.
2 Which factors are likely to be most important when deciding to locate the following businesses?
(a) hairdresser (b) an airport (c) a boat repair business (d) a horse riding centre (e) a computer game design company (f) a foreign electronics company wishing to build a manufacturing plant and create 350 new jobs.

**Portfolio tip**

*You should describe where the business is located and explain why this particular location was chosen by the owners. You should also examine why the business may wish to relocate in the future.*

## AO6 Explain the competition model within which the selected business operates and any legislative constraints affecting its ability to compete in the future

Almost every business operates in a competitive market. This means that businesses will need to consider not just their own products and prices but will need to take into account the actions of their market competitors. Some markets, such as that for savoury snacks, are fiercely competitive whereas in other markets there may be little or no competition. There are a number of different **competition models** that describe these different market conditions.

## Competition models

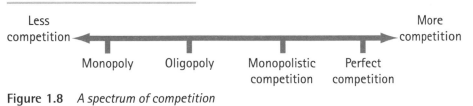

Figure 1.8 *A spectrum of competition*

## *Perfect competition*

Perfect competition is an economic model describing a highly competitive market. In this case, there are very many businesses in the market supplying a virtually identical (homogeneous) product or service. There are no brand names to help **differentiate** products. The businesses tend to be small with each having a tiny share of the overall market. The result is that they are unable to influence price (they are all 'price takers') and customers can easily shop around looking for the best deal. Competing in such a market is difficult and businesses may make only modest levels of profit. There are few examples of perfect markets but small-scale agricultural producers are often in this position. There are a considerable number of UK farmers growing vegetables and, as their produce is not branded, they have little influence over the price that they receive for their produce.

## Monopoly

A pure monopoly exists when there is only one supplier of a product or service in a market. The result of this is that:

- customers do not have any choice over the product or service that they buy – they only have a 'take it or leave it' choice
- product or service quality may suffer as the monopolist does not have to try very hard to satisfy customers' requirements
- prices tend to be higher because of the absence of competition
- a monopolist has little incentive to be innovative and bring new products to the market.

There are few pure monopolies in existence. The regional water companies, such as Thames Water, have a monopoly of water supply in their region and consumer groups sometimes complain about water quality and water prices. The Post Office has enjoyed a monopoly on letter deliveries up to the value of £1.00, though there is fierce competition in the market for parcel deliveries and courier service.

Despite the potential problems, monopolies are not illegal in the UK. However, they may be investigated by the Competition Commission if it is felt that they are acting against the interests of customers. In the UK the legal definition of a monopoly is any business with 25 per cent or more market share, which is a much broader definition than a pure monopoly.

## Oligopoly

Oligopoly is quite a common market structure in the UK. An oligopoly is a market which is dominated by a small number of firms. They tend to be large businesses and as such they are relatively powerful but competition is often quite fierce. The market for chocolate bars in the UK is oligopolistic, being dominated by Cadbury, Nestlé and Mars. There are other chocolate manufacturers but they have a small share of the market compared to the big three.

One of the key features of an oligopoly is that businesses are reluctant to compete on price. If one company cuts its price the others are likely to follow, which reduces the profits of all the firms in the industry, so oligopolists tend to use **non-price competition**. This means that they compete through branding, advertising and special promotions rather than risk a **price war**.

**QUESTIONS**

1 Why will it be difficult for a firm to raise its price in a perfect market?

2 To what extent is the UK market for (a) petrol (b) groceries oligopolistic?

## Monopolistic competition

Monopolistic competition exists where there are a large number of companies competing in a market. Businesses attempt to differentiate their products through **branding** and advertising. Businesses are able to protect their own brand name through trademarks and so, in effect, they have a monopoly of their own brand. Customers, nevertheless, have a wide choice of products or services and competition may be fierce. Competition is not solely based on price; image and quality are also important issues. The market for women's clothing in the UK tends to conform to this structure, with retailers, such as Top Shop, French Connection, New Look, Dorothy Perkins, Monsoon and many others, offering consumers a wide choice in terms of style, quality and price.

**ACTIVITY**

Find out the prices of a range of chocolate snack bars such as Twix, Toffee Crisp, Flake etc. What do you notice about their prices?

**ACTIVITY**

1 How do the following differentiate their clothing. Consider price range, age of customers, quality, style/image:
   (a) Marks & Spencer   (b) New Look   (c) Next   (d) Top Shop   (e) Ghost
2 Key in and complete Table 1.3.

| | NUMBER OF SUPPLIERS | SIZE OF FIRMS | ROLE OF BRANDING | POWER OVER PRICE |
|---|---|---|---|---|
| **Monopoly** | | | | |
| **Oligopoly** | | | | |
| **Monopolistic competition** | | | | |
| **Perfect competition** | | | | |

Table 1.3  *Illustration of the business competition models*

## Restrictive trade practices

Restrictive trade practices are aimed at reducing the amount of competition in a market and they often result in higher prices to the consumer. Some practices can be registered with the Office of Fair Trading (OFT) and these are then legal. However, if restrictive practices are not registered with the

OFT then the business runs the risk of being prosecuted under the Fair Trading Act 1973.

Some examples of restrictive practices are:

- producers forcing retailers to charge a minimum resale price (i.e. refusing to allow retailers to cut prices charged to the customer)
- refusing to supply products to retailers who sell at discount prices
- collusion between large suppliers
- forcing retailers to stock a full range of products. This means that if retailers wish to have supplies of a best-selling product from a manufacturer, they may be forced to stock other less popular products made by that manufacturer.

## Cartels

A **cartel** is an agreement made between suppliers to cooperate together to restrict competition by fixing prices and/or levels of output. Cartels usually work against the interests of the customer and so they are illegal in the UK. However, it can be difficult to prove that firms are operating a cartel. The major petrol companies in the UK are sometimes accused of operating a cartel as their petrol prices are always similar and move up and down together. If there is a suspicion that producers are operating as a cartel they may be investigated by the Office of Fair Trading.

## CASE STUDY

### Toy companies in a fix

--------------------------------------------------------------------------------

fined a total of over £20m for being involved in price-fixing. Argos suffered the heaviest fine of £15m. An Office of Fair Trading investigation found that the three companies had illegally colluded together to fix the prices of popular Hasbro toys and games. While the price-fixing agreement was in operation in 2001, both catalogues retailers were charging £17.99 for Monopoly. Following the OFT decision the price fell to below £14.

In 2003, Hasbro UK, the manufacturer of toys and games such as Action Man and Monopoly, and the catalogue retailers Argos and Littlewoods (owners of Index stores) were

1 Why do you think these companies received such large fines?
2 Why are companies prepared to act illegally to fix prices?

# Competition legislation

Since 1948 a significant amount of legislation has been enacted to encourage competition and reduce anti-competitive practices. Much of the older legislation has been incorporated into the Competition Act 1998 and the Enterprise Act 2002. Some of the key legislation is shown below:

## Monopolies and Restrictive Practices Act (1948)

This Act set up the **Monopolies Commission,** a government-funded body with power to investigate monopoly situations in the UK. At the time this was regarded as a situation where one firm had more than one-third of the domestic market. **The Monopolies and Mergers Act 1965** gave the Commission the power to investigate mergers and takeovers resulting in the creation of such a firm or involving the transfer of assets of £5m or more. The Monopolies and Mergers Commission (MMC) could recommend that the proposed takeover or merger should not proceed if it was likely to be against the public interest.

## Restrictive Trade Practices Act (1956)

This Act created a Registrar of Restrictive Practices and a Restrictive Practices Court. If businesses wished to operate agreements restricting trade, they must present them to the registrar. The onus was on businesses to prove that the agreement was not against the public interest.

## Fair Trading Act (1973)

This Act established the Office of Fair Trading (OFT) which took on the role of controlling restrictive practices in the UK. It also extended the power of the MMC, allowing it to investigate markets where businesses appeared to be colluding together. It also changed the definition of monopoly to 25 per cent or more of the market share or a significant part of a regional market.

## Competition Acts (1980 and 1998)

The 1980 Act strengthened anti-competition laws by giving the MMC the power to investigate public-sector bodies, e.g. The Post Office, and by giving the Director General of the OFT power to deal directly with businesses operating restrictive practices.

## Competition Commission

The Competition Commission was set up by the **Competition Act 1998** to replace the MMC. The Competition Commission (CC) is a government body which can investigate monopoly situations, defined as a business with a 25 per cent or greater market share. If it finds that the business is abusing its position, e.g. by charging excessively high prices or preventing new firms entering the market, it can take action against the company. Companies can be fined up to 10 per cent of turnover for up to three years. The

> ### GLOSSARY
>
> **Restrictive practices:** business practices which tend to reduce competition within the market and lead to higher prices and a poorer standard of service to the consumer. Typical restrictive practices include price-fixing and market-sharing agreements between companies known as **cartels.**

Commission also investigates mergers or takeovers which would lead to the creation of a business with 25 per cent or greater market share and it could recommend that the merger or takeover should not proceed if it would be against the public interest. The **Enterprise Act 2002** strengthened the power of the CC further, allowing it to take direct action against companies.

## CASE STUDY

### Supermarket scrap

In 2003 Morrisons, the northern-based supermarket chain, announced a proposal to take over the rival Safeway chain. This would make the new combined company the fourth largest supermarket chain in the UK. Within days, Asda, Sainsbury's and Tesco all expressed interest in buying Safeway. The Competition Commission (CC) was asked to investigate the proposed acquisitions. The CC concluded that Asda, Sainsbury's and Tesco should not be allowed to acquire Safeway as this would be against the public interest. However, the Morrisons proposal should be allowed subject to the new merged company selling off a number of its grocery stores.

1 In what ways might a takeover of Safeway by Asda, Tesco or Sainsbury's have raised concerns over competition?
2 Why do you think the Morrisons bid was allowed?

## AO7 Illustrate the growth or decline of the industrial sector associated with the business selected, in comparison with other industrial sectors

Businesses in the UK operate in a wide range of sectors, from farming to telecommunications and from oil exploration to leisure centres. This assessment objective examines the different types of business activity in the UK and some of the important trends and changes taking place in the different business sectors.

Economists categorise business activity into three main sectors known as the **primary, secondary and tertiary** sectors.

# Primary industry

Primary industries are involved in obtaining resources from the natural world. They include businesses such as agriculture and forestry. Some of these primary industries are called **extractive industries** as they extract or obtain resources from the natural environment; they include industries such as coal mining, oil exploration and water supply industries. The number of people who work in these industries in the UK is relatively small but the production of foodstuffs to feed the UK's 60 million population and obtaining natural resources for business is clearly vital for our success as an economy. In 2005, less than 2 per cent of the workforce worked in the primary sector.

# Secondary industry

Secondary industries are involved in taking raw materials and resources and transforming them into finished or semi-finished products, for example a brewery such as Greene King takes hops and barley which have been grown by farmers and combines them with water to produce a finished product, beer, which can be sold to consumers. Brewing is, therefore, a secondary process. The construction industry is also included in the secondary sector of the economy as it uses raw materials such as cement, steel and timber to produce homes, roads, hospitals, etc.

# Tertiary industry

The tertiary sector does not make products as such but it provides valuable services that consumers and other businesses are prepared to pay for. There has been huge growth in this sector of the economy over the last 50 years and over three-quarters of all workers work in the tertiary sector. Some of the largest tertiary industries are retailing, banking, transport, hotels and communications.

## Portfolio tip

*You should comment upon the level of competition in the market. Who are the main competitors and how fierce is competition? In what ways does your chosen business compete?*

## Real business

*Scottish & Newcastle plc is a major international brewing group, marketing a number of well known brands. The company can trace its origins back to 1749 and it is now one of Europe's leading brewers and is in the top 10 by sales volume in the world.*

# ACTIVITY

Working in pairs or small groups identify which sector of the economy the following belong in:
(a) a travel agent    (b) a salmon farm in Scotland    (c) a coffee bar
(d) a bakery    (e) a slate quarry    (f) a housebuilding company such as Barratt
(g) a fish freezing plant    (h) a television company such as Sky TV
(i) Asda    (j) an oil refinery    (k) Thames Water plc    (l) a chat magazine.

## Employment by industrial sector

The vast majority of workers in the UK now work in the service sector of the economy, that is, the tertiary sector. Table 1.4 shows data for employment in the UK by industrial sector.

### ACTIVITY

| | |
|---|---|
| Agriculture, forestry & fishing | 1% |
| Energy and water supply | 1% |
| Manufacturing | 13.2% |
| Construction | 8.0% |
| Services | 76.4% |
| | |
| Total | 100% |

**Table 1.4**   *Employment by UK industrial sector (2004)*
Source: Office of National Statistics (2005) www.statistics.gov.uk

Calculate the percentage of the UK workforce that work in each of the following sectors:

(a) primary   (b) secondary   (c) tertiary.

## Growth and decline by industrial sector

There have been enormous changes in UK industry over the last 25 years and the pattern of employment in the different sectors of business continues to change.

### The primary sector

Over the last 30 years the number of people working in agriculture has fallen significantly. Small farms have closed or been swallowed up by larger farms that are able to produce food more cheaply for the big supermarket chains. Changes in the European Union's (EU) Common Agricultural Policy (CAP) have also affected farmers' incomes causing some to leave the industry.

There have been similar job losses in mining and fishing.

## ACTIVITY

| | NUMBER EMPLOYED (IN THOUSANDS) | |
|---|---|---|
| | **1994** | **2004** |
| Agriculture, forestry & fishing | 599 | 415 |
| Energy and water supply | 264 | 185 |
| Manufacturing | 4,344 | 3,569 |
| Construction | 1,835 | 2,145 |
| Services | 20,265 | 24,125 |
| | | |
| Total | 27,307 | 30,439 |

Source: Office for National Statistics (2005) www.statistics.gov.uk

**Table 1.5** *Employment by UK industrial sector (1994–2004)*

1 Calculate the total number of workers working in each of the primary, secondary and tertiary industries for 1994 and 2004.
2 Plot this data on a graph.
3 Comment upon the changes observed.

## Manufacturing industry

Manufacturing is another sector that has seen a massive fall in the number of workers employed in it and during the 1980s the term **deindustrialisation** was given to this process. The trend has continued and between 1997 and 2002 over half a million manufacturing jobs disappeared. One explanation for this is that manufacturing has become more **capital intensive**. Far more technology is used in manufacturing, resulting in fewer workers being needed. A second factor is that cheaper foreign products have replaced many UK manufactured goods and some UK companies have switched production to lower-wage economies to cut costs. For example, Dyson the vacuum cleaner business, has switched some of its production from Wiltshire to Malaysia to take advantage of lower wage costs.

## The service sector

There has been a massive expansion of this sector over the last 25 years and in 2002 there were over 20 million people working in the service sector. As citizens have become wealthier the demand for services has increased. Consumers are now far more likely to eat out, have credit cards, own a mobile phone, take foreign holidays and belong to a fitness club than ever before. The service sector of the economy has grown to meet consumers' needs.

### Real business

*Vodafone made the UK's first mobile call at a few minutes past midnight on 1 January 1985. Within 15 years, the network would become the largest company in Europe and the largest of its kind anywhere in the world. By the turn of the century, almost every second UK citizen would have a mobile – one-third of them connected to Vodafone.*

Source: *www.vodafone.co.uk*

### Portfolio tip

*You need to state which sector your business operates in and you should describe any trends in the sector that may be affecting the business and compare this sector with trends in other sectors.*

## ACTIVITY

Carry out a survey either of the part-time jobs done by students in your class or the jobs done by your parents.

1 How many work in each of the three sectors?
2 Do your findings reflect the main pattern of employment outlined above?

## AO8 Carry out a presentation to explain how the selected business maintains its competitive position and propose appropriate strategies to improve this level of competitiveness in the future

To achieve this assessment objective you will need to successfully carry out a presentation which explains the various factors that are relevant to the firm in maintaining competitiveness and propose suitable strategies that would enable it to improve its competitive position. **Competitiveness** refers to a firm's ability to compete successfully with its market rivals. Many of the issues have already been addressed earlier in the unit. Some of the key areas you should address are shown below.

## Customer focus

Customer focus means that the business puts the customer at the heart of everything it does. A customer-focussed business will conduct thorough market research to identify what it is that customers want from the product or service. The company will then develop appropriate products and services to meet customers' requirements.

## Competitor watching

Businesses must be aware of what their competitors are doing. It is important to know the prices, product range and levels of service that rival firms offer. The supermarket business Tesco actually has a website which shows price comparisons with its competitors. One way of approaching this issue is to carry out a **competitor audit**. This identifies the main competitors in the market and looks at their various strengths and weaknesses.

# Suitable location

Location can be of great importance for a business such as a restaurant or department store. However, for an Internet-based business, geographical location may be unimportant. You should consider the location of your business and assess the importance of its location. You may also wish to consider whether it would benefit from a change of location.

# Suitable resources

Some types of businesses, particularly manufacturing businesses, rely heavily on a particular raw material or component. A company promoting itself as a fair trade coffee business must be able to have a reliable source of fair trade products. For some businesses, the supply of particular labour skills is of crucial importance.

# Suitable ownership

Businesses in the UK range from small sole proprietorships to large public limited companies. As a business grows, it may need to adapt its structure and consider the benefits of limited liability. As a business develops further, it may consider the costs and benefits of converting to public limited company status.

# Market penetration

Market penetration refers to how successful the business and its brands are in the market. **Market share** is a useful way of measuring how successful a business is in its market. If a business is increasing its market share, it means that it is winning business from its rivals. If a new product or brand is being launched it is important that the product can establish itself quickly in the market. It is likely that senior managers will set a target for market share as a way of measuring the success of the launch. In your presentation you should look at how successful your chosen business is within its market. Bear in mind that a business may be quite small in national terms but it may hold a significant share of a local market, e.g. a local chain of dry cleaners.

# Expansion and/or merger

Some businesses expand because they are successful and they are enjoying rising sales and profits. The Spanish clothing retailer Zara has been very successful in Spain and is now expanding into the UK. Others set about expanding as a way of gaining market share and enjoying economies of scale, such as bulk buying discounts. The supermarket group Morrisons took over Safeway as a quick way of increasing its market share and to enable it to compete with Tesco, Sainsbury's and Asda. Sometimes businesses may decide to merge together to enable them to compete more effectively. You should consider whether your chosen business has scope for expansion or whether it is content with its current scale of operation.

## Research and development (R&D)

In some markets, it is vital to maintain a stream of new products and services. This is particularly true for markets such as electronics and pharmaceutical products. Products quickly become technically obsolete and sales revenue will fall unless replaced.

## Portfolio tip

*Most students find giving a presentation a challenging experience. The keys to a successful presentation are* **preparation** *and* **practice**. *Make sure that you have covered all the key areas and that you have all the resources, such as Powerpoint slides and overhead transparencies, that you need. Practise your presentation in front of classmates before doing the assessed presentation.*

*Presentations can be challenging*

## SKILLS CHECK

**1** (a) Outline two possible aims of a private sector business.

   (b) Explain what is meant by SMART targets and explain the benefits to a business of setting such targets.

**2** Outline some of the implications of a business moving from:

   (a) partnership to private limited company (Ltd) status

   (b) Ltd to public limited company (plc) status

**3** Explain two reasons why a business might wish to change its legal status.

**4** Outline some of the key differences between:

   (a) functional organisation and matrix management

   (b) centralised and decentralised management structures

**5** (a) What is meant by the term stakeholders?

   (b) Explain, using examples, why the aims of some stakeholders in a typical business may conflict.

**6** Explain four factors that a business may take into account when deciding where to locate or relocate.

**7** Why do governments generally favour competition in markets?

**8** Distinguish between primary, secondary and tertiary industries.

**9** Give some reasons for the growth of the tertiary sector over the last 20 years.

**10** Outline some of the ways in which a firm may improve its competitiveness.

# Customer service

We all use different types of businesses in our everyday lives. We have all as customers experienced unfriendly and even rude staff who make no effort to offer a service. Research has shown that customers are likely to tell twice as many people about a bad experience than a good one.

Your work experience placement or part-time job may help you to provide the evidence needed for your portfolio. However, if you are not working, your tutor may have contacts with local businesses and may be able to arrange visits. You may use role-play exercises or a mixture of real situations and role play to provide the evidence required for the practical skills.

Practical tasks in this unit include four demonstrations of customer service in a range of situations. You will evaluate your own performance in these demonstrations and propose appropriate actions for improvement.

Successful achievement of this unit will help to develop your understanding of the importance of providing excellent customer service and of how businesses prioritise the maintenance of high customer service standards. You will learn the principles of providing excellent customer service, including adapting responses to suit different, and often complex, situations.

## This unit will cover

- AO1 Illustrate, using examples, the benefits to business of providing good customer service to both internal and external customers.

- AO2 Describe how customer service responses are adapted to the needs of the customer.

- AO3 Investigate the customer service function of a selected business and describe, using examples, its structure, operation and interactions.

- AO4 Explain how customer service standards are planned, implemented and monitored and the impact this has on the operation of a selected business.

- AO5 Demonstrate customer service, evaluate own performance (four situations) and propose appropriate actions for development.

# AO1 Illustrate, using examples, the benefits to business of providing good customer service to both internal and external customers

Customer service has been described as all the activities that affect customers' experience of dealing with a particular business. Good customer service ensures that customers leave feeling happy and wanting to come back. They will tell their friends and family, who will then tell others about the good service they have received. Many companies strive to give their customers what they want and to provide a high-quality product or service that ensures that no complaints are received.

For this section, you will need to use examples to illustrate the benefits to business of providing good customer service. Remember that the examples you choose must enable you to obtain all the evidence that you need.

## Who are external customers?

These are people who come to a business to buy its products or use its services.
The benefits to the business of caring for external customers are:

- satisfied customers
- loyal customers
- more customers through repeat business and recommendations

- increased sales
- better public image
- an edge over the competition.

## Satisfied customers

All businesses compete for customers. The success or failure of a business can depend on whether the customers are happy with the product or service they receive. It is a fairly easy task for a salesperson to sell a product to a first time customer, especially by offering incentives such as special discounts. However, the real task is to sell to that same customer on a second occasion. Although the quality of the product is obviously important, the service the customer receives will often be the determining factor.

Dissatisfied customers can be very costly to a business. Firstly, there will be the loss of income from those customers that have been lost and, secondly, extra costs will be needed to replace the lost business, such as on advertising, marketing and sales.

### Example

Mr and Mrs Carter went to Moonraker Travel, a small high street travel agency in their local town. They wanted to arrange a holiday to Majorca for 12 people. The travel agent greeted them in a friendly manner. They told her what they wanted and when they would like to go. The travel agent was able to find various alternatives and she explained these, giving details as well as prices. They chose a holiday in a first-class hotel in Palma at a special group rate. They enjoyed a wonderful holiday and have now booked a winter cruise, also with Moonraker Travel.

## Loyal customers

Customers who are happy with the service they receive are likely to return. They will feel confident with the quality of the goods, or the way they have been treated. Loyal customers are important to all businesses but are particularly important to shops and supermarkets. Research has shown that it costs on average four to five times as much to acquire a new customer than to retain an existing one.

Customers are often rewarded for their loyalty to a business. This can take many forms, from a birthday card sent as a special gesture, to simple discounts and loyalty card schemes. Many businesses now use a loyalty card to encourage customers to use their business, rather than those in competition with them. There are over 25 million loyalty cards in circulation with Tesco, Sainsbury's and Boots as the market leaders. Competition has never been fiercer. Some supermarkets are reporting even higher profits and this may be due to customers' use of loyalty cards.

## ACTIVITY

1 Select a business with which you are familiar.
2 Give at least two examples of how satisfied customers can bring benefits to that business.

*Loyalty card*

One of the benefits to businesses of loyalty cards is that they encourage customers to return; customers are enticed by the use of the card as they see it as a reward for taking their business to that store. Another very important benefit to the businesses, is that by using their loyalty cards, customers are also giving stores a lot of information about them, including their buying habits, postal addresses, email addresses and other, more personal, information. Stores are also able to target particular customers with specific products.

Although it costs a significant amount of money to set up and administer a loyalty card scheme, the benefits seem to far outweigh the costs.

## QUESTIONS

1 What are the advantages of loyalty cards to the companies that operate them?
2 What are the advantages and disadvantages of loyalty cards to customers?

## More customers through repeat business and recommendations

Customers who are happy with the service they receive will benefit that business by bringing **repeat business**. This not only enables the company to offer a greater range of products, which also leads to increased sales, but also to more income and therefore improved profits.

**Recommendation** of a business by a customer is an excellent advertisement for a business and is most valued. People feel more at ease using a business recommended by someone who has used and been happy with the product or service provided, than picking a business out of a telephone directory or newspaper advertisement. Recommendation is also very cost-effective as it saves the company money in advertising costs or special introductory offers.

**Example**

Hairport is a small hair salon run by the owner, Saleem, and three employees. Many customers have been using the salon since it opened in 1990. Saleem discusses with his customers exactly what they require, particularly where more technical treatments such as colouring or perming are required. Everything possible is done to ensure that the customers' needs are met in full so that they feel valued, with good hair design, styled professionally. Customers usually make repeat appointments before they leave the salon.

*Excellent care – professional styling*

## ACTIVITY

1  Ask your friends:
   (a) whether they have used businesses that were recommended to them
   (b) whether they still use those businesses
   (c) if they were happy to recommend those businesses to others.
2  Look in the local newspapers and see if those businesses advertise
3  Explain how repeat business might affect a company's need to advertise.

## Increased sales

Customers who are satisfied with the product they buy, or the service they receive, will return and will also tell others about that excellent customer service. As well as benefiting from more income and therefore more profits, the business will also benefit in other ways. Businesses have found that by focusing their sales efforts on loyal customers, they will increase sales. Businesses also increase sales by keeping the customer informed about what is happening within the organisation.

## Better public image

A company that provides excellent customer service will benefit from improved trade, more income and an increased reputation. All of these things will lead to a better public image. People will hear about the efforts being made by the business to offer good products (or services) and excellent customer service.

**Did you know?**

*A public image is the way in which someone or something is perceived by others.*

Some companies, however, experience adverse publicity from time to time, which causes their public image to suffer. This can be a disaster to any business and, if not rectified quickly, could cause it to close down.

## ACTIVITY

Working in groups:

1  Look through local and national newspapers. Select a business that has received adverse publicity recently – each group should choose a different example.
2  Use as many sources as possible to find out how the business has improved its public image.
3  Each group should note its findings and present these to the class.
4  Discuss each group's findings as a class.

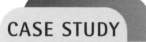

## CASE STUDY

### Barkers' Candles

Barkers' Candles is a family-owned business that makes candles and candle-making supplies in its 500 m² factory. The adjacent factory shop sells ready-made candles and everything required for customers to make their own candles.

The shop is open from 7.30 am to 7.30 pm six days a week and from 10.00 am to 4.00 pm on Sundays. There are many themed candles, including those related to food, animals, people and Christmas.

Barkers' Candles has many different customers, many of whom have been visiting the shop since it opened ten years ago.

*Barkers' Candles – lighting the way*

## *An edge over the competition*

Businesses compete with each other for customers and need to find something special that will define their business as different and superior to any other. This gives the business an **edge over the competition**. A business with no customer service policy, and even unsatisfactory quality and prices, may survive for a while if there is no competition nearby because customers will have no choice where to buy their goods or obtain their services. However, situations can change and competition may occur, offering a threat to the business which does not care for its customers.

## ACTIVITY

1   Identify and explain the benefits to Barkers' Candles in caring for external customers. Include the following categories:
    - satisfied customers
    - loyal customers
    - more customers through repeat business and recommendations
    - increased sales.
2   How can Barkers' Candles ensure a good public image?
3   What steps should the company take to ensure that they retain an edge over the competition?

## Who are internal customers?

The second part of this assessment objective is about how business benefits by caring for internal customers. The factors to be considered are:

- better level of service given by members of staff to one another
- happier and more efficient workforce
- improved job satisfaction.

   Internal customers are the employees of a company who receive service from other company employees. An organisation's employees are also its customers in that they invest their time and effort into the company in exchange for the opportunity to earn a living. How a business deals with its internal customers can be a good indication of how it deals with its external customers. Businesses can only offer a really professional service to external customers if they also offer a professional service to their internal customers. Everyone in a business serves someone and, in turn, is served by someone else within that business.

**Example**

Peter works with you in the Administration Services Unit of a manufacturing company. He asks you for a printout of the minutes of last month's Health and Safety Meeting. You give him the printout. In this instance, Peter is an internal customer and you provide the service. Later that day, you ask Peter for a copy of the agenda for next week's Health and Safety Meeting and he emails this to you. Now you are the internal customer and Peter is the service provider.

## Better level of service given by all members of staff to one another

Good customer service is vital to the success of any business. This service extends not only to external customers but also to its employees – its internal customers. Employees who have a clear definition of what their job roles are and how their jobs link into the activities required in producing goods or providing services will be more efficient. Each employee is an important link in the customer service chain. For example, in a manufacturing company, the buying department purchases the supplies required to make the goods, the manufacturing department uses these goods to make the company's products, the sales department sells them and the dispatch department ensures that delivery to the external customer is made on time. If one department fails to meet its target goods may not be delivered to the external customer on time. This could result in the business losing the customer, money having to be spent to replace this customer's business, and loss of income.

When employees work well together in a team, everything will run smoothly, work will be completed within the timescales set, customers will be happy and this will result in loyal customers, repeat business and more income and profit for the business.

People working in teams find that they can work well together if they respect each other and speak to each other in a courteous way. This can be difficult when dealing with someone in the team who you do not get on well with, but kindness and consideration is always appreciated and, in turn, you will find people are kind and considerate to you. For example, a 'please' and 'thank you' does not cost anything, but good manners show respect and this is always appreciated, no matter how old or young people are.

Working in harmony with each other will make for a happier workforce which will improve productivity and efficiency and, as a result, the product or service to the external customer.

**Figure 2.1**  *How departments rely on each other*

## *Happier and more efficient workforce*

A happy workforce will be an efficient workforce. This will directly influence external customers who will be happy with the service they receive and will return to the business and therefore improve income and profits for the business.

Building and keeping good customer relations is very important to all businesses. It is often the internal customers who identify external customers' needs. A business that meets these needs will maintain customer loyalty.

Communication can be the key to good internal customer service. It is vital that internal customers communicate effectively, not only with each other but also with external customers. Good internal customer service improves the morale of the workforce – they will feel valued – and productivity will improve as a result. This in turn will lead to more income and more profits for the business. A company that cares for its staff and provides excellent internal customer service also ensures that staff will want to stay, thus reducing costs in recruiting staff when people leave. There may also be less likelihood of absenteeism due to stress-related illnesses. A business that has a high turnover of staff is often not a happy organisation and people may be reluctant to work for that company.

Those businesses that organise and implement a good complaints procedure, which enables staff to take action when external customers make a complaint, will ensure that there is less aggravation from customers. Staff can become stressed when customers keep complaining, especially when nothing seems to be done to put things right. A good complaints procedure will ensure that staff can deal with customers' complaints, or refer them to a senior manager if necessary. Where a

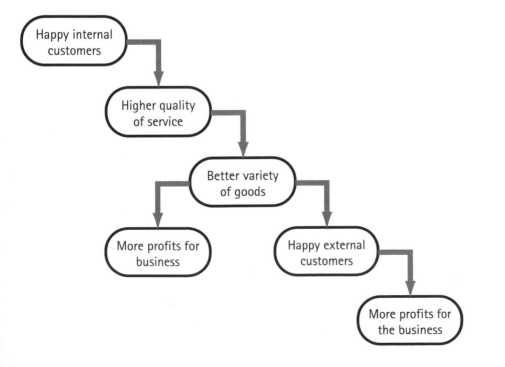

**Figure 2.2** *A happy workforce brings benefits to a business*

complaints procedure is not clear and does not work well, staff can find it difficult to deal with customers' complaints. This can lead to unhappy staff, unhappy customers and possibly even to the loss of the customers altogether.

Some businesses measure internal customer satisfaction by surveying their staff and asking them what could be improved and how. Questionnaires are used quite extensively to find out from staff exactly what is happening day to day in a business. Staff are better placed to do this and their feedback can be very important to the success of a business.

Performance measurement is also very important in that it will help identify problems. For example, the purchasing department may have goals concerning stock levels at any one time, the manufacturing department may have to complete orders on time and the sales department may have sales targets to meet.

It is important that businesses regularly measure the satisfaction levels of internal customers in an effort to identify ways in which improvements can be made. Businesses will review the effectiveness of the service to both internal and external customers and make improvements where necessary. This may mean new procedures or improving existing ones. The review will also identify training required for new staff or existing staff, who may need to be updated on new techniques or skills. This will lead to an improvement in staff morale as they will be more confident. They are also more likely to be loyal to their company.

### Example

Rosa works in a garden centre and has just completed training in customer care. She hopes that the training will not only help her to deal with customers but also help her to gain promotion. She now feels more confident in dealing with complaints and knows that she can refer any difficult complaints to her team leader. Rosa says that her team is very friendly and everyone works efficiently. Her company shows that it cares by providing training to ensure that she can handle all situations. In providing training the company is also demonstrating its commitment to Rosa, making her feel more secure in her job.

## QUESTIONS

1. What could be done where you work to provide a better level of service to the employees?
2. What could your company do to ensure that you and your work colleagues are a happy and efficient workforce?

## *Improved job satisfaction*

When people work well together, the feeling of harmony often reaches out to the external customers as well.

Work that is produced on time can often lead to bonuses being paid. Employees can also take advantage of perks such as free holidays, the use of a company car or van, commission on sales, etc. This all leads to job satisfaction. A happy workforce will be more efficient; more productivity leads to more income.

## CASE STUDY

### *Abbot Pine*

Abbot Pine has manufactured pine furniture since 1976 when Peter Abbot started making high-quality pine tables and chairs for his family, friends and neighbours in a shed in his garden. He was so successful that Abbot Pine Furniture Ltd was formed in 1985. The furniture is manufactured in a purpose-built factory and is produced to high-quality and exacting standards. Over 1,000 pieces of furniture are produced every week and delivered by the company's fleet of trucks and vans to the company's showrooms.

The majority of Abbot Pine's customers are people looking for a range of furniture for their home. However, the company also sells to schools, offices, hotels and guesthouses throughout the UK.

The company employs skilled craftspeople who offer a made-to-measure and colour-matching service. The company guarantees that all the furniture is made from quality pine.

**Working in pairs, discuss the ways in which Abbot Pine Furniture benefits by caring for its internal customers. You should include:**

(a) a better level of service given by all members of staff to one another
(b) a happier and more efficient workforce
(c) improved job satisfaction.

## AO2    Describe how customer service responses are adapted to the needs of the customer

In this section, you will investigate how customer service responses are adapted to the needs of the full range of an organisation's customers, using examples to illustrate your findings.

Different customers are likely to have different levels of intelligence, language and communication. It is very important, therefore, to treat them with tact and patience. It is important to try to match your use of language to that of the customers, without being patronising.

You need to describe how customer service responses are adapted to customers' needs for the following types of customers:

- individuals
- groups
- people of different ages
- people from different cultures
- non-English speakers
- people with specific needs, e.g. wheelchair access
- young children
- business people.

## Types of customer

Businesses are very diverse and the nature of the business will have a bearing on the type of customers who use it. This will, to some extent, also influence the responses required to meet all the needs of the customers. For example, the way in which a dentist deals with customers, who may be anxious or in pain, will be very different to the way in which a golf professional deals with customers who he is teaching to play golf.

### Individuals

There are likely to be many different situations where you will deal with individual customers. These situations will be on a one-to-one basis, either face to face or using the telephone.

### Face to face

You should aim to be polite and friendly. Keep eye contact at all times, but be careful that the customer does not interpret this as staring. Watch out for non-verbal signs (body language) that may indicate how the customer is feeling. Research has shown that approximately 54 per cent of what we learn from customers comes from their body language; 37 per cent comes from the tone of their voice; and just 9 per cent from what they say. For example, if a customer is red-faced, throwing his arms around, using an aggressive stance or clenching his fists, these are all signs that he may be angry. You will then be able to decide how to deal with him.

Dealing with a customer face to face may involve a complaint. Stay calm at all times, no matter how angry the customer is or how loudly he is shouting at you. By speaking in a calm and reassuring manner and keeping eye contact, you are likely to calm the customer so that you can find out what the problem is. Never lose your temper as this can make a fraught situation worse. If you know the customer, perhaps because he is a regular, use his name, e.g. 'I will do whatever I can to help you, Mr Wilson. I'm sure we can sort out your problem.'

*Face-to-face communication*

### Example

Malik is a waiter in Swan's Coffee Shop, where customers can enjoy a variety of hot and cold snacks and drinks. He serves customers at tables, taking their orders and endeavouring to provide a quick and efficient service. Recently, the coffee shop was very busy when a customer suddenly stood up, shouting and waving his arms. He complained that he had asked for tea but was served coffee. Malik stayed calm and quickly apologised for the mistake, ensuring his voice was not too loud and his tone was soft. The customer immediately quietened and returned to his seat. Malik replaced the coffee with a pot of tea, and some biscuits with the compliments of the shop. The customer was happy and everyone continued chatting, eating and drinking in a calm, peaceful environment.

## ACTIVITY

Working in groups, compile a notice detailing a step-by-step approach for dealing with a customer in a face-to-face situation. On completion, the whole class should discuss each group's findings.

## Telephone

When you answer the telephone to a customer you can't see how the customer is feeling, as there are no body language signals to guide you. It is helpful to remember that approximately 85 per cent of what we learn from people over the telephone comes from the tone of their voice and just 15 per cent from what they say.

It is important to answer the telephone as promptly as possible and to smile as you do so. This ensures that you are in good humour when you answer the phone. Give your name and department, if appropriate. Be polite and friendly. As soon as the customer starts speaking, the tone of her voice will tell you whether she is happy, displeased or downright angry. You should bear in mind that the customer may have a problem that is causing some distress. She may well be complaining about something. Your first words and the tone and volume of voice you use are vital. If you don't handle the situation carefully, you could make it much worse. If the customer has a problem and you cannot help, tell the customer that you will find out and phone her back. However, do not just promise to phone back, give her a time when you will do so. For example, 'I'm very sorry that I can't answer your question at the moment. I will find out and ring you back before 11 am.' Then you must be sure to ring the customer before 11 am or ensure that someone else does so. It is very frustrating for customers when they do not know what is happening so your prompt call to them will prevent them having to ring again and possibly having to start all over again, with a different member of staff.

### QUESTIONS

1 Why is it important to answer the phone promptly?
2 Give five tips on dealing with customers on the telephone.
3 Outline what you would do if you could not help the customer.
4 Describe the routine you should follow for ending a call with a customer.

## Groups

Dealing with a group can be quite overwhelming, especially if there is a large number of people who can be boisterous and noisy. It is important to wait until you have the attention of all members of the group before you try to speak to them. Position yourself so that everyone in the group can hear what you are saying, even if they can't see you. Endeavour to find out if anyone in the group needs to be able to read your lips and take appropriate action. You may need to use questions and answers to check that everyone has heard what you have said and that they have understood. Remember that people tend to talk quickly when they are nervous. Try to ensure that you speak slowly and clearly. Some people in the group may be shy or have particular problems. Give them the opportunity to speak to you alone, away from the group. Stand to one side while the group disperses to enable anyone who wishes to speak to you to do so.

Remember, everyone likes to feel appreciated – deal with groups of people, even large groups, as kindly and courteously as possible.

## People of different ages

You should respond to people of different ages in different ways. For example, you would treat a young child in a very different manner to a very old lady. A young child may become separated from his or her parents; an older person may become confused, or have difficulty with sight, hearing or mobility. Both will need patience and kindness.

You will quickly learn to assess a situation and adjust the tone and volume of your voice to fit that situation. You will also speak slowly to ensure that people can understand what you are saying. You should find body language of help when dealing with people of different ages. For example, you will often be able to gauge whether an older person has heard and understood what you have said by the way they express themselves. Look particularly at their faces for significant signals such as a look of puzzlement, frowning, etc.

Young people, including teenagers, can be very independent and you should treat them with as much patience and tact as you would any other age group.

Adults should be treated with respect and tolerance. They can be difficult to deal with at times but you should always use kindness and patience, however difficult they may be to deal with.

**ACTIVITY**

Give an example of how you dealt with a group of people, including details of where this occurred and what type of people were in the group.

### Example

Francis works in a motorcycle shop, selling and repairing motorcycles. A group of young teenagers came into his shop. They were boisterous and noisy and playing about with the bikes. Francis was worried that they would knock the bikes over and perhaps damage them. The lads were keen to buy a bike but were not old enough to ride one on a public road.

*Motorcycles for sale at 'Young Rider'*

## ACTIVITY

Look at the example. What advice would you give to Francis on dealing with this situation?

## People from different cultures

People using a business may be from a different culture. It may be that they do not understand British customs, even fairly simple ones such as queuing. Many food stores try to ensure that their range of food caters for all people, whether they are vegetarian or have special dietary requirements for religious reasons. In large towns and cities, clothes shops often try to offer clothing which is appropriate for all customers. Many restaurants and cafés offer menus that cater for all dietary needs. It is very important that any complaints are handled with care and are logged so that senior management are able to amend procedures and policies.

## Non-English speakers

Communication may be difficult when you are dealing with someone who cannot speak English and whose language you do not understand. Some businesses employ staff who are fluent in languages other than English. Customers may carry a phrase book with them and this may help when trying to communicate. However, where there is no phrase book some communication may be possible with hand signals, pointing, drawing pictures, etc. Some customers may have a little understanding of English – speaking slowly will help them understand you. Do not be tempted to raise your voice – shouting will not help understanding and will probably upset them.

## ACTIVITY

1  Describe the problems that may arise when dealing with people of different cultures.
2  Explain how you would deal with a customer who doesn't speak English.

## People with specific needs

People with specific needs may be those who are wheelchair users, hard of hearing, or who have problems with their sight or mobility. All businesses must ensure that disabled people have access to their premises. Customers with hearing problems may use loop systems, which reduce background noise, to help them hear more clearly. Others may be able to lip read or to use sign language. Remember to speak slowly and clearly when communicating with people who lip read. They need to see your lips in order to read them, so try to avoid turning away from them as you speak. Some businesses provide training in sign language for their staff and there may be someone within your company who is a competent signer. Sometimes, simply writing things down can be a tremendous help.

However, some people with specific needs can be self-sufficient and independent – you should always ask if you can help them; never assume that they need your help!

## ACTIVITY

You work in a petrol station when a disabled customer arrives to put petrol in her car. She appears to be having difficulty getting out of her car. Explain the action you would take in order to help the customer.

## Young children

Young children need particular care. They may have become separated from their parents and may be frightened and anxious. When talking to them, get down to their level so that your eyes and theirs are level. Speak to them in a quiet, gentle voice to find out whether or not they have understood what you have said to them. Some young children may not be able to tell you their name, they may be crying so much that they cannot speak. You must ensure the safety and security of children who are in your care, however temporary.

### Example

Jenni works on the customer service desk of a large supermarket in a seaside town. A customer brought a distressed young girl to her. The child had become separated from her parents and she was sobbing so loudly that she could not speak. Jenni took her hand and, talking to her gently all the time, sat her down in a quiet area and asked a colleague to put out a call over the store's loudspeaker. The parents soon arrived at the desk but before Jenni allowed them to take the child away, she made quite sure that they were, indeed, the child's parents.

## Business people

Most contact with business people is via email, fax or telephone, rather than face to face. You should bear in mind that business people may bring in large amounts of income to your organisation, making them regular customers. Those who are particularly favoured by your organisation may expect special treatment. Your company may have a policy or procedure for dealing with business people and you should comply with this at all times. Business customers can be difficult to deal with by demanding special favours, such as discounts, reduced prices or extra services. If you have any doubts when dealing with business customers, ask your team leader or supervisor for help. Remember, patience, tact and kindness, and, above all, try to keep smiling.

## CASE STUDY

*Maxim's Adventure Park*

Josef Maxim established Maxim's Adventure Park in 1992. He wanted to build a park that would be a recreation playground for children of all ages. He grew up in a small village and was keen to give people, especially children, the opportunity to hold and feed domestic animals.

Maxim's Adventure Park opened with a small pets' corner and a takeaway outlet. Very soon the park had become so successful that Josef began to think about expansion. His children were then aged 14 and 16 and they convinced him that the park should provide attractions, such as rides, go-karts and bumper boats for all the family, including parents and older children.

Today, Maxim's has many attractions, including a massive rollercoaster, a splash zone, a pirate-themed restaurant, and a huge range of other entertainments. Many of the activities are under cover so there is always plenty to do even when it rains. Local organisations and companies also use the park for corporate events and team-building sessions.

1 In groups of three, discuss how Maxim's Adventure Park adapts its customer service responses to the needs of one of the following categories:
   ● individuals
   ● groups
   ● people of different ages
   ● people from different cultures
   ● non-English speakers
   ● people with specific needs
   ● young children
   ● business people.

2 Each group should make notes on a flipchart and present their findings to the class.

3 Discuss each group's findings as a class.

The second part of this assessment objective is about how customer service responses are adapted to deal with:

● predictable and unpredictable situations

● providing knowledge and information to different types of customers

● adapting information for customers with different levels of understanding

● dealing with sensitive issues and adapting what is said or written to customers

● situations where the customer must be referred to someone else

● legal requirements that must be met concerning information supplied to and records held about customers.

# Predictable and unpredictable situations

Most of the everyday work of staff in customer service could be classified as predictable – requests for information, queries about pricing and stock levels, and complaints. Long queues can form in some stores in the period immediately after Christmas when people come back to exchange their unwanted presents, and companies usually employ more staff to ensure the best possible customer service. A company's procedure for handling all these predictable situations will be specific and easy to follow, and training will be provided to ensure staff can confidently handle all situations.

Unpredictable situations can be more tricky and it will often be necessary for staff to refer to senior staff for advice.

### Example

Jigna works as an administrator for Cath's Cleaners, a small company offering a cleaning service to offices and householders. One day a regular customer phoned to inform her that some money was missing from her home. She had noticed it after the cleaner had finished work there that day. Jigna was calm and sympathetic, taking care not to upset the customer. She explained that she could not deal with the situation but that Cath, the owner, would contact her immediately. Jigna then phoned Cath to tell her what had happened.

## ACTIVITY

In groups of three, select a business and discuss predictable and unpredictable situations that may occur in that business. Make a list of at least three predictable and two unpredictable situations.

# Providing knowledge and information to different types of customers

When providing knowledge or information to customers, you should take into consideration many aspects, such as their age, any special needs they may have, whether they speak English, to ensure that you cater for each customer's individual needs. For example, in a restaurant an old person requiring information may not hear clearly or may have difficulty reading the menu.

It is very important that you have good product knowledge. Customers vary in the information they need; some require simple details, while others need detailed technical information, depending to some extent on the type of business. Good product knowledge is also important for good customer relations and will give staff confidence. Companies will organise staff training, not just in customer care but also in its range of products.

# Adapting information for customers with different levels of understanding

Some customers have a lower level of understanding than others. When talking to customers, you should soon realise whether they have understood what you have said. Look out for a puzzled look, or a frown. You may need to speak more slowly and clearly. You may need to ask questions to try to elicit what it is that they have not understood and you may need to repeat what you have said. You may find it necessary to take the customers to one side to give them special individual attention, away from other customers.

# Dealing with sensitive issues and adapting what is said or written to customers

There are many situations where great care, tact and sympathy must be used when dealing with customers. They may have problems or needs which are rather sensitive. In these cases, the customer would normally be taken to one side or to a room somewhere, so that his or her needs can be explained in privacy, with appropriate displays of empathy from the staff.

### Example

Dulcie works in Babies R Us, a shop that sells everything for new and expectant mothers and babies. A man walked into the shop, obviously embarrassed and reluctant to approach her. Dulcie went up to him and asked him if she could help. The man was very embarrassed but Dulcie managed to find out that his wife had just given birth to their daughter prematurely and unexpectedly. His wife had made a list of some personal items that she needed and had asked him to buy them for her. Dulcie was able to show him to the various displays and discreetly put the items in a basket for him. She talked to him, putting him at ease all the time and he left happily with his purchases.

## ACTIVITY

Working in pairs, look at the example and discuss how Dulcie would have handled this situation had the customer been the man's mother-in-law.

There may be occasions when letters that are written to customers may need to be adapted to suit particular circumstances. For example, a hotel may send a standard letter to customers who cancel their holiday booking just days before they are due to arrive. This may stress that the deposit that customers have already paid will be retained to cover expenses such as administrative costs and those involved in finding new customers. However, in the case of a customer cancelling due to bereavement, the deposit would be returned to the customer with a note of sympathy.

# Situations where the customer must be referred to someone else

Some situations will need to be referred to someone else, particularly senior staff. It may be that you do not have the experience or product knowledge required. Never be tempted to bluff your way through a situation. Customers will soon realise that you are unsure of yourself. If you cannot help, be honest and tell the customer, and then call for a senior member of staff to help.

## ACTIVITY

Describe a situation in the workplace where it would be necessary to refer a customer to someone else.

# Legal requirements that must be met concerning information supplied to and records held about customers

The Data Protection Acts of 1984 and 1988 give individuals the right to know if inaccurate information about them has been disclosed, lost or retained. They also have right of access to any personal information that is held by a company.

There are seven rights under the Data Protection Act:

1 The right to find out what information is held on a computer and within some manual records.
2 The right to prevent anyone processing information that may cause damage or distress.
3 The right to prevent processing of information for direct marketing purposes.
4 The right to object to decisions made only by automatic means, e.g. there has been no human involvement.
5 The right to compensation for damage and distress caused by any breach of the Act.
6 The right to rectification, blocking, erasure and destruction of inaccurate information.
7 The right to ask the Commissioner to assess whether the Act has been contravened.

## Portfolio tip

*In order to provide the portfolio of evidence required for this assessment objective, you will need to clearly explain, using a range of relevant examples, how customer service responses are adapted to the needs of the full range of customers.*

# AO3 Investigate the customer service function of a selected business and describe, using examples, its structure, operation and interactions

In this section, you will choose a business and investigate the customer service function of that business. You will use examples to help you describe its structure, operation and interactions.

If you work in a small family business, the owner may be willing to help you gather the information you need. In a larger organisation, you may have access to information through a team leader or supervisor.

## Definition of the customer service function

Customer service includes all the activities that affect a customer's experience of dealing with a particular business, whether it is to buy its products or to use its services. These activities may include how customers' needs are satisfied and the way they are treated by staff. It embraces getting to know the customers, learning what they want and ensuring that they get it. It is also about businesses creating systems and providing training that enable staff to give the best possible service to customers. Businesses need customers; without them they would be forced to close.

## The structure and operation of the customer service department

In some smaller organisations, such as a sole trader, the owner would handle customer service, as well as all the other business functions. In larger organisations, the structure of a customer service department will vary depending on the size and type of business. Customer service may be a part of the marketing or sales departments. Many companies recognise the importance of customer service to their businesses and ensure that it is given its own department, with a manager overseeing its work.

All members of staff in a business will have some responsibility for customer service. Management will devise procedures for dealing with customers and will arrange training for staff in customer care and dealing and communicating with customers. Training will cover aspects such as:

- product knowledge – on both new and existing products, as well as additional skills that may be required to ensure good product knowledge

- completing customer records – enquiries, complaints, feedback
- dealing with customer complaints – procedures for handling, recording and providing feedback to senior management
- when to ask for help from colleagues or senior staff
- dealing with feedback from customers.

## CASE STUDY

### *The Best Plaice: Customer Service Department*

The Best Plaice is a private limited company with its head office in Torquay. It has six combined restaurant and takeaway enterprises and ten takeaway outlets throughout Devon and Cornwall. The company is owned by the Osman family.

At present, each Best Plaice outlet serves fish and chips, alternative foods such as sausages, a selection of home-made desserts and hot and cold drinks. The fish is bought in bulk daily from Brixham fisheries. The batter and desserts are made in a small factory adjacent to the head office. These products are transported by the company vans to the outlets on a daily basis. Each outlet, however, buys its own potatoes, but only from local growers.

Each Best Plaice outlet has a manager who is responsible for the day-to-day operations of the company. This includes staff management, overseeing operations (such as purchasing)

and customer service, including the handling of enquiries and complaints. Every manager has an assistant manager who takes control in the manager's absence. Also employed in each outlet are chefs, waiting staff and kitchen staff, who are all provided with uniforms and name badges. Kitchen staff are also responsible for cleaning. New staff attend induction training at head office, which includes sessions on food hygiene and health and safety, ensuring high standards are maintained and that employee loyalty is assured. Staff in all outlets are responsible for customer care.

Head office staff monitor each outlet to ensure that the company's customer service policy is being implemented. This is achieved by:

- holding regular meetings with the manager of each outlet
- computerised links to each outlet
- regular staff updating and training
- regular quality control checks
- regular staff information, such as news sheets
- analysis of customer feedback.

The company insists on very high standards of customer service and strives to give customers exactly what they want – the best quality fish and chips, cooked to perfection, served in a friendly manner and at a fair price.

# How the needs and expectations of the customer influence every stage of the business activity cycle

The needs and expectations of customers will vary from business to business, depending on the products or services involved. Most customers will expect to be able to buy products or use services

- of the right quality at a fair price
- at a place that is convenient for them
- at a time that is convenient for them.

All the customers' needs will be met within an organisation by a number of employees working in different departments. Customer service staff will constantly interact with staff in other departments. For example, they will work closely with marketing staff to ensure that the company is delivering what the customer wants. They will liaise with production staff to ensure that goods are made to the specifications that the customer requires. Human resources staff will be responsible for employing suitable staff (or issuing guidelines for recruitment) and will organise appropriate customer service staff training.

## CASE STUDY

### The Best Plaice: Customer influence

The directors of the company work closely together to ensure that customers always have what they want. All departments hold regular meetings, which directors normally attend. These will monitor the organisation of the business as well as feeding back any complaints from customers.

The production and customer service departments work together to ensure that quality control checks are carried out, both in the production of the batter and desserts and at the outlets where the customers purchase the food.

The marketing and customer service departments meet regularly to discuss feedback from customers to ensure that the company is meeting customers' expectations.

# How customer service interacts with other internal departments

The customer service department will constantly monitor customer satisfaction and will liaise with other internal departments on aspects that need to be improved or where consideration should be given to changing procedures, or to offering new products. These departments may include, for example:

- marketing – to carry out customer surveys and primary market research

- production – to ensure that the right products are available, to amend quality control processes where appropriate, and set new deadlines if needed

- distribution – to ensure that customers have their goods delivered on time.

Where a complaint has been received, the customer service department may need to liaise with other internal departments, particularly if the problem is a technical one or has serious implications for the company.

## How customer service interacts with external customers

Customer service staff need good communication skills to be able to deal with external customers in face-to-face situations and via the telephone. They are likely to offer advice, provide information, give assistance, resolve problems and complaints, and offer services to the customers to ensure that they have exactly what they need, when they need it. They may also occasionally need to write a letter to a customer, perhaps in response to one that has been received, complying with a company's house style.

Customers will expect staff to have good knowledge of their company's products, know how they work, be able to demonstrate them, and to do all this in a friendly and helpful way. Of course, customers also want good quality products at reasonable prices. However, research has shown that the service the customer receives can make the difference between a customer being happy and returning in the future or going elsewhere.

The way in which staff deal with customers is vitally important. First impressions stay with customers and they will be deciding whether to do business with an organisation within the first minutes of contact with a member of staff. A friendly greeting and a smile will help the staff/customer relationship. Staff should always be polite and show **empathy** wherever possible. Body language should always be appropriate, as should the tone of language and pitch of voice, when interacting with external customers. Staff must always give customers their full attention. They should not hesitate to refer a customer to a senior member of staff if they are unable to help for any reason.

### Portfolio tip

*In order to provide the portfolio of evidence required for this assessment objective, you will need to carry out a comprehensive investigation of a selected business. You should demonstrate a thorough understanding of the structure of the customer service department and how it operates and interacts with internal departments and external customers.*

### GLOSSARY

To display **empathy** is to show that you understand how someone is feeling; having sympathy for their feelings.

## CASE STUDY

*The Best Plaice: Interaction with external customers*

--------------------------------------------------------------------

All staff, whether at head office or in the outlets, are responsible for customer service. They are expected to offer a friendly and helpful service at all times. Staff are trained at induction sessions and at regular intervals in different aspects of customer service. There is great stress on hygiene and cleanliness.

The company's procedure for dealing with customers is as follows:

1   Greet the customer – and smile.

2   Find out what the customer wants.
3   Listen carefully to what the customer is saying.
4   If appropriate, ask questions to clarify anything.
5   Repeat any requests the customer has made – for example, to ensure that orders are correct.
6   Take action to fulfil the customer's requirements.
7   Keep smiling!

## ACTIVITY

Ask your tutor to arrange for a local businessperson to come to your class to give a presentation or talk, with the aid of a DVD or video if possible, on the structure, operation and interactions of the customer service function of his or her business. It may then be possible to arrange for you to visit the customer service department to see how the department functions at first hand and to question staff working there.

## AO4   Explain how customer service standards are planned, implemented and monitored, and the impact this has on the operation of a selected business

All organisations need to plan, implement and monitor customer service standards. A company's existing customers are important assets and businesses will do their utmost to ensure that they keep their customers. With no customers, there is no income and therefore no profits and no business. Keeping existing customers is important because finding new ones can be expensive and time-consuming.

In this assessment objective, you will need to access the customer service standards that your selected business uses to measure their customer service performance. You may use the same business that you used in the previous assessment objective, or you may choose a different business, if you prefer.

# Planning customer service standards

Companies must plan their customer service standards in order to ensure that they survive. In today's harsh business climate, those companies which plan ahead, with both internal and external customers in mind, are more likely to succeed than those who make no plans and will therefore soon find that they have no customers.

## Setting aims, outlining measurable benchmarks

Most companies understand the importance of ensuring that customers are provided with what they require. Companies must have standards against which service can be measured and then if targets are not being achieved action can be taken.

## Setting aims

Ways in which companies set aims for customer service standards will vary from business to business. They will vary between companies offering different goods or services and even between companies offering similar products or services.

## CASE STUDY

*The Best Plaice: Setting customer service aims*

------------------------------------------------------------------------

The company has set aims for customer service standards and these are constantly reviewed. They are:

- to reinforce the company's position as the top provider of fish and chips in the South West
- to provide customers with:
  - quality fish and chips, cooked to perfection every time
  - excellent service that is reliable and consistent
  - what they want, when they want it
  - an efficient service performed by friendly, helpful staff
  - a system for dealing with any complaints quickly and efficiently.

## Outlining measurable benchmarks

Benchmarks are points of reference that are used by businesses to set a minimum level of service, quality and quantity that the customer service system must reach in order to meet their objectives. Benchmarks are realistic, understandable and, most importantly, measurable.

---

## CASE STUDY

### The Best Plaice: Benchmarks

The Best Plaice directors have set benchmarks for the level of service they expect their customers to receive at every outlet, whether in a restaurant or a takeaway.

- The exterior and interior of each outlet should always be clean and well maintained.
- Easy access to outlets is essential – dedicated parking spaces must be made available to customers at all times.
- The entrance to each building must be easily accessible.
- When taking telephone orders, the telephone must be answered within four rings and staff must be friendly, helpful and have a good telephone manner.
- Staff must make a good first impression. Their appearance is one of the most important factors in contributing to a positive first impression.

- When customers enter, they must be greeted promptly in a friendly manner – and with a smile.
- Staff must make personal contact with customers within two minutes of them entering.
- Staff should listen carefully to the customer, nod encouragement, use questions to clarify any detail and repeat what has been said.
- Staff will ensure compliance with health and safety regulations and high standards of hygiene at all times.
- Food must be served within ten minutes of the order being taken.
- Staff will be trained so that the service they offer customers is of the highest quality.

---

### GLOSSARY

**Qualitative performance indicators**: non-numeric indicators, such as judgements or opinions.

**Quantitative performance indicators**: numeric indicators.

## Designing qualitative and quantitative performance indicators

Performance indicators are used by many businesses to enable them to determine what is being achieved in their business and how the service can be improved.

**Qualitative performance indicators** may include staff/management relationships, customer satisfaction, employee morale, quality and taste of product and customer loyalty. **Quantitative performance indicators** will include sales and profit levels, speed of service, customer retention, the number of complaints received about staff and/or products or services, the percentage of orders resulting from visits to customers by salespeople, and responses to marketing material sent out.

Public services also set performance indicators. Examples are the number of urgent cases meeting the eight-minute target set by the government (ambulance) and the proportion of police officers available for frontline policing (police).

## CASE STUDY

### *The Best Plaice: Performance indicators*

Qualitative performance indicators designed by the company include:

- customer satisfaction – including monitoring of a recent customer feedback programme
- quality and taste of product
- employee morale – level of staff turnover
- levels of staff absenteeism – indicators of staff unhappiness and possible stress.

Quantitative performance indicators include:

- the speed of service – that customers receive their food within ten minutes of ordering, or that there are no more than two people at the till at any one time
- sales levels – have they dropped or risen?
- profit levels – have these increased or decreased?
- the number of complaints received about the food and service
- the number of complaints received about staff.

# Implementing and monitoring customer care standards

Companies that wish to ensure continued success not only need to set up good customer care standards but also ones that can be monitored.

## *Providing staff training on raising customer service standards*

Most companies include sessions on customer service in their induction training programmes and some provide at least a full day's training dedicated to customer service. Often new staff will attend training at an organisation's head or regional offices, which would then be reinforced by training at the local level. Training usually includes a presentation giving examples of dealing with different customers. It may also include role plays involving different scenarios, such as dealing with problems or complaints, with different types of customer, such as young children, business people and those with specific needs. When the induction session is complete, training usually continues, being undertaken by local staff to ensure that customer service standards are always maintained.

## Meeting performance indicators

Companies constantly monitor the performance indicators that they have designed to see whether they are being met, and if not, to determine why not and to take direct action to rectify matters. For example, is the product of good quality? What are the customers' opinions on taste? Are the customers receiving the goods they ordered within the time set? Have the levels of sales fallen below those set and expected for the time of year?

## Measuring performance

There are many ways in which performance can be measured and these include:

- sales levels
- conducting surveys of customers as they leave the business premises
- postage-paid questionnaires, comment cards and forms left in very accessible places
- special facilities for customer feedback on an organisation's websites, such as 'Contact us' buttons
- emailing customers – including electronic survey panels

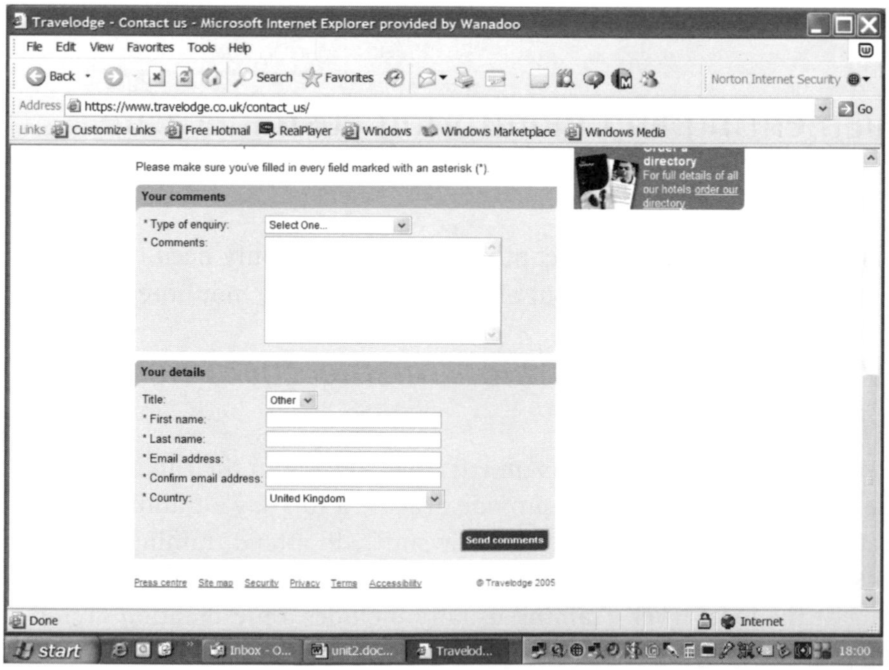

**Figure 2.3**   *Give feedback through a website's Contact Us facility*

- postage-paid questionnaires which may be handed to customers or sent to their homes
- occasional telephone calls to customers to gauge customer service levels
- personal or telephone interviews – for use by internal and external customers
- suggestion boxes – internal and external customers
- complaints about staff
- complaints about products or services.

## CASE STUDY

### *The Best Plaice: Measuring performance*

To monitor each outlet's performance, staff regularly hand customers questionnaires with clipboards and pens. Each one targets a particular aspect of the business and customers are able to complete these while waiting for their food to be prepared and cooked.

Results of a recent questionnaire on freshness and quality of produce resulted in 96 per cent satisfaction in the restaurants but only 58 per cent in takeaways. The major reason given was that customers said that takeaway food was too greasy and suggested more time for food to drain before wrapping. The directors discussed this as a matter of urgency and decided that they wished to stay with their policy of 'fish cooked to order' but the procedure was changed to ensure that food was drained for at least two minutes before serving, but at the same time ensuring that it remained hot.

**Figure 2.4**   *The Best Plaice questionnaire*

How often do you visit **The Best Plaice**?
Please tick one box

First visit ☐   Once a week ☐
Once every two weeks ☐
Once a month ☐   Once every two months ☐
Less often ☐

Please rate the following by ticking the appropriate boxes

|  | Very Good | Good | Fair | Poor |
|---|---|---|---|---|
| Staff welcoming | ☐ | ☐ | ☐ | ☐ |
| Order taken efficiently | ☐ | ☐ | ☐ | ☐ |
| Speed of service | ☐ | ☐ | ☐ | ☐ |
| Please rate the service you received | ☐ | ☐ | ☐ | ☐ |

Please indicate, in minutes, the time taken to serve you today: _____ minutes

Please indicate whether you are

| a local | a tourist | on business |
|---|---|---|
| ☐ | ☐ | ☐ |

Thank you for taking the time to complete this questionnaire

**The Best Plaice**

## Monitoring performance

Customer service performance will be monitored constantly by businesses to ensure that their customers are getting what they want, when they want it. This monitoring is carried out in a variety of ways:

- inspection by unknown company staff to witness customer service at first hand – to ensure that standards are being maintained
- regular staff meetings
- mystery shoppers who, acting as customers, visit an organisation to buy a product or use a service – the staff are not told in advance of the shopper's visit
- monitoring telephone conversations – to assess speed of answering and technique used
- staff appraisals.

## CASE STUDY

### The Best Plaice: Monitoring performance

Head office staff regularly visit outlets to buy food at takeaways and also use the restaurants. They may take their families with them to add authenticity. Staff are not warned in advance.

The company has recently decided to use a system of mystery shoppers, managed by an external organisation. Soon a visit has been made, a report is completed and a copy sent to head office. This is discussed at the monthly managers' meetings and action is taken. Mystery shoppers also telephone an outlet with an order to assess speed of answering and telephone skills, and will then visit the premises to collect the order. Occasionally, senior management will discuss a suggestion or complaint received via a mystery shopper.

## Reviewing performance and taking action

Businesses need to know which customers are very pleased or very dissatisfied. Then they can take steps to ensure that matters are rectified, where appropriate. Staff are informed when they have been praised. Any suggestions for improvement are considered and put into practice where appropriate.

The following are some of the ways in which performance is reviewed and the action that would be taken:

- action plan to improve areas that have been criticised and to maintain those areas that have been satisfactory
- strong negative feedback is immediately investigated
- suggestions and praise are acted upon

- senior management is informed – this helps measure achievement and to take steps to improve further
- implement any changes to procedures
- further checks on progress
- let the customer know what action has been taken
- put information on the website – for internal and external customers
- regular meetings to discuss performance indicators, customer satisfaction and the performance of the customer service function
- brainstorming sessions with customer service staff managers and senior staff to come up with ways of rectifying problems and improving standards.

## CASE STUDY

### *The Best Plaice: Reviewing performance*

The company places great stress on the importance of reviewing customer service performance and taking action promptly. If strong negative feedback has been received regarding a part of the service or concerning a member of staff, this is investigated immediately by head office staff. Where complaints are received, an action plan is devised to ensure that a complaint is dealt with quickly, that the customer is contacted and that any necessary changes to the company's procedures are implemented.

A new webcam system facilitates regular meetings with managers. Brainstorming at the monthly managers' meetings has resulted in some new procedures in the company's customer service standards which, it is hoped, will lead to higher sales levels.

The company's newsletter is a useful tool for keeping staff informed on performance reviews and any action taken by the company. It is published quarterly and every employee is given a copy.

## *Procedures for handling customer complaints*

All businesses have to deal with customer complaints. Most businesses have a procedure for staff to follow when dealing with these. If the complaint is handled successfully, the customer is likely to use the business again. Careful handling of complaints is often seen as a way to keep ahead of competitors. However, customers must know what an organisation's complaints procedure is. Complaints should be handled courteously, quickly and with sympathy, and feedback given to the customer as to the outcome.

## CASE STUDY

### The Best Plaice: Complaints procedure

If a customer makes a complaint, staff will deal with it immediately, following the company's procedures. The details will be logged in the complaints book. This is a duplicate book – the top copy is sent to head office who will write to the customer directly. The company's procedure for handling complaints is:

- listen sympathetically to establish what it is that the customer is complaining about
- nod your head to show understanding – and keep smiling

- apologise – even if you do not think the fault lies with the company
- record the details in the complaints book and send the top copy to head office
- offer a solution – such as a free meal
- take follow-up action, such as a letter of apology or phone call from your manager to tell the customer what action has been taken.

## Customer information and helplines

There are many different methods of informing customers and some of these are:

- websites containing detailed information
- notices displayed on notice boards
- leaflets and information sheets available in stores
- frequently asked questions (FAQs) on websites
- mail shots – these can be personalised
- emails – known as 'spam'
- newsletters
- special buttons and hot spots on websites, for example to find the nearest store
- customer service advice helplines – usually with a freephone telephone number.

*Leaflets contain useful information for customers*

# Impact on resources

Many companies strive to ensure that their customer service is of the highest quality. However, where problems are identified, remedies must be implemented and these will have an impact on the company's resources.

## *Resources (human, financial, time, physical)*

If some aspects of poor customer service have been identified, such as poor product knowledge or staff's inability to use products, then staff training may be needed. This will have cost, time and staff implications. It will cost money to organise the training, to transport staff to the place of training and to replace the member of staff for the time they are away from their place of work. Staff will also have to make the effort to attend the training.

The investigation of complaints can also be costly in terms of time and money. Several members of staff may be involved in resolving the complaints and records will need to be completed. This will take time and cost money. Where a customer has complained about a member of staff, this may result in a verbal warning. If it is not the first complaint, it may result in a written warning or even dismissal.

Improved communication within an organisation can be expensive. Telecommunications have improved to such an extent that instant communication is now the norm, but this can be expensive. However, the costs of installing modern systems such as videoconferencing and webcams may be offset by the savings made – staff will not have to travel to meetings, for example.

Where a need is identified for improvement to the physical structure of a company, for example improved disabled access (ramps, rails etc.) or health and safety warning stickers, this will also have cost implications, in time and money.

> **Portfolio tip**
>
> *In order to provide the portfolio of evidence required for this assessment objective, you should comprehensively explain how the selected business's customer service standards are planned, implemented and monitored. There should be clear links between the planning, implementation and monitoring of standards and the impact on the resources of the business. Research should be extensive and relevant, and conclusions should be drawn.*

## AO5   Demonstrate customer service, evaluate own performance (four situations) and propose appropriate actions for development

In this section, you will demonstrate good customer service by taking part in customer service interactions with four different customers, at least one of which should be an internal customer. You will then evaluate your performance in these demonstrations, recommend any changes to your approach and identify any training which may lead to an improvement in your ability to deliver more effective customer service.

The factors that follow may help you to improve your performance when delivering customer service.

## Presentation – dress, posture, personal hygiene

First impressions are vital. Customers who form good first impressions when they first meet staff are more likely to become regular and loyal customers.

> **QUESTIONS**
> 1  When you are a customer, what factors influence your first impressions of the person serving you?
> 2  Does your first impression influence your decision to use a business?
> 3  Might it persuade you to go elsewhere?

### Dress

Customers expect staff to wear appropriate clothing. Casual but smart may be suitable for some jobs, but this does not mean that staff can turn up for work wearing dirty clothes.

For many staff, dress is not a problem because their companies provide a uniform. Some have strict rules regarding shoes, many do not permit trainers.

### Posture

Good posture is not only vital to a person's wellbeing, but is also important for first impressions. Staff should endeavour to keep a straight back, with shoulders back and head up. Someone who stoops may suffer long-term health problems. People sitting at a desk should also remember to keep good posture at all times. If sitting at a computer, for example, their back should be well supported by an easily adjusted chair.

### Personal hygiene

Personal body odour is caused by bacteria and can be offensive, especially when working with food. Staff should make every effort to avoid body odour by showering regularly and using a good deodorant. Clean clothes are also very important; clothes should be washed regularly in order to kill odour-causing bacteria. Regular visits to the dentist are also essential to prevent bad breath which may be caused by gum disease or rotten teeth. Smoking can also be a cause of bad breath. Some simple measures such as brushing and flossing your teeth regularly and using a mouthwash can help.

# Communication – face to face, on the telephone, in writing

Ways of communicating with customers include face to face, by telephone, or by writing to them. The most important point to bear in mind is that you must be polite at all times. However you are provoked, however angry the customer may be, you must always remain in control – polite and attentive and never angry, or too weary to bother.

The best way to judge how customers are feeling is to use your eyes and ears. Listen carefully to what they have to say and take note of their body language – a customer who is tapping their feet may be frustrated. A customer's actions and manner will determine the way you approach and speak to that customer.

If you are speaking to a customer on the telephone, listen carefully. Within a short time, you will be able to judge how the customer is feeling.

When answering the telephone:

- answer the phone within four rings if at all possible

- as you pick up the phone, take a deep breath and smile – this will help ensure that you are in good humour

- give the business name, followed by your name, slowly, so the customer knows who they are talking to; a business will often have a standard greeting that you must use

- use effective listening skills to help you concentrate on what the customer is saying

- find out what the customer is phoning about as soon as you can – don't interrupt; use open and closed questions to help you clarify what the customer wants to say

- make notes; record the important points

- tell the customer what you intend to do; if you need to put the phone down, inform him or her

- if you can't deal with the complaint immediately, tell the customer you will need to phone back – give a specific time (e.g. before 4 o'clock)

- always phone back on time, even if you haven't managed to resolve the matter

- before completing the call, ensure that the customer puts down the phone first – this ensures that you will not appear to be rude or end the call prematurely.

*Speak to customers – with a smile!*

When writing to a customer, often in response to a letter, you will need to ensure that you find out all the information needed to reply. You should ensure that your letter is well laid out and conforms to your company's house style. You should use an appropriate manner and tone; for example, if you are responding to a customer complaint, you should include an apology and detail the action taken.

## Personality – showing interest, attentiveness and responsiveness

### ACTIVITY

Compare someone who is moody and unresponsive with someone who is bright and friendly. Who do you think would most make an impression with customers? What sort of impression would they make?

When dealing with customers, your first priority will be to find out exactly what their needs are. You can then decide what action to take. Customers appreciate being treated by staff who show an interest in them and in what they are saying. It also makes them feel valued. To be an effective listener, you need to listen carefully and not to interrupt. Make notes while you are listening. Use closed questions to help you identify the customer's requirements. For example, you might start with a simple 'Do you need any help?' or 'Do you have a receipt?' If you need more detailed information, use open questions such as 'When did you buy this?' or 'Do you remember who served you?' You might find it useful to summarise what the customer has said to you and to use questions to clarify anything.

Remember to watch for the customer's body language. This will help you to gauge how they are feeling. Look out for gestures, posture, facial expressions and willingness to maintain eye contact with you.

When dealing with customers, try to ensure that you use appropriate body language:

- smile and give positive signs, such as nodding your head, while they are talking

- keep eye contact with the customer – this gives the impression of openness

- try not to fiddle, e.g. with your hair or with jewellery.

## Product knowledge – full and accurate

Staff need to have a full and accurate knowledge of the products or services that their company sells or offers. Training is often given to ensure good product knowledge and this may be included in induction training and backed up by regular updating sessions. A customer will soon realise if a member of staff does not have good product knowledge and perhaps tries to bluff his or her way through a situation. The customer may even walk out!

## Knowledge of products and services sold by the business

As well as good knowledge of the company's products, staff need to know how these work. For example, a person working in an electrical shop may be asked how a microwave works. The customer would not get a good impression if that person didn't even know how to open it – and would probably go elsewhere to buy. If staff are unsure, they should ask their team leader or supervisor as it may be possible for them to try out products when the store is not busy. Training sessions devised especially for product awareness and how to demonstrate products efficiently could also be arranged.

*Good product knowledge is vital*

## Meeting customer needs

In this section, ideally as part of your work or work placement, you will demonstrate the practical skills of customer service to at least one internal and two external customers. You may be able to provide the evidence required by working on your centre's reception desk, or admin or training offices. If it is not possible for you to do this as part of your work, then it is acceptable for you to carry out the practical skills through role play, but the simulations should be realistic and involve people who are not known to you.

You should demonstrate customer service in four of the following situations for both internal and external customers:

- offering advice
- providing information
- after-sales service
- relaying messages
- answering questions
- dealing with complaints
- handling feedback.

You should consider, first of all, the situations you could use to meet customer needs. Ask your team leader, supervisor or tutor for advice. You must use face-to-face interaction, written communication and telephone conversation in your demonstrations. If you choose to deal with a complaint as one of your situations, you should remember to follow the procedure set out by your centre or company for this.

You will need to think about how you will provide the evidence required for your portfolio. For example, your team leader or supervisor (or your tutor if he or she is visiting you at the time) can complete a witness statement.

## Offering advice

A situation may arise where you must give a customer advice. Consider the situation you could arrange to provide the evidence required, for example advising an external customer face to face about how to use a microwave.

### ACTIVITY

Role play a situation where you give advice to a customer, either face to face, in writing or by telephone. Consider whether this will be to an internal or external customer and what sort of advice you could give.

## Providing information

You may need to provide information to a customer. For example, you may receive a telephone call from an external customer asking for information about your new products.

### ACTIVITY

Role play a situation where you give information to an internal or external customer, either face to face, in writing or by telephone.

## After-sales service

Demonstrating an after-sales service to a customer may involve you being approached by a customer who has bought something that does not work correctly, or is faulty and needs repair under its warranty. This is likely to be face to face or by telephone.

### ACTIVITY

Role play a situation where you provide an after-sales service to an external customer either face to face or by telephone.

## Relaying messages

It may be convenient to use this situation to demonstrate a customer service interaction with an internal customer. For example, you may receive a telephone call, take a message, and then deliver it.

## ACTIVITY

Role play a situation where you relay a message to a customer, either face to face or by telephone. Consider offering this service to an internal customer.

## Answering questions

You may answer a customer's questions in a number of ways, but face to face or by telephone would be the most usual. For example, you may be working in your centre's examinations office and receive a phone call from a parent who asks you various questions about a specific examination.

## ACTIVITY

Role play a situation where you answer an internal or external customer's questions, either face to face, in writing or by telephone.

## Dealing with complaints

Customers' complaints may be handled face to face, in writing or by telephone. For example, you may receive a complaint about speed of service from an internal customer face to face.

## ACTIVITY

Role play a situation where you handle a complaint from an internal or external customer. Consider using written communication.

## Handling feedback

This feedback could result from a customer's suggestion or complaint. For example, an external customer may approach you with a completed comment card which you discuss with her face to face.

## ACTIVITY

Role play a situation where you handle feedback from an internal or external customer. You may find face-to-face communication convenient for this.

### Portfolio tip

*You must take part in customer service interactions in four different situations and with at least one internal and two external customers. You must demonstrate effective customer service via face to face, written and telephone interaction.*

### Portfolio tip

*In order to provide the portfolio of evidence required for this assessment objective, you must take part in customer service interactions with four different customers (real situations or simulated). You must demonstrate effective customer service to include at least one internal and two external customers via face to face, written and telephone interaction. You must then evaluate your own performance for each of the four situations, and recommend any changes to your approach or training needs necessary to improve your ability to deliver more effective customer service.*

*You should ensure that you submit a completed witness statement for each of the four situations. You and your assessor (who may be your tutor) should sign and date each one.*

## Evaluate own performance and propose appropriate actions for development

As soon as you finish each situation, you should make notes about what went well and what could be improved. Ask the people who witnessed your demonstrations for feedback.

Consider how you could improve your performance. What could you do to provide a more efficient service to the customer? You may be able to identify some training that might help you. You may be able to recommend changes to your company's procedures. Most companies use feedback from their staff, as it is the staff who are in closest contact with the customers. If something is not working well or needs amending often the staff are the first to know. If a customer has complained, staff are often the best people to know what to do to rectify things and to prevent it happening again in the future.

## SKILLS CHECK

**1** What is the definition of customer service?

**2** Who are the internal customers of a company?

**3** What methods of research could be used to identify the types of customers who use a specific business?

**4** What are an individual's rights under current data protection legislation?

**5** Describe how customer service responses are adapted to meet the requirements of customers who are wheelchair users.

**6** Identify a business that has an edge over the competition. Explain how the business has successfully achieved this and how they can continue to do so.

**7** Explain the word 'empathy'. Give an example of the use of empathy when meeting the needs of a customer.

**8** Give one example of qualitative and two examples of quantitative performance indicators.

**9** Design a flow chart outlining a procedure for handling customer complaints.

**10** List ways in which customers can obtain information, including helplines.

**12** Explain why appearance, posture and personal hygiene are important when dealing with customers.

**13** Why is it necessary to answer a phone within four or five rings?

**14** Explain why it is important to show interest and be attentive when dealing with customers.

**15** Explain why self-evaluation is important.

# Business communications

You use a range of communications every day, talking with family and friends, by mobile phone, texting and so on. To complete this unit successfully, you will need to produce evidence to show that you understand how to use verbal and written communications for specific

purposes, both ICT based and non-ICT based. You will use the Internet for research and communications purposes and ICT software for communication and presentation. Finally, you will show that you understand the impact of ICT on business practice.

You will need to produce evidence to achieve the seven assessment objectives that are contained in the specification and which are given below.

## This unit will cover

- AO1 Use verbal methods for communication in a work-related context.
- AO2 Use written methods for communication in a work-related context.
- AO3 Use the Internet for research and communication purposes.
- AO4 Use suitable software for communication purposes.
- AO5 Use word processing software for the presentation of information.
- AO6 Use presentation software to support a verbal presentation.
- AO7 Investigate and evaluate the impact of ICT on business practice.

# AO1 Use verbal methods for communication in a work-related context

In your portfolio, you will need to provide evidence of using verbal communication that are suitable for different business scenarios, including:

● face-to-face discussion

● telephone discussion

● presentation

● meetings.

## Verbal methods of communication

### Face-to-face discussions

Businesses use face-to-face discussion for many reasons, such as providing opportunities for people to resolve problems, to decide on particular systems required, or to highlight issues that need to be shared.

Face-to-face discussions could involve just two people (e.g. staff review or appraisal), a group of people (e.g. a team meeting) or a large gathering (e.g. a project meeting). Discussions are useful if you need a quick response, compared with writing a letter which may take time to consider what to write, to order what you write, to produce the letter, to wait for it to be delivered and then wait for the reply.

Another advantage of using discussions is that you are able to see the participants and gauge their non-verbal communication (body language). This is very useful as you can see if what they are saying is backed up by their gestures and facial expressions and their willingness to keep eye contact. For example, if a person constantly puts his hand in front of his mouth, this can be a sign of anxiety. You can also use body language to put people at their ease. This can be an effective way to start a discussion on a positive note and encourage full participation.

When taking part in a discussion, ensure you speak clearly and slowly. Try to remain calm, even though this may be difficult at times, especially if people become agitated and voices are raised as a result. People tend to speak more quickly when they are angry and understanding can be lost, with the result that the discussion is unlikely to be successful.

*A face-to-face discussion*

Try not to interrupt people when they are speaking. Listen carefully and courteously and wait until they pause or finish speaking before beginning to speak. This is not always as easy as it sounds! People may interpret any interruption as rudeness and important detail can be lost when people 'talk over each other'.

Before any discussion, it will be important to ensure that all participants understand the purpose of the discussion. It may be helpful to elect someone to take charge, to ensure discussions flow smoothly and that everyone has an opportunity to take part. This can also help prevent one person monopolising the discussion. It can also be helpful to elect another person to take notes and to record any decisions or important points.

## ACTIVITY

1 Working in groups, discuss the factors that will make a successful discussion.
2 Each group should nominate a reporter to note on a flipchart the main points agreed by that group during the discussion.
3 Each group should then present their findings to the whole class in order to agree on the main points of a successful discussion.

## *Telephone discussion*

Telephone discussions are useful when distance makes face-to-face discussions difficult. They are also useful because they result in an immediate response to gain information or advice, or resolve problems.

When you talk to friends on your mobile phone, your call will probably involve a discussion of some sort, even if it is only to agree when and where to meet – this is a form of telephone discussion.

Video phones and videoconferencing can help people to see each other during a telephone discussion, although the use of this technology is not widespread, especially among smaller firms. Unless you have access to these facilities, it will not be possible to see the people you are talking to and you will not have the benefit of body language to help you, as with face-to-face communication. However, you can gain a lot of information from the tone and volume of a person's voice, especially if you are speaking to someone you know. Even with someone you do not know, you will often be able to tell quite quickly if they are happy, sad or angry.

Before commencing a telephone discussion, you should ensure that you are clear about what you wish to achieve during the discussion. Make good preparations well before you start the discussion. Prepare a list of questions to ask – if nothing else, it might help to get the discussion started. Speak clearly and make sure your language, tone and the volume of your voice is appropriate to the person you are talking to. Take notes of important points and facts – you can then refer back to these at any time should it be necessary. Be careful to listen attentively and try not to interrupt, as some of the discussion can be lost in this way.

## Presentation

Businesses use presentations for a number of reasons. They can be made by one person, or sometimes a team of people, to a group, using audio and/or visual aids. Presentations are often made in business to highlight new products, to explain facts and statistics (possibly with the help of charts and graphs) and to give information on specific topics.

Even people who are used to public speaking can be nervous about getting up and making a presentation. There are things you can do to help you feel more confident such as preparation, practice and good audio visual aids, such as well presented slides.

Good preparation is vital to a successful presentation. Once you have decided on the topic, you will need to carry out thorough research into that topic. You will then need to work out what information you want to present and to consider what exactly you want your audience to know when you have finished your presentation. You should make a plan of how you will present the information and in what order.

More detailed information concerning presentation slides and delivery may be found on page 126 onwards.

## ACTIVITY

1 Working in pairs, prepare a short presentation – of no more than two minutes in length.
2 Your topic should be one of which you have good knowledge and feel confident in presenting to an audience, such as your favourite sport, football team, or type of music.
3 You do not need to prepare slides for this presentation or to use computer software or screens but you may use alternative audio/visual aids if you wish, such as posters, flipchart, etc.
4 Deliver the presentation to a group of at least three colleagues.
5 Ask your audience for comments on your performance to help you in future presentations. If possible, you may wish to video your presentation.

## Meetings

In business, meetings may be formal such as an Annual General Meeting (AGM) or a meeting of the board of directors, or it may be informal, such as team meetings or sales meetings.

You will need to organise a meeting, prepare all the documentation required, run the meeting, take notes and record all important points and decisions.

Try to give people attending the meeting 24 hours' notice, or even longer if this is possible. When notifying them, include the reason the meeting is being held and the agenda. This will ensure that people have time to think about what they may contribute, such as different ideas for the running of a specific project.

You should think about the meeting room well before the meeting is due to start. Make sure that tables and chairs are arranged so that everyone will be able to hear and see everything that is going on. Consider also what you will say and make a list of any questions you may wish to ask.

During the meeting, you should endeavour to keep control so that the audience can keep up with what is happening. The pace should be neither too fast, nor too slow. If it is too fast, people may not be able to keep up; too slow and people may lose interest. It will also be necessary to keep to the agenda and not allow people to introduce other topics. Make sure everyone is given the opportunity to take part.

## Meetings documentation

For your portfolio, you will need to produce evidence that you have organised a meeting and prepared all the documentation required. Before a meeting can take place, several things must be confirmed:

- the purpose of the meeting
- the date, time and place where it is to be held
- the people required to attend
- documentation required.

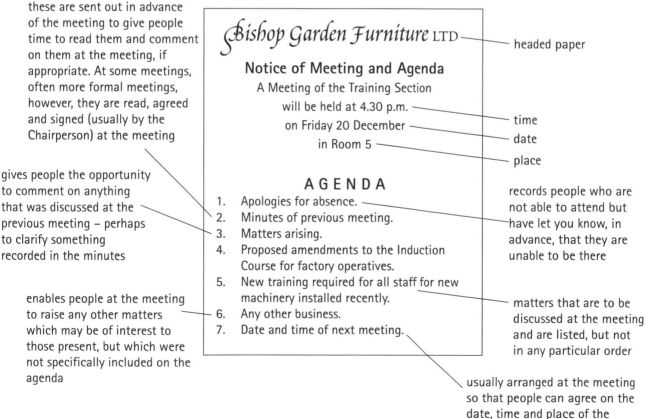

these are sent out in advance of the meeting to give people time to read them and comment on them at the meeting, if appropriate. At some meetings, often more formal meetings, however, they are read, agreed and signed (usually by the Chairperson) at the meeting

gives people the opportunity to comment on anything that was discussed at the previous meeting – perhaps to clarify something recorded in the minutes

enables people at the meeting to raise any other matters which may be of interest to those present, but which were not specifically included on the agenda

**Bishop Garden Furniture** LTD — headed paper

### Notice of Meeting and Agenda
A Meeting of the Training Section
will be held at 4.30 p.m. — time
on Friday 20 December — date
in Room 5 — place

### AGENDA
1. Apologies for absence.
2. Minutes of previous meeting.
3. Matters arising.
4. Proposed amendments to the Induction Course for factory operatives.
5. New training required for all staff for new machinery installed recently.
6. Any other business.
7. Date and time of next meeting.

records people who are not able to attend but have let you know, in advance, that they are unable to be there

matters that are to be discussed at the meeting and are listed, but not in any particular order

usually arranged at the meeting so that people can agree on the date, time and place of the next meeting

**Figure 3.1** *An example of a notice of meeting with agenda*

**GLOSSARY**

**Agenda**:
details of items that
will be discussed in a
meeting.

One document, called a **Notice of Meeting and Agenda** is used to tell everyone when and where the meeting will be held and details of what will be discussed and the order of discussions. Some items always appear on an agenda, as shown in Figure 3.1.

The **Chairperson's agenda** is produced for use by the Chairperson, who is the person appointed to chair the meeting – to ensure it is held in an orderly and proper manner. It is a copy of the Agenda with space on the right-hand side for the Chairperson to make notes. These are usually only used at a formal meeting, such as of the board of directors.

**Minutes** are taken during a meeting and are kept as a record of the proceedings. A person is nominated to take the minutes (very often referred to as a 'secretary') and these may be recorded in a special book or may be

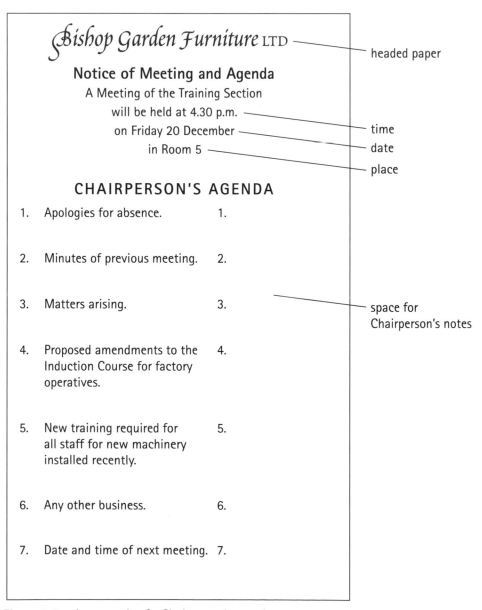

**Figure 3.2** *An example of a Chairperson's agenda*

word processed and filed. They are kept as brief as possible to ensure that only important facts are recorded.

The secretary would write the minutes in the past tense and in the third person: for example, 'It was agreed', 'Alex Parrott reported'. Minutes are signed and dated by the person who chaired the meeting, when all those present have agreed that they are a true and accurate reflection of what took place. Some businesses use an 'Action' column to identify people who are asked to take some type of action during the meeting, for example to find out some information or to present a report at the next meeting.

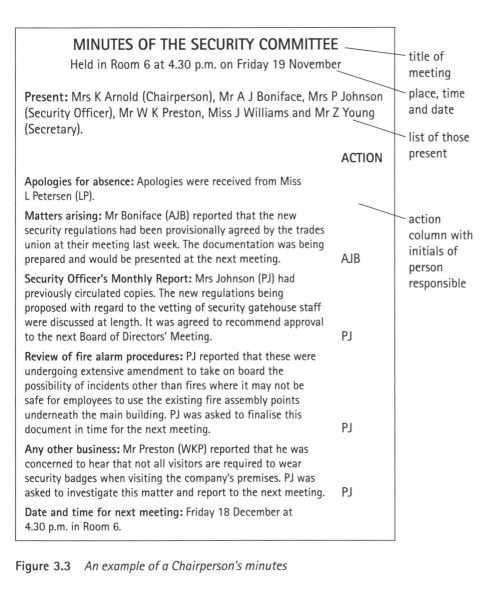

**MINUTES OF THE SECURITY COMMITTEE** — title of meeting
Held in Room 6 at 4.30 p.m. on Friday 19 November — place, time and date

**Present:** Mrs K Arnold (Chairperson), Mr A J Boniface, Mrs P Johnson (Security Officer), Mr W K Preston, Miss J Williams and Mr Z Young (Secretary). — list of those present

ACTION

**Apologies for absence:** Apologies were received from Miss L Petersen (LP).

**Matters arising:** Mr Boniface (AJB) reported that the new security regulations had been provisionally agreed by the trades union at their meeting last week. The documentation was being prepared and would be presented at the next meeting.   AJB — action column with initials of person responsible

**Security Officer's Monthly Report:** Mrs Johnson (PJ) had previously circulated copies. The new regulations being proposed with regard to the vetting of security gatehouse staff were discussed at length. It was agreed to recommend approval to the next Board of Directors' Meeting.   PJ

**Review of fire alarm procedures:** PJ reported that these were undergoing extensive amendment to take on board the possibility of incidents other than fires where it may not be safe for employees to use the existing fire assembly points underneath the main building. PJ was asked to finalise this document in time for the next meeting.   PJ

**Any other business:** Mr Preston (WKP) reported that he was concerned to hear that not all visitors are required to wear security badges when visiting the company's premises. PJ was asked to investigate this matter and report to the next meeting.   PJ

**Date and time for next meeting:** Friday 18 December at 4.30 p.m. in Room 6.

**Figure 3.3** *An example of a Chairperson's minutes*

**Portfolio tip**

*In order to provide the evidence required in your portfolio for this assessment objective, you will need to communicate fluently and confidently, engaging and meeting the needs of the audience.*

*You should demonstrate a high level of competency in using a range of verbal communication methods that are suitable for different business scenarios. Your evidence may include documentation such as notice, agenda and minutes, notes, prompt cards, presentation slides and audio/video recordings if appropriate. Detailed witness statements must support your evidence.*

## CASE STUDY

*Bryant Automotive Parts*

---

You work as an administrator at Bryant Automotive Parts who distribute spare parts to retailers and garages. You report to Mrs Camara, who is the office manager.

She has asked you to call a short meeting of the staff at lunch time today. There are several items for the agenda and these are:

- weekly checks of vehicles – these are not being carried out correctly or recorded in the appropriate vehicle log books
- reporting absenteeism due to illness – staff need to comply with the company rules about telephoning before 8.30 a.m.
- staff holidays – no more than two van drivers may be on leave at the same time and no more than one van driver and the relief driver at one time.

Mrs Camara has told you that your branch manager, Mrs Olya Defarge, will be attending.

1 Organise the meeting for Mrs Camara, using colleagues to take the roles of the staff, as well as Mrs Camara and Mrs Defarge.
2 Create and word process the agenda. Circulate the agenda to all participants (colleagues).
3 The colleague taking the part of Mrs Camara should act as Chairperson.
4 You should take the part of 'secretary', taking notes during the meeting so that you can produce the minutes.
5 On completion of the meeting, prepare and word process the minutes.

# AO2  Use written methods for communication in a work-related context

Businesses use a variety of methods of written communication and these include:

- memos
- reports
- notices
- letters

## Methods of written communication

Before writing anything, you should decide on the *purpose* of your communication. There are four main purposes:

- to request information
- to provide information

- to give instruction
- to attract potential customers/participants.

Then you should think about what you wish to include in your communication. Be careful to use the correct tone, for example a letter to a friend would be much more informal and casual than one written to a chief executive. Think about the people who will be reading your communication – try to put yourself in their place.

You will also need to identify the advantages and disadvantages of each written communication method.

# Memos

Memos are used in business as internal notes that enable people working for the same organisation to communicate with each other. They may be used to request information, provide information or to give instruction.

Ask your tutor if you have access to a template that you could use for preparing memos. If not, you will need to key in the headings yourself.

In a memo, the heading 'MEMO' may be displayed in a larger font size, but the text in the memo itself should be in a smaller size.

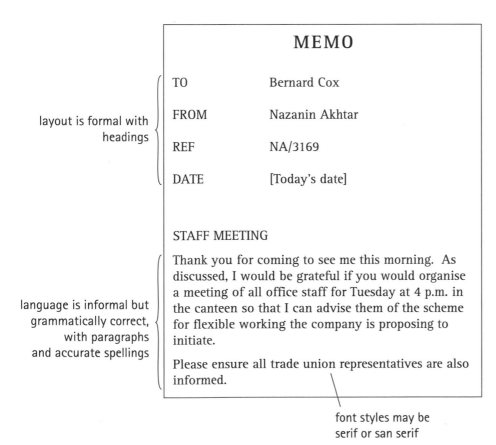

layout is formal with headings

language is informal but grammatically correct, with paragraphs and accurate spellings

font styles may be serif or san serif

**MEMO**

TO             Bernard Cox

FROM        Nazanin Akhtar

REF           NA/3169

DATE         [Today's date]

STAFF MEETING

Thank you for coming to see me this morning. As discussed, I would be grateful if you would organise a meeting of all office staff for Tuesday at 4 p.m. in the canteen so that I can advise them of the scheme for flexible working the company is proposing to initiate.

Please ensure all trade union representatives are also informed.

**Figure 3.4** *An example of a memo*

Many companies specify the font and size to be used, such as Arial 11, Times New Roman 12 or Comic Sans 10, and care should be taken to follow the house style laid down. If there is no house style, then choose a font that is clear and easy to read.

> For this paragraph, Palatino 12 font has been used, an example of a serif font. Notice that the characters are more fancy.
>
> compare with:
>
> Arial 12 font has been used for this paragraph, an example of a sans serif font. Notice that these characters are plain; they have no fancy "tips".

**Figure 3.5**  *An example of fonts*

Many people prefer to use a serif font, e.g. Times New Roman or Bookman Old Type, as the characters tend to be easier to read than those produced with sans serif fonts. For example:

> This paragraph has been produced in sans serif font Arial 11. Can you easily distinguish between the word "modem" and the word "modern"? Similarly, an initial capital I can be mistaken for a lower case l or a figure 1.

**Figure 3.6**  *Is this text clear?*

The word 'modem' could be mistaken for the word 'modern' and there are other words which can also cause ambiguity.

| ADVANTAGES | DISADVANTAGES |
|---|---|
| • Permanent written record of what has been said | • No confirmation of receipt |
| • Can be personal to one person or sent to a large number of people | • No immediate response |
| • Economical means of communication | • Can be lost during delivery |
| • Internal mail system gives cheap, quick delivery | • Response may not be delivered so no way of knowing whether received |
| • Easy to communicate with work colleagues without having to find them to speak to them face to face | • Emails are often preferred as they are instant and provide quick response and feedback |
| • Includes the date – may be useful if proof required at later stage | |

**Table 3.1**  *Advantages and disadvantages of memos*

## ACTIVITY

1 Using a word processor, recall a memo template if one is available to you, or key in the memo headings.
2 Prepare a memo to your tutor incorporating the main points of the discussion from the activity on page 91 on what makes a successful discussion.

## *Reports*

A variety of reports are used in business and these may be quite long and detailed, giving information or research results, or may be quite short, giving brief details on a specific topic. They may request information, record facts, interpret information, present suggestions, provide information and include conclusions and recommendations.

Reports have set conventions and layout, which make them very recognisable.

REPORT ON STRESS IN THE WORKPLACE — main heading

**Introduction**
The directors expressed concern at the high levels of office staff absenteeism due to stress in recent months. They asked me to investigate this and to recommend how this should be eliminated.

— double linespacing makes it easier for the reader, however this makes photocopying costs higher so that single linespacing often preferred

logical sequence for the content summarising the information, which may be divided into sections with topic headings

page 2/2

introduction

**Conclusion**
Many of the office staff are suffering stress and it seems to be affecting our more experienced staff, many of whom are struggling to cope with information technology.

conclusions and recommendations provided at the end of the main facts

**Recommendations**
I recommend that staff undertake IT training as soon as this can be arranged.

language is formal, third person, and grammatically correct with accurate spellings

Peter Arnold
HR Manager

[Today's date]

fonts and house style set by a company should be adhered to but Arial 11 or 12 or Times New Roman 11 or 12 is acceptable

layout should include dates and page numbers. Appendices can be useful to include examples of documentation or other facts which support those in the report and these are attached to the report, but are usually given separate page numbering to the report itself

**Figure 3.7** *Example of a report providing information*

| ADVANTAGES | DISADVANTAGES |
|---|---|
| • Permanent record, kept on file for future | • If badly prepared can be difficult to understand |
| • Clear, structured format – easily recognisable | • Time-consuming to compile |
| • Has stated clear aims | • Purpose may not be clear |
| • Logical sequence – can be easy to reference back | • Good report writing needs experience and possibly training which has cost implications |
| • Includes information required to meet aims set | • Report writer needs good standard of grammar, spelling etc. |
| • Use of template makes it easy and quick to use | • Can be too long and complicated |
| • Can be targeted to a specific audience | • Important detail may be lost |

Table 3.2 *Advantages and disadvantages of reports*

## ACTIVITY

1 Draft a short report providing information to your tutor. Ensure you set out your report using appropriate format and conventions as detailed above. Save and print one copy.
2 On completion of your report, read it through and consider:
   (a) Have you used a normal layout, appropriate font and style?
   (b) Is the language you have used appropriate?
   (c) Does the introduction explain the subject and purpose of the report?
   (d) Is the content of the report in a logical sequence?
   (e) Has all the important information been included?
   (f) Could the use of charts, graphs, drawings or illustrations be of help?
   (g) Does the report achieve what you intended?
3 Amend your report, if necessary; save and print a copy.

## Notices

Notices are used for many purposes in business. The most familiar is to notify staff of some company news, a forthcoming event or a social gathering. They are normally displayed on a general noticeboard, where they can be seen by the majority of staff, and also in the canteen or staff rest room. They are used to provide information and to attract potential customers/participants.

More formal notices that are necessary for legal reasons include health and safety notices. Some companies and hospitals, etc., also use notices to display photographs of all the staff working in a particular area.

There is no formal layout for notices. An example is shown in Figure 3.8.

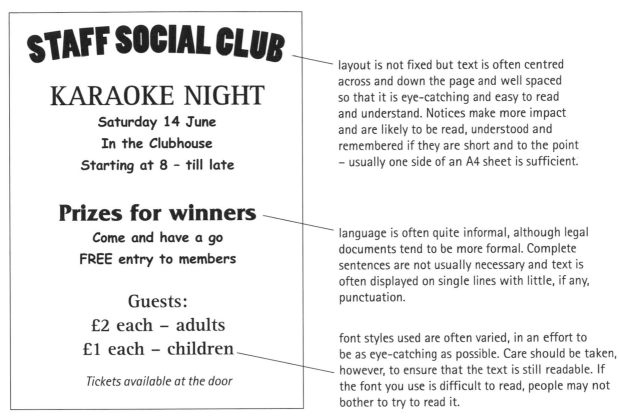

layout is not fixed but text is often centred across and down the page and well spaced so that it is eye-catching and easy to read and understand. Notices make more impact and are likely to be read, understood and remembered if they are short and to the point – usually one side of an A4 sheet is sufficient.

language is often quite informal, although legal documents tend to be more formal. Complete sentences are not usually necessary and text is often displayed on single lines with little, if any, punctuation.

font styles used are often varied, in an effort to be as eye-catching as possible. Care should be taken, however, to ensure that the text is still readable. If the font you use is difficult to read, people may not bother to try to read it.

**Figure 3.8** *An example of a notice*

| ADVANTAGES | DISADVANTAGES |
|---|---|
| ● Can be used to communicate with many people | ● May not receive an immediate response |
| ● Economical means of communication | ● Could be easily destroyed or damaged |
| ● Display of notice can provide constant reminder | ● Not suitable for conveying important information as no guarantee people will read it |
| ● Can be very eye-catching and colourful | ● Could be removed or covered up with other notices |
| | ● Relies on people regularly looking at the noticeboard rather than being delivered to individuals |

**Table 3.3** *Advantages and disadvantages of notices*

## Portfolio tip

*Any letters that you produce for your portfolio should be displayed on letterheaded paper. You may use a pre-printed letterheading or you may wish to ask your tutor if you have access to a template. It is quite acceptable to use your centre's letterheading. You would normally include your name in the complimentary close and sign the letter yourself. If you are preparing your own letterhead, it is not necessary to include clipart, but you may if you wish.*

## ACTIVITY

Using a word processor, prepare a notice that provides information. Make sure that all the information is displayed on one sheet of A4 paper. Use your skill to produce an eye-catching notice and on completion, save and print a copy.

## *Letters*

Letters are used in business to communicate with other companies, customers, suppliers and so on, but can also be used to communicate with employees, such as formal letters enclosing contracts of employment or when dealing with disciplinary cases or an **employee's grievance**. Letters may be used to request or provide information, give instruction, or attract potential customers/participants. Figure 3.9 shows an example of a common layout used in business:

### GLOSSARY

**employee's grievance**: a complaint made by an employee against management or other employees; it may concern a breach of contract.

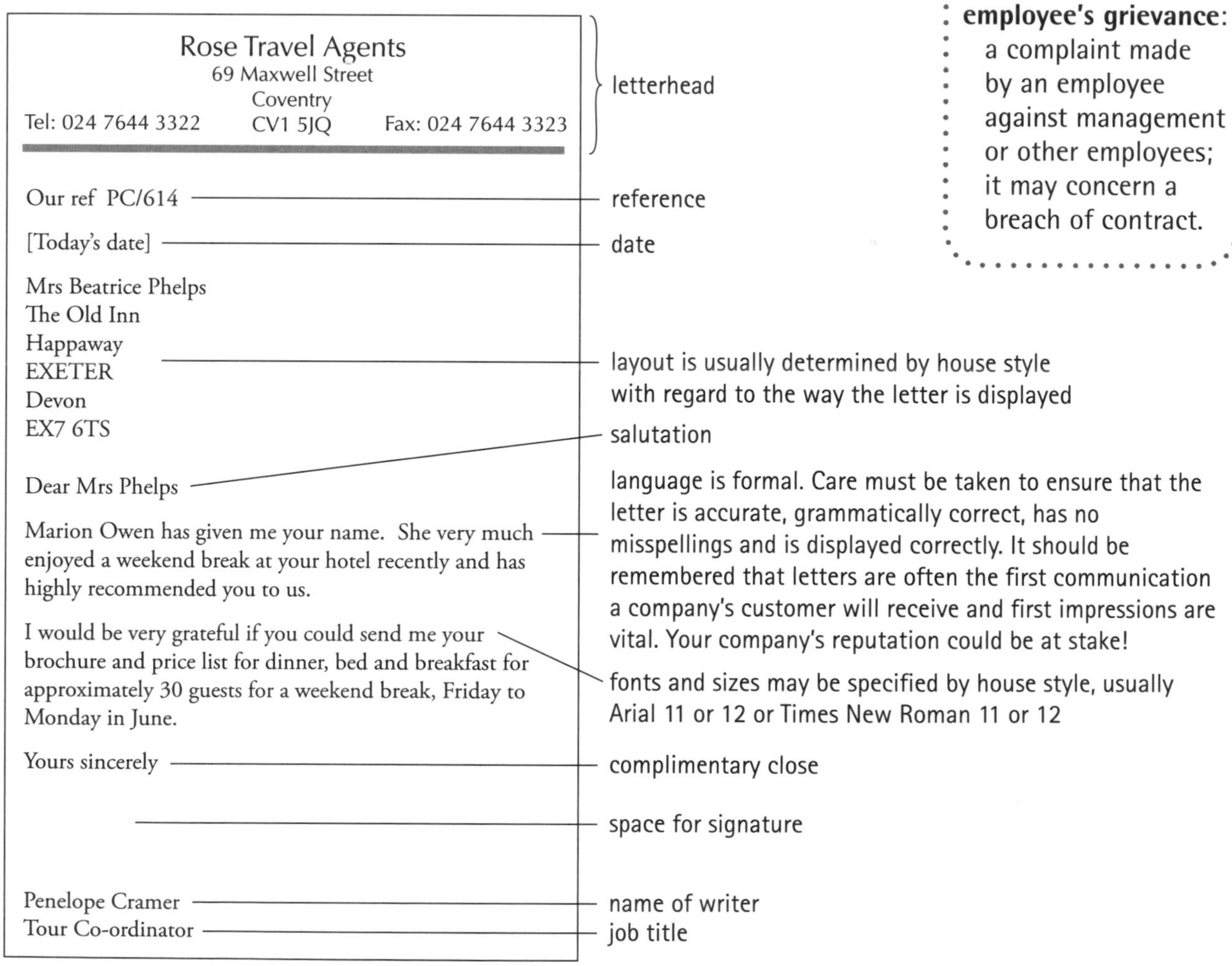
Rose Travel Agents
69 Maxwell Street
Coventry
Tel: 024 7644 3322 CV1 5JQ Fax: 024 7644 3323

Our ref PC/614

[Today's date]

Mrs Beatrice Phelps
The Old Inn
Happaway
EXETER
Devon
EX7 6TS

Dear Mrs Phelps

Marion Owen has given me your name. She very much enjoyed a weekend break at your hotel recently and has highly recommended you to us.

I would be very grateful if you could send me your brochure and price list for dinner, bed and breakfast for approximately 30 guests for a weekend break, Friday to Monday in June.

Yours sincerely

Penelope Cramer
Tour Co-ordinator


**Figure 3.9** *An example of a business letter showing common layout*

# Standard business letters

There are many occasions when businesses wish to write to a number of their customers. They may produce an individual letter to each one but that would be time-consuming and expensive. They could opt to write a general letter with a salutation such as 'Dear Customer'. However, a word processor's mail merge facility to produce a personalised letter which is addressed to each individual customer is preferable.

> **Portfolio tip**
>
> *In your portfolio it is acceptable to produce a standard generic letter rather than spending time inserting merge codes etc.*

---

**Central Garage**
Brookfield
Newton Abbot
TQ12 7JJ
Tel: 01626 365411

---

Our ref  VGT/12 ———————————— layout may be determined by house style

[Today's date]

Dear Customer ——————————————— salutation

As a loyal customer, we are writing to advise you that we have won a contract with Panther Cars offering us the major dealership with their company in the south west of England.

As you already know, Panther Cars are top of the range executive cars, offering comfort as well as a high ———— language is formal, must be grammatically specification.  All cars have leather interior, cruise control and correct, with no misspellings air conditioning or climate control.  Prices are very competitive and for the next three months, we are pleased to offer all our loyal customers a special 10% discount on the purchase of a new car.

We would be delighted to show you the complete range if you would like to call in and see us. ——————— fonts and sizes may be specified by house style, usually Arial 11 or 12 or Times New Yours sincerely Roman 11 or 12

——————————————— signature after the complimentary close adds another personal touch

Victor and Gordon Titus
Owners

**Figure 3.10**   *An example of a standard business letter*

> **Portfolio tip**
>
> *In order to provide the evidence required in your portfolio for this assessment objective, you will need to use a variety of methods of written communication in work-related contexts. You should demonstrate a high level of competency.*
>
> *The formats and conventions adopted (such as language, tone, layout, fonts) should be appropriate for the purpose for which they will be used. The four purposes of communication must be included within the documents, such as requesting and providing information, giving instruction or attracting potential customers or participants. All documents should be well expressed and informative, containing appropriate details. You must also identify the advantages and disadvantages of each method of written communication.*

## CASE STUDY

### A J Landscape Gardeners

Ayesha Maxwell started her own landscape gardening business three years ago. She has several regular customers who range from private home owners to various retirement home complexes. Jordan Browne set up his gardening business in the same town as Ayesha just a year ago and offers various gardening services such as mowing, pruning, digging, planting, etc.

Ayesha and Jordan met recently at a Garden Exhibition at a local hotel and have now formed a new partnership – A J Landscape Gardening. This enables them to combine their talents and expertise and make use of their individual skills to grow the business. They have just won a contract to landscape and maintain the grounds of The Old Manor Country House Hotel, a large hotel conference centre complex 10 miles out of town.

They now share the same mobile telephone number, so that customers can contact them easily at any time and have set up their office at Ayesha's home. They have also set up a new website: www.aj_landscape.co.uk.

**Create a standard business letter to A J Landscape Gardeners' customers and inform them of the changes and the advantages these will offer customers. You should use normal formats and conventions. Save and print one copy of the letter.**

| ADVANTAGES | DISADVANTAGES |
|---|---|
| • Permanent written record of what has been said – kept on file for future reference | • No confirmation of receipt |
| • Easy to send personal letter to many individuals | • No immediate response |
| • Can promote professional image of company | • Can be lost during delivery |
| • Produced on good quality paper with professional letterheading and logo enhances company image | • Takes time to prepare and produce |
| • Easy to produce extra copies | • Could damage a company's image if poor letter |
| • Includes the date – may be useful if proof required at later stage | • May take long time for reply to be received |
| | • Professionally printed letterheads can be expensive |

**Table 3.4** *Advantages and disadvantages of letters*

## AO3  Use the Internet for research and communication purposes

The Internet is used for many different purposes such as to find information and also to communicate.

**Figure 3.11**  *The Kelkoo website*

## Role and function of an ISP

An ISP provides access to the Internet. There are thousands of companies which now offer Internet access to businesses, people at home and people on the move. Before anyone can gain access to the Internet, it is necessary to establish an account with an ISP, examples of which are BT, NTL, Wanadoo and Tiscali.

Access to the Internet can be gained by using a dial-up service or broadband. A web-hosting service can also be offered. Most companies offer broadband and millions of people throughout the UK now have access to broadband in their own homes.

> **GLOSSARY**
>
> **ISP:**
>   Abbreviation for Internet service provider.

## Types of search engines

There are two major types of search engine – individual and meta search engines.

## Individual search engines

These are large databases of web pages through which the search engines search when you enter your key words. Examples are Altavista (www.altavista.com), Google (www.google.co.uk), HotBot (www.hotbot.com), Lycos (www.lycos.com) and Yahoo (www.yahoo.com).

## Meta search engines

These search the databases of individual search engines and they do not have their own databases. Examples of these are Dogpile (www.dogpile.com) and Ask Jeeves (www.ask.co.uk).

# Portal websites

Businesses set up **portal websites** so a directory of websites appears on the one website. Facilities include products for sale, news, weather information, email, stock quotes, phone and map information, and sometimes a community forum.

Some companies have set up portal websites to offer a complete service to their customers. One of these is www.kelkoo.co.uk (see Figure 3.11), which offers price comparisons on thousands of products and services. Another web portal is www.yahoo.co.uk, which offers links to other companies' websites offering a vast range of services and products for sale.

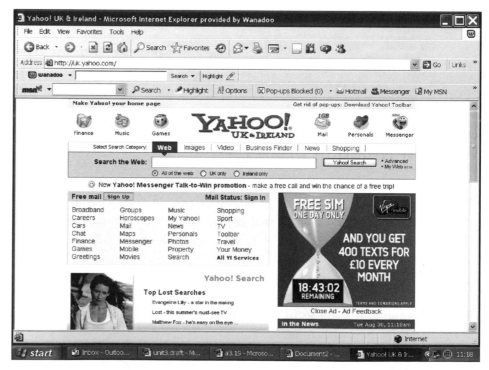

**Figure 3.12** *An example of a portal website*

## ACTIVITY

Your tutor has been asked by your centre's social club to organise an evening out for all staff. This will be either:

- a canal narrowboat trip
- 10-pin bowling or
- paintballing.

Use a search engine to search the Internet to find the following information and use the table to record your findings:

(a) at least one example for each of the activities – no more than 20 miles away from your centre

(b) the cost of the different categories: adults, senior citizens and children under 16 years of age

(c) the opening hours of each of the venues

(d) on completion of your research, prepare a letter to your tutor, giving the results of your research.

(e) attach a list of the websites you visited and the information you found during your research. This can be presented in a simple table with headings.

| Websites visited | Summary of research findings |
|---|---|
|  |  |
|  |  |
|  |  |

## Favorites

If you wish to save a website that you found particularly useful, or would like to visit it again, you can add that website address to a menu called 'Favorites'. (This is known as '**bookmarking**' on some browsers.) The easiest way to do this is to click on the Favorites menu at the top of your homepage screen. Click on Add to Favorites and click OK. When you wish to visit this website again, you will simply click on the Favorites menu and select the stored website address from the list displayed.

## Editing

A company website is likely to need constant updating – the information contained within it may alter with time and most companies recognise the importance of having up-to-date information on their websites. Visitors to a website are not normally able to edit a website. Most companies have software available to them that enables them to amend text and images or to input additional data so that they do not have to pay a professional website designer every time they wish to make changes. Some larger companies may employ people whose job it is to maintain the firm's website. This enables changes to be made quickly and ensures that the website is up to date.

> **GLOSSARY**
>
> **bookmarking**: storing a link to a particular website so you can easily return to it (also known as Favorites).

## *Printing of web pages*

To provide evidence of your research on the Internet, you may print a copy of a web page if that is appropriate. Use the Print Preview function to tell you how many pages there are in the particular section of the website that you are looking at. You can then decide which individual page you wish to print and select this detail on the Print menu. You can also see whether you need to print in landscape format to ensure that all the data will print in full. If in doubt, ask your tutor for advice on printing and printers.

# Copy and paste text and clipart

Instead of printing web pages from a website, it may be more convenient to use just a small part of a web page as useful evidence for your portfolio. It is possible to copy and paste text and images from a website. However, if you decide to do this you must reference the website clearly in any documents that you produce, otherwise you may contravene copyright legislation.

To copy and paste some data:

1. Ensure you have a blank page opened in MS Word.
2. Ensure you have the relevant website displayed:
   - use the mouse to highlight text and/or images you wish to select
   - right-click the mouse and select Copy
   - switch to the MS Word document and ensure cursor is in the exact position where you wish to insert the website data
   - right-click the mouse and select Paste
   - the data selected should now appear within the blank MS Word document.
3. Now insert a short sentence referencing the website you have copied and pasted from.

This is an example of data that has been copied and pasted from a website:

*In October 2004, The Victoria University of Manchester and UMIST came together in an historic merger to create Britain's largest unitary university, a move which also of course brought together the two largest academic conference players in the North. **The really good news** for our clients is that they now have access to a much wider and more flexible range of facilities, and a wealth of experience in our conference team.*

We are proud to be a member of the *Meeting Industry Association (MIA)* where we have achieved *Hospitality Assured Meetings accreditation.*

**Figure 3.13** *Selected data pasted from a website*

Clipart is a collection of pictures, images, icons, buttons, sound and video files that can be inserted into word processing files or web pages. Clipart can be used to illustrate a particular piece of text.

## ACTIVITY

Use a search engine to find information that is of particular interest to you.
Use the copy and paste facility to insert a paragraph of text and an image
from the web page you find, detailing the information for which you searched.

# Advanced search features

When using a search engine, you may find you are given thousands of
options in response to your key words. It is possible to refine a search to
give you fewer options when trying to find specific information. For
example, if you were to search for some information on Sir Winston
Churchill and enter the word 'Churchill', you are likely to be given
thousands of options including Churchill tanks and products and services
offered by various companies named 'Churchill'. To refine a search:

1. ensure you are connected to the Internet and that your browser is loaded
2. use the search engine www.google.co.uk
3. enter the words Winston+Churchill. (The use of the + sign narrows the
   search and gives you a better chance of finding the specific information
   you want.)
4. refine the search further by opting for the UK results only
5. from the list, choose the website www.number-10.gov.uk
6. you should now have a biography of Sir Winston Churchill.

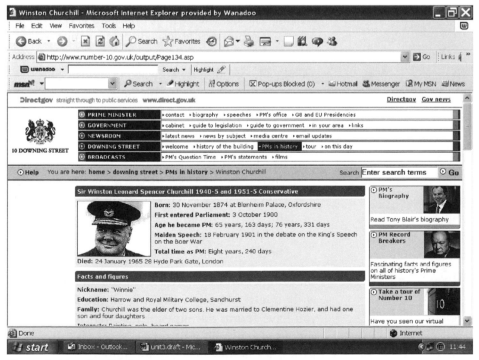

**Figure 3.14**  *A refined search*

## Portfolio tip

*In order to provide the evidence required in your portfolio for this assessment objective, you will need to undertake extensive research using the Internet. The research will be directly relevant to a specific work-related context. Resource lists should be submitted as evidence of your research.*

## ACTIVITY

Search the Internet for the following:

1 A description of kevlar – include at least one paragraph of text and an image of a kevlar product. Copy and paste into a word processing document and print a copy.
2 A recipe containing pistachio – copy and paste into a word processing document and print a copy.
3 A description and an image of how white sugar cubes are produced – copy and paste into a word processing document and print a copy.
4 Produce a list of the websites visited and a summary of the information.

## CASE STUDY

### Suzi's Dog Walking Service

Suzi Chu has just left college and wishes to start her own business, caring for people's dogs while they are at work and while they are away on holiday. She is very fond of dogs and has been offering a service to her neighbours and friends during the summer holidays. Her parents are willing to support her and have offered sufficient finance for her to buy a small van for her to use to get to her customers and to transport the dogs when appropriate. Suzi is very keen but is not sure where to start. She has asked you for some help.

Suzi would like you to do some research into other businesses that offer a dog walking service. She does not have access to a computer and would like you to carry out research on the Internet to find people who are already offering a dog walking service. She needs information specifically on:

- the kind of service they provide
- the number of times they visit each dog per day
- how long each visit lasts
- whether they offer a different service to different categories, e.g. some dogs are very large and others extremely small
- how much they charge.

**On completion of the research, you should write a letter to Suzi including all the details you have found during your research. You should also attach a list of websites visited with brief details of what you found.**

# AO4 Use suitable software for communication purposes

Businesses use electronic mail (email) to communicate with other businesses, customers, suppliers and its own employees, who also use email to communicate with each other. In this assessment objective, you will:

● send, receive and delete emails

● send and receive attachments within emails

● use an online message system.

Ask your tutor for information on the email system you can use for your studies. You should have your own email address so that you can send and receive messages. For the purposes of this assessment objective, we will use MS Outlook Express, but you may use any email system, including webmail such as Hotmail. However, you should ensure that printouts will provide clear evidence of header information such as *To, From, Subject, Sent (or Date)* as well as the attachments.

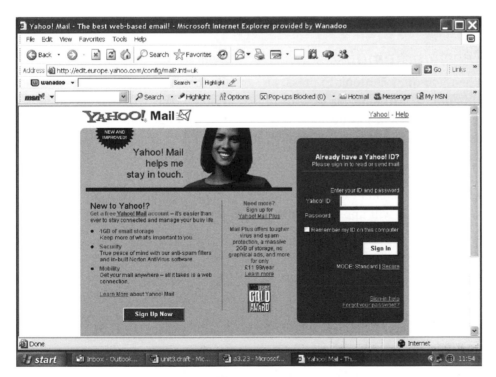

Reproduced with permission of Yahoo! Inc. © 2006 by Yahoo! Inc. YAHOO! and the YAHOO! logo are trademarks of Yahoo! Inc.

**Figure 3.15** *Example of a webmail ISP*

# Send, receive and delete emails

You should ensure that you include in your portfolio examples of sending and receiving emails, and evidence of deletion of emails should also be provided. Check that you are able to print emails from your Inbox and Sent Items folder.

## Sending emails

Beware of sending emails without giving them a great deal of thought. It can be too easy to send an email by just one click on the mouse. Always consider carefully what you have said and how you have said it *before* you send it – or you may regret it! Use this as a guide to sending an email:

1. Ensure you are connected to the Internet – access your email software, e.g. Outlook Express.
2. Create an email to a colleague – be very careful to enter the email address accurately or it will not be delivered.
3. Enter an appropriate subject heading.
4. Enter at least 15 words in your message, e.g. ask your colleague to meet you this evening.
5. Use the spellchecker to check for errors.
6. Double-check that the email address is accurate.
7. When you're happy that everything is accurate, send the message.
8. Check in the Sent Items folder that the email has been sent (see Figure 3.16).

## Receiving emails

When you open Outlook Express, any emails that have been sent to you will automatically appear in your Inbox, although this will depend on how your email system has been set up. The list of messages will display the email addresses of people who have sent you emails and the subject, date and time sent.

Look in your Inbox to see if you have received a reply from your colleague to the email below. To access it, simply double click on the message and it will appear. If only part of the message is displayed, click

| **Going to the match?** | |
|---|---|
| **From:** | tye.j@tigermail.co.uk |
| **To:** | dixon.v@tigermail.co.uk |
| **Sent:** | 14 February 2006 11:06 |
| **Subject:** | Going to the match? |

Hi Victor

Are you going to the match tonight?  Bob, Mary and Jon are going to meet me at the usual place outside the club at 7 o'clock.  Can you meet us there?  Please let me know ASAP.

Josh

| **Re: Going to the match?** |
| --- |
| **From:** dixon.v@tigermail.co.uk<br>**To:** tye.j@tigermail.co.uk<br>**Sent:** 14 February 2006 12:32<br>**Subject:** Re: Going to the match? |

Hi Josh

Yes, I'd love to see the match. See you at 7, usual place.

Victor


-------Original Message ---------

**From:** tye.j@tigermail.co.uk
**To:** dixon.v@tigermail.co.uk
**Sent:** 14 February 2006 11:06
**Subject:** Going to the match?

Hi Victor

Are you going to the match tonight? Bob, Mary and Jon are going to meet me at the usual place outside the club at 7 o'clock. Can you meet us there? Please let me know ASAP.

Josh

**Figure 3.16** *An example of an email and reply*

on the maximise button – top right-hand corner of your screen. Print a copy of the message – notice, the 'RE:' in the 'Subject' indicates that your colleague has correctly used the reply facility.

## Deleting emails

It is good practice to delete unwanted email messages on a regular basis. You would normally only do this when you have replied to an email received. To delete an email message:

1. click on the email message you wish to delete
2. click on the Delete option – centre top of your screen: it has a large red cross
3. the email will disappear.

You will also need to delete your replies from the 'Sent' folder on a regular basis.

However if, after deleting an email, you realise you do need it after all, you will find it in the Deleted files folder and you can easily retrieve it from there. At regular intervals, you should delete files permanently from the Deleted files folder. If you do not, you will find your email system will not run so efficiently.

The easiest way to provide evidence of deleting an email is to produce screen prints 'before' and 'after'. For example:

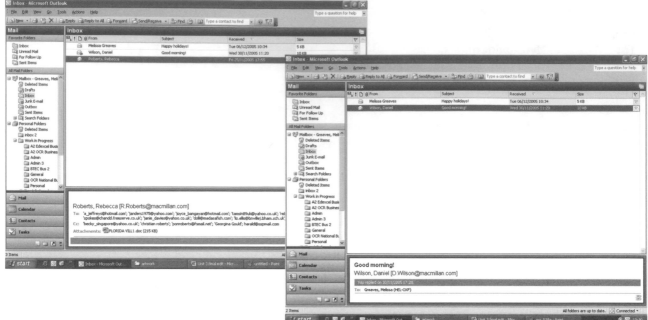

**Figure 3.17** *A 'before' and 'after' check for email deletion*

## ACTIVITY

Send an email to a colleague, attaching a copy of a file, photograph or picture, and ask for a reply. Print a copy of the email, clearly showing the attachment and the message.

## ACTIVITY

1 Ask your tutor or a colleague to send you an email. Look in your Inbox and click on the email you have received. Print a copy of the email.
2 Send a reply to the email – make sure that RE: (or similar) appears in the Subject panel. Print a copy of the email from the Sent Items folder. Delete the email you received from your tutor or colleague.

# Send and receive attachments within emails

Anyone with an email address can send and receive attachments and these may be photographs, files or pictures.

## Send attachments within emails

To send an attachment to a colleague:

1. Create a new message to your colleague, using an appropriate subject.
2. Key in an appropriate message and include your name at the end of the message.
3. Click **Insert** and then **File Attachment**.
4. The File Attachment menu will drop.
5. Go to the **Look In** box and you will see a drop-down arrow on the right. Click on this and select the drive and folder required and click on the filename required.
6. Once you have selected the file name in the Look In box, click **Attach**.

## GLOSSARY

**Virus**:
A program that can automatically copy itself and spread infection, rather like a human virus, by invading programs or disks without the user necessarily knowing. It can then cause severe disruption to the operator of that computer.

| **New car** | |
| --- | --- |
| **From:** | student133@hotmail.com |
| **To:** | student142@hotmail.com |
| **Sent:** | 14 February 2006 13:57 |
| **Attach:** | HPIM0091.JPG |
| **Subject:** | New car |

Hi Philip

I'm attaching a photo of my new car. It's great isn't it! Let me know what you think. Are you getting a car for your 18th – what are you hoping to get? Send me an attachment of a picture of the car you'd like.

Josh

| **Re: New car** | |
| --- | --- |
| **From:** | student142@hotmail.com |
| **To:** | student133@hotmail.com |
| **Sent:** | 14 February 2006 14:06 |
| **Attach:** | Sierra.jpg |
| **Subject:** | Re: New car |

Hi Josh

It looks great – I like the colour. I don't know yet if I'm getting a car for my 18th. I'd like a red or blue Sierra – here's a picture of one.

Philip

-------Original Message ---------

**From:** student133@hotmail.com
**To:** student142@hotmail.com
**Sent:** Tuesday, 14 February, 2006 13:57
**Subject:** New car

Hi Philip

I'm attaching a photo of my new car. It's great isn't it! Let me know what you think. Are you getting a car for your 18th – what are you hoping to get? Send me an attachment of a picture of the car you'd like.

Josh

**Figure 3.18**  *Attachments with emails*

7. The filename of the attachment will appear in the **Attach** panel in your email's header.
8. Send the message (see Figure 3.18).

## Receive attachments within emails

You should be aware that attachments can be dangerous to the health of your computer! **Viruses** can be easily transmitted by email attachments. You should be very sure before you open an attachment that you know the person who has sent the email. Ask your tutor if your computer is protected from viruses by up-to-date virus protection software. To receive an attachment follow this procedure:

1. Check your Inbox for a reply to the message you sent to your colleague (see p 114).
2. Click on the message – notice the paperclip-shaped icon on the right-hand side of the header area in the bottom half of the screen.
3. Access the attachment by clicking on the paperclip.
4. A file name should be displayed in the menu.
5. Click on this filename.
6. A Mail Attachment menu will now be displayed asking you if you wish to open the attachment – click on Open.
7. Word will automatically open the document and it should appear.
8. The document is now available to you to edit it or to print it.

## ACTIVITY

Access an online message system and send a message to a colleague. Your tutor will give you details of how to access the system and will witness you using it.

## Use online message system

An online message system enables you to chat online via text in real time and is faster than email. You type a message and will see it displayed on the screen as you type it. The person you are communicating with will also see it displayed on his/her screen as you type and will then type some text in reply. Some systems also enable you to talk to others using a computer microphone and to use a webcam to view others in real time and in colour. An example of an online message system is AOL's Instant Messenger, which allows you to send instant messages and is a free service.

## Portfolio tip

*Your use of email should be highly competent and should include evidence of sending and receiving emails in relation to a specific context. You should also include evidence of receiving and sending file attachments. You should demonstrate a high level of competence using an online message system and should ask your tutor to provide a witness statement as evidence.*

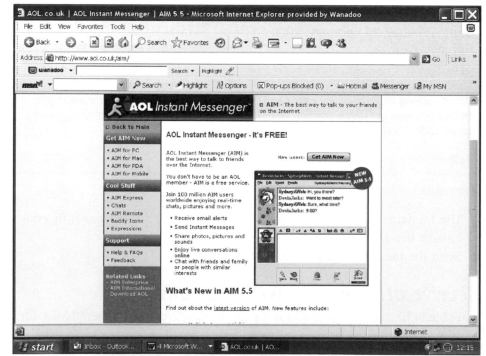

Figure 3.19 *An example of an online message system*

# AO5 Use word processing software for the presentation of information

Many of the assessment objectives in this unit require evidence that you will produce using a word processor; for example, a memo for AO2 that may contain results of research carried out for AO3.

You may use any word processing system to produce evidence for your portfolio. The information given below is generic so that it can be used on any word processing system, e.g. MS Word, Lotus, Works, Corel WordPerfect. If you have difficulty accessing or using any of the facilities and functions mentioned, ask your tutor for advice or use the Help facility within your word processor.

## Creating, editing, saving and printing text files

All these functions are vital if you wish to ensure professional, well-displayed documents, which are easy to access should you need to amend or re-print them at any time.

### Creating text files

When you open a word processing program, a new blank document will normally appear automatically. If a blank document is not displayed, then click on the New Blank Document icon.

### Editing text files

When writing, editing or entering text, you are likely to make errors – everyone does, but the important thing is that you check your work thoroughly and correct errors before submitting your work! There are no short cuts – for good, professional-looking documents, you need to check your work carefully. Using a spellchecker is a good first check of text you have entered but you should not rely on this as your only proofreading method. For example, a spellchecker would not pick up the incorrect use of 'principal' and 'principle'. Use grammarcheckers with care – often they will advise you to amend a sentence for American English (if a US program) which is not always appropriate for a British English document. You should read what you have typed; looking for errors and at the same time making sure that it makes sense.

### Saving text files

You should save your work regularly when working on a document – just in case there is power loss or a problem with the software. In this way, you won't lose your work. Saving every couple of minutes is not too often, as those people who have lost work because they haven't got into the habit of saving will verify!

You should agree with your tutor the filenames you will use and where your work can be saved. You may be using a network and may be given your own secure area on the network or you may use removable media such as a CD or flash stick/pen on which to save your work. You should make back-up copies of files on removable media and should take great care to keep these safe and secure at all times and to keep them with you. Otherwise, when you have some unexpected free time, you will be very frustrated when you remember that your floppy disk is at home. On completion of your work, save once more, just to be sure.

## Printing text files

You need to check with your tutor what printer is available for your use and what arrangements need to be made, if any, such as access codes. Some centres charge for using printers and require you to have a smart card to gain access to a printer, while others have software that counts the number of pages you print so that charges can then be levied.

Figure 3.20 shows the printing options available via the Print Menu.

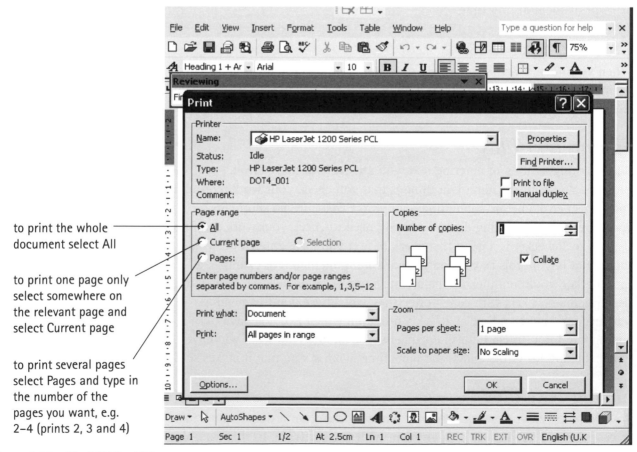

to print the whole document select All

to print one page only select somewhere on the relevant page and select Current page

to print several pages select Pages and type in the number of the pages you want, e.g. 2–4 (prints 2, 3 and 4)

**Figure 3.20** *The MS Word Print menu*

Before printing a document, you should proofread your work on screen and make any changes needed. When you are happy that the document is free from error, you should use **Print Preview**. This facility allows you to check that the document is presented in the way you want. It is particularly useful with multi-page documents. If you decide to make some changes, you can note the page number, return to the document by closing Print Preview, go to the appropriate page and make the amendments. Then use Print Preview again to check that the amendments you have made are correct – it's cheaper than constantly printing!

Colour printers would be very useful, especially when printing presentation slides, notices with colour fonts or documents where graphics have been imported, but are more expensive to use. You can keep the cost down by printing in black only for evidence purposes. It is also cheaper to use 'draft quality' rather than 'normal quality' or 'best quality'. Good quality A4 paper should be used, with 80 gsm considered as the minimum quality.

# Text formatting and page layout

There are various functions available that will help you to format text and to alter the layout to enhance the appearance of a document.

## *Text formatting*

It is possible to change the appearance of text and to use different spacing and alignment.

**Font styles and sizes**, including word art, font colour, emphasis such as bold, italics, underlining, capitals and shading, can all be used to enhance a piece of work. Symbols can also be very useful and are easy to access.

01626 112455

 at the above address

Figure 3.21   *Example symbols*

**Linespacing** can be altered for a whole document or just a paragraph or section of text. You can use single, double or treble linespacing, the latter being used in legal offices for the production of first drafts but can be useful if you have produced a rough draft and need plenty of space between text to write your amendments.

**Alignment** may include left and right alignment or centring. Some businesses have a house style that includes full justification for all documents – that is, both left and right margins are justified. Others prefer that text is left justified – the left margin is justified, the right margin is ragged. However, text that is justified can produce large spaces between words, especially if the words are lengthy and the margins are wide. You should consider changing from full justification to left justified text if this happens as it can make a document look strange and difficult to read because text does not flow so well.

In the documents you produce for your portfolio, you may use full or left justification, but you use one or the other consistently within a document.

Centre alignment is used mostly for display of text, as in a notice, but it can be very effective when used for headings. Right alignment is used for single lines of text, e.g. to align some words at the right margin, but is not usually used for whole paragraphs of text.

**Indenting** of text can be very helpful to draw people's attention to some text for a particular reason. It is particularly effective if used when text is fully justified and text is indented from both left and right margins, but indenting just from the left margin can also be effective.

**Headers and footers** are useful to include details about the document you are producing and have automatic options for page numbers, filenames etc. The header area is usually used for displaying a heading and the footer area for page numbering and filename, but there is no hard and fast rule. **Page numbers** should be inserted on all documents with more than one page of text. Any style is appropriate, but for a long document the style 'page x of y' is particularly useful as it is easy to see if a page is missing. **Filenames** can be displayed but are best inserted after the file has been given the name you wish to use. A smaller font size can be very effective (e.g. point 10 for a footer, while the remainder of the text is in point 12).

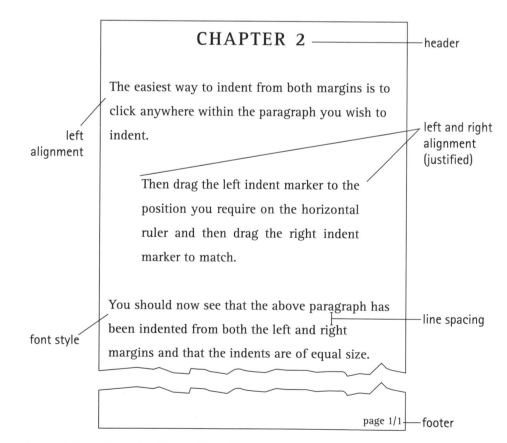

**Figure 3.22** *Example of formatting of text*

## Page layout

To change the way a document is set out, you need to use a page setup (or similar) function. Here you can alter the margins and paper orientation (either landscape or portrait) but remember, if you alter the margins, they will normally be changed for the whole document, not just one section of it. If you wish to change the margins for just one section of text, for example one paragraph, you will need to indent the text from the left and right margins.

Professional, well-displayed documents are usually produced using equal margins. If you want to use wider margins than the default (usually 2.5 cm), then you can easily change them, but you should consider changing the left and right margins of a document to give balance.

## ACTIVITY

1 Create a new document. Enter the following text:

Christmas Fair

Buckland School are holding
their Christmas Fair
starting at 10.30 am
on (insert date)
at The Old Manor
Buckland
¼ mile from the village
free transport will be provided

There will be lots to see and do and refreshments will be available:

Father Christmas
Mince pies and mulled wine
Cake stall
Tombola
Raffle
A huge variety of gifts
Sweets and chocolates
and much, much more

Please come along and support us

*All money raised at this year's Christmas Fair will be donated to the After School Club*

*If you would like more information about the Fair, please contact Morice Khan*

*01225 224433*

2 Change the left and right margins to 3.5 cm. Centre some text and use single and double linespacing.
3 Change some of the text as follows:
 - use different font styles and sizes, word art, shading and font colour (if colour printing is possible)
 - use bold, italics and underlining.
 Insert at least one symbol. Save your work, using the filename underline{enhance1} and then insert this filename in the footer area of your document. Spellcheck, proofread on screen carefully and print a copy.
4 Working in groups, peruse the notices that have been produced and discuss whether changes to the appearance have enhanced the appearance of the documents or made it more difficult to assimilate the information. Edit the document, if appropriate, and re-save and re-print.

# Inserting graphics and numerical data

**Graphics** can be charts, graphs, clipart and horizontal dividers. Charts and graphs will break up the text and illustrate what you are saying. Clipart is useful to present your reader with an image to back up your words. Horizontal dividers can break up the text and further enhance your document.

Charts and graphs can be imported into a document from a spreadsheet file, but you need to ensure that you position these accurately so that they do not obscure any text. The clipart that is available to you depends on what your word processor has and whether you have access to other programs or to the Internet, where more clipart can be found.

**Numerical data** is usually aligned so that it can be seen and interpreted easily, and to do this decimal tabs are often used to ensure that the decimal points are aligned in any sums of money.

| ITEM | DESCRIPTION | COST (£) |
| --- | --- | --- |
| Printer | Inkjet colour | 125.65 |
| Scanner | Flat bed scanner | 52.50 |
| Camera | Digital camera | 89.00 |

**Table 3.5** *Table to show alignment of decimal point*

## ACTIVITY

1　Recall the file <u>enhance1</u> saved in the previous activity.
2　Insert clipart in an appropriate position; this may be any clipart of your choice.
3　Ensure that none of the text has been obscured by the clipart.
4　Enter the following data, ensuring the decimal points are aligned:

*Christmas Show*

*Our Christmas Show will be held in the School Hall on Wednesday, Thursday and Friday next week. Tickets are available from the school office:*

| | |
|---|---|
| *Adults* | *£4.00* |
| *Senior Citizens* | *£3.20* |
| *Children under 16* | *£2.00* |
| *Family ticket* | *£18.50* |
| *(max 2 adults, 4 children)* | |

5　Save the file and print a copy.

## Use of text boxes

Text boxes can draw attention to specific information. They may be shaded or unshaded. However, if you decide to use a shaded box, it is important not to make the shading too dense or it will not be possible to read the text within the box. Text boxes may be positioned in precise locations within a document and the exact size can be specified. Different font styles and sizes and centre alignment may also be used to enhance the text within a text box (see Figure 3.23).

## ACTIVITY

1　Recall the file <u>enhance1</u> and insert a shaded text box at the end of the text, in the centre of the page, 6 cm wide by 1.5 cm high. Include the text:

*We hope to raise more than last year.*

2　Centre the text within the box and use italics for all the text in the text box.
3　Save and print a copy.

Staff may claim certain expenses:

- The cost of telephone calls may be claimed but an itemised bill must support claims.

bullet points ———

- Stationery costs may also be claimed, but receipts must be attached to your claims.

Please note that the procedure to be followed when sending a fax is given below.

1. Load the document correctly.

numerical ———
points

2. Dial the fax number and check that it is correct.

3. Press the send button.

text boxes ———

Text boxes can be any size and may be shaded by using colour, as here, or with different shades of grey.

This text box is unshaded. Note the use of a distinctive font to draw attention. Text can also be centred within the text box.

table ———

| ITEM | CODE NO | PRICE (£) |
|------|---------|-----------|
| Hanging basket | 291 | 24.75 |
| Picnic hamper (large) | 568 | 105.50 |
| Fishing basket | 569 | 22.00 |

columns ———

**SUMMER MAGIC**

Baskets and containers ensure even the dullest corner of your garden can burst with colour. Almost any plant lends itself to container growing.

Pouches are amazing and versatile new containers. They are so easy to use. Plants in pouches need less watering than those in baskets.

We are very happy to welcome visitors to our centre. Our opening hours are very generous – why not call in to see us.

Or you may prefer to order a catalogue. Why not visit our website www.plantscolour.co.uk? Or, if you prefer, contact Julius Grand on 01626 346781.

**Figure 3.23** *Example of layout of page*

# Use of bullets

A bullet is a small graphic, the most common of which is a large dot. However, bullets can be virtually any graphic you wish, including small pictures. Bullets are very useful in a list, but where a sequence is involved numbers are preferred. When using bullets or numbers, the text is often indented so that the bullets or numbers stand alone at the left. This makes it easy to read and will look very professional.

## ACTIVITY

Recall the file <u>enhance1</u> and insert bullet points to the four lines of text beginning 'Father Christmas' and ending 'A huge variety of gifts'. Save and print a copy.

# Use of tables

Tables can be very helpful as they can help to display material very clearly. They also act as good breaks in text. Gridlines can be inserted to separate rows and columns. Any columns with sums of money should be aligned at the decimal points.

## ACTIVITY

1   Create a table and enter the following data:

| Item | Code No | Price £ |
|------|---------|---------|
| Hanging basket | 291 | 24.75 |
| Picnic hamper (large) | 568 | 105.50 |
| Fishing basket | 569 | 22.00 |

2   Ensure that text in columns is left aligned and that numbers are aligned at the decimal points.
3   Show all gridlines.
4   Save and print a copy.

# Use of columns

Columns are useful to present information, just as you would find in a newspaper. You can divide a document into two, three or more columns of text. The text will flow from the bottom of one column to the top of the next and if you want the columns to be of equal length, you can insert a column break to force the text to move to the top of the next column. You can change the width of a column and reduce the space between the columns if you wish. Text can be formatted in the same way as full line text. Full justification can be used, as in newspapers, but left justification is also acceptable.

## Portfolio tip

*The documents you produce for your portfolio should show that you have covered the full range of word processing software functions competently and independently.*

## ACTIVITY

Recall file enhance1 and insert a full page border. You may use any border of your choice. Save and print a copy.

## Use of borders

Full page borders can be easily inserted into a document and these may be plain or fancy (see Figure 3.24). Their use is particularly helpful when producing eye-catching documents such as notices, invitations, etc. As well as full page borders, borders can be inserted around a paragraph of text.

# AO6  Use presentation software to support a verbal presentation

Presentation software can be used to put together a presentation, to help you present your information professionally and efficiently. This software is used to create an electronic slide show, which is made up of a series of slides. These can contain eye-catching text, graphics, bulleted items and animation.

In this section, the information given is generic to any presentation package, so that it can be used in software such as Corel Presentations and MS PowerPoint and different editions such as 1997, 2000, 2003. Ask your tutor for help and guidance if you have any difficulties, or use the Help facility that is available within the presentation software.

## Creating, saving and editing a new presentation

When you open a presentation program you need to select a blank slide. You might then find it useful to create a 'master' slide as this allows you to insert fonts and sizes, colour and clipart which will then appear on other slides within the presentation (see Figure 3.24). If you then decide to change these features, you can simply revisit the master slide at any time and make the changes. It is very important that your slides are consistent, with the same designs and colours throughout to identify each one as part of a series. An audience may find it distracting if the slides are a mixture of designs, colours, etc. The use of a master slide will ensure that all the slides in the presentation are consistent.

Save your presentation once you have created the master – use an appropriate filename. Get into the habit of saving on a regular basis to reduce the risk of losing work.

You should use a spellchecker to check for errors and then proofread your text very thoroughly. Your audience will probably be quick to point out errors because of the large font size and the small number of words in your slides. So make quite sure there are none for them to find!

# Entry of text, graphics and spreadsheet data

You should aim to keep your slides simple – restrict each slide to 5–7 main points. If necessary, use more slides with less information on each.

## *Entry of text*

Make sure you use a large font, not less than 24 point. Use easy-to-read serif fonts, although headings in san serif can be eye-catching. Remember that a slide on your computer screen may look fine, but when viewed from the back of a room, will it still be readable?

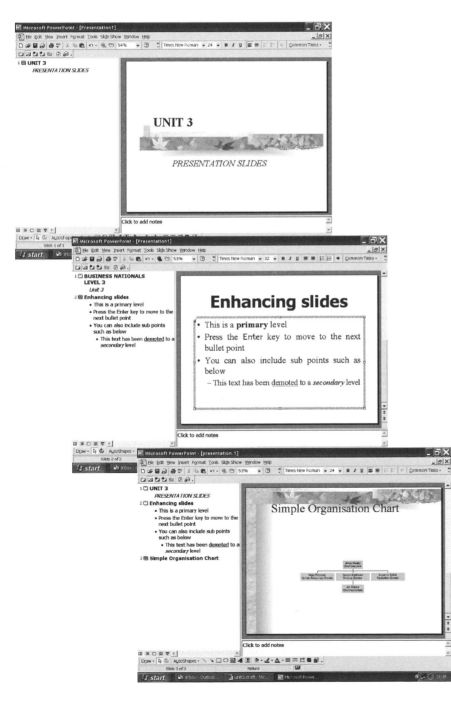

**Figure 3.24** *A slide presentation*

### Enhancing text

Your software will have a variety of functions that will help you to enhance your slides. However, too much enhancement can be overwhelming and the message can be lost!

Remember, though, that all text formatting should be carried out on the master slide. Functions include:

- emphasis, such as bold, italics and underlining
- justification
- bullet points – with different levels
- font styles and sizes.

## Graphics

Graphics can include clipart, graphs and charts (including organisation charts, pie and bar charts). Clipart can easily be inserted and can add interest to a slide.

## Spreadsheet data

Spreadsheet data can be imported from another program if required, but charts and graphs can be created from within the presentation software. If you want to create a chart that is not displayed, there should be a facility that will enable you to select a different chart.

Organisation charts are used primarily to show the people who work for a company. When you select a template with an organisation chart, chart boxes automatically appear into which you can enter the names and job titles, if appropriate. There are several levels – top, second, co-worker and subordinate (see Figure 3.24).

## Background graphics

It is possible to choose a colour for the background but you should do this with care as too dark a background will make it impossible to read the text and too bright a colour can shimmer. However, by choosing the text colour carefully, some very striking presentations can be achieved. Some companies have a house style with the background colour, logo and so on already set up so that all slides created by any employee will use the same logo, style, colours, etc.

## Animation

It is possible to apply animation to text and graphics. For example, if you are using a bulleted list, you might find it useful to show just one bullet at a time. You can then control the animation with the mouse during your presentation. If you wanted to grab your audience's attention, you could animate a graphic so that it would appear to 'fly' across the slide.

# Printout formats

Although your presentation is likely to be displayed using a computer, projector and screen, you may want to print your slides in the first instance, to check that they look professional, well displayed and that they are accurate. Also, you may not have any projector or screen facilities and may need to use overhead projector transparencies (OHTs) or you may wish to provide your audience with handouts of your slides.

## *Print range and options*

Figure 3.25 shows the various print ranges and options available.

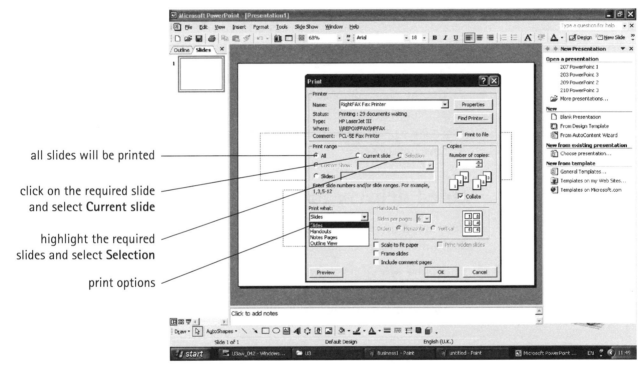

Figure 3.25  *Examples of print ranges and options available*

## *Slides*

This option enables you to print slides and by choosing one of the print range options, to select all the slides or just one slide.

## *Handouts*

You can print six thumbnail images on each page which you can then use to hand to your audience so that they can follow your presentation more easily. You can also create handouts that give space on the right for your audience to make notes during the presentation – in PowerPoint this is done by selecting three slides to a page.

## Notes pages

You will probably want to make notes to help you with the delivery of your presentation. These can be added to your slides and you can keep these for yourself only or you can print them for your audience if you wish them to see your notes!

## Outline view

This displays all the text you have included on all slides. You can use it to rearrange text, bullet points, paragraphs etc. It is also useful as it enables you to check that you have not left out any important points and you can then easily make any amendments needed.

### ACTIVITY

1 Return to the case study on Suzi's Dog Walking Service (page 110).
2 Use the main points contained within your letter to Suzi to prepare presentation slides.
3 Produce handouts – three to a page.
4 Save and close.

# Varied delivery formats of presentation

There are many options available for delivery of a presentation. The more usual one is onscreen but there are other options:

- Self-running presentation – this is useful if a company has set up a presentation for use at a trade show or exhibition; the presentation will run unattended and will restart when it has completed the slide show.

- Online meeting – this enables the leader of a meeting to control a presentation to others online; the participants can view the slides on their computer screen.

- Presentation broadcasting, using video and audio – a presentation can be broadcast over the web and is used by companies to present to groups who may be in remote areas abroad.

- Overhead transparencies – slides can be printed in colour or black and viewed via an overhead projector (OHP).

- Paper printouts – a presentation can be made using printouts and can be effective if colour printing is of a high quality. It is also useful to have paper printouts in case of power failure or problems with the software – you will then have a backup.

- 35 mm slides – presentation slides can be transferred to conventional 35 mm slides and shown with a projector.

# Preparing and delivering a presentation

Your presentation will be based on research you have previously carried out (as part evidence for AO3). A successful presentation is one that manages to convey a message to an audience, using slides to reinforce the message.

Decide what equipment you will need, e.g. computer software projector and screen, and any audio/visual aids you will use to help you engage the audience and keep their attention. You should be absolutely sure you know how to use the software and projector. This will not only help boost your confidence, but there is nothing worse for a nervous speaker than being faced with equipment that he or she does not know how to operate and, possibly, no one available to help. All this, perhaps, with the audience waiting and watching!

When planning your presentation, always start at the beginning – a good, snappy introduction will grab the audience's attention and keep it to the end. Be sure to tell your audience your objectives. Then move on to give them the facts or information you wish to give. Prepare presentation slides and audience handouts – all participants will then have a printed version and this will help them to follow your presentation.

## Portfolio tip

*Use language, tone and style appropriate to the audience, speak clearly and make sure your audience can hear you.*

*You should maintain eye contact with your audience and be confident, using positive body language.*

## *Presentation delivery skills*

You will probably be very nervous – that is quite natural. However, the more preparation you do, the more confident you will feel. During the presentation, keep eye contact with your audience and move around a little

– don't stand in one place the whole time but, on the other hand, don't move around so much that it becomes a distraction.

Structure your presentation carefully – start at the beginning by introducing your topic, informing your audience what it is you want to present to them. Then give them the facts, using statistics, graphs, charts, and so on to help you. Finish by giving them a summary. Then thank them for their attention and ask them if they have any questions.

## Research and planning

Thorough preparation is vital. You will need to carry out thorough research of your topic and then to make a plan of how you intend to present the material you have discovered.

Think about how you will end your presentation. A brief summary may be useful – but don't try to bombard your audience with yet more facts at this late stage. Thank them for their attention and then ask them if they have any questions.

It is highly recommended that you practise your presentation before the 'real' thing – a colleague may be prepared to help you. You will be able to judge the running time of your presentation, ensure your audio/visual aids work well and, if not, you will have time to remedy things.

Once you have prepared your slides, have a rehearsal and work out the timings. Ask a colleague to help you. Make any adjustments to the slides in the light of feedback received.

## Organisation of materials

As soon as you have decided on the slides you will use, you should consider whether you will make any notes and whether these will be for your own use only or whether you will share them with your audience. You can then make prints of these well beforehand. If you are planning to give your audience handouts so that they can make notes on printouts of your slides, you also need to do this well in advance.

During your rehearsal, ask your colleague to look at your notes and handouts and get feedback which you can then use to make your presentation even more professional.

The day before the presentation, ensure that all your materials are in order. Printouts of handouts and notes are stacked ready to be handed out. Slides are in the correct order and the projector and computer are available for your use on the day. You should also make sure you know how to operate the projector and software!

## Team working and performance review

You and your colleagues can work together as a team to practise presentations before you do it 'for real'. Take it in turns – one giving the presentation while the others act as the audience and then change round,

---

### Portfolio tip

*In order to provide the evidence required in your portfolio for AO6, you will need to demonstrate a high level of confidence in the delivery of the presentation, having carried out detailed research (as evidence for AO3), planned effectively and organised materials. Your slides will enhance the verbal presentation and fully support your message. The whole presentation will be delivered in a highly professional manner, with effective use of presentation techniques. You should ask your audience (including your tutor) to complete witness statements to be submitted as evidence. Copies of handouts, notes and slides will further enhance your submitted portfolio.*

giving everyone a chance to take part. In this way you can get valuable feedback from them on how your presentation slides and style could be improved. You will probably be very nervous and the more practised you are, the more confident you will become.

You should also carry out a review of your own performance, both during the rehearsal and the live presentation. Was there anything you could have done to improve your delivery? What feedback did you get from your audience?

## ACTIVITY

Return to the activity on Suzi's Dog Walking Service (page 110). Use the slides you have already prepared from your research to deliver a 10-minute presentation to a group of three of your colleagues and your tutor, if possible. On completion of the presentation, ask the group for feedback in order to help you improve your next presentation.

## AO7 Investigate and evaluate the impact of ICT on business practice

Recent research has shown that more than half of British households have access to the Internet and more than half of these are via broadband. These figures are rising continuously.

Many businesses, large and small, have been able to use ICT in their organisations in a variety of ways. For example, a small firm, employing just two people and located in an isolated rural area, provides medical supplies and since setting up their website have found it difficult to cope with orders received, from within the UK and abroad.

## Growth and application of e-commerce; potential of e-business, website, e-marketplaces, e-customer relationship management; e-personnel management

The use of **e-commerce** is growing rapidly. Companies are using ICT to grow their businesses at a time when customers are becoming familiar with the facilities that e-commerce offer and are feeling more confident buying online.

> ### GLOSSARY
>
> **E-commerce (or electronic commerce)**: The buying and selling of goods or services via computers.

## Growth and application of e-commerce

The growth of e-commerce has been steady and has opened up new opportunities for many businesses. Many are able to make use of easier, faster and better access to information, which often leads to less paperwork and improved efficiency. For example, a small company which prints community newsletters is able to receive and send artwork using email from/to customers rather than having to wait for delivery of drafts or printed hard copies dispatched by customers using postal delivery. It also means that the company can give customers more time to prepare their newsletters, ensuring that their articles are up to date.

The impact of e-commerce will vary, depending to some extent on the type of business. For example, many manufacturers and suppliers are linked so that orders can be placed and processed electronically. Stock control databases are used to track items and payment is also made electronically. This system is much quicker and cheaper than paper-based methods and also saves on warehouse space as materials can be delivered and used on the same day.

## Potential of e-business, website, e-marketplaces, e-customer relationship management

E-business can enhance productivity and increase cost-effectiveness and competitiveness of any business, large or small. For example, a medium-sized company, with regional offices, battling to survive in the face of fierce competition, centralised all its customers onto one database. Now the company can easily communicate with its customers, prepare accounts and arrange delivery times, using just one set of information instead of a muddle of sources.

Many businesses have set up their own websites, which enable them to give customers essential information about their products, but also enable customers to buy those products without having to leave their homes.

E-marketplaces are vast and growing rapidly. For example, supermarkets such as Sainsbury's enable customers to order all their shopping needs via the Internet, choose convenient delivery slots and then await delivery. Many people who work are taking advantage of this. They can order via the Internet from their homes, go to work and then await delivery on their return home. The stores give additional benefits by using loyalty cards to obtain information about their customers and their buying habits and can also communicate with customers by email.

E-customer relationship management provides a more interactive way of communicating with customers. In the past, customers had personal contact with sales staff, but nowadays they can simply access a company's website to order online and telephone the company's **call centre** to make an enquiry regarding the order, expecting the staff there to have access to the details concerning the customer's order – no personal, face-to-face communication.

**Figure 3.26**  *Buy a DVD without leaving home*

An e-customer relationship management system can be set up by a company to ensure information is shared about customers across all functions of the organisation, e.g. production, sales, marketing, despatch, finance. It ensures that customer service is improved by providing systems such as efficient order tracking.

## E-personnel management

Staff working in an e-commerce environment often work in large centralised centres which require fewer managers. Staff performance can be easily monitored and managers are able to match staff accurately with the skills required for particular services. Up-to-date powerful computers are necessary for efficient, cost-effective systems, and training of staff may be required, especially where constant upgrades are necessary. All of these have cost implications. Where companies offer a 24-hour service, staff may be required to work early mornings and nights. Some companies require staff to be bilingual.

Some larger organisations have an electronic system that keeps a record of all staff details, holidays, sickness, pay etc. For example, if a member of staff wishes to book a day's holiday, the system will email that person's manager for approval.

## The rise of call centre based/online customer support systems

Customers now have access to customer support systems via the telephone or the Internet and these have been set up by companies as part of their drive to improve customer care.

### The rise of call centre based customer support systems

The use of call centres is increasing and businesses, such as utility companies, computer hardware and software customer support (help desks) and mail order firms, are using them to interact with their customers. Staff may make calls to customers to remind them that their payment is overdue or to sell a product or service. They may receive calls from customers to obtain information, report a fault or request help.

Once a call centre has been set up, staffing costs are the most significant expense, and this is the main reason cited by companies for switching their call centre operations to countries such as India and the Philippines where there are English-speaking graduates available who often earn just one-tenth of equivalent UK employees.

### The rise of online customer support systems

There are many different customer support systems that are available online and these include company websites that contain detailed information in order for customers to make purchases, as well as FAQs (frequently asked questions) for customers to use as a first port of call in order to answer queries. Many websites also include **hot spots** and icons that customers can click on to get further information. For example, if a customer wished to purchase a printer from a firm's website, there would be hot spots that the customer would click on to gain information about the range, types and prices of printers available, speed of printing, running costs, availability of ink supplies, etc.

> **GLOSSARY**
>
> **hot spot:**
> a link on a website that will connect with further pages of information concerning a product or service.

## Automation of business functions (electronic payment/money transfers, high-density data transfer and the impact on postal services)

For many people, the Internet has become their normal method of purchase. Customers are able to visit a website, search the range of products displayed, select an item, arrange delivery and pay online, all completely automatically and without intervention from a human being.

## *Electronic payment/money transfers, high-density data transfer*

People used to pay for their goods by cash or cheque and received a paper sales receipt. This system is still used by some shops, but the majority have moved over to electronic payment, 'swiping' the customer's card through a machine. The sales assistant then enters the sales figure and the details are passed to a bank for approval. People using the Internet to purchase goods can also make use of electronic payment and enter their credit or debit card details on a secure website.

Money transfers are used by people who need to send or receive money quickly, often from outside the UK. A money transfer service is offered by various companies, such as PayPal and Western Union, who will provide a quick service, accepting payment for the money transfer by debit or credit card.

CD-Rs, CD-RWs and DVDs are used at present for high-density data transfer as these offer a cheap and fairly robust system of transferring data. Research is ongoing in this area and companies are investigating technology such as holography to find out if recording massive amounts of storage on one medium, for example 100 films on a disk the size of a CD, would be feasible.

### GLOSSARY

**CD–R:**
a compact disk that can be read only; no information can be stored on it.

**CD–RW:**
a compact disk that can be written, erased and rewritten.

**holography:**
a scientific term related to three-dimensional optical recording.

## CASE STUDY

### *Prism Jewellery*

Julienne Mablethorpe started making earrings as a hobby ten years ago. She gave them to friends and family and then starting selling her jewellery at craft shows and car boot sales. The business grew and Julienne decided to expand. Customers asked her for jewellery to complement the earrings and she now makes matching bracelets, necklaces, brooches and pendants. Gothic pewter jewellery is particularly popular. She has advertised in a local free newspaper but the response was disappointing. Advertising in national newspapers and magazines is very expensive, so she now feels the time is right to look at other ways of selling her jewellery.

She has no knowledge of computers but friends have told her that she should set up her own website. She is not convinced as she feels the costs would be too high.

## Impact on postal services

Electronic communications used by many companies, such as email, wireless technology and electronic payments, have led to a decline in letter post, a decline which is likely to accelerate in the future. Research has shown that the total volume of post has declined in recent years as companies turn to technology to communicate with their suppliers, customers and staff. It is not only businesses that are turning away from postal services – many people are now using email and e-cards instead of sending letters and traditional greetings cards. However, parcel post has increased as people have become more IT-proficient and have the confidence to make use of e-commerce.

## Portfolio tip

*In your portfolio, you will need to produce a comprehensive evaluation based on an extensive investigation into the impact of ICT on business practice.*

## ACTIVITY

Julienne has asked you to research the possibility of setting up her own website, with an electronic payment system, so that customers can search through the pages of jewellery on her website and choose what they would like, order instantly and pay for it automatically.

1 Carry out research using the Internet, investigate other websites offering pewter jewellery for sale.
2 Produce a list of the websites you have visited, giving a brief summary of your findings.
3 Investigate a system of electronic payment that could be used by customers to pay at the time of order.
4 Prepare and produce a report for Julienne that describes the results of your research. Use normal formats and conventions in your report.

## SKILLS CHECK

1. Give two advantages of face-to-face discussions.

2. Give one reason why you should not interrupt someone during a telephone discussion.

3. Explain why it is important to plan a presentation and describe the steps you would take in your planning.

4. Identify five items that you should include on an agenda for a meeting.

5. Explain how a Chairperson's Agenda differs from a Meeting Agenda.

6. Describe the style of language used to record minutes and explain the purpose of an 'Action' column.

7. Identify the main purposes of written communications and give one example of each.

8. Give the advantages and disadvantages of letters.

9. What does ISP mean?

10. How would you identify whether the reply facility had been used when replying to a received email?

11. Explain how you could identify whether there was an attachment to an email.

12. What is meant by an instant online message service? Give an example.

13. Name five ways in which you could change the appearance of text using a word processor.

14. When creating presentation slides, explain how you would insert font styles/sizes, background colour and a logo so that all these features appeared on all slides.

15. Identify the steps you would take to insert a column or bar chart within a slide.

16. How would you print audience handouts so that three slides appear on a page with space alongside for notes.

17. Explain what is meant by e-commerce.

18. Give one example of electronic payment.

# Unit 4  Finance for business

## Getting started

A lot of students do not relish the thought of a finance unit as they believe their mathematical skills will be insufficient to cope with the demands of such work. Do not panic, this unit is not about complex calculations. The focus of your learning will be on the interpretation of published accounts.

If you intend to work within a business environment you will need the necessary skills to be able to interpret financial information and understand its possible implications for your employer or yourself if you become self-employed.

*What do you think all these figures mean?*

Throughout AO1 and AO2 all financial examples will be based on the accounts of Plainford Ltd for the years 2003/04 and 2004/05. Subsequent exercises will be based on two further sets of accounts for two similar businesses, Breakthrough Ltd and Headway Ltd. You will find all of the accounts at the end of AO1. If you work through the examples and set exercises you will gain the skills necessary to tackle the model assignment set by OCR for this unit. This has been structured to allow you to achieve all of the assessment objectives through the completion of set tasks. Look closely at the results of your investigation in order to avoid jumping to obvious conclusions. There will be no right or wrong answers. You will be awarded the higher grades for well presented, logical and clearly justified responses to the tasks.

To complete this unit successfully you will need to produce evidence to demonstrate that you can interpret, evaluate, and analyse financial statements that have been supplied for your use. You will also need to make recommendations and judgements about a business's future performance. To achieve the higher grades you must link the different assessment objectives to produce an overall picture of the financial health of your chosen business.

*This unit will cover*

- AO1 Explain and interpret features of a business organisation's profit and loss statement.

- AO2 Explain and interpret features of a business organisation's balance sheet.

- AO3 Interpret financial performance using a range of ratios.

- AO4 Make recommendations based on the preparation and analysis of a cash flow forecast.

- AO5 Identify and evaluate costs involved in the purchase of business assets.

- AO6 Explain the role in the economy of a range of financial institutions.

- AO7 Analyse the impact of the economic environment on business performance.

# AO1 Explain and interpret features of a business organisation's profit and loss statement

In this section you will learn about the different sections of a profit and loss statement. You will then be able to use the figures presented within a profit and loss statement to interpret the financial health of the business being investigated.

## What is a profit and loss statement?

A profit and loss statement summarises a business's income and expenditure over a set period of time. It is an historical document which represents facts. It calculates two profit figures – gross profit and net profit. Gross profit is the profit made when only the expenses related to the sale of the product have been included. The net profit is the gross profit minus all of the general expenses of the business. Some of the net profit will be paid to the Inland Revenue in tax.

### Example

You are about to go into business selling secondhand cars. You purchase the first car for £2,000 and sell it for £2,500. In order to sell the car you spent £50 on advertising.

| | |
|---|---|
| Sales | £2,500 |
| – Purchase of car | £2,000 |
| **Gross profit** | £ 500 |
| – Advertising | £ 50 |
| **Net profit** | £ 450 |

## ACTIVITY

You have purchased a further two cars for £6,000. You sell the second car for £4,000 and the third car for £3,500. You spend a further £100 on advertising and £40 on telephone calls. Calculate the gross and net profits.

## ACTIVITY

In small groups write down the reasons you think businesses are required to produce profit and loss accounts. Compare your ideas with the rest of the class.

## Why do businesses prepare profit and loss accounts?

Small businesses, such as sole traders, have to comply with less legal legislation when producing their final accounts, so for the purpose of this unit we will consider why limited companies are required to produce final accounts.

## To monitor performance

All businesses need to know how they are performing throughout the year. If sales suddenly start to fall this trend needs to be quickly identified and remedial action taken. It is quite common for large plcs to publish interim accounts six months into their financial year. These accounts allow shareholders to monitor how the business is performing.

## To comply with legislation

Public limited companies are regulated by the Companies Acts 1985 and 1989 concerning the preparation and publication of financial statements. They are required to submit a copy of their accounts annually to Companies House. Companies with a turnover greater than £1 million are also required to have their accounts audited. The auditors are appointed each year at the annual general meeting. The auditors examine the company's books and accounts and their report states whether or not the accounts give a true and fair picture of the business's financial health. The report and financial statements are given to the shareholders at the annual general meeting.

The Inland Revenue also receive the final set of accounts so that they can calculate how much corporation tax must be paid. Customs and Excise require final accounts figures to be submitted every three months so that the business's VAT liability can be calculated.

## To formulate strategic plans

By looking at past financial facts and figures it is possible for a business to identify trends, whether good or bad, and make plans to improve or build upon them. For example, if a particular line has been selling really well it might be worth increasing production, backed up with a new marketing campaign to try and improve an already developing existing market. This may be at the expense of a less popular product.

# Features of a profit and loss statement

In order to illustrate the different features of profit and loss statements the examples are going to make reference to two sets of final accounts. These appear on pages 152–155.

## Sales revenue

Sales revenue is the total amount that has been received by the business for the sale of its goods or services. Sales revenue will relate to the period stated within the accounts, usually a 12-month period. Sometimes large businesses produce interim accounts which cover the first six months of their trading period to illustrate to their shareholders how the business is performing.

The sales revenue stated will be the total value of all goods or services sold. Some of these goods or services may not have been paid for by the customer yet, and therefore sales revenue does not always correlate to the amount of money a business has received in payment.

## ACTIVITY

Look in one of the major newspaper's (e.g. *Guardian, The Times, Independent*) business section. Find a report on a business that has just issued its final accounts and another that has just released its interim results.

*Plainford Ltd, engineering works*

### Example

If we look at the accounts of Plainford Ltd we can see that total sales revenue has increased from £195,000 to £230,000, an increase of £35,000.

This could also be shown as a percentage change.

$$\frac{\text{Difference between the two years}}{\text{Original amount}} \times 100 = \text{Percentage change}$$

$$\frac{35,000}{195,000} \times 100 = 17.95\% \text{ increase}$$

In the example the sales revenue has increased by nearly 18 per cent. This could be due to the following reasons:

- more products sold by the business – penetration into new markets
- lower sales price has increased the number of products sold

- reduced competition

- economic – there may have been an interest rate decrease so people have more money available to spend on the product. This is known as an increase in disposable income

- change in tastes and fashions has lead to an increase in demand – e.g. increase in the use of gyms due to increased health awareness, DVD players replacing video players.

## QUESTIONS

Using the accounts of Breakthrough Ltd and Headway Ltd, answer the following questions.

1   What was the sales revenue for Breakthrough Ltd?
2   What was the sales revenue for Headway Ltd?
3   Which one has the highest sales revenue? Why do you think this is?

## Cost of sales, materials/stock, opening and closing stock

All of these items are closely related and therefore we will consider them together within this section. When a business buys in items to sell on they are known as purchases. For example, a newsagent would have to purchase newspapers, sweets, ice creams and cigarettes to sell on to the general public.

## QUESTIONS

What is the difference between the purchase price of goods and the selling price?

Financial accounts usually run over a period of 12 months. At the end of each financial year a business will still have some of its purchases unsold. These items are known as closing stock. The closing stock of one year becomes the opening stock of the following year. In order to ascertain the value of the stock that a business is holding at the end of its financial year it will conduct a physical stock check. Some stock may have become damaged, obsolete or out of date and so have a reduced value. Stock records are adjusted so that the financial value stated in the accounts is 'true and fair'.

### Example

Let's consider a sweet shop whose financial year runs from 1st January to 31st December. When the shop opens on 2nd January the value of all the sweets in the shop, the opening stock, is £2,000. Throughout the year the shop buys in a further £12,000 of purchases – all the different sweets they are selling on to the customer. On the 31st December the owner adds up the value of all the sweets which remain in the shop unsold. This adds up to £3,500. This is the closing stock of the sweet shop.

| | |
|---|---|
| Opening stock | £ 2,000 |
| + Purchases | £12,000 |
| – Closing stock | £ 3,500 |
| **Cost of sales** | **£10,500** |

The example illustrates that the cost of sales is the total cost of the purchases after adding opening stock and deducting closing stock for the financial year.

Businesses that manufacture goods do not always buy in complete items to sell on. They buy in **raw materials** which they use to produce their products. A business making wooden furniture would have to buy in wood, glue, screws, metal, etc. These would be recorded as raw materials in their accounts.

## ACTIVITY

A hardware store's financial year runs from 1st January to the 31st December. When the shop opened on the 2nd January 2003 the opening stock was valued at £4,700. Purchases during the year amounted to £37,000. When the shop closed on 31st December the closing stock was valued at £3,400. Calculate the cost of sales.

### Example

Within the profit and loss statement of Plainford Ltd we can see that the only figure stated is cost of sales. The cost of sales has fallen from £87,000 in 2003/04 to £82,000 in 2004/05. This is a decrease of £5,000. The percentage change would be:

$$\frac{5,000}{87,000} \times 100 = 5.75\% \text{ decrease}$$

The reduction in the cost of sales could be due to the following reasons:

- the business has found a cheaper supplier
- there has been less wastage
- by bulk buying or paying for received goods more quickly the business may have secured discounts, making the goods cheaper to buy in.

Note 1 in the accounts shows the breakdown of stock and purchases. This illustrates that the business has been trying to reduce the amount of stock held. At the beginning of 2003/04 the business had stock valued at £28,000. By the end of 2004/05 closing stock had been reduced to £22,000. Holding excessive stock can be expensive for a business for the following reasons:

- it ties up money – the business has paid for the stock but is still waiting to sell it on to the customer

- there may be insurance costs
- it takes up storage space, which may cost money
- it may become out of date or damaged or it may be pilfered.

### QUESTIONS

Using the accounts of Breakthrough Ltd and Headway Ltd, answer the following questions.

1  What is the cost of sales for Breakthrough Ltd?
2  What is the cost of sales for Headway Ltd?
3  What do you think is the reason for the difference?
4  What is the value of the opening and closing stock for Breakthrough Ltd?
5  What is the value of the opening and closing stock for Headway Ltd?
6  Explain the disadvantages of holding too much closing stock.

## *Expenditure*

All businesses incur other expenses which are known as 'expenditure', which can include items such as employee wages, electricity and gas used in heating etc. It will also include expenses such as stationery, postage and the interest and capital repayments on any loans that the business may have.

Within the accounts of limited companies these items are not illustrated individually. Within the accounts of sole traders and partnerships the amounts may be listed individually.

It is important for businesses to monitor their expenditure. The higher the level of expenditure the lower the profit will be. Businesses that are able to keep a tight control on their expenses are those that will remain most competitive in the market place.

**Example**

In the accounts of Plainford Ltd the total expenses for the year 2003/04 amount to £87,000. They have increased to £98,456 for the year 2004/05. As the sales have increased an increase in expenses would be expected. The important question is - has the increase in expenditure been greater or lower than the increase in sales?

$$\frac{\text{Expenses for year 2004/05} - \text{expenses for year 2003/04}}{\text{Expenses for year 2003/04}} \times 100$$

$$\frac{11,456}{87,000} \times 100 = 13.17\%$$

From our previous calculations we can see that sales increased by 17.95 per cent but expenses by only 13.17 per cent. This shows that Plainford Ltd have been able to control their expenses. This could be due to the fact that they have been able to make use of economies of scale.

### GLOSSARY

**Economies of scale:** The more you buy the cheaper you are able to buy it. A business may be able to secure discounts and improved unit price due to the quantity it is ordering.

**QUESTIONS**

Using the accounts of Breakthrough Ltd and Headway Ltd, answer the following questions.

1 What is the total expenditure of Breakthrough Ltd?
2 What is the total expenditure of Headway Ltd?
3 Explain and justify which business you think has the greatest control over their expenses.

# Depreciation

Fixed assets are items that are purchased by the business for a specific purpose and not for resale. Fixed assets would include items such as buildings, equipment, computers and vehicles. All of these items would be used within the business and have a life expectancy of more than one year. Due to their high initial cost, fixed assets cannot be charged directly to the profit and loss account in the year they were purchased. If this were to happen, the net profit figure would be dramatically reduced and not reflect a 'true and fair' picture of the trading results of the business.

It is recognised that fixed assets will deteriorate through wear and tear and reduce in value from year to year. It is a well known fact that as soon as you purchase a new car and drive it off the garage forecourt it loses a considerable amount of value.

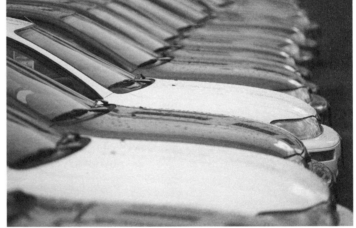

In accounts, fixed assets are depreciated. Every year an amount is deducted from their value. Depreciation is deducted from gross profit the same as other expenses in the profit, and loss account. By doing this the fixed assets will be valued correctly, all the relevant wear and tear and age has been taken into consideration. By charging depreciation against net profit each year it has the effect of spreading the cost of the fixed asset over the number of years that the business uses the asset.

*How much am I worth now?*

### Example

In the accounts of Plainford Ltd depreciation is one of the expenses being charged under the heading 'Financial'. The other expense is the capital repayment of a loan, which is £5,000 per annum. The depreciation charged in the year 2003/04 amounted to £6,000, but in the year 2004/05 depreciation amounted to £11,000. These figures will be further explained under the heading 'Depreciation' in AO2.

## ACTIVITY

1 Explain what is meant by the term depreciation.
2 Explain why fixed assets are not directly charged to the profit and loss account in the year that they were purchased.

## Taxation

We all have to pay tax and businesses are no exception. Limited companies have to pay corporation tax on the profits that they make as they have a separate legal identity to their owners. Corporation tax is set at varying rates according to the amount of profit the business has made. For the sake of the examples used, corporation tax has been charged at the rate of 22 per cent.

### Example

Within the Plainford Ltd accounts you can see that corporation tax for the year 2003/04 was £2,640 and for the year ended 2004/05 it was £9,007. The tax liability has increased due to increased profits.

### QUESTIONS

Using the accounts of Breakthrough Ltd and Headway Ltd, answer the following questions.

1 How much corporation tax did Breakthrough Ltd charge to their accounts?
2 How much corporation tax did Headway Ltd charge to their accounts?
3 Why are they different?

## Net and gross profit

Gross profit is sales revenue less cost of sales. It represents the amount of money a business has made from the sale of their goods after deducting the total cost of the purchases. It does not include the running expenses of the business.

Net profit is gross profit less the running expenses of the business. This is the final profit a business has made after all costs have been deducted. In the accounts of limited companies three different types of net profit can be shown:

- Net profit before interest is the profit the business makes prior to the deduction of the interest that has been paid on external borrowing, e.g. a bank loan. This can also be known as the operating profit.

- Net profit after interest is the profit after interest has been deducted.
- Net profit after taxation is the profit the business can distribute to its shareholders as the liability for taxation has been deducted.

### Example
In the accounts of Plainford Ltd the gross profit for the year 2003/04 was £108,000 but this rose to £148,000 in 2004/05. This is an increase of £40,000.

The percentage change would be:

$$\frac{40,000}{108,000} \times 100 = 37.04\% \text{ increase}$$

This shows that the business has experienced a higher percentage increase in gross profit than the percentage increase in sales. This percentage change in gross profit indicates that the business has managed to reduce its cost of sales.

The net profit after interest has also increased from £12,000 to £40,944. This is a percentage change of:

$$\frac{28,944}{12,000} \times 100 = 241.2\% \text{ increase}$$

The business has kept its expenditure under very tight control even though sales have increased.

### QUESTIONS
Using the accounts of Breakthrough Ltd and Headway Ltd, answer the following questions.

1  What is the gross profit and net profit after interest of Breakthrough Ltd?
2  What is the gross profit and net profit after interest of Headway Ltd?
3  Comparing the two companies, which one do you think has the better control over their expenses? Justify your answer.

### Portfolio tip

*In order to achieve this assessment objective you should comprehensively describe and interpret the features of the selected business organisation's profit and loss statement, and use this information to analyse the financial situation of the selected organisation.*

# Profit and loss statements to be used with examples

## PLAINFORD LTD - ABBREVIATED ACCOUNTS

| Taken from Plainford Ltd annual report and accounts 2004/05 | £ 2004/05 | £ 2003/04 |
|---|---|---|
| Sales | 230,000 | 195,000 |
| Less cost of sales (note 1) | 82,000 | 87,000 |
| Gross Profit | 148,000 | 108,000 |
| | | |
| Less expenses | | |
| Financial | 16,000 | 11,000 |
| Administration | 76,000 | 70,000 |
| Other | 6,456 | 6,000 |
| | 98,456 | 87,000 |
| | | |
| Net Profit before interest | 49,544 | 21,000 |
| Interest (note 2) | 8,600 | 9,000 |
| Net profit after interest | 40,944 | 12,000 |
| Corporation tax | 9,007 | 2,640 |
| Net profit after taxation | 31,937 | 9,360 |
| Profit and Loss accounts b/fwd | 5,626 | 8,266 |
| Less proposed dividend | 24,000 | 12,000 |
| Profit and Loss accounts c/fwd | 13,563 | 5,626 |
| Balance Sheet Details | 2004/05 | 2004/04 |
| Fixed Assets (note 3) | 164,970 | 148,838 |
| Current Assets | | |
| Stock | 22,000 | 16,000 |
| Debtors | 19,500 | 21,250 |
| Bank | 12,600 | 9,870 |
| Total current assets | 54,100 | 47,120 |
| | | |
| Creditors - amounts falling due within one year (note 4) | 79,007 | 58,832 |
| Net current liabilities | -24,907 | -8,712 |
| Total assets less current liabilities | 140,063 | 140,126 |
| | | |
| Creditors amounts falling due after more than one year (note 2) | | |
| Bank loan | 45,000 | 50,000 |
| Total assets less total liabilities | 95,063 | 91,126 |
| | | |
| Capital and Reserves | | |
| Authorised share capital | | |
| 100,000 ordinary shares at £1 each | 100,000 | 100,000 |
| | | |
| Issued share capital | | |
| 60,000 ordinary shares at £1 each | 60,000 | 60,000 |
| Profit and Loss accounts | 13,563 | 5,626 |
| General Reserve | 21,500 | 21,500 |
| Shareholders funds | 95,063 | 91,126 |

Table 4.1 *Profit and loss statement – Plainford Ltd*

## Notes to the accounts

### Note 1

|  | £ 2004/05 | £ 2003/04 |
|---|---|---|
| Opening stock | 26,000 | 28,000 |
| Purchases | 78,000 | 85,000 |
| Less closing stock | 22,000 | 26,000 |
| Cost of goods sold | 82,000 | 87,000 |

### Note 2
Loan taken out in 2003/04.
£50,000 over 10 years at an interest rate of 8%

### Note 3 Fixed asset schedule 2003/04

| Fixed Assets | £ Cost | £ Depreciation to date | £ Net Book Value |
|---|---|---|---|
| Buildings | 120,000 |  | 120,000 |
| Vehicles | 49,000 | 23,912 | 25,088 |
| Computers | 5,000 | 1,250 | 3,750 |
|  |  |  | 148,838 |

#### Fixed asset schedule 2004/5

| Fixed Assets | £ Cost | £ Depreciation to date | £ Net Book Value |
|---|---|---|---|
| Buildings | 120,000 |  | 120,000 |
| Vehicles | 77,000 | 34,530 | 42,470 |
| Computers | 5,000 | 2,500 | 2,500 |
|  |  |  | 164,970 |

### Note 4
**Creditors – amounts falling due within one year 2003/4**

|  | £ |
|---|---|
| Creditors | 41,192 |
| Corporation tax | 2,640 |
| Proposed dividend | 12,000 |
|  | 55,832 |

Creditors – amounts falling due within one year 2004/05

|  | £ |
|---|---|
| Creditors | 46,000 |
| Corporation tax | 9,007 |
| Proposed dividend | 24,000 |
|  | 79,007 |

**Table 4.2** *Notes to the accounts – Plainford Ltd*

### Profit and Loss accounts for year ended 31st December 2005

|  | Breakthrough Ltd | Headway Ltd |
|---|---|---|
|  | £ | £ |
| Sales | 240,000 | 360,000 |
| Less cost of sales (note 1) | 144,000 | 252,000 |
| **Gross Profit** | **96,000** | **108,000** |
| Less expenses |  |  |
| Financial | 31,608 | 31,488 |
| Administration | 7,142 | 12,512 |
| General | 6,000 | 10,000 |
| Total expenses | 44,750 | 54,000 |
| Net Profit | 51,250 | 54,000 |
| Less interest (note 2) | 3,250 | 0 |
| **Net Profit after interest** | **48,000** | **54,000** |
| Less corporation tax | 10,560 | 11,800 |
| Net Profit after tax | 37,440 | 42,200 |
| Net Profit and Loss accounts b/fwd | 21,000 | 34,000 |
| Less proposed dividends | 20,000 | 42,000 |
| Net Profit and Loss accounts c/fwd | 38,440 | 34,200 |
| **Balance Sheet as at 31st December 2005** |  |  |
| **Fixed Assets (note 3)** | 281,432 | 425,952 |
| **Current Assets** |  |  |
| Stock | 52,000 | 60,000 |
| Debtors | 72,000 | 72,000 |
| Bank | 34,000 | 12,000 |
|  | 158,000 | 144,000 |
| Creditors - amounts falling due within one year (note 4) | 80,160 | 130,600 |
| **Total assets less current liabilities** | **359,272** | **439,352** |
| Creditors falling due more than one year | 50,000 |  |
| **Total assets less total liabilities** | **309,272** |  |
| **Captial and Reserves** |  |  |
| Authorised share capital |  |  |
| 500,000 Ordinary shares at £1 each | 500,000 | 600,000 |
| Issued Share Capital |  |  |
| 250,000 Ordinary Shares at £1 each | 250,000 | 400,000 |
| Profit and Loss accounts | 38,440 | 34,200 |
| General Reserve | 20,832 | 5,152 |
| **Shareholders Funds** | **309,272** | **439,352** |

**Table 4.3** *Profit and loss statements – Breakthrough Ltd and Headway Ltd*

## Notes to the accounts

### Note 1

| | Breakthrough Ltd | Headway Ltd |
|---|---|---|
| | £ | £ |
| Opening stock | 72,000 | 40,000 |
| Purchases | 124,000 | 128,000 |
| Less closing stock | 52,000 | 60,000 |
| Cost of goods sold | 144,000 | 252,000 |

### Note 2
**Breakthrough Ltd**
Loan taken out this year. £50,000 over 10 years at an interest rate of 6.5%

### Note 3
**Fixed asset schedule**

| Breakthrough Ltd | £ | £ | £ |
|---|---|---|---|
| | Cost | Depreciation to date | Net Book Value |
| Factory | | | 175,000 |
| Equipment | 125,000 | 37,000 | 88,000 |
| Vehicles | 36,000 | 17,568 | 18,432 |
| | | | 281,432 |

**Fixed asset schedule**

| Headway Ltd | | | |
|---|---|---|---|
| Factory | | | 300,000 |
| Equipment | 220,000 | 129,888 | 90,112 |
| Vehicles | 52,000 | 16,160 | 35,840 |

### Note 4
**Breakthrough Ltd**
Creditors - amounts falling due within one year

| | £ |
|---|---|
| Creditors | 49,600 |
| Corporation tax | 10,560 |
| Proposed dividends | 20,000 |
| | 80,160 |

**Headway Ltd**
Creditors - amounts falling due within one year

| | £ |
|---|---|
| Creditors | 76,800 |
| Corporation tax | 11,800 |
| Proposed dividends | 42,000 |
| | 130,600 |

**Table 4.4** *Notes to the accounts – Breakthrough Ltd and Headway Ltd (year ended 31st December 2005)*

# AO2 Explain and interpret features of a business organisation's balance sheet

In this section you will learn about the different sections of a balance sheet. You will the be able to use the figures presented within a balance sheet to interpret the financial health of the business being investigated

## What is a balance sheet?

A **balance sheet** illustrates the value of a business at a set moment in time. It lists all of the assets (what the business owns) and deducts the liabilities (what the business owes). The resulting figure is the value of the business at that moment in time.

**Example**

Joe runs his own fruit and vegetable stall. He owns the following items:

| | |
|---|---|
| Market stall | £1,500 |
| Van | £3,000 |
| Cash register | £ 500 |
| Stock | £ 400 |
| Money in bank | £2,700 |
| | **£8,100** |

Joe owes the following money:

| | |
|---|---|
| Stock not yet paid for (creditors) | £ 900 |
| Loan to the bank for van | £1,500 |
| | **£2,400** |

The value of Joe's business = £8,100 - £2,400 = £5,700

*Joe's market stall*

## ACTIVITY

Pansy has a flower stall at the same market as Joe. She owns her market stall (£1,600) and a small van (£4,000). She has a bank loan of £3,100. She has a stock of flowers worth £250. She owes £120 for flowers she purchased this week. Calculate the value of her business.

All of the above-mentioned items will have special names within a balance sheet. We are now going to look at what these are.

# Why does a business need to produce a balance sheet?

## As a measure of the business's value

If the owners of a business wanted to sell, a balance sheet gives the owners and potential buyers a value from which a sales price can be negotiated.

## In order to make plans

The balance sheet illustrates the **working capital** of the business. This is the difference between the current assets and current liabilities. If a business has more current assets than current liabilities they have a good working capital ratio. This means that they have sufficient funds available to meet their immediate debts. A business that does not have adequate funds to meet their debts will soon find themselves with cash flow problems.

The balance sheet will help a business identify any problems that it might have. For example, a business may be holding too much stock. Excess stock means the business has money tied up doing nothing. This situation could hinder the business making payments to suppliers. Once a **liquidity** problem has been identified the business should be able to start rectifying the problem. This could involve selling off some stock in a sale, or reducing the amount being ordered. Another scenario that could be highlighted in the balance sheet is that the business has too many debtors, customers who still owe them money. This could be solved by the introduction of a credit control system. Somebody in the company would have to take over the responsibility of chasing customers who have not paid their bills within the 30 days allowed.

> **GLOSSARY**
>
> **Liquidity:**
> The funds a business has available to pay its immediate debts. This looks at whether the business has sufficient money in the bank to pay all the people it owes money to in the immediate future.

## In order to borrow from external sources

The balance sheet would also form part of the business plan presented to external lenders of finance if a loan was being sought. If the business was seeking extra funding from outside sources they have to prove that (a) the business is capable of meeting the required repayments and (b) they have sufficient assets within the business to secure the loan. External sources will look at the balance sheet to find out how much the fixed assets of the company are worth. If they are worth more than the value of the loan required the fixed assets can be used as security. For example, if a business wanted to borrow £20,000 and they had buildings worth £120,000 the lender of the loan would be reassured that if the business got into financial trouble they would get their £20,000 back by making the business sell its buildings.

## Tax authorities

The Inland Revenue produces regulations which state that businesses which have a turnover above a set limit must submit a balance sheet as part of their final accounts. Failure to do so could incur penalties.

## ACTIVITY

Plainford Ltd may wish to expand in the future and may need to raise further finance through another bank loan. In groups, decide the purpose of preparing a balance sheet when trying to secure a loan for external finance.

# Features of a balance sheet

We now need to look at the different features of a balance sheet and discover what each section means.

## Assets and liabilities

Assets are the items that the business actually owns. They are broken down into fixed assets and current assets. Liabilities are the debts of the business. They are broken down into current liabilities and long-term liabilities.

## Fixed assets

Fixed assets are items purchased in order to perform a job within the business and not to be sold on. They have a life expectancy of more than one year. Fixed assets include items such as buildings, equipment, machinery, vehicles, fixtures and fittings, and computers. Fixed assets cannot be charged directly against net profit as they would distort the net profit figures from year to year. They are depreciated over their expected life span. Depreciation is dealt with fully below.

## Current assets

Current assets are items that can be turned quickly into cash if required. Current assets are considered to be the 'life blood' of the business. In the balance sheet they are listed in the following order:

- stock (closing)
- debtors
- bank
- cash.

They appear in reverse order of liquidity. This means how quickly they can be turned into cash. Stock is the least liquid of all the items as you need to find a buyer before you receive any cash. The buyer will then turn into a debtor and when they pay for the stock the money will either be kept as cash or put into a bank account.

### Example

The fixed assets of Plainford Ltd increased from £148,838 to £164,970. Note 3 shows that this was due to the purchase of a new vehicle.

The value of the current assets increased from £47,120 to £54,100 from 2003/04 to 2004/05. Upon further investigation it can be seen that the value of the closing stock increased by £6,000. An increase in stock can reduce the overall liquidity of a business as it is money tied up doing nothing. There is also a danger that the stock being held may become damaged or out of date. It also takes up storage space. Debtors (people who owe the business money) have fallen by £1,750. Plainford Ltd may have introduced a system of credit control and started to limit the amount of credit that they allow their customers, or they may have been actively chasing people who have not paid their bills within the specified time period. The bank balance has also shown an increase of £2,730.

### QUESTIONS

Using the accounts of Breakthrough Ltd and Headway Ltd, answer the following questions.

1 What is the value of the fixed assets for Breakthrough Ltd?
2 What is the value of the fixed assets for Headway Ltd?
3 What is the value of the current assets for Breakthrough Ltd?
4 What is the value of their debtors?
5 What is the value of the current assets for Headway Ltd?
6 What is the value of their debtors?
7 Which business holds most stock? What are the disadvantages of holding too much stock?
8 Analyse the current assets of both businesses. Which one do you think is in the most stable position? Justify your answer.

## Current liabilities

Current liabilities represent those debts that must be paid within one year. Within the accounts of public limited companies these are also referred to as creditors – amounts falling due within one year. In the balance sheet there will often just be one total figure under the heading of net current liabilities. However, there will usually be a note within the accounts which breaks the total figure down.

Current liabilities will include:

- creditors
- corporation tax due
- proposed dividends
- bank overdraft.

These are all amounts which the business owes to other people and must be paid within the year.

### Example

If we look at the balance sheet for Plainford Ltd we can see that the creditors – amounts falling due within one year – have increased from £55,832 to £79,007, an increase of £23,175. A detailed breakdown of the figures is supplied in note 4 attached to the accounts. It can be seen that creditors have increased by £4,808. This is slightly unexpected as the value of purchases actually fell by £7,000. The increase has also been caused by the dividend being doubled for the year 2004/05.

### QUESTIONS

Using the accounts of Breakthrough Ltd and Headway Ltd, answer the following questions.

1 Which business has the highest amount for creditors falling due within one year?
2 Using note 4 attached to the accounts, suggest and justify your reasons for this difference.

## Long-term liabilities

These are loans that have been made to the business from external sources and will be repaid over an agreed number of years. These could include:

- bank loans
- business mortgages
- debentures.

If a business wishes to raise £10,000 they could issue a debenture to a third party. This would carry a fixed interest rate and a date by which it must be redeemed. Debentures are often secured on the business's fixed assets and therefore if the business were to get into financial trouble the third party would receive their money from the sale of the fixed assets.

**Example**

If we look at the balance sheet for Plainford Ltd we can see that there is an outstanding bank loan of £50,000 taken out in 2003/04 for 10 years at an interest rate of 8 per cent (note 2).

> **QUESTIONS**
>
> Using the accounts of Breakthrough Ltd and Headway Ltd, answer the following question.
>
> Which business has creditors falling due in more than one year?

# Debtors

Debtors are people that the business has sold goods to on credit. They will make payment for their goods within an agreed time scale. This is usually 30 days. In order to maintain a high level of liquidity a business must ensure that it keeps a close eye on the value of its debtors. The longer people take to pay, the greater the risk they will never do so.

# Creditors

Creditors are people that the business owes money to for goods and services received on credit. The business will be required to pay for these goods within a specified time period. If a business does not pay its suppliers regularly it may gain a poor reputation and find it increasingly difficult to secure credit in the future. The business may also lose the benefit of any discounts for large and regular orders.

*Fleet of business vehicles*

**GLOSSARY**

**Net book value:**
the amount of money that a fixed asset is worth should it be sold at that moment in time. In the accounts it will be calculated by deducting all the depreciation from the cost of the asset.

**GLOSSARY**

**Residual value:**
the amount of money that the fixed asset could be sold for when it has finished its useful life within the business. With some pieces of equipment and machinery this could simply be a scrap value.

## Depreciation

In AO1 we saw that depreciation is the amount of money that is deducted from the value of fixed assets to take into account wear and tear. The amount deducted each year from the original cost of the asset should give a true reflection of the asset's true **net book value**. There are two methods by which fixed assets can be depreciated.

## Method one – Straight line or at cost

Using this method, the owners of the fixed asset have to consider two things:

- how long they will use the asset for in the business
- what its **residual value** will be when the business no longer needs it.

The straight line method is calculated using the following formula:

$$\frac{\text{Cost of fixed asset - residual value}}{\text{Number of years to be used in business}} = \text{amount to be depreciated each year}$$

### Example

A transport business buys a new lorry for £120,000. Its estimated life in the business is 10 years. After 10 years it will be sold for £15,000.

$$\frac{120,000 - 15,000}{10 \text{ years}} = £10,500$$

Every year over the next ten years £10,500 will be charged against the profit of this business.

**Calculation of depreciation over a three year period**

| | | |
|---|---|---|
| Purchase lorry | £120,000 | Net book value at purchase |
| Year 1 depreciation | £ 10,500 | |
| | £109,500 | Net book value after 1 year |
| Year 2 depreciation | £ 10,500 | |
| | £ 99,000 | Net book value after 2 years |
| Year 3 depreciation | £ 10,500 | |
| | £ 88,500 | Net book value after 3 years |
| Total depreciation over 3 years = | £ 31,500 | |

## Method two – Reducing balance

Using this method the fixed asset is depreciated by a set percentage each year. The percentage calculation is performed on the reducing value of the fixed asset as illustrated below.

### Example

As in the example above, a transport business buys a new lorry for £120,000 to be depreciated by 20 per cent per annum using the reducing balance method.

| Purchase price | £120,000 | Net book value at purchase |
|---|---|---|
| Year 1 depreciation | £ 24,000 | |
| | £ 96,000 | Net book value after 1 year |
| Year 2 depreciation | £ 19,200 | |
| | £ 76,800 | Net book value after 2 years |
| Year 3 depreciation | £ 15,360 | |
| | £ 61,440 | Net book value after 3 years |

Total depreciation over 3 years = £ 58,560

As you can see from the two examples above, the amount of depreciation differs. A greater amount of depreciation has been charged using the reducing balance method. If the calculations were to continue, the depreciation charged to the profit and loss statement would gradually become more using the straight line method as the percentage calculation for reducing balance is performed on the decreasing value of the asset.

The value shown for the fixed asset on the balance sheet is its net book value. If the fixed asset were to be sold at any time this is the price the business hopes they would receive.

### Example

In the accounts of Plainford Ltd it can be seen that the value of the fixed assets has increased by £16,132. These figures are explained in note 3.

Note 3 is a breakdown of all the fixed assets that are owned by Plainford Ltd.

Within a fixed asset schedule there are three different figures:

- at cost
- depreciation to date
- net book value.

At cost represents the price that was paid for the fixed asset. By studying the at cost figures you can see if any new fixed assets have been purchased in the year.

Depreciation to date is the total amount of depreciation that has been charged against the fixed asset.

The net book value is the amount of money you would receive if the fixed asset were to be sold.

The fixed assets have increased in value because the business purchased a new vehicle in the year 2004/05. Within this set of accounts buildings are not depreciated as their value increases rather than decreases. Vehicles have been depreciated using the reducing balance method. However, computers have been depreciated using the straight line method. This is because computers very quickly become out of date and obsolete. They are depreciated over four years with no residual value.

**QUESTIONS**

Using the accounts of Breakthrough Ltd and Headway Ltd, answer the following questions.

1  Which business has the highest value of fixed assets? Use note 3 attached to the accounts.
2  Have the factories been depreciated? Why do you think this has happened?
3  Which business has the highest value of equipment at cost?
4  What do the three values for equipment for Breakthrough Ltd and Headway Ltd tell us?

## Capital

Capital is the money that has been put into the business by its owners. In the case of Plainford Ltd it is the total value of the shares and includes any money that is held within reserves. If you look at the balance sheet for Plainford Ltd you will see that the capital value of the business in 2003/04 was £91,126 and in 2004/05 was £95,063. The capital figure is also the same as all the assets added up less all the liabilities.

**Portfolio tip**

*In order to achieve this assessment objective you should comprehensively describe and interpret the features of the selected business's balance sheet.*

**QUESTIONS**

Using the accounts of Breakthrough Ltd and Headway Ltd, answer the following questions.

1  What is the value of the capital in Breakthrough Ltd?
2  What is the value of the capital in Headway Ltd?

# AO3  Interpret financial performance using a range of ratios

In this section you will learn how to calculate and interpret accounting ratios. You will gain the ability to assess a business's profitability, liquidity and efficiency using ratio analysis.

Without the use of ratios it is very difficult to compare one business with another or even two different years of the same business. You may be able to see that sales have increased, but it then becomes difficult to calculate if gross or net profit has increased by the same percentages.

Ratio analysis only works effectively if you compare 'like with like'. If you tried to compare Asda with Ford your results would be very different and not comparable as they operate within different sectors.

# Limitations to ratio analysis

Although an extremely useful tool when analysing the financial health of a business it must be remembered that the results do have limitations, and therefore must not be considered in isolation of other factors. Some of the possible limitations are:

- ratios illustrate what has happened in the past – based on historic accounts
- it is impossible to compare two businesses that are very different
- ratios do not disclose the future plans of the business
- ratios depend on skill of workforce
- ratios depend on business location
- ratios depend on quality of customer base
- ratios depend on age of fixed assets – will they need to be replaced in the near future?
- ratios depend on business's relationship with their suppliers.

The ratios that we will be looking at fall into three categories:

- profitability
- liquidity
- efficiency.

# Profitability ratios

Profitability ratios help assess whether a business has met its objectives by assessing the amount of gross or net profit made by the business in relation to the business's turnover or the assets or capital available to it. It enables managers and owners to compare the profitability of the business over a period of time.

## *Return on capital employed (ROCE)*

This ratio is often considered to be the most important of the profitability ratios. It looks at the relationship between the capital and the net profit earned. Investors in a business will expect this ratio to be higher than a percentage rate they could earn from placing their money in a savings account.

$$\frac{\text{Net profit after interest}}{\text{Shareholder funds (Capital)}} \times 100 = \text{ROCE}$$

**Example**

Looking at the accounts of Plainford Ltd we can see that the ROCE calculation for the two years is as follows:

| 2003/04 | 2004/05 |
|---|---|
| $\frac{12{,}000}{91{,}126} \times 100 = 13.17\%$ | $\frac{40{,}944}{95{,}063} \times 100 = 43.07\%$ |

In the year 2003/04 every £100 invested in the business earned just over £13.17. This rate of return is higher than an individual could earn if they invested their money in a normal savings account.

In the year 2004/05 there had been a big increase in the rate of return. Every £100 invested in the business now earns £43.07. This would make this business a very good option to buy shares in as the capital employed is earning a very high rate of return.

---

**QUESTIONS**

Using the accounts of Breakthrough Ltd and Headway Ltd, answer the following questions.

1  What is the ROCE for Breakthrough Ltd?
2  What is the ROCE for Headway Ltd?
3  Compare the two results. Which business is performing well? Justify your answer.

---

## Gross profit margin

This ratio illustrates the relationship between the amount earned through sales and the cost of sales. It represents the amount of gross profit earned for every £100 worth of sales.

$$\frac{\text{Gross profit}}{\text{Sales}} \times 100 = \text{Gross profit margin}$$

**Example**

Looking at the accounts of Plainford Ltd we can see that the gross profit margin calculation for the two years is as follows:

| 2003/04 | 2004/05 |
|---------|---------|
| $\frac{108,000}{195,000} \times 100 = 55.38\%$ | $\frac{148,000}{230,000} \times 100 = 64.35\%$ |

In the year 2003/04 for every £100 of sales the gross profit was £55.38. This increased in the second year to £64.35. This indicates that the business has managed to reduce the cost of their purchases. This could have been due to a change in supplier, or being able to secure discounts for bulk orders.

---

**QUESTIONS**

Making reference to the accounts of Breakthrough Ltd and Headway Ltd, answer the following questions.

1  What is the gross profit margin for Breakthrough Ltd?
2  What is the gross profit margin for Headway Ltd?
3  Compare the two results. Which business has the most control over their purchases? Justify your answer.

## Net profit margin

This ratio illustrates the relationship between the amount earned through sales and the total expenses of the business. It represents the amount of net profit earned for every £100 worth of sales.

$$\frac{\text{Net profit}}{\text{Sales}} \times 100 = \text{Net profit margin}$$

**Example**

Looking at the accounts of Plainford Ltd we can see that the net profit margin calculation for the two years is as follows:

| 2003/04 | 2004/05 |
|---------|---------|
| $\frac{12{,}000}{195{,}000} \times 100 = 6.15\%$ | $\frac{40{,}944}{230{,}000} \times 100 = 17.80\%$ |

In the year 2003/04 for every £100 of sales the net profit was £6.15. This increased to £17.80 net profit in 2004/05. This illustrates that the business was able to increase its sales while at the same time controlling their level of expenses. Their total expenses have not increased at the same rate as their sales and they have therefore been able to raise their net profit margin. This has increased the profitability of the business.

### QUESTIONS

Using the accounts of Breakthrough Ltd and Headway Ltd, answer the following questions.

1 What is the net profit margin for Breakthrough Ltd?
2 What is the net profit margin for Headway Ltd?
3 Compare the two results. Which business has the most control over their expenses? Justify your answer.

# Liquidity ratios

Liquidity ratios look at a business's ability to pay its immediate debts. Does the business have sufficient funds to pay their creditors, expenses and loans on time?

## Current ratio

This ratio compares the current assets against the current liabilities and indicates whether the business has sufficient short-term funds to meet their short-term liabilities.

$$\frac{\text{Current assets}}{\text{Current liabilities}} = \text{x:1}$$

**Example**

Looking at the accounts of Plainford Ltd we can see that the current ratio calculation for the two years is as follows:

$$
\begin{array}{cc}
\textbf{2003/04} & \textbf{2004/05} \\
\dfrac{47,120}{55,832} = 0.84{:}1 & \dfrac{54,100}{79,007} = 0.68{:}1
\end{array}
$$

In 2003/04 the business had 84p available to pay every £1 of debt. By 2004/05 this situation has deteriorated and the business now only has 68p available to repay every £1 of debt.

These figures mean that the business could experience liquidity problems in the future and they have a higher level of short-term debt than funds.

In the past it was practice to state that the 'best' current ratio for a business was 2:1. However, it is now widely accepted that there is no 'best' current ratio. When analysing the current ratio of a business you need to establish the 'normal' current ratio for that type of industry. If the business under investigation has a lower current ratio this may indicate the possibility of liquidity problems in the future.

> **QUESTIONS**
>
> Using the accounts of Breakthrough Ltd and Headway Ltd, answer the following questions.
>
> 1  What is the current ratio for Breakthrough Ltd?
> 2  What is the current ratio for Headway Ltd?
> 3  Will either business suffer from liquidity problems in the future?

## Acid test ratio

This ratio deducts stock from the current assets as it is the least liquid. The ratio's purpose is to see if a business has sufficient liquid funds to pay its immediate debts.

$$
\frac{\text{Current assets} - \text{stock}}{\text{Current liabilities}}
$$

**Example**

Looking at the accounts of Plainford Ltd we can see that the acid test ratio calculation for the two years is as follows:

$$
\begin{array}{cc}
\textbf{2003/04} & \textbf{2004/05} \\
\dfrac{47,120 - 16,000}{55,832} = 0.56{:}1 & \dfrac{54,100 - 22,000}{79,007} = 0.41{:}1
\end{array}
$$

In 2003/04 the business had 56p available to pay every £1 of its immediate debts. The situation has once again deteriorated in the second year and the business now has only 41p available to meet every £1 of immediate debt.

This again indicates that the business may find it difficult to pay its current liabilities on time.

It must be remembered that no matter how profitable a business is, it may fail unless it has adequate liquid funds.

# Efficiency ratios

Efficiency ratios assess how efficiently a business has used its resources. Has it made the best possible use of resources or could things be improved in the future in order to improve the overall profitability of the business?

## Stock turnover calculation

This ratio looks at how often a business turns its stock round. It enables a manager to analyse how effective their stock control system is. A reduction in stock turnover could represent a slowing down of trade. Stocks are not being sold and therefore piling up in the warehouse.

$$\frac{\text{Cost of sales}}{\text{Average stock}} = \text{x times}$$

(Average stock is calculated by adding opening stock and closing stock together and dividing by two.)

**Example**

If we look at the accounts of Plainford Ltd we can see the stock turnover calculation for the two years is as follows:

| 2003/04 | | 2004/05 | |
|---------|---|---------|---|
| $\frac{87,000}{27,000}$ | = 3.22 times | $\frac{82,000}{24,000}$ | = 3.42 times |

2003/04 Average stock = £28,000 + £26,000/2 = £27,000
2004/05 Average stock = 26,000 + 22,000/2 = £24,000

The results above show that in 2004/05 the stock turnover has increased slightly to 3.42 times per year. This is not a particularly high turnover and could indicate the business should consider tighter stock control. By looking at the stock figures in the accounts the business has been trying to reduce the amount of stock that it holds.

**QUESTIONS**

Making reference to the accounts of Breakthrough Ltd and Headway Ltd, answer the following questions.

1 Calculate the stock turnover calculation for Breakthrough Ltd.
2 Calculate the stock turnover calculation for Headway Ltd.
3 Compare the two results. Which business has most control over their stock? Justify your answer.

## Debtors collection period

Debtors are people or companies that owe a business money for goods or services received. It is usual practice within business to allow customers a 30-day period in which to pay for the goods and services received. This ratio shows the relationship between credit sales and the level of debtors. It calculates how many days on average it takes the business to collect its debts.

$$\frac{\text{Debtors}}{\text{Credit sales*}} \times 365 \text{ days} = \text{total number of days it takes debtors to pay}$$

* Often within accounts it is impossible to distinguish between credit and cash sales. If this is the case you will need to use the total sales figure.

### Example

Looking at the accounts of Plainford Ltd we can see that the debtors collection period for the two years is as follows:

| 2003/04 | 2004/05 |
|---------|---------|
| $\frac{21,250}{195,000} \times 365 = 40 \text{ days}$ | $\frac{19,500}{230,000} \times 365 = 31 \text{ days}$ |

Plainford Ltd has managed to reduce their debtors by £1,750. This is against a background of increased sales. Their debtor collection period has now been reduced to 31 days, which is very good. It can be assumed that the business has put into place a system of credit control which will include chasing late payment. This appears to have been effective.

**QUESTIONS**

Using the accounts of Breakthrough Ltd and Headway Ltd, answer the following questions.

1 Calculate the debtors collection period for Breakthrough Ltd.
2 Calculate the debtors collection period for Headway Ltd.
3 Compare the two results. Which business has most control over their debtors? Justify your answer.
4 How can a business reduce its debtors collection period?

## Creditors collection period

Creditors are people or companies that the business owes money to in the immediate future. This ratio shows the relationship between credit purchases and the level of creditors.

$$\frac{\text{Creditors}}{\text{Credit purchases*}} \times 365 \text{ days} = \text{total number of days it takes to pay creditors}$$

\* Often within accounts it is impossible to distinguish between credit and cash purchases. If this is the case you will need to use the total purchase figure.

### Example

Looking at the accounts of Plainford Ltd we can see that the creditors collection period for the two years is as follows:

**2003/04**                                      **2004/05**

$\dfrac{41,192}{85,000} \times 365 = 177 \text{ days}$          $\dfrac{46,000}{78,000} \times 365 = 216 \text{ days}$

The figures illustrate that Plainford Ltd have serious problems paying their creditors. The payment period has risen by 39 days. This is not a good situation and could result in the business experiencing problems with their suppliers. They may receive a bad credit rating, with suppliers refusing to supply them with goods and services on credit. The business is also not able to benefit from discounts offered for prompt payment.

### QUESTIONS

Using the accounts of Breakthrough Ltd and Headway Ltd, answer the following questions.

1  Calculate the creditors collection period for Breakthrough Ltd.
2  Calculate the creditors collection period for Headway Ltd.
3  Compare the two results. Which business has most control over their creditors? Justify your answer.
4  What could be the consequences of a business having a very long creditors collection period?

### Portfolio tip

*In order to achieve this assessment objective you will be required to calculate a range of ratios and interpret their meaning. You will then need to compile an analysis and evaluation and make a conclusion of the business's current financial health. Use the Plainford Ltd case study as a model.*

## CASE STUDY

### Plainford Ltd – Analysis of financial health

The profitability of this business is very good. The ROCE has increased to 43.07 per cent. This represents an earning of £43.07 per £100 invested. An investor would find it hard to find a better rate of return for their money.

The gross profit margin has also shown an improvement of 8.97 per cent. The gross profit is now earning £64.35 for every £100 of sales. This illustrates that the business has been able to control its costs of sales in relation to an increase in sales of nearly 18 per cent. This indicates that the business may have been able to find a cheaper supplier or taken advantage of discounts for bulk buying. These theories are not backed up when the creditors collection period is analysed. This currently stands at 216 days. This is unacceptable and in the long term will cause problems with suppliers.

The net profit margin has also increased dramatically from 11.65 per cent to 17.8 per cent. This would indicate that the business has taken very strict control over the expenses of the business.

The liquidity ratios for this business are quite worrying. Their current ratio indicates they currently only have 68p available to meet every £1 of debt. This has fallen by 16p. Things look even worse when stock is deducted to calculate the acid test. The rate drops to just 41p to meet every £1 of debt.

The efficiency ratios paint a varied picture. Currently, the business is turning its stock over 3.42 times per year, which is a slight increase on last year. This could indicate that the business is holding too much stock. When looking at the stock figures, the business has been trying to reduce the amount of stock they currently hold, which could help their liquidity problems.

The debtors collection period is excellent, with debtors taking only 31 days to pay. It is obvious that the business has a good system in place to chase late payers. As mentioned above, the creditors collection period is far too long. Suppliers are not going to maintain good relationships with this business unless they start paying on time.

### Recommendations

Plainford Ltd appears to be a very profitable business, however they do have liquidity problems, which means that they are taking far too long to pay their suppliers.

On further examination of the accounts, I would recommend that the business reduces the amount of stock that it currently holds. This will free up money to pay off creditors. It would also improve their stock turnover ratio. I also suggest that they consider the proposed dividend of £24,000. Would it be better to use some of this money to reduce the level of creditors?

## ACTIVITY

Pull together all the results so far for Breakthrough Ltd and Headway Ltd. Compile an analysis and evaluation of their current financial health. If you were offered the chance to invest in one of these businesses which one would you choose? Justify your answer.

## AO4 Make recommendations based on the preparation and analysis of a cash flow forecast

In this section you will learn how to prepare simple cash flow forecasts. You will also learn how to interpret and make recommendations based on either the cash flow forecast you have created or one that has been supplied within the OCR model assignment.

## What is a cash flow forecast?

The purpose of preparing a **cash flow forecast** is to establish how much money the business has available throughout the period by looking at its income and expenditure. A cash flow forecast will only ever be as good as the quality of the predictions being made. It is therefore vital that the most accurate information is made available in order to develop detailed estimations of the financial position of the business. When this has been established it is possible to make decisions based on the results. Businesses compare their cash flow forecasts with the actual figures when known. Any major differences in figures will be investigated to find out why they occurred. This procedure is known as variance analysis and is critical in order to ensure that the next year's cash flow forecast is accurate.

*Where has all my money gone?*

# Elements of a cash flow forecast

A cash flow forecast is made up of different sections which will be explained in detail below. The explanations will be based on the cash flow forecast for Plainford Ltd (see Table 4.5).

## *Income breakdown*

The first section in a cash flow forecast is where the incoming money is recorded. This can consist of:

- sales revenue – money received from the sale of goods or services by the business
- capital – extra funds that have been put into the business by the owners
- sale of shares – if a limited company were expecting to sell some shares during the time span of the forecast the amount due to be received will appear within this section
- loans – money that has been borrowed from external sources
- sale of fixed assets – if the business is considering selling any fixed assets during the time span of the forecast this will also be recorded in this section.

### Example

Looking at the cash flow forecast for Plainford Ltd we can see that the only income came from sales. The sales figures had been estimated using the following assumptions:

- sales would increase by 10 per cent over the year
- the sales variations were based on the previous year's sales figures.

## *Expenditures*

This section records all the money a business spends. It is broken down into different categories. These could include:

- purchases – items that have been bought in for resale
- raw materials – materials used in the manufacture of a product
- electricity, gas, water etc. – also known as utility expenses
- wages – payments made to employees for work done
- administration expenses – which could include postage, stationery, computer cartridges etc.
- motor expenses – the costs associated with running a fleet of vehicles
- interest and capital repayments on loans
- corporation tax – tax paid on the profits of a limited company

- dividends – money a business may decide to pay to its shareholders
- any other expense relevant to the type of business.

## Monthly allocation of outgoings

In order to compile the cash flow forecast, managers will have to estimate what they expect their monthly outgoing to be in the future. In order to make these 'guesstimations' they will look back at previous figures and trends. Managers may undertake investigations to see if they can find cheaper suppliers, better deals in order to control expenditure in the future etc.

## ACTIVITY

In groups, estimate how much you will spend over the next month. Do you all spend your money on different things? Who spends the most money?

**Example**

Looking at the cash flow forecast of Plainford Ltd (Table 4.5) we can see that its expenses range from purchases to dividends. When all the expenditure has been recorded it must then be totalled. This gives the total expenditure figure (b).

| PLAINFORD LTD | | | | | | | | |
|---|---|---|---|---|---|---|---|---|
| Cash flow forecast for six months January–June 2006 | | | | | | | | |
| Income | January | February | March | April | May | June | July | Total |
| Sales | 20,000 | 20,000 | 20,000 | 21,000 | 21,000 | 21,000 | 21,000 | 144,000 |
| Total Income (a) | 20,000 | 20,000 | 20,000 | 21,000 | 21,000 | 21,000 | 21,000 | 144,000 |
| Expenditure | | | | | | | | |
| Purchases | 7,000 | 7,000 | 7,000 | 7,350 | 7,350 | 7,350 | 7,350 | 50,400 |
| Interest on loan | 720 | 720 | 720 | 720 | 720 | 720 | 720 | 5,040 |
| Wages | 6,000 | 6,000 | 6,000 | 6,000 | 6,000 | 6,000 | 6,000 | 42,000 |
| Administration expenses | 5,800 | 5,800 | 5,800 | 5,800 | 5,800 | 5,800 | 5,800 | 40,600 |
| Corporation tax | 9,007 | | | | | | | 9,007 |
| Dividend | | 24,000 | | | | | | 24,000 |
| Total Expenditure (b) | 28,527 | 43,520 | 19,520 | 19,870 | 19,870 | 19,870 | 19,870 | 171,047 |
| Opening balance (c) | 12,600 | 4,073 | -19,447 | -18,967 | -17,837 | -16,707 | -15,577 | |
| Cash inflow/outflow (d) | -8,527 | -23,520 | 480 | 1,130 | 1,130 | 1,130 | 1,130 | |
| Closing balance (e) | 4,073 | -19,447 | -18,967 | -17,837 | -16,707 | -15,577 | -14,447 | |

Table 4.5 *Cash flow forecast – Plainford Ltd (January–June 2006)*

## Cash brought forward and balances

The cash brought forward is the amount of money that the business has available to spend at the end of each month. In order to understand opening and closing balances you need to know how to balance the cash flow.

The cash brought forward or **opening balance** is the amount of money the business has at that moment of time (c).

The **cash inflow/outflow** (d) is calculated by subtracting the total expenditure figure (b) from the total income figure (a). If the figure is positive it constitutes an inflow. If negative it will be an outflow (the business has spent more than it received). If the figure is negative it must

either be shown as a minus figure, -8,527, or in brackets (8,527).

The **closing balance** is the amount of money the business has left at the end of the month. It is calculated by adding the opening balance to the cash inflow/outflow. The closing balance of month one becomes the opening balance of month two.

Having the skills to budget your own finances will be a very useful tool throughout your whole life. It will be especially useful if you are intending to go to university and want to limit the amount of debt you finally leave with.

## ACTIVITY

In order to complete this activity you can work in small groups. As a group, undertake some research to find out how much it costs to live away from home while attending university. Create a realistic cash flow forecast to show your expected income and expenditure. Having completed the cash flow, are there any areas where you could try and reduce your expenditure? Are there any ways you could try and increase your income?

### Example

Looking at the cash flow forecast for Plainford Ltd we can see the opening balance was £12,600. This is the amount of money the business has in their bank account on 1st January 2006. In January the business has a cash outflow as their expenditure was greater than their income, due to the payment of corporation tax. The next major outflow is the payment of the dividend of £24,000. It is evident that the business has insufficient funds to meet this payment as it pushes the closing balance to a negative (£19,447). To make this payment, an overdraft or short-term loan would have to be arranged with the bank, which would further stretch the cash flow as it would attract interest payments.

Plainford could investigate whether they could increase their sales predictions further. Would a new marketing campaign be useful to stimulate new demand? The business could look at the relationship between sales and purchases. Could this ratio be increased by looking at alternative suppliers or negotiating discounts for bulk buying?

It looks like the business should reduce its dividend payments to £10,000 payable in February and July. This would mean that the business would need to arrange a small overdraft to cover the months of February and July. Using this suggestion, the new cash flow forecast is shown below.

| PLAINFORD LTD | | | | | | | | |
|---|---|---|---|---|---|---|---|---|
| Revised cash flow forecast for six months January–June 2006 | | | | | | | | |
| Income | January | February | March | April | May | June | July | Total |
| Sales | 20,000 | 20,000 | 20,000 | 21,000 | 21,000 | 21,000 | 21,000 | 144,000 |
| Total Income | 20,000 | 20,000 | 20,000 | 21,000 | 21,000 | 21,000 | 21,000 | 144,000 |
| **Expenditure** | | | | | | | | |
| Purchases | 7,000 | 7,000 | 7,000 | 7,350 | 7,350 | 7,350 | 7,350 | 50,400 |
| Interest on loan | 720 | 720 | 720 | 720 | 720 | 720 | 720 | 5,040 |
| Wages | 6,000 | 6,000 | 6,000 | 6,000 | 6,000 | 6,000 | 6,000 | 42,000 |
| Administration expenses | 5,800 | 5,800 | 5,800 | 5,800 | 5,800 | 5,800 | 5,800 | 40,600 |
| Corporation tax | 9,007 | | | | | | | 9,007 |
| Dividend | | 5,000 | | | | | 5,000 | 10,000 |
| **Total Expenditure** | 28,527 | 24,520 | 19,520 | 19,870 | 19,870 | 19,870 | 24,870 | 157,047 |
| Opening balance | 12,600 | 4,073 | -447 | 33 | 1,163 | 2,293 | 3,423 | |
| Cash inflow/outflow | -8,527 | -4,520 | 480 | 1,130 | 1,130 | 1,130 | -3,870 | |
| Closing balance | 4,073 | -447 | 33 | 1,163 | 2,293 | 3,423 | -447 | |

**Table 4.6** *Revised cash flow forecast – Plainford Ltd (January–June 2006)*

## ACTIVITY

Using the cash flow forecast illustrated below for Headway Ltd, comment on the business's financial position. How would you suggest they improve their cash flow position?

| HEADWAY LTD | | | | | | | | |
|---|---|---|---|---|---|---|---|---|
| **Cash flow forecast for six months January–June 2006** | | | | | | | | |
| Income | January | February | March | April | May | June | July | Total |
| Sales | 33,000 | 33,000 | 33,000 | 33,000 | 33,000 | 33,000 | 33,000 | 33,000 |
| Total Income | 33,000 | 33,000 | 33,000 | 33,000 | 33,000 | 33,000 | 33,000 | 33,000 |
| **Expenditure** | | | | | | | | |
| Purchases | 16,500 | 13,200 | 13,200 | 13,200 | 13,200 | 13,200 | 13,200 | 13200 |
| Wages | 2,000 | 2,000 | 6,000 | 6,000 | 6,000 | 6,000 | 6,000 | 6,000 |
| Administration expenses | 1,000 | 2,000 | 3,000 | 3,000 | 3,000 | 3,000 | 3,000 | 3,000 |
| Corporation tax | 11,800 | | | | | | | 11,800 |
| Dividend | | 42,000 | | | | | | 42,000 |
| New van | | | | | | 16,400 | | |
| **Total Expenditure** | 31,300 | 59,200 | 22,200 | 22,200 | 22,200 | 38,600 | 22,200 | 217,900 |
| Opening balance | 12,000 | 13,700 | -12,500 | -1,700 | 9,100 | 19,900 | 14,300 | |
| Cash inflow/outflow | 1,700 | -26,200 | 10,800 | 10,800 | 10,800 | -5,600 | 10,800 | |
| Closing balance | 13,700 | -12,500 | -1,700 | 9,100 | 19,900 | 14,300 | 25,100 | |

**Table 4.7** *Cash flow forecast – Headway Ltd (January–June 2006)*

The reasons a cash flow forecast is produced are outlined below.

# Reduce the risk of insolvency

Just because a business has made a profit does not mean that it will have the liquid funds necessary to keep it financially afloat, and many profitable businesses have failed due to liquidity problems.

One of the reasons a business may have liquidity problems is because it has been unable to collect what it is owed regularly and on time. Another reason may be that the business has purchased too much stock which is now sitting idle in the warehouse. The stock has been paid for but until it is sold no money will come into the business. Worse still, the stock could be out of date, damaged or obsolete, so its ability to earn money in the future has also decreased.

The cash flow forecast will highlight these situations. It shows a business when it will have insufficient funds to pay its immediate debts. It is at this point that management should take action. One course of action could be to limit the amount of credit offered to customers, start chasing up late payments and undertake more stringent credit checks on new customers. If the business is holding too much stock it may decide to try special offers such as buy one get one free, a 'sale', or to undertake a marketing campaign in order to try and stimulate sales. Another course of action could be to identify where specific cuts could be made and to undertake some cost cutting within the business. All of this information and consequent plans will help reduce the risk of a business becoming insolvent.

## Obtain short-term funding

The cash flow forecast will illustrate months when the business will have insufficient funds to meet its immediate debts. For example, this could be due to a large order for which payment will not be received for two months. The cash flow will illustrate this potential problem to management, who can arrange short-term finance to cover this period of time. This could involve the business negotiating a bank overdraft, which will be much cheaper if pre-arranged with the bank. Alternatively, the owners of the business may wish to loan the business some funds to cover the shortfall.

## Adjust cost base

A cash flow forecast clearly illustrates the estimated expenditure of a business over a set period of time. It is often an excellent opportunity for management to review the current spending levels of the business, whether they are fully justified and if costs can be cut. On a more positive note, a cash flow forecast could illustrate periods when the business has excess funds over expenditure. Management could decide that a pay increase for employees is affordable or that they can afford to purchase a new fixed asset or undertake the planned redevelopment program for the site.

During the preparation of a cash flow forecast a manager may be required to undertake some research into different costs. New suppliers may be contacted to see if products can be purchased at a cheaper rate. Negotiations may take place which identify discounts that could be available for larger orders. Managers will have the opportunity to fine-tune all expenditure ensuring that they are able to secure the best deals possible whilst sustaining the quality required. It is not always the cheapest product that proves to be the best.

## React to cash flow predictions

If sales revenue is falling management could decide to undertake a new marketing campaign in order to place the product back in the customers' eye. While this will cause a further outflow of money, it would be hoped that eventually this will be recovered by an increase in sales and eventually an increase in the flow of money into the business.

Another reaction to a poor cash flow performance will be the requirement to find alternative finance to cover the excess of outflow over inflow. This could be in the form of a pre-arranged bank overdraft, or a short-term loan from the owners of the business. The cash flow forecast may highlight the need for the business to consider longer-term financial borrowing. The business may wish to undertake a large marketing campaign in order to launch a new product. The development of the new product has already severely reduced their liquidity, it will take time to establish itself in the market and is therefore not expected to show high returns for at least 18 months. In order to launch the desired marketing campaign and to reduce the risk of insolvency problems, the business may decide to take out a bank loan over five years. This will give it sufficient funds to undertake its proposed marketing campaign as well as maintaining sufficient liquidity levels until the new product has established itself in the market.

The cash flow forecast may also illustrate products that are no longer selling well and those that are doing particularly well. This information will help managers decided how to schedule production. It may be necessary to reduce the production levels of goods that are currently not selling well and are forming stock piles in the warehouse.

## Portfolio tip

*In order to achieve this assessment objective you should prepare the selected business organisation's cash flow forecast. You should then analyse the financial health of the business and make recommendations for improvements.*

## ACTIVITY

Complete Berkley Ltd's cash flow forecast using the information supplied below. Recommend and justify how Berkley Ltd could improve its current financial position.

**Sales** – January £10,000, February £11,000 and March £10,000
**Purchases** – £13,000 in February
**General expenses** – £9,000 per month
**Opening balance on 1st January** – £3,200

# A05   Identify and evaluate costs involved in the purchase of business assets

In this section you will learn that making major purchases within a business has to be considered very carefully to ensure that the right product is purchased, at the best price and, more importantly, that the business can actually afford the payments related to the required item.

## Purchase decision making

There are two kinds of purchases that a business can make. The first kind of purchase is those items purchased with the sole intention of being re-sold to the customer. These items can also be referred to as stock. The second kind of purchase is fixed assets. This section will analyse the total costs of purchasing fixed assets, which include:

*Fixed assets include tools, equipment and machinery*

- the original price of the asset
- costs linked to the finance arrangements
- opportunity cost – how else could the business have used the money.

## ACTIVITY

Look at your notes for AO1 and review the definitions of purchases and stock. How do they fit into the trading profit and loss accounts of a business?

## ACTIVITY

Look at your notes for AO2 and review the definition of fixed assets.

In today's competitive world being efficient is often the key to reducing the cost of manufacturing a product. To achieve this businesses are often required to invest in expensive equipment and machinery. The example below will be used to clearly illustrate the points within this section.

### Example
Precision Engineering manufacture a range of filters that are used in the production of domestic gas boilers. The business has been operational for 15 years but its machinery is now out of date, slow and unreliable. The time has come to modernise the factory. To do so will cost the business in

*Production line at Precision Engineering*

excess of £300,000. The business cannot raise this amount of money internally. It would need to borrow at least £250,000 to complete the refurbishment program. Owners Paul and Janet have been looking at the different suppliers of the machinery they require. Each supplier offers a slightly different deal, and their machines all have different features and capabilities. It is decision time. What should Paul and Janet consider before making their final decision?

# Evaluating product cost

## *Stage one*
Paul and Janet must first consider exactly what they want the new machinery to do. They are the experts in their own field and would be

advised to talk to their workforce to ascertain the business's specific requirements.

## Stage two

Having agreed what the precise requirements of the machinery are they then need to contact possible suppliers to see what they have on offer. Having discussed their requirements with each supplier they then need to consider:

- which supplier will offer them the most adequate equipment
- the financial deal each supplier is offering
- the after-sales service that they offer, whether they service the equipment free, what guarantees they offer etc.

## Stage three

Having worked out what type of machinery they need the next step is to calculate the **cash inflow** that the machinery will generate. When the cash inflows have been calculated it is possible to decide whether the investment in the machinery is going to be beneficial to the business.

## Stage four

Having completed the preliminary investigations Paul and Janet have chosen their machinery from HI Technology Ltd. They have been given a quotation of £320,000. HI Technology Ltd has agreed that the refit could take place over a period of two years. Stage one would cost £235,000, with the second stage being completed in the second year at a further cost of £85,000. Paul and Janet now have to consider how they will raise the required amount of finance.

> **GLOSSARY**
>
> **Cash inflow:**
> This is the money that the new machinery will bring into the business. The amount is calculated by adding up the value of the items the machinery will produce and taking away all the running expenses.

## Interest rate costs

Paul and Janet have agreed that they will try and raise the required finance through a bank loan. They are hoping to arrange a loan of £185,000 for a period of 10 years, with the possibility of an extension during the second year if profits have not increased sufficiently to raise the second payment of £85,000. Prior to their meeting with the bank manager they have prepared their forecast profit and loss accounts and cash flow forecast. This will enable the bank manager to see if their estimated increases in production and costs are realistic and sufficient to allow them to meet their future repayments to the bank.

Paul and Janet were offered the loan at a variable interest rate of 7.6 per cent. This means that their yearly interest payments will be:

$$\frac{185,000}{100} \times 7.6 = £14,060 \text{ for the first year or £1,171.67 per month}$$

This would not include the capital repayment of £18,500 per year or £1,541.67 per month. Combined, this gives Paul and Janet increased costs of £2,713.34 per month for the first year.

A variable rate loan means that the cost of borrowing rises with rising interest rates. This increase in costs will either have to be absorbed through their own profits, or a price increase would be required. On the other hand, if interest rates fall Paul and Janet's payments would decrease, which could result in a period of higher profits.

A fixed rate loan will have a higher rate of interest but means that the business repayments remain the same regardless of fluctuations in the rate of interest, thus enabling Paul and Janet to budget more effectively.

## ACTIVITY

Investigate the current interest rates for commercial borrowing.

1  Work out what the repayments would be for a £75,000 loan taken out over 5 years.
2  What would be the increase in the payments if interest rates rose by 0.5 per cent?
3  What would be the decrease if interest rates fell by 0.5 per cent?

## Leasing costs

One of the key decisions that Paul and Jane have to make is how to finance capital items. They want to invest in the best and most efficient equipment to stay ahead of their competitors. However, there will be many demands on their capital.

Leasing can be an alternative method for asset purchases which enables a business to invest in new machinery without making a large capital outlay which could severely affect their liquidity. Leasing is very popular for the purchase of capital items such as plant, machinery, computers and commercial vehicles.

Leasing equipment allows a business to spread the cost of an asset over a period of time. The business will therefore be able to earn money from the use of the asset and put their working capital to an alternative use. Under a leasing agreement a finance house (lessor) purchases the fixed asset and then leases it to the business (lesser) for a fixed monthly fee over an agreed period of time. At the end of the lease the lesser does not have automatic right of ownership.

### Benefits of leasing

Below is a list of what are considered to be the overall benefits of leasing rather than directly purchasing fixed assets:

- immediate access to the equipment

- fixed rentals enable easier budgeting – repayments are not subject to fluctuating interest rates

- working capital can be put to other uses – for example, the purchase of more stock/raw materials in order to increase production and hopefully sales

- upgrade options – you are able to upgrade equipment in line with the developments in modern technology

- tax efficiency – all payments are tax deductible from net profit

- agreements can be made to suit customers – repayment terms can run from 1 to 7 years and could, depending on the company selected, include holiday periods, irregular profiles and stepped rentals.

## Lease versus buying directly

Paul and Janet would have to carefully consider how they could finance their expansion plans. Leases and loans are simply two different methods of finance. One finances the use of the equipment and the other finances the purchase of the equipment.

It is not easy to decide which one is best. Paul and Janet will have to consider their own personal circumstances and preferences. Is the opportunity to have new equipment every two years with no major repair risks more important than long-term cost savings? Are long-term cost savings more important than lower monthly payments? Is ownership more important than low up-front costs and no down payment?

When you buy equipment you pay for the entire cost of the equipment regardless of how much you use it. You typically make a down payment and then capital repayments plus interest payments set at a rate determined by the loan company. You make your first payment a month after you sign your contract. When you have finished paying off the loan you own the equipment and can continue to use it without any further costs.

When you lease equipment you pay for the portion of the equipment's cost which you have used. You can choose whether or not to make a down payment. Your monthly payments will be similar to the interest rate on a loan. You make your first payment at the time you sign your contract.

### Example

Paul and Janet lease a piece of equipment for £30,000 and use it for 2 years. At the end of the 2 years the lessor decides that the equipment has depreciated by £12,000. Paul and Janet pay £12,000 plus finance charges and fees. If they purchase the equipment with borrowed money they would pay the entire £30,000 but would own the equipment at the end of the term. This example illustrates why leasing offers significantly lower monthly repayments.

*Should Janet and Paul purchase or lease?*

## ACTIVITY

Paul and Janet are not sure whether to borrow money to purchase their fixed assets outright or to lease them. Suggest and justify what you think they should do.

## Opportunity cost

This is a very simple concept to remember. You can only spend money once. When you have made a decision and spent your money the opportunity cost is all the other items you chose not to purchase instead. For example, if you spent £2.50 on bus fares this morning the opportunity cost could have been buying breakfast when you got to school or college, buying some stationery or a tub of popcorn at the cinema.

Businesses have to think very carefully about how they spend their money. If they tie all their money up in the purchase of new fixed assets it may leave them short to buy raw materials, pay the wages, meet rent payments etc. These would all be considered opportunity costs.

## ACTIVITY

Write down all of the items that you have purchased over the last few days. Then make a list of all the other things you could have purchased instead. These items are the opportunity cost. Looking at your two lists have you spent your money wisely?

## AO6　Explain the role in the economy of a range of financial institutions

There are a variety of financial institutions with whom you may have already had dealings. Most of you will have a bank account, and maybe even a savings account, which might still be with a building society. You will probably already have a basic knowledge of the different types of services that some of the institutions we are about to investigate offer to members of the general public and businesses.

Throughout this assessment objective we will be looking at the role the following institutions play within the economy. Remember to focus your evidence on the role these institutions play and not just the services they offer.

## High street banks

These organisations can be seen on most high streets. Their purpose is to supply a financial service to both the public and business organisations.

## ACTIVITY

In groups, create a list of all the high street banks you can think of.

Banks are public limited companies with their shares quoted on the Stock Exchange. Their aim is to make profits which will be distributed to their shareholders.

Over recent years banks have seen a huge growth with many expanding by buying up a variety of other businesses in order to expand the services that they offer to the general public. By buying up other businesses to expand their own portfolio they also reduce their competition. In the long run this could cause problems for us, the consumer, as there will be fewer companies in the market place offering different products and services.

## CASE STUDY

### Lloyds TSB Group plc

The merger between Lloyds Bank and TSB took place in 1995 and made it one of the largest forces in domestic banking.

In June 1999, TSB and Lloyds Bank branches in England and Wales were re-branded Lloyds TSB. Branches in Scotland came under the new brand of Lloyds TSB Scotland, which now has 185 branches stretching from the Northern Isles to the Mull of Galloway.

Scottish Widows joined the Lloyds TSB Group on 3 March 2000. This combination created one of the UK's largest providers of life, pensions, and unit trust products.

On 1 September 2000, Lloyds TSB Group subsidiary, Lloyds UDT, acquired Charter Trust Group Ltd and ACL Autolease Holdings Limited, the UK consumer finance and contract hire subsidiaries of Standard Chartered Bank.

The Lloyds TSB Group has over 15 million customers and 67,000 staff.
Source: www.mediacentre.lloydstsb.com

As you can see Lloyds TSB has expanded in a number of different ways in order to extend their portfolio of products.

1 **Identify all of the different products that Lloyds TSB are now able to offer through their expansion programme.**
2 **Do you think that allowing businesses to become so large is good for the consumer? Justify your answer.**
3 **Describe the products that you think Lloyds TSB are able to offer to personal customers.**

## GLOSSARY

**Standing order:**
This is where a customer completes a mandate stating that the bank is to pay a certain person/business the same amount on set dates; this could be weekly, monthly or as directed by the customer.

Lloyds TSB is not the only high street bank to have extended the services that it is able to offer its customers. Through these mergers the role of high street banks has changed considerably over time. Through their expansion they are now able to offer an extremely diverse range of products and services. In fact a customer need only go to one bank in order to sort out all their financial needs. Their role in the economy today is to provide customers with a full range of products and services which include:

- current accounts
- deposit accounts
- **standing orders** and **direct debits**
- insurance
- loans and mortgages
- debit and credit cards
- pensions
- telephone banking, Internet banking.

## ACTIVITY

Find out what the difference is between a debit card and credit card.

Another major service that banks offer is assistance to small businesses, especially those just starting up. Lloyds TSB have created four different banking relationships. These include:

- Business Partner – an in-depth face-to-face relationship with a business manager covering every aspect of planning and managing a business. The manager will take an active role making suggestions, seeking opportunities and identifying challenges.

- Business Focus – a face-to-face relationship with a business manager who will focus on the financial aspects of the business.

- Business Response – a telephone-based one-to-one relationship with a business manager who will know all about your business when you call. They will act as a sounding board and suggest solutions to business issues and point out opportunities as they arise.

- Business Express – a telephone-based relationship giving a business direct access to a team of business managers who will be able to provide solutions and answer any queries asked of them.

Barclays bank offers new businesses a starter pack, including a disk which contains cash flow and profit and loss templates and a business plan to help it get started. The pack also includes booklets entitled 'Thinking of starting a business?' and 'Setting up and running your business'.

To clarify what a bank's role is within the economy let us think what would happen if they disappeared overnight. People would no longer have somewhere to safely store their money, and there would be fewer organisations available to offer credit facilities, loans and mortgages. This could reduce people's ability to spend and cause a recession in the economy. Businesses would struggle to raise the funds to start up and this could cause loss of employment opportunities and a reduction in the amount of products and services available for people to buy.

Therefore the role of the bank in the economy is to:

- finance and support businesses which support growth within the economy

- enable people to store their money safely – earning interest

- offer people credit facilities in order for them to make purchases, such as houses, cars, which in turn stimulates the economy

- help people to plan their future (pensions). Sound pension advice will help people to continue to spend when they have retired and hopefully will allow an aging population to be self-sufficient in their old age

● provide insurance against unforeseen risk. Insurance helps replace items that are lost or damaged through accidents and can supply an income in the sad occurrence of early death within a family.

## ACTIVITY

Investigate another high street bank and see what services they offer to new business start ups.

## Merchant banks

Merchant banks are banks that specialise in the activities that facilitate trade and commerce. They deal in international finance, long-term loans to companies and underwriting. Merchant banks do not offer services to the general public. British merchant banks have been increasingly taken over by foreign investors and the only sizeable participant left is Rothschild. Merchant banks offer the following services to businesses:

● They act as issuing houses for new shares on the Stock Exchange. When a business wishes to float on the Stock Exchange they will put up a set number of shares for sale. If these shares are not purchased, the merchant bank acting on their behalf will buy the shares back. This process is known as underwriting.

● They provide loans to businesses.

● They give advice on business problems.

Merchant banks will invest money directly in suitable businesses that might be considered too high a risk by the high street banks. Because the ventures are higher risk they will charge higher rates of interest.

Therefore the role of merchant banks in the economy is to help launch new companies onto the Stock Exchange, and provide loans advice and guidance. They support the development and growth of business which in turn will support the growth of the economy and its wealth within the country.

## Building societies

Building societies are known as mutual societies. This means they are owned by their investors. Any profits that they make must be shared out with their customers. Their main aim is not to make profit for shareholders and this can therefore enable them to offer favourable interest rates to their investors and borrowers.

The UK Building Societies Act of 1986 opened the way for competition between building societies and commercial banks and introduced the procedures for **demutualisation** of a building society.

A wave of demutualisations followed in the 1990s. The Woolwich and Halifax both became public limited companies. The sale of shares enabled them to undergo a period of growth and expansion. They were able to increase the range of products and services that they offered their customers. Investors in the business at the time of demutualisation received bonuses and shares within the newly formed company. Borrowers became losers in the change over as there was an increase in the cost of loans and many local branches closed.

## ACTIVITY

In groups, investigate how many building societies there are in your area. Compare the services they offer to those of the high street banks. Do you think demutualisation was a good idea?

One of the most widely recognised building societies which has fought hard to keep its mutual status is the Nationwide. The Nationwide building society offers the following services to their customers:

- current accounts
- savings accounts
- credit cards
- mortgages
- insurance (including building and contents, health and income protection, life, mortgage and travel)
- Internet banking
- travel money
- overdrafts
- loans
- commercial lending and commercial mortgages.

The role building societies play in the economy is to provide a safe place for people to invest their money. This then enables other people to borrow this money to purchase houses. By stimulating and funding the housing market it enables the economy to continue to grow. By retaining a mutual status they are able to offer their borrowers better deals and are therefore able to continue to compete with the major high street players.

# Bank of England

The Bank of England is the central bank of the United Kingdom. It has always been fondly known as the 'Old Lady of Threadneedle Street'. The bank was originally founded in 1694 and was nationalised in 1946. It gained operational independence in 1997.

*The Bank of England*

The bank stands at the centre of the United Kingdom's financial system and is committed to promoting and maintaining a stable and efficient monetary and financial framework as its contribution to a healthy economy.

Originally the bank was most recognised through its production of bank notes. However, it is now more recognised through its interest rate decisions. In 1997 the bank was given operational independence enabling it to set interest rates at a level which would maintain a stable economy, without interference from the government.

Interest rates are set by the Monetary Policy Committee. It is their role to set interest rates with the aim of maintaining inflation at the target level of 2 per cent. The interest rate is the rate at which the bank lends to banks and other financial institutions.

The Bank of England is also responsible for maintaining the financial stability of the country which enables the economy to function efficiently. It analyses and promotes initiatives to maintain and strengthen the financial system, and watches financial developments in order to identify any potential threats to financial stability. The Bank has arrangements in place for handling financial crises should they occur and is known as the 'lender of last resort'. In order to perform this role the Bank works closely with Her Majesty's Treasury and the Financial Services Authority, the regulator of banks and other financial institutions in the UK.

## ACTIVITY

Undertake an investigation to find out what the current rate of interest is and when it last changed. Why did the Bank of England decide to change the base rate? Did it go up or down?

## European Central Bank (ECB)

The role of the ECB is to make decisions on monetary policy for those countries participating in the monetary union, and sets a common interest rate for the countries that have entered the euro zone. Its main aim is to maintain price stability. Price stability has been defined by the ECB as a 'year-on-year increase in consumer prices of no more than 2 per cent'. This contrasts with the UK approach where the Bank of England's target level of inflation is 2 per cent.

The ECB is part of the European System of Central Banks (ESCB). The ESCB consists of all the central banks in the EU plus the ECB. The Bank of England is part of the ESCB, even though the UK has not joined the euro, and will take part in some of the ESCB's operations.

## ACTIVITY

Find out which countries that have joined the euro zone. What is their current rate of inflation? Is it higher or lower than in the UK?

# The London Stock Exchange

The London Stock Exchange is one of the world's oldest, able to trace its origins back more than 300 years. It started life in 17th-century London and was based in the coffee houses of the time. In 2000 the Stock Exchange transferred its role as UK Listing Authority with HM Treasury to the Financial Services Agency and shareholders voted to become a public limited company.

The Stock Exchange provides a market for the buying and selling of 'issued' or 'used' shares. Businesses raise their finances outside of the Stock Exchange but the state of the market influences the ease with which this can be achieved.

To be able to sell its shares on the Stock Exchange and become a listed company a business has to meet the requirements of the Stock Exchange. These are outlined in 'Admission of Securities for Listing Rules of the Stock Exchange'. The main requirements are outlined below:

- minimum capitalisation of £700,000
- at least 25 per cent of shares must be offered for sale to the public
- five years or more full trading accounts must be published.

## *The economic role of the Stock Exchange*

The Stock Exchange encourages the general public to invest in businesses because they have access to a market where they can get their money back. In the 1980s with the sale of the public utilities (water, gas etc.) and the demutualisation of the building societies a lot of people suddenly either had the opportunity to invest in shares or were given them. This greatly increased the number of shareholders within the country.

The Stock Exchange enables companies to raise large amounts of money which they can then invest in expansion or new machinery. This enables businesses to expand and increase production, which can lead to increased employment and therefore greater wealth within the country. If this were not possible goods may not be able to be produced so cheaply, unemployment would be higher and the general wealth of the country would be lower. Our standard of living can therefore be affected by the Stock Exchange.

The government also uses the Stock Exchange to raise finance by selling government bonds. Without this facility there would be fewer and more costly public services and taxation might have to be increased to raise funds.

A large proportion of investment in the Stock Exchange is through large institutional investors. These large institutions invest money on behalf of investors, in order to fund pensions, life insurances, endowment mortgages etc.

In the 1980s a lot of endowment mortgages were sold with the idea that the return from investment in shares would not just pay off the original borrowing but would also supply a lump sum pay off. Unfortunately the Stock Exchange has failed to perform as well as originally predicted and these policies are often now worth much less than originally predicted when sold.

The Stock Exchange provides a means of valuing businesses for takeovers and mergers. Their value is based on their share price and the number of shares issued.

## Portfolio tip

*In order to achieve this assessment objective you should explain the role of a range of financial institutions within the economy, and discuss how they may affect the selected business organisation. Some of the organisations may have a direct effect on the businesses, others may have a more discreet and indirect effect.*

## ACTIVITY

Using a broadsheet newspaper or the Internet, choose five businesses that are currently listed on the Stock Exchange. Plot their share prices over the course of a week. Have they gone up or down? Explain the trends that you have found.

# AO7 Analyse the impact of the economic environment on business performance

Within this section you will learn that businesses do not work in isolation. Whilst businesses are able to control what happens internally they can often only predict what might happen to them externally. The external environment can affect the decisions that they make and the financial stability of their customers. There are a number of external influences that can affect a business. Some of the external influences will have a much greater direct affect on a business's performance than others.

## Inflation

This is the increase in the price of goods measured over a set period of time, usually monthly, quarterly or annually. Inflation is measured by the

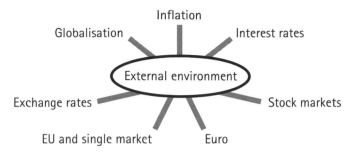

Figure 4.1 *External influences that can affect a business*

government using a tool known as the retail price index (RPI). The government has a set basket of shopping which they use to compare how much it costs one month against the next. The increase in price is known as the rate of inflation. The housing market is not included within this index. The government's current inflation target is 2 per cent. However, at the time of writing (May 2005) inflation was stable at 1.9 per cent.

## What is the impact of inflation on production and trade level?

If, due to rising inflation, the raw materials that a production business needs to buy keep increasing in price the business will have a number of options:

- They can increase the price of their products to maintain profit. If they take this route they may find that their customers are no longer able to purchase their products, meaning demand and profits will fall. If their competitors do not raise their prices will the business lose its competitive edge?

- They can absorb the increase in the price of raw materials and therefore possibly suffer from reduced profits.

- They can look for a cheaper supplier. However, a cheaper supplier could mean lower quality raw materials which might affect the overall quality of their products.

If a business operates in a luxury market it might soon discover that its sales are falling because people can no longer afford to pay for luxuries.

In simple terms, the impact of inflation on production and trade levels:

- reduces profit as raw material prices increases
- could increase the price of products being produced – further fuelling inflation
- could decrease peoples' ability to purchase goods and services.

## What is the impact of inflation on investment?

Money invested in a savings account will be losing value if the interest paid on the account is less than the current rate of inflation. This would discourage people from saving as they feel that their money is actually losing and not gaining value.

### ACTIVITY

In groups, make a list of all the items that you have purchased today. Write down how much they cost you. Try and think back to last year. How much did they cost then? Ask your parents if they remember what they cost 10 years ago.

## What is the impact of inflation on prices?

Inflation is the increase in the cost of products and services.

There are two main causes of inflation:

- Demand pull – this is where there is a greater demand for products and services due to the increased spending power of consumers. This creates an excess of demand and therefore prices increase.

- Cost push – the higher costs of raw materials and labour cause rising costs of production.

Both of these causes of inflation have the effect of raising prices.

## What is the impact of inflation on wages and salaries?

When the price of goods and services keep rising consumers are able to purchase less and less with their disposable income. Employees need to maintain their standard of living and will therefore demand higher wages. Increased demands for increased wages will fuel cost-push inflation.

### Did you know?

*Standard of living is measured by the amount of money that a person earns and the type of goods and services that they choose to purchase. If consumers' wages are being eroded by inflation they will not be able to maintain their standard of living.*

# Interest rates

The interest rate is the amount that businesses and individuals are charged to borrow money. The higher the interest rate the more expensive borrowing becomes. If you look back at your notes from AO6 you will recall that the Bank of England is responsible for setting the base rate. In August 2005 the base rate had been reduced to 4.5 per cent to maintain the stability of the economy. Interest rates are increased in order to curb consumer spending and to try and maintain a low rate of inflation.

## *What is the impact of interest rates on production?*

### Increased interest rates

Businesses that have external borrowing will find that the interest charged on their loans will increase. This will have the effect of reducing their profits. In order to overcome this loss of profits the business could raise their prices but this might have the adverse effect of reducing their competitiveness and will also fuel cost-push inflation.

When interest rates are high businesses may decide not to borrow further and may halt any ideas for the expansion or purchase of fixed assets. In terms of production, increased interest rates could limit expansion and plans for future growth. It may also mean that as the overall expenditure of the business has risen, the business needs to look at ways to increase productivity or reduce expenditure. In the worst possible scenario a business may not be able to meet the increased payments and would have to cease trading.

In terms of trade levels, increased interest rates also hit the consumer. The cost of their own personal borrowing will have increased, limiting the amount of goods and services that they are able to purchase. For example, when interest rates are high the demand for luxury cruises may decrease. The demand for basic food will remain stable, but people may stop buying expensive cakes and biscuits.

### Decreased interest rates

Businesses that have external borrowing will suddenly find that the interest on their loans has decreased. This will allow them to spend the extra money on other areas of the business. They might also decide to keep their loan repayments the same in order to pay off the loan quicker.

With more money available a business may decide to expand its product range, improve production techniques etc. In times of low interest rates businesses will be looking to expand in order to meet increased consumer demand. If the business has investments these will be earning them less and this money might be better used within the expansion process.

When interest rates fall consumers' own loan repayments will decrease. They will have more money available to spend on different products and services. This could stimulate demand and encourage businesses to increase production levels.

## What is the impact of interest rates on investment?

When interest rates are high the amount of interest that can be earned in a savings account will increase. This will have the effect of encouraging people to save their money. The Bank of England increases interest rates in order to try and curb inflation. The idea is to reduce consumers' ability to spend and encourage them to invest their money in savings.

When the Bank of England decides to decrease interest rates they are reducing consumers' outgoings and therefore stimulate demand within the economy. It will also have the knock-on effect of discouraging people from investing their money in savings accounts as their money will be earning less interest.

## What is the impact of interest rates on prices?

This is much more of a difficult area to predict as there are many more variables involved. As we have seen above an increase in interest rates will have the overall effect of reducing the disposable income of consumers. This means that they will have reduced spending power. Businesses may therefore decide to lower their prices in order to retain their customers. However, if they are already having to absorb increased costs due to an increase in their own interest repayments this might not be possible. An increase in prices could put their product out of the reach of consumers.

When interest rates fall consumers have more money available to spend. This enables them to stimulate an economic boom, by demanding more goods and services. If a business suddenly has a surge in demand they may consider increasing their prices. Having raised their prices a business may suddenly find that they have lost their competitiveness and start to lose their customer base. On the other hand, a surge in demand may enable a business to increase their levels of production, take advantage of economies of scale and therefore reduce the price of their products and services. A reduction in prices could also stimulate further increases in demand.

## What is the impact of interest rates on wages and salaries?

Interest rates will not have a direct effect on wages and salaries. However, they will have an indirect effect. If interest rates rise consumers who have mortgages and loans will be suffering from higher repayments which will in turn decrease their disposable income. In order to combat a reduction in their standard of living employees may try and negotiate higher wages and salaries.

## ACTIVITY

Work in small groups. You have just been given £5,000. Investigate all the different banks and building societies in order to locate the highest earning account available. Having established the institution and type of account you are going to invest in, calculate how much interest the original investment will earn over a five-year period. Present your ideas to the rest of the class.

# Stock markets

The economic health of the Stock Exchange is measured through the FT Index (FTI). A rise in the FTI is considered to be good as it denotes confidence in the stock market – people are continuing to buy and sell shares. A fall is considered to be bad news. It could mean that a lot of shareholders are trying to sell their shares and there are insufficient buyers to purchase them. It would indicate a lack of confidence in the economy. Small shifts of the FTI on a daily basis are of little importance because they could simply come down to large investment companies changing the types of shares/investments that they purchase because they predict a change in the external environment. For example, if a large investment company thought that interest rates were about to fall they might shift their portfolios into bond investments because the prices of bonds will rise as rates fall. Long-term shifts in the FTI would be much more influential and could indicate a loss of confidence in the economy.

*Trading on the London Stock Exchange*

## *How does the stock market affect production?*

If the stock market is stable or rising, businesses will have confidence in the economy and will be able to continue producing at their current levels, and maybe consider increasing productivity through investments. On the other hand, if the stock market is unstable with the FTI moving downwards, businesses may lack the confidence to expand production.

## *How does the stock market affect investment?*

Investments on the stock market can be from the general public, but also from major investment companies with portfolios that include insurance, pensions etc. If the stock market is rising these investments will increase and their returns to investors will be good. However, if the market is falling the return to investors will be much smaller and therefore investments will be curtailed.

An example of this is endowment mortgages. In the mid-1980s people were encouraged to take out endowment mortgages. Endowment policies were from reputable financial businesses and the premiums were invested in the stock market. Customers were informed that their policies would not only pay off their mortgages but would also earn a considerable amount of money due to the booming stock market. Unfortunately the stock market trends did not continue and many people are now left with endowment policies that will not cover the original cost of their mortgage.

## How does the stock market affect prices, wages and salaries?

The stock market reflects confidence in the country's economic future. If this is felt to be strong, demand will be high and businesses will be able to raise their prices. However, if the trend is falling then people's confidence in the economy is not high. Businesses will probably be hesitant about making large investments or raising their prices, as demand for goods and services may be falling. In times of economic boom, backed up by a strong stock market, employees may be able to negotiate large pay rises. The reverse will be true in times of economic gloom and falling confidence in the stock market.

## ACTIVITY

Work in groups. You have just been given £10,000 which needs to be invested on the stock market. Investigate two potential companies that are listed on the London Stock Exchange that the group would like to invest in. Prepare a short presentation clearly justifying your choice.

# Exchange rates

The exchange rate is how much foreign currency we can purchase for our sterling pounds. For example, at the time of writing (May 2005) £1 = $1.88 (US) dollars. If you were going on holiday to America you would need to buy some dollars to use while there. Similarly, businesses must buy foreign currency to pay for imports or investments abroad. If a business sells its goods abroad (exports) their customers will have to buy pounds to pay for them. The exchange rate is based on the supply and demand for each currency.

## How do exchange rates impact on production and trade levels?

If the value of the pound falls British goods and services become cheaper abroad. This is because the foreign buyers will be able to get more pounds for their currency.

For example, let us assume that the exchange rate is £1 to $1.88. If we sold an antique table to an American customer for £700 this would have cost the American customer $1,316. If the value of the pound fell and the exchange rate became £1 to $1.55 the American customer would pay $1,085 for the table.

If the pound falls in value British goods become more appealing abroad and therefore exports could increase. This could cause a rise in production levels in this country. When the pound falls it also means that imports become more expensive and therefore people could be encouraged to purchase British-made goods, stimulating British manufacturing.

The opposite is true if the value of the pound increases. When the pound is very strong exports become expensive and therefore export trade can often fall. This will have the effect of reducing production in this country.

As exchange rates fluctuate on a daily basis it can mean that profit margins on exports and imports can increase or decrease quickly and substantially, and it can make it very difficult for a business to forecast production costs.

## *How do exchange rates impact on investments?*

There is a link between interest rates and exchange rates. Banks and other large-scale investors move their money around the world looking for the best possible short-term interest rates. If the UK interest rates go up then it becomes an attractive place for these investments. If the interest rates are high in the UK it generally leads to a strong pound. A low interest rate is more likely to weaken the strength of the pound against other currencies.

## *How do exchange rates impact on prices, wages and salaries?*

If exports are priced in foreign currencies, sales could be lost or profits reduced if the relative values change. This will ultimately mean that wages and salaries would be unlikely to rise and could even fall.

### ACTIVITY

You are about to book a holiday but cannot decide where to go. One of your considerations is to get the best exchange rate you can. Investigate what the different exchange rates currently are around the world. Where do you think you would like to go on holiday to get the best value for your money?

## The European Union and the single market

The European Union is known as a customs union, meaning that free trade in goods, services and labour should exist between all the member countries. In effect this means that if you wanted to go and work in France the only restriction might be your ability to speak French. In order to encourage member states to trade within the union there are trade barriers against non-member states such as taxes on their imports, known as tariffs.

The European Union is the biggest single economy in the world, so there are significant incentives for countries to join if they want easier access to consumers. The Maastricht Treaty of 1991 aimed to promote greater 'harmonisation' between the members on social issues, taxation, health and education.

The development of the single market has involved the passing of 300 different measures. These have included:

- common standards for EU products so that they can be sold all over the EU

- tax alignment in the EU to eliminate tax advantages from locating in certain countries – the UK has been criticised for low taxes on profits and low non-wage labour costs for employees

- free movement of people

- reduction in paperwork and customs posts across the EU to promote trade

- free movement of investment capital between member states. This has created some mergers of firms such as SEAT and VW and insurers like Commercial Union and the French insurer Victoire.

The Social Chapter of the Maastricht Treaty guarantees basic rights to employees in member countries, such as:

- the right to join a trade union

- the right to take industrial action

- the right to be consulted and informed on company plans

- equal rights for men and women

- a minimum wage and a maximum working week of 48 hours

- four weeks minimum paid holiday per year.

## How does the European Union impact on production and trade levels?

As can be seen from above the EU has given businesses the largest market place in the world. British firms are now able to trade freely within the European Union, taking the opportunity to make use of further economies of scale. However, they also face more competition, and they have had to improve productivity and efficiency in order to compete within this extensive market place.

## How does the European Union impact on investment?

It has enabled countries to move currency freely around in order to find the best interest rates for short-term investments.

## How does the European Union impact on prices?

The size of the market place has expanded, giving businesses greater opportunity to extend their customer base. If a business is in a niche market it might be able to stimulate sufficient demand to enable it to increase its prices. It is more likely that within this expanded market place a business will now be competing against much larger businesses and will need to reduce its prices in order to remain competitive.

## How does the European Union impact on wages and salaries?

As can be seen above Britain has had to comply with legislation that has been agreed and set by the European Union. This has included elements of the Social Chapter. Britain now has a minimum wage which ensures that everybody receives a set basic rate of pay. In October 2004 this was raised to £4.85 per hour for an adult over the age of 22. This has increased the cost of wages for some businesses and as a result they may have had to reduce their workforce, raise prices or accept reduced profit margins. Britain has also had to accept the Working Time Regulations which stipulates that employees must not be expected to work over 48 hours per week.

# The euro

The European Union comprises 25 member states. Twelve of those states chose to adopt the euro on 1st January 2000. Having a single currency and economic and monetary union strengthens Europe's role in international trade. The euro is now taking an important role as an international investment and reserve currency.

In order to join the euro each country had to meet stringent economic rules which had been laid down in the Maastricht Treaty under Article 121.1. These are briefly outlined below:

- Price stability: inflation rate was not to exceed that of the three best performing countries by more than 1.5 per cent.

- Public finances: government deficit was not to be above the reference point of 3 per cent of gross domestic product (GDP) and the level and evolution of the government debt compared to the reference value of 60 per cent of GDP.

- Exchange rate stability: must have remained within the normal margins of the exchange rate mechanism of the EMS without severe tensions of devaluation for at least two years.

**Figure 4.2** *Symbol for the euro*

- Long-term interest rates: long-term interest rate was not to exceed that of the three best performing countries in terms of price stability by more than 2 percentage points.

A single currency allows the European Union's single market to function more efficiently and makes it more conducive to growth through:

- elimination of exchange rate fluctuations
- the reduction of uncertainties allows businesses to plan their investments more easily
- elimination of transaction costs which arise from transactions taking place in different currencies
- price transparency
- enhanced competition
- increased opportunities for consumers
- more attractive opportunities for foreign investors.

## How does the euro impact on price, production and trade levels?

Those countries that have adopted the euro are now able to trade more freely with the other euro zone countries. The elimination of exchange rate fluctuations allows them to trade within the euro area by reducing risks and uncertainties for both exporters and importers. Independent research has suggested that the euro has already created significant growth in trade within the euro areas. The adoption of the euro has made price comparisons much easier, encouraging greater competition and leading to lower costs in the short to medium term. Wholesalers and traders can buy from the cheapest source, putting pressure on companies trying to charge higher prices.

## How does the euro impact on investment?

A large single market has enabled investors to do business throughout the euro area with minimal disruption and enables businesses to take advantage of a more stable economic environment. Savers are now able to benefit from a wider and diversified choice of investment opportunities. Private and corporate borrowers are able to reap the benefit of better funding opportunities because money is easier to raise on capital markets.

## How does the euro impact on wages and salaries?

The euro will have no direct effect on wages and salaries. It may cause greater competition for skilled employees as they are able to move and work freely within the European union, and as a result cause an increase in wages and salaries.

## ACTIVITY

Work in two groups. One group investigates the advantages of joining the euro and the other group investigates the disadvantages of joining. Once all the investigations have been completed hold a class debate.

**Figure 4.3** *Globalisation encourages free world trade*

# Globalisation

Globalisation is the ability of countries to trade goods and services around the world. One of the driving forces of globalisation has been the development of telecommunications in general and the Internet in particular. The end of World War II saw multinational companies producing and selling not only in their own domestic markets but also to nations around the world. This development enhanced the progress of international trade which has grown 16 times since 1950, reflecting the lowering of tariff barriers. The growth in the trade of services has been even greater. The fall of the Berlin Wall and the collapse of the Soviet Union ended the cold war and led to a further increase in international trade.

International trade is supported by international organisations. The roles of the major organisations are outlined below.

- **World Trade Organization (WTO)** was established in 1995 to administer the rules of international trade agreed to by its 123 member countries.

- **International Monetary Fund (IMF)** was established in 1946 to:
  - promote international co-operation on finance
  - encourage stability in exchange rates and promote orderly systems for exchanging money between countries
  - provide temporary assistance for countries suffering balance of payment problems.

- **World Bank** provides loans to poor countries for development projects.

- **United Nations** has become a promoter of globalisation, believing that individual states have responsibilities to both their own citizens and to the world society as a whole. It supports the case for reform of international institutions to make them more representative.

## How does globalisation impact on price, production and trade levels?

The growth of globalisation, and the lowering of barriers, such as tariffs and import quotas, enables countries to trade freely. This will increase the opportunities a business has to export or import goods and services. It will also encourage greater competition, which means that businesses have to keep their production costs to a minimum in order to be competitive in world markets.

The WTO makes it more difficult for countries to favour their domestic industries over imports from other countries. British companies therefore have to compete with imported goods that are cheaper than those produced in Britain. Imported goods are often cheaper because of reduced labour costs in third world countries. The WTO believes that the growth of trade between countries increases the wealth of everyone. Trade encourages the production of goods and services by those who are the most efficient, therefore maximising the availability of goods and services at the best price.

## How does globalisation impact on investment?

Businesses will be able to move their money around different countries freely to seek out the best short-term returns.

## How does globalisation impact on wages and salaries?

It is often quoted that exports increase jobs and imports reduce jobs. It is not this simple as most exports also depend on some imports. For example, an exporter of training shoes might import the boxes they are sold in.

Lowering import barriers makes export industries even more efficient and competitive in world markets. Countries that lower trade barriers concentrate their national energies in industries they are good at, and where they have an international advantage. The subsequent growth will create employment and maybe an increase in wages.

However, some unions oppose globalisation as they believe that it lowers wages and workplace standards. They argue that globalisation encourages the trade in goods produced in countries which do not allow unions to defend their workers' rights. These businesses are able to undercut the price of goods produced in countries where unions defend workers' rights. This leads to a 'race to the bottom' as the markets are won by those with the lowest standards.

## Portfolio tip

*In order to achieve this assessment objective you should analyse the impact of the economic environment on production and trade levels, investment, prices and wages and salaries. You should also consider the impact of the economic environment on the selected business organisation.*

## SKILLS CHECK

1. Why do businesses construct a profit and loss account?

2. Explain the following terms:
   (a) sales revenue
   (b) opening and closing stock
   (c) net and gross profit.

3. Why do businesses depreciate their fixed assets?

4. Explain the following terms:
   (a) current liabilities
   (b) long-term liabilities
   (c) current assets.

5. Give three examples of fixed assets.

6. Write out the formulas for the following ratios:
   (a) ROCE
   (b) net profit margin
   (c) acid test.

7. Explain why a cash flow forecast is prepared.

8. How is the cash inflow/outflow calculated in a cash flow forecast?

9. What does the term 'closing balance' mean in a cash flow forecast?

10. Explain the meaning of opportunity cost.

11. Outline the advantages and disadvantages of leasing rather than purchasing fixed assets.

12. What is the difference between high street banks and merchant banks?

13. What is the major role of the Bank of England in the economy?

14. Analyse the impact of an increase in interest rates on businesses.

# Marketing for business

To survive and be successful, businesses must provide products and services that customers wish to buy. Marketing is the business process of **identifying** and **meeting** customer wants, **profitably**. Even excellent products can fail in the market if a business does not market them effectively to its customers.

The aim of this unit is to give you knowledge and understanding of marketing theory and techniques that are used by businesses. You will learn about concepts such as the **marketing mix** and how it is applied to a product or service. You will look at market research and how businesses analyse their markets. To complete this unit successfully you will need to address the six assessment objectives in the specification and to achieve AO2-AO6 you must produce evidence based upon a proposed new product or service or the relaunch of an existing one.

*Piccadilly Circus at night showing illuminated brand names*

## This unit will cover

- AO1 Demonstrate how the four elements of the marketing mix influence decisions about how a product is marketed.

- AO2 Undertake a market analysis and complete market research for the selected product or service.

- AO3 Use marketing models to define the selected product or service the market.

- AO4 Recommend and justify a pricing strategy for the selected product or service.

- AO5 Suggest and justify a method of distributing the selected product or service from manufacturer to consumer.

- AO6 Recommend and justify the use of promotional techniques for the selected product or service.

# AO1   Demonstrate how the four elements of the marketing mix influence decisions about how a product is marketed

The marketing mix refers to the way in which a business markets its products or services. The marketing mix is made up of four elements, sometimes referred to as 'the 4 Ps': product, price, place and promotion. Each one of these elements must be given careful consideration when deciding how a product or service is marketed.

Figure 5.1 *Marketing mix*

A business supplying specialist components for the aircraft industry will take a very different approach to its marketing compared to a manufacturer of a consumer product such as shampoo. The aircraft component may only have one potential customer and it must meet the customer's precise specifications whereas shampoo will be sold to a mass market comprising perhaps millions of consumers.

## Product

The product or service is clearly of crucial importance in determining the marketing mix. It may be a physical product such as a body spray or it may be a service such as a car insurance policy. The business must have a very clear idea of what the product or service means to the customer. On one level, a car is merely a means of transport but a car such as a Porsche or a Rolls Royce conveys messages about the status of the owner. Image is irrelevant when marketing building materials such as sand and cement but is very important when marketing designer clothes. A life assurance policy offers no direct benefit to the person taking it out, other than the sense of providing financial security for dependents. Effective marketing must inevitably take these important issues into account.

*A new improved product*

Businesses must ensure that products meet the needs of customers and market research is a way of identifying what customers want. Manufacturers may bring out new products or adapt old ones to meet changing customer expectations. New versions and editions help to keep the product attractive to customers.

## Pricing

For some products price is absolutely crucial but for others it is not always the most significant factor. Businesses such as easyJet rely heavily on offering cheap, 'no-frills' air services but business travellers flying to the USA will expect a higher quality service and the ticket price is less important to them as comfort is an issue and as their employer may be paying. In many cases, the quality, image or brand name is of far greater importance than price. When purchasing a wide range of consumer products, customers rarely buy the cheapest available.

### QUESTIONS

How important is price to you when buying? In pairs or groups, consider whether you would buy the cheapest possible product in the following cases? If not outline other factors which may be more important to you.

(a) a DVD player
(b) a wedding dress
(c) a car insurance policy
(d) a pair of training shoes
(e) a box of chocolates to be given as a gift.

## Place

Place refers to where the product is sold and how it gets to the customer. The term **distribution channel** describes the route by which the product gets from the producer to the final customer. A **mass market** consumer product such as a Mars bar is likely to be available in a wide range of outlets whereas a Rolls Royce car can only be purchased from a limited number of authorised dealers. It is important for businesses to match up the product with the most appropriate distribution channel. Marketing an up-market product in a down-market outlet will be ineffective in terms of sales and may well damage the image of the product.

### QUESTIONS

Where are the following products available?

Comment upon the number and type of outlets used to sell them.

(a) a packet of crisps
(b) a branded perfume such as Chanel or Christian Dior
(c) a music CD
(d) a saxophone
(e) a surf board
(f) holiday insurance.

### Portfolio tip

*You will need to have a good theoretical knowledge of the marketing mix but you also need to be able to apply it to the product that you have chosen to market.*

## Promotion

Promotion involves informing customers about products and services and persuading them to buy. Promotion also covers a broader range of activities, including free gifts, sponsorships and public relations activities. These promotional techniques are addressed in detail in AO6.

It is important to recognise that the 4 Ps are not independent of each other and the whole 'mix' must fit together logically. A product that is built using high-quality materials will have to be sold at a relatively high price to cover costs. This means that it will be marketed at higher income customers and so the business will need to think of the most effective way of reaching those customers. Getting the marketing mix wrong may lead to poor sales, damage to the **brand image**, disappointed customers and a host of other potential problems. A business such as the watch makers Rolex may well sponsor yachting or professional tennis tournaments but would never use a 'buy one get one free' promotion. A mass market product such as toothpaste will need to be available through a wide range of distribution channels across the whole country and will probably need a large sales force whereas a product sold by mail order or the Internet will need only a small sales team.

## AO2   Undertake a market analysis and complete market research for the selected product or service

Market analysis involves examining the current state of the market and analysing the position and performance of the business and its products within the market. This will also involve looking at competitors and other outside factors. Detailed market analysis will form the basis for a future marketing strategy for the business. Some useful techniques for market analysis are outlined below.

# SWOT analysis

SWOT analysis is a useful business tool which managers use to analyse how well a product, brand or company is performing in its market. SWOT stands for:

S   trengths
W   eaknesses
O   pportunities
T   hreats

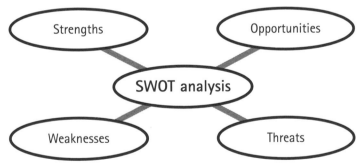

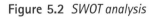
**Figure 5.2** *SWOT analysis*

**Strengths** are the advantages that the business has over its rivals in the market. These may include things such as having a high-quality product, excellent distribution network or an original design. Sony is known internationally for high-quality electrical goods while Ryanair offers very low prices on its airline tickets. It is important that managers are honest when assessing the strengths of the business or product.

**Weaknesses** are on the other hand those areas in which the product or brand is not performing as well as rivals. For example, the business may have a smaller range of products than its rivals or a weaker distribution network. Marks & Spencer has suffered from poor profitability in recent years, largely as a result of its disappointing range of women's clothing. Complaints from customers about products and services will often be a way of highlighting some areas of weakness within the business.

**Opportunities** are circumstances that the business is able to take advantage of and exploit, such as a major competitor in the market going into liquidation or a change in fashions or tastes. For example, a relaxation of licensing laws will create opportunities for pubs and bars to open longer hours. If a celebrity is spotted wearing a brand of clothing or an accessory such as sunglasses, then this can become a great promotional opportunity for the business.

**Threats** are factors which may damage the performance of a business, such as increased levels of competition in the market or changes in the law. For example, if the government decides to open up postal delivery services in the UK to greater competition it would undoubtedly threaten the profitability of the Post Office and the jobs of some Post Office workers.

Strengths and weaknesses are **internal factors** that the business has some control over. Opportunities and threats come from the **external environment** outside the business. They cannot be controlled but they cannot be ignored. Once the managers of a business have carried out an assessment of these issues, then SWOT analysis can provide the basis of a future strategy. The business will need to look hard at any weaknesses and try to put them right. The managers of the business will need to consider how opportunities can be exploited.

## CASE STUDY

# What Happened to WH Smith

In October 2004 WH Smith announced a pre-tax loss of £135m, one of the worst losses in its history. This was largely the result of exceptional charges of £200m relating to unsold stock and restructuring costs. Nevertheless, pre-tax profit before the exceptional items was £67m, down from £102m the previous year, and retail sales fell by 2 per cent.

WH Smith has been in existence for over 200 years and has 673 stores, many in prime high street and station locations. However, in recent years the company has faced tough competition in its main markets from specialist retailers and the supermarkets. Despite the fact that the WH Smith brand name enjoys a high level of customer recognition, many observers feel that the business lacks a distinct retail identity on the high street. Some business commentators feel that WH Smith competes in too many markets while others feel that it should seek out new areas of opportunity.

1 What different types of products does WH Smith sell? Which broad markets does the company operate in?

2 List WH Smith's main retail competitors in its different markets.

3 Produce an outline SWOT analysis for WH Smith.

Tip: You may find it helpful to go to the WH Smith website: www.WHSmith.co.uk

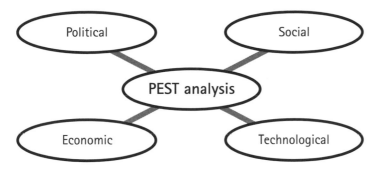

**Figure 5.3** *PEST analysis*

# PEST analysis

PEST analysis is a management tool for analysing some of the external forces that act upon a business. The business does not have any control over these forces but it will have to be aware of them and respond to them if it is to remain competitive in the market. Businesses need to be aware of changing market trends and the political and economic climate. PEST stands for political, economic, social and technological factors.

## *Political factors*

Changes in government and changes in the laws passed by the government may have a big impact on the business. For example, when the Labour government was elected in 1997 it introduced a minimum wage for the first time in the UK. This increased costs for a number of businesses in low pay industries such as catering and cleaning. Similarly, when all forms of tobacco advertising were banned in the UK this had a big impact on the marketing activities of tobacco companies. More recently, the government has decided to relax controls on gambling and pub opening hours, which will affect these industries.

## *Economic factors*

Businesses are inevitably affected by economic forces. The economy may move through periods of growth and recession, the Bank of England may change interest rates and the value of the pound may rise and fall against other currencies. These economic changes may influence consumer spending in the UK and they may change business costs. During 2004 and 2005, the world oil price rose significantly, raising costs for a range of businesses but particularly transport businesses which are heavy users of diesel and petrol.

## *Social factors*

Over periods of time consumer tastes, fashion and habits change. These trends may have important effects upon UK businesses. It is obvious that in industries such as fashion and music, styles change and businesses need to

*Sports car designed to appeal to women*

adapt if they are to remain competitive. The growth of female employment in the UK over the last 30 years means that women's spending power in the economy has increased significantly and businesses need to be much more aware of this when marketing products. Traditionally, sports cars were marketed at a predominantly male audience but demand from affluent female professionals has grown rapidly. There has been a significant increase in the number of drinks aimed at young women over the last ten years.

## Technological influences

Changes in technology will threaten some existing businesses while creating opportunities for others. The mobile phone industry has grown massively over the last decade and Vodafone has become one of the UK's largest businesses. The Internet has created great opportunities for businesses such as the low-cost airline easyJet and the bookseller Amazon, and now, apparently, even the Queen has an iPod! Over the same time period, certain products and businesses have become virtually obsolete. Many electrical retailers are, for example, ceasing to stock VHS videos as the demand for DVDs has grown rapidly. Downloading of music from the Internet, both legally and illegally, has had a detrimental effect on music CD sales in the UK.

### QUESTIONS

1. Identify one recent change in the law or a proposal to change the law that would have an effect on business in the UK and outline the possible impact of such a change.
2. Identify an economic issue that may currently be affecting UK business.
3. Identify a product, fashion or music trend that is currently enjoying increasing popularity.
4. Describe a new piece of technology that is gaining popularity with consumers.

## Market segmentation

Markets can often be broken down into smaller sub-markets called **segments** as a way of analysing customers and their behaviour. For example, within the market for magazines we can further segment the market into men's magazines and women's and into general interest and specialist hobby magazines. Markets can be segmented using a number of important characteristics. Some of the most commonly used factors are shown below.

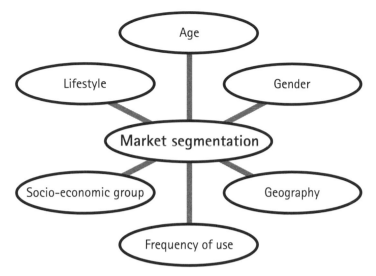

**Figure 5.4** *Market segmentation*

## Gender

Gender is an important factor when analysing the market for many consumer products. Cosmetics and tights are purchased almost exclusively by women whereas the majority of motorbikes are purchased by men. This inevitably influences the marketing and promotion of these products.

## Socio-economic group

Income and social class is another important issue when analysing markets and buying behaviour. The assumption is that those who belong to a particular social group will have similar preferences and habits. An expensive product such as a luxury sports car or a designer-label suit will inevitably be aimed at higher-income customers, whereas value-brand sausages are likely to be aimed at lower-income customers such as students.

The most commonly used social classification is the National Readership Survey (NRS). The NRS social grade definitions have been in use for several decades and are shown below.

| SOCIAL GRADE | SOCIAL STATUS | OCCUPATION |
|---|---|---|
| A | Upper middle class | Higher managerial, administrative or professional |
| B | Middle class | Intermediate managerial, administrative or professional |
| C1 | Lower middle class | Supervisory or clerical, junior managerial, administrative or professional |
| C2 | Skilled working class | Skilled manual workers |
| D | Working class | Semi and unskilled manual workers |
| E | Those at lowest level of subsistence | State pensioners or widows (no other earner), casual or lowest grade workers. |

**Table 5.1** *National Readership Survey social classification*

## Age

Age may be a relevant factor in some cases. Extreme sports equipment will be aimed at a relatively young 16-30 age range whereas stairlifts and walk-in baths have a much older target market. It is easy to categorise and target customers by age, though for some products and services it is not always particularly relevant.

## Frequency of use

This can be looked at in two ways. Firstly, customers can be categorised in terms of whether they are frequent buyers or just occasional users of a product. The business should focus its marketing on retaining its core customers but also try to bring in more occasional users and find ways of transforming them into regular users. It is common to find that 20 per cent of customers account for 80 per cent of sales. This is known as the '80/20 rule' or the Pareto Effect. An alternative approach is to look at the product itself. Is it purchased only every few years like a washing machine or purchased weekly like instant coffee or toilet rolls?

## Lifestyle

Some products will appeal only to those customers or potential customers who have a particular lifestyle, for example busy working mums or young professionals. This may be a life choice such as vegetarianism or be linked to particular cultural, religious or ethnic backgrounds.

## Geography

A business may group its customers based on geography, e.g. it may distinguish between domestic and overseas customers. A business may sell more of its product in certain regions of the UK or it may find that customers in different regions have different tastes and preferences, e.g. the soft drink Irn Bru sells mainly in Scotland. Some businesses structure themselves according to geography, e.g. the marketing department may be based on UK regions such as the South East or Wales.

## The validity and viability of segmentation

At times it may appear that crude stereotyping is being used but it is important for business to try to identify valid groups which share certain common characteristics such as tastes and lifestyles or which have similar spending patterns. This can then help a business to develop an effective marketing strategy and develop a marketing mix to target the product at potential customers and not waste marketing resources on groups who are unlikely to buy the product or service. It may be possible to break down a market into very small segments but at some point the number of potential customers may be so small that the market segment is not **viable** for the business. This means that the small number of customers makes it not worthwhile for the business to bother targeting them. Small niche markets such as this may, however, be very attractive to smaller firms.

# Consumer targeting

Informing potential customers about products and persuading them to buy is vital for the success of most consumer products in competitive markets. If a market can be accurately segmented the business can then begin to target key groups of customers and potential customers. If a business can develop an accurate picture of who buys the product or service and the main characteristics of those customers (known as a customer profile) it can then create an appropriate marketing mix. A whole industry exists to compile data on consumer spending habits, preferences and trends which is known as market intelligence. Retailers' loyalty cards potentially provide businesses with a wealth of information about how much customers spend and on what products. This means that if Sainsbury's is planning to bring out a new range of low fat, low salt products, it can target customers who already purchase healthy option products. This is likely to be more cost-effective than a mail-shot to all loyalty card holders.

## The Target Group Index

Market research companies such as **Target Group Index (TGI)** provide market research surveys and provide a means of describing target groups for consumer goods and services. Questionnaires are sent to thousands of households in the UK and the results are used to compile reports on spending patterns, attitudes and consumer profiles. These reports provide market intelligence which can assist businesses to understand their target markets and provide the basis for communicating with target groups.

## ACORN system

The **ACORN** (A Classification of Residential Neighbourhoods) system is another useful marketing tool. The ACORN system is a database built upon the principle that people living in similar neighbourhoods will tend to have similar purchasing and lifestyle habits. Therefore, a postcode can reveal valuable market research data. At its simplest level it can reveal whether the household is located in a block of flats or whether it is rented or owner-occupied. A business selling gardening products by mail order can therefore send out catalogues to addresses in localities with a high percentage of households that are owner-occupied with large gardens and avoid wasting its resources on flats without gardens. This approach will never be completely reliable but it can help businesses to target their market.

# Market research

Market research is the process of identifying what products and services customers want and how much they are prepared to pay for them. It may also identify trends, gaps in the market and the success of recent campaigns. A **market-centred** business will devote considerable resources to obtaining this information. If products and services can be developed which closely match customers' needs, then it should be much easier to sell them. If a company's products are out of touch with customers' needs then they stand less chance of success in the market.

Market research information can be categorised into **primary** and **secondary** information. Numerically based data is known as **quantitative** data whereas consumer opinions and views about products are known as **qualitative** data.

Both types of data information are of value to a business.

## Secondary information

Secondary information is data that is already available in published form. The business itself should have information on things such as past sales, the geographical distribution of customers, seasonal trends, average customer spend etc. This internally held information, sometimes called **backdata**, is cheap and easy to obtain and also is not available to competitors. However, there will be other external secondary data that a business can gain easy access to, such as government statistics, industry surveys, reports by pressure groups and press articles, which will provide useful information about the market.

## Primary information

Primary market research involves collecting information about customer behaviour and market trends first hand. This process can be time-consuming and expensive but it will provide the business with up-to-date market information that will not be available to competitors. The business may carry out market research itself or employ a specialist market research company. It must also decide upon the most appropriate research method, for example observation of customer behaviour or surveys, and may consider methods such as personal and telephone interviews, postal surveys, consumer panels and focus groups. Each method has its advantages and drawbacks. Personal interviews may allow detailed exploration of the respondent's preferences but they can be costly and time-consuming. Focus groups can be a very effective way of obtaining qualitative information about customer perceptions of value, brand image and taste in a relaxed setting but once again this can be time-consuming. Postal surveys are cheap but the response rate is low and results may not be representative.

Businesses can make use of widespread market research groups such as MORI, Gallup and NOP to conduct research on their behalf, though this is likely to be too costly for smaller businesses.

.......................................
: **GLOSSARY** :
.......................................

**Secondary information:**
This is also called **desk research** and is information that is already available in published form.

**Primary information:**
This is also called **field research** and is data that has been collected for a specific purpose.

# Questionnaire design

A questionnaire is a structured series of questions and is a valuable tool for market researchers. However, considerable thought must be given to the design of a questionnaire if it is to produce useful information that marketing decisions can be based upon. The starting point is to decide what the purpose of the questionnaire is and what information is needed. The questionnaire designer will need to devise questions which are clear and unambiguous and which will lead to useful information for marketing purposes. **Closed questions** will lead to yes or no answers enabling quantitative information to be gathered, e.g. 67 per cent of those questioned preferred Brand X to Brand Y, while **open questions** will provide useful qualitative information, e.g. reasons why consumers prefer Brand X to Brand Y. **Multiple-choice questions** allow respondents to choose from a number of pre-determined options and allow the researcher to limit the range of responses (see Figure 5.5). It is usually sensible to test the questionnaire out on a small number of people to identify any potential problems before beginning full-scale research.

---

**closed question**
*Do you have a pension plan ?*                          Yes            No

**multiple-choice question**

*How far did you travel to Northway*    0-4 miles    5-10 miles   10+ miles
*Shopping Centre today ?*

**open question**

*What features attracted you to this product ?*

---

**Figure 5.5**  *Questions for a questionnaire*

## *Sample sizes*

If a business has a comparatively small number of customers or offers a customised service, such as a wedding planner, then it can discuss individual client requirements. However, if the business operates in a mass market selling its product to millions of customers, then it will not be able to seek feedback from each individual customer. In these cases, it will carry out research by selecting a sample of its customers or potential customers. The group that the sample is selected from is known as the **population**. The bigger the sample, the more representative of the total population and the more accurate the results are likely to be. However, interviewing a large sample will be expensive and time-consuming. The business will, therefore, need to decide how large its budget for market research is and this will determine the size of the sample. Samples can be random, stratified or based on quotas, depending upon the size of the survey and the type of data required.

**Figure 5.6** *Market research data presented in a visual format*

## Findings of market research

Once information has been collected, it will need to be analysed and the findings presented in a convenient format. Closed questions will enable the researchers to compile quantitative data, e.g. 71 per cent of respondents did not have a pension plan. Open-ended questions will provide feedback on issues such as brand image, changes customers might like to see in the product or service, and a wide range of other qualitative information which can help to inform the company's future strategy.

Market research findings may be presented in a written report but quantitative data may be presented in a visual format. Presenting data as a pie chart or in the form of a graph can give the research results much greater visual impact. The level of analysis and the way in which the data is presented will depend upon the final user of the information.

# AO3 Use marketing models to define the selected product or service

A number of business theories or models have been developed which are of value in assessing the position and performance of products and services in the market. The first of these considered is the product life cycle theory.

## Product life cycle theory

Product life cycle theory likens all products and services to living creatures which have a certain life span and go through a number of different phases in their lives. These phases have implications for the level of sales and for cash flow in the business. Some products such as Marmite have been on the market for decades while others have a life span of only a few weeks or months, e.g. a computer game linked to the 2006 World Cup.

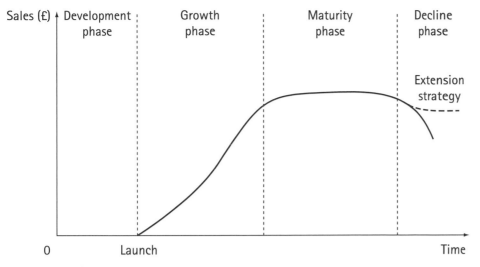

**Figure 5.7** *Phases of the product life cycle*

## Development phase

In this phase, the product has not yet been brought to the market. It is still being developed and tested. Sample batches may be produced to conduct trials and test marketing prior to the launch of the product. During this period no revenue is generated as the product has not yet been launched and there are likely to be high development costs. Cash flow is therefore negative in this phase so a business must be confident that it has sufficient finance to develop new products.

## Launch phase

Launch occurs when the product or service is first introduced to the market. Launching a new product will usually involve high promotional costs as potential customers will have to be made aware of the new product and encouraged to buy it through advertising and other techniques. There is always a risk that the product will fail to establish itself in the market.

## Growth phase

If the product is able to establish itself in the market this suggests that the initial market research was correct and sales begin to grow. Sales revenue will start to flow into the business and the new product begins to gain market share. This growth phase may continue for months or even years for some products but for others, e.g. a new (seasonal) Spring fashion, it may be for only a few weeks or months.

## Maturity phase

In the maturity or mature phase the product is well-established in the market and sales are high. The product is generating revenue for the business but the market is becoming saturated and there is no further growth in sales. A product such as Kit-Kat has been in this phase of its life for many years. Products in this phase generate revenue which can be used to develop new products.

## Decline phase

In this phase sales and sales revenue begin to fall. This can occur quite quickly, leading to the product being taken off the market. In other cases, a product may continue for years in gentle decline. The business may be unwilling to kill it off if it is still generating significant levels of sales revenue. A business may use an extension strategy to prolong the life of a product. This may involve making changes to the packaging or running special promotions. Car manufacturers often bring out special editions of a successful older model, e.g. with alloy wheels as standard, while they are developing a completely new model.

## A balanced product portfolio

Product portfolio means the range of products or services that a particular business sells. Product life cycle theory suggests that because of the cash flow implications, a multi-product business should aim to have a number of different products at different stages of their life cycles. Products in the mature phase will generate cash to finance the development of new products while new products are needed to replace those coming to the end of their lives.

### ACTIVITY

1. Working in pairs or groups, give two current examples of products or services in each of the following phases.
   (a) launch phase  (b) growth phase  (c) maturity phase
   (d) decline phase.
2. What problems might a business have which has most of its products in
   (a) the development phase?
   (b) the decline phase?

## Mapping

Mapping involves identifying where a product fits into its market. Key factors such as price or quality may be used in mapping. For example, within the market for breakfast cereals, Special K is aimed at diet-conscious women whereas Frosties is aimed at the children's market.

# The Boston matrix

The Boston matrix was developed by the Boston Consulting Group in the USA as an alternative way of analysing the performance of a product or service in its market. The Boston matrix considers **market share** and **market growth**.

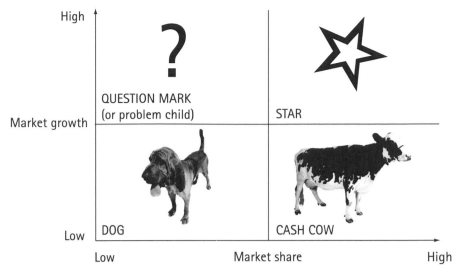

**Figure 5.8** *The Boston matrix*

**Stars** are products or brands which have a high market share in a high growth market. They generate a great deal of revenue for the business and enhance its reputation in the market, e.g. the Apple iPod has a large market share in the rapidly growing market for downloading music from the Internet.

**Cash cows** have a large market share in a low growth market. These products tend to be in the mature phase of their life cycle. They are very familiar to their customers and they generate high sales volumes and revenue for the business. Kellogg's Cornflakes are the market leader in the market for breakfast cereals but this is a fairly low growth market.

**Problem child (or question mark)** these products operate in a high growth market but have not been able to win a large market share. It may be possible to transform them into stars with a few simple changes to the product's marketing mix. However, the business may decide to remove them from the market.

**Dogs** are products which have only a low market share in a low growth market. This means that they generate comparatively small amounts of revenue and they may actually be damaging the firm's image or reputation. Dogs should generally be removed from the market to avoid wasting resources.

*The iPod MP3 player*

## Ansoff's matrix

Ansoff's matrix is another useful tool for analysing the approach to marketing strategy taken by a business. The matrix plots markets against products, and suggests that a business can follow one of four basic marketing strategies.

**Market penetration** is a relatively straightforward strategy which involves selling more of the existing product in an existing market. It will need to encourage existing customers to buy more of the product or attract new customers. The business may use various promotional techniques or price cuts to achieve this goal.

## ACTIVITY

Identify one product or service in each of the four Boston Matrix categories currently on sale in the UK.

| Products | | Markets | |
|---|---|---|---|
| | | Existing | New |
| | New | Product development | Diversification |
| | Existing | Market penetration | Market development |

**Figure 5.9** *Ansoff's matrix*

**Product development** involves developing new products or services to sell in the existing market. For example, a yoghurt manufacturer may decide to bring out a new range of low cholesterol yoghurts and milk drinks.

**Market development** involves selling the existing product in new markets. This may involve moving into overseas markets and exporting products that have been successful in the domestic market for the first time. This is inevitably risky as the business is moving into an unfamiliar market.

**Diversification** is in many ways the riskiest strategy as it involves selling new products into new markets. Launching a new product or service into a competitive market is always risky but launching a new a product into an unfamiliar market is particularly so. The Virgin Group has, over the years, diversified into areas such as train services and mobile phone services.

## Product planning and development

We have seen above that a number of models can be used to analyse the performance of a product or service in its market and form the basis of a future marketing strategy. When developing an approach to marketing a business must decide which particular characteristics of its product it wishes to emphasise. Some products are heavily marketed on a **unique selling point (USP)**. The Dyson vacuum cleaner was the world's first bagless vacuum cleaner and this was its USP. McCain Micro Chips are heavily promoted as frozen chips which can be cooked in the microwave. Shell petrol claims to have a unique engine-cleaning additive.

However, not all products can claim to have a unique or unusual feature. A product may be marketed using a successful **brand name**, so United Biscuits, for example, may launch a new biscuit under their McVities brand name. Customers know and trust the brand name and will probably be willing to try the new biscuit. The owners of a brand name may have a particular strategy for that brand. Rolex is a prestigious brand name in watch making and the company is careful to market its products in ways which protect its image. Lombard Direct is a loan company which tries to project a friendly and approachable image with customers arranging loans conveniently over the phone. Other companies may rely heavily on the product's name or use eye-catching or distinctive packaging, e.g. Jif Lemon Juice and Kit-Kat, to market the product. Packaging can be simply functional to contain or protect the product but it is also a marketing opportunity to promote a distinctive logo or brand image.

**ACTIVITY**

Can you think of any products or services that are currently being marketed with a USP?

A Jif Lemon containing lemon juice

## AO4 Recommend and justify a pricing strategy for the selected product or service

Price is an important element in the marketing mix. In general, price will be linked to the customer's perception of value for money and quality. Generally, as the price of a product is reduced demand for it tends to rise and vice versa. Therefore, one obvious way to boost sales is to offer discounts and price cuts. The concept of **price elasticity of demand (PED)** measures how sensitive customers are to price changes. With some products, a small per cent price change will lead to a much larger per cent change in demand and so demand is said to be **price elastic**. With other products, such as petrol or tobacco, even a large price rise will not reduce demand much and so these goods are said to be **price inelastic**. Therefore, a business should have an understanding of price elasticity before making price changes.

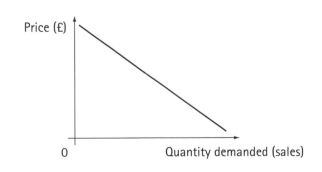

**Figure 5.10** *Demand curve*

## ACTIVITY

Calculating price elasticity of demand

$$\frac{\% \text{ change in demand}}{\% \text{ change in price}} = \text{price elasticity of demand (PED)}$$

If the result is greater than 1 = ELASTIC
If the result is less than 1 = INELASTIC

# Pricing strategy

## Cost-plus pricing

In a non-competitive market or in a market where customers are not very sensitive to price, businesses may be able to set prices based solely on their own costs and the profit margin they require. This is a traditional *cost-plus* approach:

Average cost + profit margin = selling price

Nowadays, comparatively few firms are able to set their own price without taking the prices of competitors into account. Water companies such as Thames Water enjoy a local monopoly of domestic water supply but their prices are regulated by Ofwat.

## Penetration pricing

This approach to pricing a new product or service involves initially setting a low price so that the product can become established in the market. This is vital in highly competitive markets such as women's magazines and chocolate confectionery. The price can later be raised so that it is more in line with competitors' prices once the product is established and brand loyalty has developed.

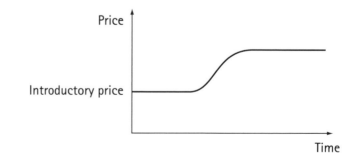

**Figure 5.11** *Penetration pricing*

## Skimming

Skimming involves initially setting a high price for a newly launched product. This can only be an option if the new product or service has technologically advanced features or a unique selling point (USP) that is not offered by the competition. A high price can be charged to 'skim' the market and recoup development costs. However, as rival firms develop their own products, the price will then tend to fall. For example, laptop computers, digital cameras and DVD players have all fallen in price now that they are widely manufactured.

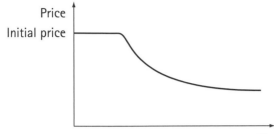

**Figure 5.12** *Skimming*

## Psychological pricing

Psychological pricing plays upon customers' notions of quality and value for money. Some businesses always set prices such as £9.99 or £6,999 ('a new car for under seven thousand pounds'). This method of pricing suggests a discount. Other businesses deliberately price in whole pounds, e.g. £40. Designer-clothing and perfumes are usually priced this way and Marks & Spencer usually price non-food items this way. The aim is to promote the idea of quality rather than suggest a discount.

## Price discrimination

This involves charging different prices for the same product or service in different market segments. For example, a standard rail return fare to London may be £34, while an off-peak return may cost only £17. The aim is to encourage non-commuters to take their journeys outside of peak times. Commuters have no choice about when they travel and so can be charged a higher fare. BT (British Telecom) operates a similar peak rate and off-peak rate system for phone calls. However, price discrimination can only work where there are separate market segments and customers in one market segment cannot sell the product or service on to customers in another segment.

## Premium pricing

Premium pricing involves charging a higher than normal price to promote an image of quality or exclusivity. Stella Artois lager is promoted as 'reassuringly expensive'. Products in Tesco's Finest range are sold at higher prices than Tesco's usual own brand products. The aim is to appeal to more discerning shoppers in higher socio-economic groups.

# Pricing determinants

A whole range of factors may influence the actual price charged for a product or service. Some of the main factors are outlined below.

## *The level of market demand*

If a product is very popular in the market then businesses supplying it are able to exploit this position by charging higher prices. This is particularly the case where there is high demand but supplies of the product are limited or even fixed. The number of tickets available for the FA Cup Final or a pop concert will be strictly limited so high prices can be charged. On the other hand, it will be necessary to offer discounts to sell a product that is unpopular within the market.

## *Competition*

Generally, when setting price a business cannot ignore the actions of their competitors. In a highly competitive market, a business will find that it will lose customers if it charges a price well in excess of those of its rivals. It may be able to charge more for a higher quality product or service but it will always have less freedom of action than a business operating in a market with little competition. Clearly, a monopolist has much more control over the price it sets for its products.

**Predator or destroyer pricing** involves setting an unrealistically low price for a time to put pressure on weaker competitors. Market share is gained and some rivals may be forced out of the market. For example, a national car hire firm could cut its prices in one area to force smaller, local firms out of business. The dominant firm will then be able to raise its prices as competition has been removed.

## *Customer types and market segments*

The price that a business can charge may also be influenced by the type of customers it has. For example, a farmer whose main customer is a supermarket chain such as Asda will find that he or she has little control over the price they receive for their produce as it is the supermarket that determines how much they will pay. As we have seen in the case of rail commuters, a business can charge a higher price to a market segment in which customers have little or no choice over whether they use a service.

## *Consumer behaviour and expectations*

In some markets the expectations of customers play an important role. Once customers have got used to the idea of the current market price for a product it may be difficult for a business to alter its price. Firms may experience customer resistance if they try to raise price above the going rate or an attempt to cut price may lead customers to believe that product quality has dropped. Cutting the price of a designer label product could actually lead to a fall in sales as its image of exclusivity may suffer.

## Distribution channels

The **distribution channel** of a product is the route by which it gets from the supplier to the final customer. Mass market products, such as crisps, must be sold at competitive prices through a very wide range of distribution outlets, including supermarkets, corner shops, canteens, sports halls etc. As customers are able to buy the product from a variety of sources, retailers are likely to charge similar prices. However, if the product is only sold through a restricted range of outlets, the customer is less able to shop around and prices are likely to be higher. A consumer wishing to buy a new Harry Potter novel will be able to choose between bookstores, supermarkets and Internet book suppliers who are all forced into offering discounted prices.

## Research and development (R&D) costs

As we have seen when looking at the product life cycle, some products are costly to develop. These costs will be reflected in a higher price when the product is launched as the business will seek a large profit margin to recover its research and development costs. Technologically advanced products are inevitably more expensive when first launched to recoup R&D costs (skimming).

## Macroeconomic issues

The price that can be charged for a product may be influenced by the state of the economy. In an economic downturn or **recession**, businesses may find that they are forced to cut prices if they wish to maintain sales as consumer incomes fall. Conversely, in a booming economy businesses may be able to charge higher prices as customers have higher disposable incomes.

> ### Portfolio tip
>
> *You are required to recommend and justify a pricing strategy for your product or service based upon the level of competition in the market or any other relevant factors. It is essential that you base your strategy on your own research into the market.*

## CASE STUDY

### Eurotunnel

In June 2005 Eurotunnel, the operator of the Channel Tunnel, announced price cuts in an attempt to win back customers. Eurotunnel's trains carry cars and lorries through the tunnel. Travellers taking their cars on Eurotunnel can now pay as little as £49 one way if they book in advance and avoid peak times. The company made losses of £540m in 2004 and saw revenues fall by 7 per cent.

1 What is the thinking behind the price cuts?
2 Who are Eurotunnel's main competitors?
3 What factors are cross-Channel travellers likely to take into account when deciding which form of transport to use?
4 What evidence is there that Eurotunnel uses price discrimination?

# AO5 Suggest and justify a method of distributing the selected product or service from manufacturer to consumer

Manufacturers or producers must decide upon the most effective way of getting their product or service to the final customer. The route by which products reach the final user is known as the distribution channel (or chain). In some cases there is a direct link between the manufacturer and the consumer whereas in others a complex chain of intermediaries may exist.

## Direct supply

Direct supply is when the manufacturer or producer deals directly with the final customer. For example, a farmer may decide to open a farm shop to sell produce directly to consumers rather than sell produce to retailers or wholesalers. The farmer will probably receive more profit on each item sold as the retailer's profit margin is cut out but will not have guaranteed buyers for the produce and this will make it difficult to predict cash flow. The farm will also have to organise its own marketing and promotional activity. A manufacturer may choose to set up a factory shop or sell its products via mail order or over the Internet which will have similar advantages and drawbacks.

*A lorry transporting goods to a supermarket*

# The use of intermediaries

The traditional distribution chain for a manufactured consumer product is illustrated below. It would typically involve **wholesalers** and retailers acting as intermediaries between the manufacturer and the consumer. The wholesaler's role is to buy in bulk from the manufacturer. The manufacturer then only has to deal with a small number of wholesalers each placing large orders. The wholesaler then 'breaks bulk' and sells the product on in smaller quantities to retailers who sell to the consumer. In this situation, there are three businesses receiving a profit margin: the manufacturer, the wholesaler and the retailer.

Nowadays, large supermarket chains such as Tesco and Asda perform their own wholesaling functions. They buy in large quantities direct from manufacturers which enables them to negotiate low unit prices and cut out the wholesaler's profit margin. This means that a lower price can be offered to the customer or the retailer is able to enjoy a higher profit margin. A manufacturer of a new ice-cream which it hopes to sell in a supermarket

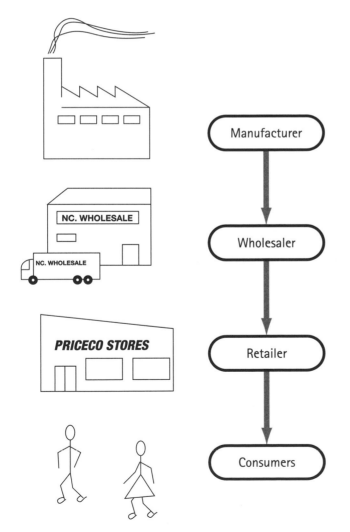

**Figure 5.13** *Traditional distribution channel*

will have to persuade the supermarket chain to give freezer space to its product and perhaps displace rival products. Failure to develop an adequate distribution network will have serious consequences for a business.

Some businesses make use of intermediaries called **agents**. This is often the case when a business first begins to export its products. It may employ an agent in the country it is exporting to. This agent will have a better understanding of the overseas market and may have customer contacts and be able to create a distribution network in that country. However, this agent will obviously charge a fee for their services or may operate on a commission basis.

Some catalogue companies such as Littlewoods have agents who generate business for the company among their family, friends and neighbours and receive commission on sales.

## CASE STUDY

### UK Tyros

UK Tyros Sports Ltd are a successful manufacturer of sports and fitness clothing and equipment. As the UK market is becoming increasingly competitive, the company has decided to market their products in France for the first time.

**Assess the advantages and drawbacks of Tyros employing an agent as opposed to setting up their own distribution network in France.**

# AO6 Recommend and justify the use of promotional techniques for the selected product or service

There are a wide range of promotional techniques that a business can use. These can be divided into **above the line** and **below the line** techniques. Whatever method a business chooses, it must be cost-effective.

## Above the line promotion

Above the line promotion involves using what are called **independent media** to promote the firm's products or services. Popular examples of this type of promotion include television, national and local press and radio advertisements. Some of the most important and popular forms of advertising products and services in the UK are outlined below.

## Newspapers

Newspapers may be national (covering the whole country), regional or local. Some are published daily, such as the *Daily Mail*, while others are weeklies, such as the *News of the World*. A popular tabloid newspaper such as the *Sun* may sell over 3 million copies per day and be read by double that number of people across the whole of the UK. On the other hand, a free weekly newspaper may be read by only a few thousand people in a particular area. Newspaper advertising is useful for businesses of all sizes.

The cost of advertising in a newspaper or magazine is related to the numbers of readers, known as the **circulation.** The *Sun* sells over 3 million copies per day and it will be read by an even larger number of people, so an advertisement placed in this paper will reach a very large audience, so it can be a very effective way of advertising a mass market product such as a new toothpaste or breakfast cereal. However, a full-page colour advertisement in a popular tabloid newspaper may cost as much as £35,000 for one day.

Obviously, only large businesses with big advertising budgets, such as Ford or PC World, can afford to place advertisements such as this. Small and medium-sized businesses are much more likely to use regional and local newspapers. Advertising costs will be lower as these papers will have a smaller circulation. However, a smaller business may well only attract customers from the local area and the local press may well be the ideal way to attract customers. Businesses such as restaurants and car dealerships are likely to make use of local and regional newspapers.

*Advertisement from a local paper*

## ACTIVITY

Why are you likely to see an advertisement for the Citroen C3 in the *Daily Mail* but not an advertisement for a local restaurant?

One of the advantages of newspaper advertising is that the information is in a permanent format. Customers can be given details about the product or service, prices, contact numbers and addresses and they can keep this information and refer to it later. Newspapers are often provided in public libraries and are left in places such as works' canteens and doctors' waiting rooms and so will be read by far more people than those who actually buy them.

## Magazines

Magazines are another popular means of advertising. These advertisements, again, have the advantage of being in a permanent form and magazines are often still being looked at several months after they were published. Magazines can be used to target a particular audience. *Nuts* is a popular weekly read mainly by young men while *Bella* is a general interest magazine read mainly by women. Some magazines are aimed at a particular hobby while others are aimed at people who work in certain type of industry, e.g. *Campaign* is aimed at those in the marketing industry.

Table 5.2 shows a readership profile of a fictitious celebrity gossip magazine *Look Here*, showing the percentage of readers by age and gender.

*A range of popular magazines*

| AGE RANGE | FEMALE | MALE |
|-----------|--------|------|
| 16–25 | 30 | 6 |
| 26–49 | 42 | 5 |
| 50+ | 16 | 1 |

**Table 5.2** *Readership for* Look Here

### QUESTIONS

1  What use could potential advertisers make of this type of information?
2  In which type of magazine are you likely to find an advertisement for (a) a strong lager (b) a new Disney film release (c) make-up removal wipes (d) pet insurance (e) online gambling (f) a new range of healthy eating foods for kids?

## Television

Television has transformed advertising in Britain over the last 50 years. Advertising of products is not permitted on the BBC but only on commercial television channels such as ITV, Channel 4 and Sky. These channels rely on charging businesses to advertise their products. Television advertising generates billions of pounds in revenue every year which enables television companies to produce and buy programmes. The ITV network is made up of a number of regional companies such as Meridian, Carlton and Granada. A business with a regional customer base might decide to advertise on its local ITV channel. A national company may choose to advertise its products on all of the ITV networks. This would be a way of reaching millions of households all over the country but it is very expensive. The cost of placing an advertisement will vary depending upon the number of likely viewers.

Television advertising is able to use strong visual images and music to send out messages about the product. Most television advertising is **persuasive** rather than informative and it can be a very effective way of reaching millions of potential customers and developing a brand image. However, the cost of making a good quality advertisement is high, particularly if it involves using a well-known celebrity. The advertiser will then have to pay thousands of pounds for a slot at peak viewing time. This means that television advertising is not an option for small and medium-sized businesses. It is also not suitable for communicating a lot of technical information about products.

## Ratings war

'Ratings' refers to the number of viewers watching a programme. The more viewers that a programme has then the more that the television company can charge for advertising in breaks during that programme. It has already been mentioned that the cost varies according to the size of the audience. Granada reaches far more viewers than West Country Television so it is more expensive to advertise on Granada. In a similar way, more people will watch *The X Factor* than *Countdown* and so advertising during a commercial break in *The X Factor* will cost more than during a less popular programme.

**Real business**

In 2005 it would have cost over £80,000 for a 30-second advertising slot in the centre break of Coronation Street networked across all of the ITV regions.

| VIEWING FIGURES FOR WEEK ENDING 26 JUNE 2005 | | |
|---|---|---|
| Top 5 programmes | Day | Figures |
| Eastenders | (Fri/Sunday BBC1) | 10.8m |
| Coronation Street | (Fri ITV1) | 9.8m |
| Emmerdale | (Mon ITV1) | 7.8m |
| New Tricks | (Mon BBC1) | 7.0m |
| Casualty | (Sat BBC1) | 6.7m |
| | | |

Source: Broadcast Audience Research Board (BARB), www.barb.co.uk

**Table 5.3** *Viewing figures for Top 5 TV programmes*

## ACTIVITY

1  What type of products and services tend to be advertised on television at the following times? Give reasons for your choices.
   (a) weekday mornings   (b) during half time of Champions League football (c) Saturday mornings.
2  In pairs or small groups, identify four television advertisements that you currently like and explain what you find appealing about them. How much information do they provide about the product that is being advertised?

## Cinema

Cinema attendances declined during the 1980s with the growth in videos but they recovered strongly during the 1990s. Films can be categorised by age and type, e.g. action, comedy, romance, so the audience can be targeted quite effectively by advertisers. A new Disney animation will have a large number of children and their parents in the audience whereas a French film with English sub-titles will have a very different type of audience. There are limited opportunities for advertising in the cinema, such as before and after the feature film, and many people will take little notice. However, like television advertising, cinema advertising can make use of music and strong visual images to capture people's attention and create a brand image.

## ACTIVITY

What type of products and services tend to be advertised at your local cinema?

## Radio

There has been huge growth in commercial radio over the last 20 years. Like the independent television companies, commercial radio stations earn income by charging businesses to advertise their products and services. Independent radio stations in the UK target many different types of audience and different parts of the country. Stations may specialise in playing particular types of music, e.g. classical music, Asian music, jazz or hip hop, while some rely heavily on listener phone-ins and chat shows. Some stations are national, e.g. Virgin, but the majority are regional or local, e.g. Capital covers London while BRMB covers much of the West Midlands.

Independent radio stations generally have a good knowledge of who their typical listeners are in terms of age, gender and lifestyle at different times of the day. This is known as the **listener profile**. This enables businesses to target a particular audience with their advertising. The cost of advertising tends to vary according to how many listeners the advertisement is likely to reach and the quality of the advertisement itself. Radio advertising can be a relatively cheap and effective way for local and regional businesses to advertise. People are able to listen to the radio while doing other things such as driving, working or waiting in a dentist's surgery. This can be an advantage but the drawback is that listeners are often not really concentrating and are unlikely to remember phone numbers and contact details unless they are frequently repeated.

## ACTIVITY

1 Which independent radio stations do you listen to?
2 List some of the products and businesses you hear advertised on radio.
3 Why do you think they have chosen to use local radio?

## *Outdoor advertising*

'Outdoor' covers a range of different approaches to advertising, including posters, advertisements on the side of buses and taxis, balloons and hoardings at football and other sports grounds. The various types of outdoor advertising have some of the advantages of newspaper and magazine advertising in that they are in a permanent format and they can target potential customers in a certain area or who have a particular interest. Billboards at prime sites, such as near traffic lights at a busy road junction, can be relatively expensive to advertise on and they may be vandalised. Some companies have their own hot air balloons in amusing or interesting shapes to help promote their products at outdoor events during the summer months, e.g. the annual Bristol Balloon Fiesta. This is unlikely to be an option for small and medium-sized businesses.

## ACTIVITY

1 Copy out (or key in) and complete the table showing the advantages and drawbacks of the various types of above the line advertising.

| Advertising media | Advantages | Drawbacks |
|---|---|---|
| National newspapers | | |
| Local newspapers | | |
| Magazines | | |
| Television | | |
| Local radio | | |

2 In pairs or groups, contrast the typical reader/listener/viewer profiles for each of the following:
   (a) *Heat* magazine and *4-4-2* magazine
   (b) The *Financial Times* and the *Sun*
   (c) The *Chart Show* on Radio 1 and *Woman's Hour* on Radio 4
   (d) Hollyoaks and Newsnight.

*Outdoor advertising*

# Below the line promotion

We have seen that television and press advertising is known as 'above the line' promotion.

Below the line promotion involves all the other promotional activities that businesses use, such as trade promotions, competitions, sponsorships, discounts, prize draws, money-off coupons etc.

## *Sales promotions*

Sales promotions aim to encourage customers to buy more of the firm's products. We are all familiar with money-off coupons, free gifts with magazines, prize draws and BOGOF (buy one get one free) deals! Food stores, such as Iceland, often offer link purchases such as offering free oven chips if the customer buys a certain brand of beefburger. For expensive items such as cars or furniture, a business may offer its customers special credit terms such as two years' interest-free credit to encourage them to buy.

*Buy one – get one free*

## ACTIVITY

State whether each of the following is an example of **above the line** or **below the line** promotion:

(a) an advertisement in a local newspaper
(b) a 50p off the next purchase price coupon issued in a supermarket
(c) a 30-second television commercial
(d) an e-mail sent to previous purchasers of a product informing them of a new update.
(e) free entry into a prize draw for the first 100 purchasers of a product
(f) an in-store demonstration of a new food processor
(g) a 15-second advertisement on local radio
(h) a free gift attached to the front of a magazine.

## *Public relations*

Public relations (PR) involves trying to present the business and its products to the general public in a more favourable light. PR activities are not always about selling more products in the short term. PR activities are often aimed at creating a particular image for the business, e.g. that a business cares about the environment or supports its local community. A local printing business may spend a few hundred pounds sponsoring a local school football team. This is unlikely to increase its sales but it may improve its image locally and if the team is successful it may gain some extra publicity. A firm may try to appeal to its customers by promising to donate a sum of money to charity for every item sold.

## Press releases

If a company, such as Coca Cola or Sony, are to release a new product or set up a big new sponsorship deal they may well decide to issue a **press release** or hold a **press conference** to inform the media of their plans. The company presents its news to an audience of press, television and radio journalists and it may allow questions. This will generate considerable publicity for the business. Small and medium-sized businesses may try to get articles about themselves into the local press or try to be interviewed on the local radio station.

## Sponsorship

We are all very familiar with sponsorship of sports teams and major sporting events. Sports stars and celebrities are often used to endorse products, meaning that a celebrity is linked with a particular product. Companies obviously believe that there are benefits in being associated with high-profile events or celebrities. A number of football stadiums and even many television programmes are now sponsored.

### Real business

In October 2004 Arsenal signed a £100m deal with Emirate Airlines. Their new ground at Ashburton Grove will be named the Emirates Stadium.

*Sponsors of the football club*

Not only are some television programmes sponsored by companies but **product placement** deals mean that a company pays the film or programme makers to have its products shown prominently in a programme or film. In recent years, James Bond films have often clearly shown Sony, BMW, Philips and other well-known branded products being used by the hero. The company knows that films such as this will be seen by large audiences internationally and that their brand will benefit from this association.

## Lobbying

Lobbying is a technique which involves individuals or businesses bringing pressure to bear on government policy-makers to change the law to promote or protect their interests. Some retailers are lobbying government to remove restrictions on Sunday trading while trade unions are lobbying government not to make such a change, so that shop workers are protected.

## ACTIVITY

1   In pairs or small groups, identify the sponsor(s) of the following.
    (a) *Hollyoaks*   (b) *Emmerdale*   (c) the London Marathon
    (d) Chelsea Football Club   (d) your local football team
    (e) *The X Factor*.
2   Why do you think that the brands/companies that you identified above have chosen these particular sponsorships ?
3   Which famous people are associated with the following products or brands?
    (a) Sainsbury's foods   (b) Renault Clio   (c) Walkers crisps
    (d) John Smith beer   (e) L'Oreal hair products.

## *Point-of-sale promotions*

Point-of-sale promotions are used to support the product at the point where it is actually sold to the customer. This may include attractive displays in the store or leaflets and posters giving information about the product. It may involve video or other demonstrations of the product in use and kitchen gadgets or cleaning products are sometimes promoted this way in department stores. Some products are shown through interactive displays on a computer screen.

   Supermarkets often run promotional offers on particular drinks or food products and give away free samples for customers to try in store. This is then often backed up with money-off coupons or other special offers to encourage customers to buy the product once they have tried it. Certain parts of supermarkets, such as the end of aisles, are known as 'hot spots' because they tend to generate higher levels of sales. Items which are being heavily promoted that week may be prominently displayed in one of these hot-spot areas to catch the customer's eye and increase sales.

Retailers may use more subtle ways to encourage customers to buy particular products such as careful lighting, music and smells. In-store bakeries and coffee shops not only provide customers with products but the aromas of bread and coffee may appeal to customers' sense of smell and lead to them buying more products.

*Point-of-sale display*

## Branding

Branding is a hugely important idea in the promotion of products. Brands such as Ford, McDonalds, Sony, Heinz and Nike are recognised across the world and these companies spend huge amounts of money promoting their brand name. Branding helps customers to recognise products and it gives them reassurance about the quality of products. Branding is often linked in with a particular logo, design feature or distinctive packaging. Apart from obvious logos, businesses may use particular colour schemes for their stores and vehicles and use distinctive lettering or layout on their business stationery and signs. The aim is to make the particular brand or business stand out from its competitors and perhaps to develop a **corporate identity**. The black and white Nike livery, for example, is recognised around the world. Businesses may also use 'jingles' and catchlines and slogans, e.g. L'Oreal's 'You're worth it', to reinforce their brand image.

*Advertising icon*

## ACTIVITY

1  Briefly describe the brand logos of the following products.
   (a) Adidas   (b) Churchill Car Insurance   (c) French Connection clothing
   (d) Heinz foods   (e) Parker pens   (f) Vodafone   (g) Legal & General
   insurance   (h) Apple Mac computers   (i) Kelloggs corn flakes
   (j) Lloyds TSB Bank.
2  List five well-known product catchlines or slogans.

## Exhibitions and trade fairs

Some businesses, particularly those which sell commercial and industrial products rather than consumer products, may decide to promote their products and services heavily at exhibitions and trade fairs. Almost every industry will have its own specialist fairs, for example the annual Boat Show at Southampton is an important promotional opportunity for yacht builders, sail makers and a host of other businesses providing marine products and services.

## Direct marketing

Direct marketing involves directly approaching customers. This may include sending mail shots or emails, telephone selling or off-screen selling on the Internet. We are all familiar with receiving telephone calls at home from double glazing, power and finance companies during the evening and receiving promotional 'junk mail' through the post.

The Internet has created new opportunities for direct selling. The budget airline company Ryanair sells all of its flight tickets directly to customers over the Internet. Similarly, Tower Records sells large numbers of CDs from its website and regularly contacts customers with details of special offers and new releases. The clothing retailer Cotton Traders has a small number of stores but sells mainly by mail order. Computers and word-processing software has meant that a business can send an apparently personalised letter to thousands of households across the country. The company simply purchases a mailing list giving names and addresses of potential customers. It can then contact them, addressing them by name, and it can vary the contents of a fairly standard letter to take account of local or other differences.

The Internet enables even small firms to email large numbers of potential customers at minimal cost. Once again, a business simply buys a list of email addresses of potential customers and then contacts them with details of products and special offers. As with 'junk mail' some people are irritated by this 'spam' but it can be a cheap, promotional tool. This form of direct

## ACTIVITY

In pairs or small groups, consider the following:

Despite the popularity of the Internet with home users, only a comparatively small number of businesses have been successful in selling their products to consumers over the Internet.

1  What types of product are commonly purchased over the Internet?
2  Why are customers happy to buy these products over the Internet?
3  What types of product are customers less willing to buy over the Internet and why is this?

marketing tends to be at its most effective when it is used to target people who have already purchased the product before. An individual who has purchased a book or DVD over the Internet is likely to make repeat purchases in the future. The big supermarkets which operate loyalty cards have a huge database of customers and they know which type of products they prefer to buy. This means that they are able to target particular customers with special offers and new products and services. For example, if a supermarket is bringing out a new range of cat food it can target customers who already purchase cat products.

## Viability of marketing communications

The size of the budget that is available will obviously influence the amount and type of promotional activity that the business undertakes. We have seen that television advertising can have great influence on customers and can be particularly effective with mass-market products such as cereals, cosmetics, beer etc. However, it is expensive and therefore not an option for small businesses serving a local market.

Producing simple fliers and posters or paying a person to walk around a busy shopping precinct with posters displayed on sandwich boards are all relatively cheap ways in which a local business could advertise its products or services. However, if a chocolate manufacturer such as Cadbury is to launch a brand new product it will need to use media which are capable of reaching a mass audience and this will inevitably cost a lot more.

### *Factors influencing the effectiveness of promotion*

Promotional material is like any other piece of communication. Businesses are sending out a message to a target audience. A business must consider the viability of each of the communication methods being considered. The cost must be assessed against the likely effectiveness of each method. A simple model of communication is shown below.

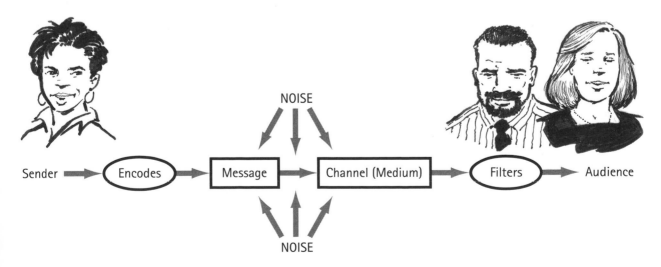

**Figure 5.14** *Simple communication model*

A simple example of a promotion may help to illustrate this. Sliklips are running a television advertisement to promote their new lip gloss. In this case the sender is the company and the message is that they have a new product on the market. The chosen medium is television and they believe that their receivers or audience are mainly women in the 16–40 age group.

Factors which will influence how effective the promotion is include:

- **How messages are encoded.** Code refers to the format that is used for the message. Messages may be in text such as 'Special offer – 50 per cent off' or they may use images or logos or music. Advertisements for Guinness and Stella Artois lager are complex and stylish pieces of promotion which offer little or no information about the products but are all about developing a distinctive image.

- **Receiving messages.** The message may not always have the desired effect on the receiver. The message may not be clearly understood by the receiver for a number of reasons to do with their age, culture, level of education or because the message itself is not clear. It may be that too much jargon is used or the language level is too high or too low for the audience. Many people are put off computers and financial products by the jargon that they encounter.

- **Reactions to the message.** Generally, the purpose of promotion is to increase sales or lead to a more positive image of the product. The use of a celebrity such as David Beckham to promote a product is based on the view that the receivers of the message will have a positive view of the footballer. However, if the receiver dislikes footballers and David Beckham in particular, then the promotion may not be successful with that individual.

- **The attention span of the watcher or listener.** A promotional poster is a permanent format that the reader can look at for as long as they wish to. However, if they are driving their car at the time, they may have only a few seconds to take in the message. Similarly, a 15-second radio advertisement can be effective but the majority of the audience will not be listening closely and they will not recall information such as a phone number unless the advertisement is repeated regularly.

## ACTIVITY

In pairs or small groups, consider the following:

1 Identify four advertisements that make use of a celebrity. Why do you think the particular celebrity was chosen?

2 Identify two advertisements that you feel are not effective and give your reasons.

## *Barriers to the promotional message*

There are a number of things that can prevent the promotional message achieving its purpose and these are known as **interference**:

- competing messages
- attention span
- filtering
- distortion
- noise.

## Competing messages

Every day most of us receive thousands of sounds and images. Many of these are very familiar, some are new and interesting, while others seem irrelevant. A promotional message will have to compete with many others and if it cannot get our attention it is not effective. An advertisement for a new car will be competing with many other promotional messages from rival car manufacturers.

## Attention span

A customer who has gone to a car showroom with the aim of buying a new car is likely to want to spend quite some time with a sales representative. However, a 15-second television advertisement during the commercial break in a film may be missed by viewers who have gone to fetch a drink or largely ignored by those who are chatting.

## Filtering

Most of us have ideas and prejudices about what we like and don't like. Sometimes the audience may interpret a message in a way that the advertiser did not expect. This could be because the message is unclear or ambiguous or the audience received it at an unexpected time or through an unexpected medium. The advertisement may be supported by a piece of music that the listener does not like or show images that the viewer finds patronising or annoying.

## Distortion

The message may not be communicated effectively because of some sort of interference. The message may be delivered too quickly, or the language used may be unsuitable for the audience. There may also be a technical problem with the chosen medium, e.g. a website crashes or the reception of a radio signal is poor.

## Noise

This may refer to physical noise which means the listener may not hear the message properly or it can mean other background interference which may make it harder to communicate the message.

# Constraints upon promotional and marketing activity

Businesses in the UK are able to choose how much they spend on promotional activities and they can decide upon the methods they will use to promote their products and services. However, it is important that the material in advertisements or promotional activity does not break the law or damage the image of the business. Promotional material is aimed at encouraging or persuading customers to buy products and services so there is a danger that businesses may make exaggerated or misleading claims to increase their sales. There are a number of legal and other constraints on advertising material which aim to protect consumers and these are included below.

## Advertising Standards Authority

The Advertising Standards Authority (ASA) is an independent body that monitors advertisements, sales promotions and direct marketing in the UK. The ASA runs the British Code of Advertising, Sales Promotion and Direct Marketing (known as the CAP code) to ensure that advertisements are legal, decent, honest and truthful. Advertisements should, also, not cause grave or widespread offence. If a complaint made by the public about an advertisement is upheld then the advertising industry will not handle the advertisement.

## CASE STUDY

### KFC

In 2005, the ASA received a record number of complaints (1,671) about a KFC advertisement in the UK for the Zinger Crunch Salad showing call-centre staff singing with their mouths full. The complaint was not upheld but KFC said that they did not plan to run the commercial again.

1 Why do you think so many viewers complained?
2 Was the ASA right not to uphold the complaint?
3 Is it necessary to have controls on advertising?

## The Independent Television Commission (ITC)

The ITC monitors broadcast advertising on television and radio and a number of rules exist to control this form of advertising. Rules cover issues such as nudity in television advertising and the use of actors and TV personalities. Actors are not allowed to appear in advertisements during programmes they appear in. For example, an actor in *Coronation Street* could not appear in an advertisement for a product in a commercial break during an episode of *Coronation Street*. Newsreaders are also prevented from advertising products, so, for example, Trevor McDonald cannot appear in television advertisements. There are also controls on products appearing in television programmes. For example, the Newton and Ridley beer served in the Rovers Return in *Coronation Street* is a purely fictitious brand and characters never ask for a branded product by name. Television companies must be careful in showing recognisable brands in its programmes, though recently a number of product placement deals have been agreed.

## Legislation

So far all of the controls that have been discussed are operated by the industries themselves. However, there are a number of laws in Britain which aim to protect the consumer from inaccurate and misleading advertisements. The main pieces of legislation that are relevant here are the Trade Descriptions Act and the Sale of Goods Act.

## The Trade Descriptions Act 1968

The Trade Descriptions Act 1968 is probably the most important legal protection for the public when considering advertising and promotional material. The Act states that claims made about products must be true and it also covers 'sales' and 'price reductions'. For example, it is an offence to claim that shoes are leather if they are not and sale items must have been on sale at the higher price for at least 28 days in the previous 6 months.

Sales notice

## The Sale of Goods Act 1994

This Act was first introduced in the nineteenth century and was one of the first laws which aimed at protecting consumers. To comply with the law, goods should be **as described**. So any claims about the content of the goods or where they are made must be true. The Trade Descriptions Act now deals more fully with this issue. Goods must also be of **merchantable quality** which means that there must not be any serious flaws or defects within them and they should be **fit for the purpose** they were bought for. For example, a pair of football boots should be reasonably hard wearing and not fall apart after one game. However, a pair of fashionable women's shoes would not be expected to stand up to heavy use. If products are defective or not fit for the purpose the buyer is entitled to a full refund. It is illegal to display notices in shops such as 'No refunds given'.

## Portfolio tip

*You are expected to recommend and justify a number of promotional techniques for your chosen product or service based on your own research findings. The techniques that you suggest should be appropriate for the product and for the size of the promotional budget that is available.*

## Pressure groups

A pressure group is a group that represents the views and interests of a particular group of people and campaigns to raise awareness of issues and bring about changes. Large, well-funded pressure groups such as trade unions act to protect the interests of their members on issues such as pay and working conditions. Other groups such as Oxfam or Friends of the Earth campaign to raise awareness of important issues with the public and put pressure on businesses and government to bring about change. If an advertisement or promotional material produced by a business causes offence or if a pressure group feels that it encourages a particular type of conduct, they are likely to complain either to the business itself or to the ASA. Anti-smoking and drinking pressure groups regularly complain about advertisements promoting these activities.

## SKILLS CHECK

1. What is meant by the term marketing mix?

2. Briefly explain the following terms: (a) SWOT analysis (b) PEST analysis (c) market segmentation.

3. Distinguish between **primary** and **secondary** market research.

4. Outline some of the key factors that should be taken into account when designing a questionnaire.

5. Explain what is meant by the term product life cycle.

6. Outline two different strategies that a business can take when deciding upon the price it charges for its product or service.

7. What is the difference between **above the line** and **below the line** promotion?

8. Give one advantage and one drawback of each of these promotional techniques: (a) a television advertisement (b) an advertisement in a local paper (c) sponsoring a local school football team.

9. Briefly explain the role of the Advertising Standards Authority (ASA).

10. What is the purpose of the Trade Descriptions Act?

## Getting started

The ultimate dream of many people is to become self-employed and run their own successful business. Unfortunately, there are not many of us who have the same skills as Richard Branson (founder of the Virgin group of companies). However, that

does not mean you and I are incapable of setting up and running our own successful business. In fact an **entrepreneur** is anyone who chooses to go it alone and make the most of a business opportunity for themselves, no matter how big or small.

If you have completed the Level 2 National Certificate in Business you will already have worked through a unit on how to run your own business enterprise. You will be aware that in order to make an idea successful it takes determination and a wide variety of skills.

Throughout the unit you are going to investigate and develop the skills necessary to become a successful entrepreneur. The unit is based on you planning an entrepreneurial activity. You will need to come up with an idea and then consider how you will develop this idea so that it could become a real business in the future.

### This unit will cover

- AO1 Provide examples of the skills, qualities and characteristics of successful entrepreneurs.
- AO2 Demonstrate the stages involved in the development of new ideas.
- AO3 Describe how to obtain finance for new ideas.

- AO4 Demonstrate the methods used by entrepreneurs to attract customers.

- AO5 Demonstrate how to value customers and build their loyalty.

- AO6 Evaluate your personal potential as an entrepreneur and recommend how these skills could be developed.

# AO1 Provide examples of the skills, qualities and characteristics of successful entrepreneurs

**GLOSSARY**

**Entrepreneur:**
Someone who starts up and runs their own business.

For more and more people, being an entrepreneur is becoming a popular career choice. In order to become a successful entrepreneur you need to have drive and ambition. Successful business people have to work long hours, be prepared to take **risks** and make quick decisions. From day one you will have to work incredibly hard, often foregoing friends and family in order to get your venture off the ground. You need to ask yourself whether you are prepared to make that kind of sacrifice and whether you can motivate yourself to put in the hours required.

Within the assessment objective we will be looking at the variety of different skills that entrepreneurs will need in order to become successful.

## Portfolio tip

*The assessment guidance for this unit is extremely detailed. You are recommended to read this section of the specifications prior to attempting the unit. Some of the main points are outlined here.*

*In order to achieve AO1 you will investigate the skills, qualities and characteristics of successful entrepreneurs. You will then build upon this knowledge. The first step is to decide what type of enterprise activity you consider could be successful. The idea does not have to be based on something which is practical for you. It is the entrepreneurial skills and qualities that you are developing and you will be assessed on these rather than the outcome of any entrepreneurial activity that you may undertake. The unit can be achieved through the demonstration of the planning stages of an enterprise. If you undertake an enterprise activity, it will not be assessed within the unit.*

*You must work independently but it is expected you will discuss your ideas with your tutor and other members of the group as well as outside agencies.*

## ACTIVITY

In groups of three or four, think of as many people as possible that you know who run their own business. Make a note of their name and occupation. Next, consider the skills that you think these people have. Is the list the same for each one? If not, why do you think they differ?

# Approach to risk taking

In order to be successful you need to be prepared to take risks. There are many different levels of risk and these depend on the individual's own personal circumstances. There are two sayings that apply:

'nothing ventured nothing gained' and 'look before you leap'.

Throughout this section we will be looking at different types of risk and investigating successful entrepreneurs and trying to evaluate the different risks they were prepared to take in order to become successful. Also, we must not forget those entrepreneurs who took risks that did not pay off – what happened to them?

Life today is full of risks – stringent health and safety laws ensure that during our everyday lives we are kept safe. If we do face risk we are given training and supplied with protective equipment and clothing to ensure that we are kept as safe as possible. All risks have to be fully assessed and then measures put into place to ensure that they do not cause anybody harm.

In real life there is very little training and certainly no equipment or clothing that will protect your money if you decide to invest in a 'high risk' business. However, if the risk pays off you could find yourself extremely wealthy but, on the other hand, should the business fail, you could lose not only your money but even your own personal possessions.

## ACTIVITY

As a group, consider the safety equipment and training you would be offered before you embarked on a whitewater rafting expedition.

## ACTIVITY

As a group, think about markets that you consider would be high risk to try and break into. These would be areas where there is a lot of competition and often high levels of investment would be needed to get them started.

## *High risk*

It is very difficult to define a high-risk venture. If a multi-millionaire invested £100,000 in a new business venture it could appear nothing more than fun. However, if someone employed in a job paying £34,000 a year, gave up their job and had to borrow sufficient funds in order to raise £100,000 to invest in a new business venture this could seem extremely high risk.

If we were to try and define high risk it would be based on the likelihood of success or failure of the venture. If the entrepreneur is trying to enter a highly competitive market which involves large amounts of capital investment this could be considered high risk. A venture could also be considered high risk if there has been insufficient investigations into the likelihood of success.

## ACTIVITY

As a group, try and think of a niche market that you could develop in your area. What product/service is needed but not provided by an existing business? Come up with as many ideas as possible. These can then be developed and used within the assignment for this unit.

## *Low risk*

A low-risk venture would be considered one where the potential entrepreneur has undertaken detailed market research, has found a niche in the market and the idea does not involve large amounts of capital in order for it be started.

### Real business

Initially, the inventor James Dyson tried to get major manufacturers interested in his design for vacuum cleaners. Unfortunately, for them, they all turned him down as they were not interested in new technology but their ability to continue selling bags worth an estimated $500 million.

In 1993, Dyson decided to take all the financial risks and manufacture his own invention. During the development years he was nearly bankrupted as he had no income. However, his belief in his invention paid off when the first Dyson Cyclone rolled off the production line from his factory in England. Within two years it was the UK's best selling vacuum cleaner.

Dyson's lack of income was not the only obstacle for the business. Very high patent fees and legal costs incurred defending his invention against patent infringement by a giant corporation also nearly bankrupted the venture.

## Positive attitude

In order to be a successful entrepreneur you have to have a **positive attitude**. You have to believe in what you are doing in order to persuade other people to 'buy into your idea/business'.

If you do not believe in your product or service nobody else is going to either. On the other hand, you must also be honest. There are stringent laws that stop businesses making false promises about the goods or services that they have on offer.

Think about all the teachers you have had throughout your time in education. Those that were enthusiastic and positive about their subject are likely to have impressed you and inspired you to learn and raised your interest/awareness of their subject. The same is true for entrepreneurs. If you are positive and enthusiastic you will soon have people believing in your product or service and then hopefully this can be converted into sales.

Let us consider market stall holders. They will often sell their wares to the general public by simply shouting prices out to a crowd. People stop and listen, process the information they hear and the enthusiasm of the stall holder is very quickly turned into sales. For example, 'There are only six sets left and you can have them, not for £20, not for £10, not even £7.50: but today's special offer of £5.' Very quickly all six sets are sold to people who, when they left home, had no idea they needed the item! The stall holder has convinced the crowd by their enthusiasm and positive attitude.

## Problem solving

No entrepreneur is going to find an easy path to fame and fortune. It is their ability to solve problems efficiently and effectively that enables them to become successful.

Problems have to be considered as challenges, clearly thought through and carefully solved. If an entrepreneur allows problems to 'get to them' they will soon burn out with all the worry and stress of the venture. If on the other hand they are seen as simply another day-to-day challenge, they will be resolved without causing the entrepreneur too much stress.

Being able to solve problems effectively involves the entrepreneur in being able to often think 'out of the box'. An entrepreneur will be able to think of solutions to problems that would not follow a normal pattern. It is this ability to resolve problems imaginatively that will enable an entrepreneur to stay ahead of the competition.

### Real business

Lena Bjorck arrived in the UK from Sweden with no qualifications. She obtained a job as a kitchen porter but quickly realised the country's service industry was not up to scratch. She saw the potential for improved services and now runs one of the country's most successful catering companies, Inn or Out Ltd.

Like Dyson, it was her own positive attitude, belief in her product/service and determination that made her successful.

### Real business

**Gary Lockton, co-founder of Deepend and Seriously Digital**
Gary Lockton developed a new media agency in 1994 with two college friends, which went from creative agency of the year to voluntary liquidation. 'One minute it was worth £25 million and nine months later it was gone'.

At the height of the new media explosion Deepgroup, the holding company for Deepend and its associated businesses, had annual revenue of £9 million and staff in eight cities. In one year it picked up 26 creative awards including Creative Agency of the Year and, in 1999, Gary was shortlisted as Young Entrepreneur of the Year in the Ernst & Young Awards.

The founders then found themselves ill-prepared to resolve the problems that the company was facing. They were not used to making tough decisions. With the benefit of hindsight Gary feels that they should have made difficult decisions earlier. 'We should have made some tougher decisions earlier before the crash. There were certain offices that were not right and we all knew probably in our hearts that they were not sustainable. But the trouble is that our culture completely clashed with it.' In September 2001, the founders placed the company into voluntary liquidation.

## ACTIVITY

Spend a few minutes considering how you solve problems on a day-to-day basis. How well do you cope with stress? How good are you at thinking up solutions to your problems?

# Flexibility and adaptability

*Flexibility is the key to success*

Entrepreneurs have to take opportunities as and when they arise and, in order to be able to do this, they will need to be flexible. Opportunities only present themselves once. An entrepreneur will rarely get a second chance to decide whether it is a good idea or not: another entrepreneur may see the same opportunity and take it. It is this ability to adapt to change that often makes the difference between those people who are able to develop fully their business ideas and those who 'plod along' just making sufficient money to live on.

Flexibility in the early years can involve working long hours in order to meet all the different needs of individual customers. This will help the business establish a regular customer base and good reputation.

Adaptability may involve listening to the changing needs and desires of your regular customers and being able to adapt your product/service to meet those changing needs. Forward-thinking businesses will be customer-driven. They will provide the goods and services their customers actually want, not those they think their customers want.

# Creativeness

Some entrepreneurs start their businesses by inventing and designing a completely new product/service. Others will re-invent or improve existing products/services. This would be considered the ultimate point of being creative. However, many successful entrepreneurs have been creative in the ways that they have presented their product/service. They may have decided that, although their product was currently on the market, it could be presented to customers in a different format.

Creativeness is the ability to see an opportunity to present or produce products or services to the general public in order to create a desire to purchase.

Creativeness can also be linked to the ability to market the business professionally. However, if an individual entrepreneur did not have these skills they could be purchased in through a marketing agency.

## CASE STUDY

### *The power of placards*

In 2003, Tony Goodman saw a golden opportunity as he was walking along the streets of Merseyside. It was not glamorous and involved a lot of flexibility. He set out to make money by walking along the streets holding placards to promote local shops and services.

He started up with £40 of his own money and one advertising banner. He now has a city centre office, a team of 80 banner holders and more than 50 clients including companies such as Pizza Hut, McDonalds and Unite Group plc.

**In what ways do you think Tony showed creativeness?**

# Intuitiveness

It is very difficult to describe or explain what **intuitiveness** actually is. However, some people do appear to be able to read a market and make the right business decisions simply based on their own 'feelings'.

It is not recommended that intuition is the only thing you need to become successful. Yours may not be very accurate. It is wise to back up any intuition with sound research in order to prove that your original idea is likely to be successful. People who have been in business for many years will have skills and experience that will enable them to trust their intuition to a much higher degree. Just start out by looking for what you think is a likely opportunity and make sure that you fully research the advantages and disadvantages of your idea.

## Real business

Tim Slade and Jules Leaver saw a gap in the market for 'been there done that' T-shirts to sell to skiing holiday makers. Their high street chain Fat Face now turns over £25 million.

Dee Edwards used her background in business-to-business marketing and Internet business strategy to start up her own business, Habbo Ltd. She saw a gap in the market to develop a graphical chat and gaming environment for teenagers. Her business saw a turnover of £1 million from the first year of trading.

# Drive to succeed

Becoming a successful entrepreneur is not going to happen overnight. It can take years of hard work and dedication. There will be highs and lows, problems and solutions. However, it is the entrepreneur that keeps on going, continues to think of new ideas, takes the risks and puts in the long hours who will ultimately reap the benefits. Unfortunately, there are not many of us who will become as successful as Richard Branson with his Virgin brand or Anita Roddick through her Body Shop. Do not become disheartened. There are many entrepreneurs out there who run relatively small businesses, enjoy what they do and earn sufficient to keep themselves and their families.

## Portfolio tip

*AO1 is based on theoretical coverage of the skills, qualities and characteristics demonstrated by successful entrepreneurs. In order to achieve the higher grades you will need to investigate some very successful entrepreneurs in order to use examples to clearly illustrate your theoretical coverage. You would also be well advised to look into some less successful entrepreneurs. The unit specification has outlined two lists but do not let these lists restrict your investigations.*

*Successful entrepreneurs:*

- *Richard Branson*
- *Anita Roddick*
- *Bill Gates*
- *Ray Kroc*
- *Walt Disney*

*Less successful entrepreneurs/products:*

- *DeLorean cars*
- *Laker Airways*
- *Sinclair C5*

## Real business

- Self-employment in the UK is increasing. In the year ended 31st December 2003, Barclays Bank saw a 20 per cent rise in new businesses started over the previous year.
- Young people are increasingly attracted to the idea of running their own enterprise. The number of young people who would like to run their own business has risen from 35 per cent in 2000 to 45 per cent in 2004.
- Young entrepreneurs are increasingly professional in their approach to their business and its success. More 18-24-year-old entrepreneurs embarking on an enterprise prepare business plans than start-ups in general. Contrary to the stereotypes, their motivation in starting a business is mainly the challenge of running their own venture and bringing their ideas to fruition rather than financial gain.
- Successful young entrepreneurs seem to exhibit an almost 'uncommon sense' of what will make an effective enterprise and they have a propensity to explore niches within a business sector that many other would have ignored or disregarded.

Source: *The Young Entrepreneurs Revisited*, a report by Gerard Darby

## CASE STUDY
*T-Hair*

-------------------------------------------------------------------------------

T-Hair, a ladies' hair salon, was started by Tanya in a small rural village about ten years ago. The village already had one small hair salon run by an elderly lady whose **target audience** was the older generation. Most local residents travelled to nearby towns to have their hair done.

Tanya's first premises were in a top floor shop above a small shopping mall. The salon could not be seen from the village square and therefore passing trade was unlikely.

Tanya's ambition was to bring a high-class hair salon to a relatively rural area where the rent of premises was considerably cheaper than in the nearby towns. She had recently left a top London salon and some of her clients were prepared to travel to remain customers. Tanya was also hoping to attract customers from the neighbouring towns. Competition was fierce but Tanya was confident that, as long as she only employed highly skilled stylists, she could make this venture a success.

In order to keep her initial costs down she rented 'a chair' to each stylist. This meant they paid her a percentage of their takings. Tanya was not tied to set salaries in the early years which helped to improve her cash flow.

After about four years she faced two challenges. A major competitor, who ran a chain of salons, moved into the village. The local bank shut down and there was the opportunity to move her salon into much bigger premises. Tanya did not hesitate: the new premises would give her a prominent position within the village and the client base had expanded sufficiently to warrant this move.

Tanya took over the lease and undertook a major refurbishment plan. The new salon was beautiful. Her choice of décor and layout really worked. The finishing touch was an extremely large bunch of fresh flowers which dominated the reception area.

Her staff were all head hunted from other top salons. Stylists had to be extremely well qualified, often having been trained and worked in London. She personally undertook customer service training for all her staff.

Tanya realised the people who could afford some of the more expensive treatments and cuts were professionals. Professional people were often unable to fit their own personal diaries into the normal opening times of a salon. Tanya took the unprecedented step to rota her staff to open the salon early in the morning and at least three late nights.

All of this worked. T-hair is an extremely successful business. Clients come from far and wide. T-hair had managed to gain and retain the major share of the hairdressing market within the local area. The venture has been so successful that Tanya is just about to open another salon.

1 Explain the risks you think Tanya took?
2 Describe how Tanya tried to reduce the risks she was taking?
3 How do you think Tanya displayed positive thinking in order to make the business the success it is today?
4 What type of problems do you think Tanya had to resolve during her ten years?
5 In what ways did Tanya demonstrate the ability to be flexible and adaptable?
6 In what ways was Tanya creative?
7 Do you think intuition played any part in Tanya's decision-making process?
8 Describe how you think Tanya showed 'drive to succeed'.

# AO2 Demonstrate the stages involved in the development of new ideas

AO2-AO6 are based on the planning of an entrepreneurial activity.

In order to achieve these assessment objectives you are required to work individually. You will need to identify a range of possible enterprise activities, reduce these down to just one idea and describe the stages involved in the development of this idea, making reference to the knowledge, understanding and skills as outlined in the course specifications.

When tackling a task like this it is often best to base your ideas on subject areas that you are familiar with. This could be your own personal hobbies and interests or businesses that you have already been involved with. Although the course specification clearly states that the business plan does not have to be based on a business idea which is practical for you, it is advisable to keep your ideas relatively simple. This will enable you to produce a realistic business plan for your venture in order to achieve AO3.

# Stages of development

No great business venture is ever just plucked out of the air. It will have been through many different stages of planning and development. At times an entrepreneur may feel progress is slow but, on other occasions, things may happen very quickly. A lot of good ideas come about through personal experience and they are then developed accordingly. The following section outlines the different stages that you will need to go through in order to achieve the assessment objective.

In order to clearly explain each stage of development of a business the example of Squeaky Clean Cars offering **franchises** to potential buyers will be outlined here.

## Squeaky Clean Cars – the business so far

If you have used the Level 2 National Business textbook you will already have met Megan and Richard as they started up their new business venture. They decided that they had found a niche market and offered a mobile car valeting service. Before they started trading they would have had to go through all of the different stages of development.

Their business has now become so successful they have decided to offer **franchises**. Other people will be able to trade under their name 'Squeaky Clean Cars'. Megan and Richard will help them with the suppliers, establish a marketing campaign and also provide some of the equipment required to start up. A new sign-written van will be included as part of the deal. The franchisee has to pay £10,500 for the licence to trade and then a percentage of their profits.

You may think this might be a good start as an entrepreneur as it has limited risk due to the fact that it is an established business throughout the country.

## Gathering information as a normal part of life (importance of 'watch, look and listen' at all times)

We are all probably unaware of all the information that we absorb without consideration throughout our daily lives. We take in sights, sounds and information and are then able to convert this into skills and knowledge we use on a daily basis. Think of how young children learn to walk and talk. It is often just through watching and listening to other people and then trying to mimic. After a lot of effort and often many setbacks children become independent, able to walk and talk.

It is similar for people who want to start up a new business venture. They will learn by investigating similar businesses.

## Squeaky Clean Cars – the new franchise

How could you gather information that would help you decide whether or not to invest in this venture?

- The first step would be to visit Megan and Richard to see how they run their business. Who does what? In what order to do they clean cars? Who is responsible for all the paper work? How much support will you receive? You could ask to join them for a day to actually see what goes on first hand.

- The second step would be to try and talk to other franchisees to see what their experiences have been like working with Megan and Richard. Do they receive the support promised? Have the customers actually materialised from the original customer list offered at the start of the franchise?

- The third step would be to go and look at alternative car washes, what services do garages and supermarkets offer? Are there any hand car washes in your area? If so, what services do they offer? How do they run their business?

- This first stage of gathering information should give you the clues on how to run the business. What would make it successful? How could you improve on the service offered by other people?

- It is also worth watching customer behaviour. Do they appear happy with the service being offered? Is there anything that could be improved upon in order to make things better?

All of this is vital information on which you can base your decision about whether the venture is actually for you.

## ACTIVITY

Think up questions that you would ask Megan and Richard if you were considering entering into a franchise agreement with them.

If you were to visit an existing franchisee, consider what you would want to see in order to help you make your decision.

## Researching old, new and niche markets

It is vital that before starting any new enterprise that sufficient **market research** is undertaken to assess the potential demand for the service/ product being offered (market research is covered in more detail in AO4).

Research must also establish exactly what customers want from the potential product/service. In today's highly competitive world the most successful businesses supply what the customer demands not what the business thinks the customer wants. Businesses have had to become more 'customer focused' in order to gain and retain their market share.

Research into old markets would involve looking back at what is currently happening within that particular market. For example, how many people still go caravanning? Research into a new market could be looking at how caravanning could be modernised in order to attract more families, or the older generation. Research into a niche market would be trying to find a gap in the market that has not yet been filled. This could be a camp site dedicated to families that include disabled members.

## Squeaky Clean Cars - the new franchise

What research would you need to undertake prior to embarking on this venture?

- To research into old markets you could investigate how much people currently spend on activities such as valeting their car. What kind of services would garages be interested in using? Have Megan and Richard been able to break into any chains of garages and if so how could this help you? You will also need to find out where your potential customers currently go to have their car washed/valeted? Do they do it themselves?

- In order to research new markets you would have to think of who to and where you could pitch this new franchise. Who would be your customers, how are you going to attract them and how much are they prepared to pay? In order to research into a niche market you will first of all have to think up a service that Megan and Richard do not currently offer. What else could car owners require? Having come up with an idea you would then need to undertake research to find out if other people think it is a service they require.

## ACTIVITY

If you were to buy the franchise licence from Megan and Richard, consider the following points:
- Who would be your customers?
- What services do you think people would require?
- What new products/services could you offer within this business proposal?
- Can you come up with a niche market?

# *Investigating competition using various means*

*Potential competition for Squeaky Clean Cars*

## Mystery shopping

This involves someone acting as a normal shopper in order to assess the level of customer service offered by the selected business. This is a very popular method of assessing customer service used by retail outlets. The purpose of a **mystery shopper** is to look for ways to improve the service received by customers. Being able to provide excellent customer service can often be one of the keys to a successful enterprise. Employees who have been identified as giving excellent customer service to a mystery shopper may receive rewards or bonuses. This should encourage employees to make sure that they offer excellent customer service throughout their whole working day.

## Buying and returning goods

In order to run a successful business you will need to know how to exceed the expectations of customers and match or improve on the customer service that is being offered by your rivals. An excellent way to gather this information is to become a customer of one of your potential rivals. This will give you insight into the services they offer and you may even get a chance to chat with some of their existing customers to find out what they think of the organisations.

Having become a customer you might then decide to find out how they deal with the return of their products. This again will give you a true insight of how the organisation works. Does it actually provide the level of services that it says it does? If not what is lacking? How well trained are their staff? All this information can be used to your advantage when considering the systems you will need in place when starting up your own venture.

## Stealth but nothing illegal

Stealth could involve getting friendly with someone who works or runs a similar business to the one you are considering setting up. You may then be able to obtain detailed information about how the business is run and any problems they have experienced. You may also choose to work within a similar business so that you can learn the ropes and find out how things are done. This could give you an excellent insight into the selected industry but it might also help you decide if this is really what you want to do. However, you must not do anything illegal in order to gain information on how another business operates.

## Squeaky Clean Cars - the new franchise

How would you use some of these tactics to find out more about Squeaky Clean Cars?

- You could visit Megan and Richard's business as a customer, or if they already know you, send a friend. This will give you first-hand experience of the service that they actually offer rather than what they state they offer. This might be two different things. You could also visit one of the established franchises to see if they offer the same levels of customer service.

- You could then try and complain about the service received at both establishments. Their response could be very enlightening. If you feel that their customer service was not as high as previously stated you may be well advised not to purchase the franchise as you do not want to be associated with a business that may start to lose its reputation.

- The other option might be to try and get a job within the business so that you can see first hand how the operation works. This would also give you excellent experience on how to run the business.

## ACTIVITY

Think of a product or service that you can obtain from different businesses. Next make a note of all the differences between the two businesses. Which one do you think offers the best deal for its customers? Justify your answer.

You could compare the different types of services offered at your local leisure centre against a private gym or you could compare two fast-food restaurants.

## Recognising opportunities

Being able to quickly recognise an opportunity and be sufficiently organised to take it, often makes the difference between a successful entrepreneur whose enterprise will grow against another who will only achieve mediocre success. Megan and Richard recognised an opportunity when they started up Squeaky Clean Cars. They have undertaken research and found that this opportunity exists within many different locations of the country. However, they lack the funds to start up all over the country, so have seen another opportunity – to sell franchises.

Being able to recognise an opportunity is a skill. Some people state that they just had a gut feeling, while others work on instinct. People who are very successful are often only too happy to boast that all they worked on was a 'gut feeling'. Those that have failed very rarely boast about their powers of instinct. After all it has just let them down – or was it just bad luck? It is recommended that until you have sufficient experience in the business environment, any decisions that you make are based on facts and detailed research. You are less likely to make a big mistake, which will usually end up costing you a lot of money, stress and ultimately heart ache.

## Squeaky Clean Cars – the new franchise

Having undertaken all of your research you will have to decide whether you feel that purchasing this new franchise is the correct opportunity for you.

- If no, you will need to look into other ideas until you find one that suits you.
- If yes, list the factors that have drawn you to the franchise.

## Addressing negativism

It is often very sensible to discuss any ideas that you have with a variety of other people and to listen carefully to their responses. They may come up with ideas that you have not thought off. They may notice problems you have missed through your natural enthusiasm.

However, do not be put off by other people's negative attitude: they may fail to see the possibilities that you do. They may also not have had the same experiences as yourself and therefore will not have the skills necessary to take the risk and give it a go. Do not forget there are some people who will never take a risk and to them the thought of being an entrepreneur would be extremely stressful. All they want is to have a secure job that pays them sufficient to allow them to do the things they choose to. That is fine. Not everybody has the skills necessary to take a risk, read the market and make a success of an enterprise and, after all, you may need employees one day!

### Portfolio tip

*In order to achieve this assessment objective think of at least two possible enterprises. Start your research by looking at the potential for both. Then select the one that you feel would be most successful.*

*You will then need to demonstrate that you have undertaken all the different stages involved in the development as outlined above. A lot of these areas overlap. Your primary research could involve you being a mystery shopper as well as conducting questionnaires, running focus groups etc. You will also need to go and investigate potential competition.*

*At the end of your research you should be able to clearly explain what your enterprise will be and justify the reasons for your choice, making reference to all the stages of development just undertaken.*

# AO3  Describe how to obtain finance for new ideas

The major stumbling block for a lot of potential entrepreneurs is being able to raise sufficient finance in order to get their enterprise started. Finance is not only needed when starting up an enterprise but also in the early stages in order to keep the business afloat. It may be several months before any income is received from customers.

There are various different ways that an entrepreneur can raise finance and some are explained below.

## Own capital

The cheapest and easiest ways to raise finance in order to start up a new enterprise is by the entrepreneur investing their own money. This is known as 'own capital'.

Own capital does not always relate to money. An entrepreneur may have brought a computer, car and other pieces of equipment that he or she already owned into the business. This would also be valued alongside the money invested in the business in order to calculate the capital the owner has contributed to the business. Investing your own money also has what is known as opportunity cost.

If an entrepreneur invests their own money into the business enterprise they are taking all the financial risk. If the venture goes wrong they could lose all their investment. If the business enterprise is a sole trader or partnership the entrepreneur will be responsible for meeting the business's debts from their own personal wealth. However, if the business has limited liability the entrepreneur will only lose the amount of capital they originally invested. Their own personal wealth is protected. For further clarification see Unit 1.

## Family and friends

If you have insufficient funds to start up your own business you may wish to try and persuade your family and friends to invest in your venture. While your own immediate family might lend you money with no conditions, it is unlikely that more distant relatives and friends will be so generous.

Your investors might well want a set rate of interest and a final repayment date. It is quite common for friends and family to lend money at a lower rate of interest than a bank or other financial institution. If the business struggles within the first few months of trading these repayments may be difficult to meet. Friends and family might be a little more sympathetic if you cannot make one month's payment and maybe cannot afford the whole amount another month. Another alternative is that your investors might want to be part of the enterprise. This could act to your benefit, having someone to consult and share the risks with, but it may also hinder the progress of the enterprise if there is disagreement over major decisions.

## Banks and other investors

Banks are able to offer entrepreneurs three main ways of raising money:

- business mortgage
- bank loan
- bank overdraft.

**ACTIVITY**

In a group, discuss how much money you could each possibly raise if you wanted to try and fund your own small enterprise in the immediate future. How would this limit the type of enterprise you could start up?

### *Business mortgage*

A business mortgage enables an enterprise to purchase land and buildings. This is a long-term loan, often 25 years, from a bank or financial institution which is secured on the assets of the business.

Securing a loan against **fixed assets** means that if the business is unable to meet its loan repayments the fixed asset can be sold and the loan paid off. Mortgages carry an interest charge which must be considered when a business decides how much it can justifiably borrow.

*High street banks offer a range of loans for businesses*

### *Bank loan*

This can be a short- or long-term loan that will also be secured on the fixed assets of the business. The bank agrees to lend the enterprise a set amount of money over an agreed time period, with regular repayments being made by the borrower. The agreement can include a fixed or variable rate of interest. A fixed interest rate is where the interest charged over the life of the loan will not change. A variable interest rate is where the rate of interest charged will go up or down according to the current interest rates being set by the Bank of England. This is known as the **bank base rate**. Repayments are based on a business paying back the original amount borrowed plus the interest to be charged over the term of the loan. Loans can often be for smaller amounts of money than a mortgage and paid back over a shorter time scale. The size of the repayments must be carefully considered when deciding how much the enterprise can afford to borrow.

**GLOSSARY**

**Fixed assets:**
Items that have a life expectancy of more than one year and will be used in order to help the business run. They include buildings, cars, machinery.

### *Bank overdraft*

This is an arrangement with the bank whereby a business can spend more money than it has in its bank account. It allows the business to borrow

## GLOSSARY

**plc:**
Abbreviation for public limited company.

## GLOSSARY

**Debentures:**
Loans that are offered for sale. They will have a set rate of interest and a final repayment date.

## ACTIVITY

Using the Internet or by visiting your local high street banks, find out how much it costs to borrow money in order to start up or expand a business venture.

What different types of products/services do the high street banks offer businesses?

small amounts of money over a much shorter time scale. The total amount that the business can overspend by is agreed with the bank and this is known as the business's overdraft limit. Should the business go over this limit it will be charged a penalty and the interest rate will be higher. This can be a convenient way to access short-term funds but does tend to carry high interest rates, making it an expensive option.

## Other investors

There are now a great range of different financial institutions that will lend money to businesses. They will all require interest to be paid back on the original amount borrowed. The higher the risk the greater will be the interest charged against the loan. Large **plcs** are able to raise large amounts of capital by selling **debentures**. Another way that people can start their own business is by seeking help from the Prince's Youth Trust.

### Did you know?

*The Prince's Youth Trust was founded in 1976 by the Prince of Wales and offers practical solutions to help young people to get their lives working. The Trust has helped many young people get started when banks and other financial institutions have considered the proposed venture too high a risk. The Trust's aim is to help people aged 18-30 who are currently unemployed or employed in part-time or low-paid jobs and who have a good idea for an enterprise. The Trust offers a start-up support which includes:*

- *a low interest loan of up to £4,000 for a sole trader and £5,000 for a partnership*
- *a grant of up to £1,500 in special circumstances*
- *a test marketing grant of up to £250*
- *ongoing business support and specialist advice such as a free legal helpline*
- *ongoing advice from a volunteer business mentor.*

## Venture capital

It can be very difficult to persuade banks and other financial institutions that your ideas are actually very good and do have the potential to earn large sums of money in the future. Banks will have to weigh up the risks of investing in your venture. They will often require assets on which the loan could be secured. This means that if your venture fails they will be able to sell your assets and retrieve their money,

**Venture capitalists** are people who are prepared to take greater risks. They will invest in enterprises that have been turned down by other financial institutions. However, in return, they often charge higher rates of interest and will also request shares in the business. The number of shares the venture capitalist requests will be dependent on the size of the loan.

This type of finance is therefore only suitable for limited companies that are able to sell shares. Venture capitalists are attracted to rapid growth and are unlikely to be suitable for businesses that require an investment of less than £100,000, or offer an annual return of less than 25 per cent on the investment.

The disadvantage of this type of investment is the high rate of returns and the requirement to give up a stake in some of your own business.

## Did you know?

**Business Angels**
*Business Angels are wealthy entrepreneurs who provide capital in return for being part of a growing organisation. If an entrepreneur requires funds of between £10,000 to £250,000 this could be one method of raising the capital. One of the disadvantages is the entrepreneur has to develop a close working relationship with their Business Angel who will expect a hands-on involvement with the venture. Business Angels can determine when and how they receive their financial rewards from the business and this may take the form of a salary.*

*One advantage is that most angels are experienced business people and can be a useful addition to the business team.*

## Share capital

If you were to start your new enterprise up as a private limited company (Ltd) you would do so by offering shares to selected people, for example family, friends or business acquaintances. These potential shareholders would buy a percentage of the shares at an agreed price. The value of all the shares issued by the business is called the **share capital**. The money raised would enable the business to start trading. The people who purchase the shares become shareholders and will have voting rights within the business. Shareholders who invest in your business idea will be able to make decisions concerning the future of the business. The number of shares they hold will determine how much power they have in the business. If the business makes a profit its shareholders will be entitled to **dividends**. This again will be determined by the number of shares that the shareholder holds.

In small limited companies the shareholders are often the people that manage the day-to day-running of the business. However, not all shareholders have to be involved with the daily activities of the business.

If in the future a business wishes to raise further finance in order to expand or invest in more modern machinery it could issue some further shares. However, the new shares can only be sold to people with the full agreement of the current shareholders.

## Did you know?

*Buying shares in a limited liability company has the advantage that should the venture experience financial problems the shareholder will only lose their original investment and will not be liable for the debts of the business.*

### GLOSSARY

**Dividends:**
The percentage of profit that shareholders may receive.

## ACTIVITY

Go back over Unit 1 and remind yourself about the advantages and disadvantages of becoming a plc.

If you have begun to consider what type of enterprise you would like to start up, would this be the suitable form of ownership?

# Government grants

A **grant** is a sum of money that has been given to an individual or business for a specific project or purpose. A grant will only cover part of the total costs involved and could be between 15 per cent and 75 per cent. The remainder of the money will have to be provided by the individual or business.

There are some grants available for businesses but their criteria are very specific and conditions vary. Examples could include people working in rural areas, businesses run by people under 25, or firms trading in a particular type of business. To secure the correct information on the current grants available entrepreneurs are advised to contact either their local authority or business adviser. Alternatively, they can contact Business Link and pay a fee to analyse grants that are available in their area.

Certain areas of the UK are set up as Enterprise Areas. A business located in or relocating to an Enterprise Area may benefit from one of several forms of Government assistance, including stamp duty exemptions, help from Community Development Finance Institutions, and neighbourhood renewal projects.

The Department of Trade and Industry recommends the Prince's Trust and Shell Livewire as possible sources of finance, support and help for young people between the ages of 18 and 30 wanting to start up their own business. There is more information on both these organisations at the end of this unit, on page 290.

## *Access to knowledge*

Some businesses link up with academic organisations in order to co-run a project of mutual interest.

## Real business

The Phoenix Fund Projects was set up by the Government in 1999 and encourages enterprise in disadvantaged communities and in groups under-represented in terms of business ownership. £44 million was allocated to the Phoenix Review Fund for the period April 2006–March 2008. The Phoenix Fund is distributed to local business support agencies, from where funding is given to local businesses. The Fund includes:

- a development fund to promote new ways of supporting business
- a network of volunteer mentors for start-up businesses
- financial support through Community Development Finance Institutions
- a Community Development Venture fund giving venture capital grants for small businesses
- special projects for city and rural areas.

## *Training*

The Learning Skills Council provides grants for training and skills development.

## *The New Deal*

This is a government strategy to get people back to work.

## ACTIVITY

You should now have an idea about what type of business you would like to start up. Do you think this would attract a grant from the Government? Justify your answer.

# Advantages and disadvantages of different sources of finance

- If you borrow money from anybody you have to make regular repayments and the loan will usually attract interest. You will ultimately have to pay back more than you borrowed.

- If you borrow from a bank or other financial institution you do not lose any control over your business and will not be required to share any profits. If you receive help from a venture capitalist you are likely to have to pay interest and lose some control of your business.

- If you issue shares you will not have the liability of a loan outstanding but you will dilute your control over the business and you will have to share any profits that you may make in the future.

*The keys to the new franchise*

## Real business

The New Entrepreneur Scholarship Scheme (NES) provides new entrepreneurs in disadvantaged areas with business support, training and start-up funding.

The entrepreneur will start off by receiving a need assessment and personal development plan. They will then get 90 hours of business support which will culminate with the creation of their business plan. When it has been decided the time is right to start the venture there is £3,500 available to help with the initial costs of the business.

## ACTIVITY

Explain how you would raise the finance necessary to invest in Megan and Richard's Squeaky Clean Cars. The cost of the franchise is £10,500.

# Obtaining finance

Any enterprise that requires finance is going to have to persuade the person or organisation with the funds that they will be able to repay this money back in the future. In order to do this you will need to produce a business plan which clearly illustrates what your business is about.

## Devising a potential business plan

If you are about to start an enterprise, your business plan must be the road map of what you intend to do and how you will go about each stage. You will need a business plan to present to a variety of people which will include potential investors, shareholders and your bank.

The purpose of the business plan is to help people mentioned above understand your personal vision and goals for the business. You will need to state how you will spend the money invested in the business and how this will benefit either the lenders of the finance or the shareholders.

It is the first document that a new start-up business will have to complete. It must be professional, accurate and detailed in order to catch the interest of potential investors or financiers. Your potential investors or financiers are going to examine the business plan very carefully in order to establish the level of risk. They have to consider: Is this enterprise worth investing my money in? What is the likelihood that I will receive a return on the investment?

## Presenting a potential business plan to potential financiers

There is no set format for a business plan. The majority of the major banks will offer help to new business start-ups. Within their packs or on CD-ROMs will be blank documents that the new entrepreneur can use in order to present their business plan.

Most business plans will include the following information.

### An introduction

This will be a brief summary of what the business hopes to do, what are its aims and objectives for the future. This should not be too long but sufficient to catch the attention of potential investors and financiers.

### Organisation chart

If this is a new business start-up which involves a number of different people it is good practice to show this within the plan. A brief outline should be given of each person's individual responsibilities.

### Competitors

There should be a description of your competitors and how your product/ service will compete against them.

## Customers

Who are your customers? Why are they going to buy your product/service?

## Marketing plan

You must state how you are going to market your product/service to your potential customers, clearly outlining any assumptions that you have made.

## Credit control

How are you going to manage credit control, monitor debtors and creditors? How will you manage stock control and other expenditure? What procedures will you put into place to ensure that financial difficulties are avoided?

If you are seeking finance you must also include the following financial information.

## Loan repayments

How will the loan be repaid? When will potential investors receive their money back?

## Cash flow forecast

This will indicate the amount of money that the business expects to have flowing in and out. It should clearly show the amount of funding needed and state any contingency plans that are in place should the business hit financial problems.

## Forecast financial accounts

The business plan will also include a forecast profit and loss statement and forecast balance sheet. These two documents will indicate the expected profit and also the assets held within the enterprise.

## *Winning support from potential financiers*

If all of your documents are well presented, based on accurate and well-researched information, you will be half way to convincing a potential investor that your enterprise is a worthwhile investment.

In order to gain the support of potential financiers it is very important to be honest and realistic in your predictions concerning revenue and expenditure. A third party will often have a much clearer idea of what the potential hazards are and can advise you accordingly.

It can feel that people are being very negative and narrow minded about your excellent idea. However, they are being realistic. Bearing these facts in mind, you will need to ensure that all your facts and figures are as accurate as possible in order to demonstrate that you do have one of the most important skills of the entrepreneur – organisation and the ability to use financial information accurately.

## ACTIVITY

Using the headings above make some brief notes outlining the type of information that you will put in the business plan for your new product/service. These notes will help you achieve the assessment objective.

## Portfolio tip

*Within Unit 4 you learnt about profit and loss accounts, what they are, why they are produced and how to interpret them. You also learnt why a cash flow forecast is produced and how to complete one. You will need all of this information in order to help you complete this assessment objective.*

# AO4 Demonstrate the methods used by entrepreneurs to attract customers

The specification states that in order to achieve this assessment objective you are required to conduct research and explain, using examples, the methods used by entrepreneurs to attract customers.

## Market research

It is vital that, before entering into any new business venture, sufficient market research is undertaken to assess the potential demand for the service/product being offered. Market research is classified into two sections – primary and secondary.

### *Primary market research*

How many times have you been stopped in the street and asked if you would participate in a survey? Do you answer their questions or keep on walking? Another popular method of interviewing people is to use the telephone. Banks, building societies and even large supermarkets call their customers to find out what they think of the business's services. If you have experienced this do you find it annoying? Do you agree to participate in such interviews?

Why do you think businesses conduct surveys?

The main reason is so that they can continually react to changing tastes and fashions and hopefully retain and expand their customer base.

There are many different ways that a business can gather information. It could question people, hold focus groups, ask the general public to try out its products or services and feedback their comments, or it could simply observe customer behaviour.

> ### GLOSSARY
>
> **Market research** is classified into two sections – primary and secondary.
>
> **Primary market research** is where the business undertakes its own research. It can do this by questioning people, holding focus groups, trial testing products or services in order to gain feedback or simply through observation.
>
> **Secondary market research** involves using data that has been collected either by another organisation or within the business for another reason.

*Market research can provide answers to questions*

Primary research is very time-consuming and can often be expensive. Another major problem can be the accuracy of the results. In order to achieve results that represent the whole of the country a large number of people need to be included in the **population**. Before undertaking market research the enterprise must first decide who its potential customers are. Will the product/service just be suitable for young people, families, male or females?

## Sampling

**Sampling** is the term used to describe how a business chooses who to question about its product or service. There are two sampling methods:

- random sampling and
- non-probability sampling.

Random sampling can be further broken down into simple, systematic or stratified.

| TYPE | DESCRIPTION | EXAMPLE |
|------|-------------|---------|
| Simple random sampling | Every member of the population has the same chance of being chosen for the survey. | This method is used when the business considers that the product could be used by any member of the population, for example toothpaste. |
| Systematic sampling | The business will question every 'nth' person. | This method is used when the product is targeted at a particular section of society.<br><br>If your school/college wanted to find out students' opinions of the canteen they could get an alphabetical list of all the students in the school/college and question every 20th person in the school/college. |
| Stratified random sampling | The business will break the population down into groups, e.g. sex, age, occupation. Each one of these groups is then randomly sampled. | This method is used when the product is aimed at the whole population and the business wants to ensure it manages to talk to everyone within each selected group.<br><br>For example, a business wants to find out people's opinions on a new flavour crisp. They have decided to divide the population according to age. They will then randomly sample each selected age group. |

**Table 12.1** *Different methods of random sampling*

**GLOSSARY**

**Population:**
This is the total number of people who are involved in the research.

**ACTIVITY**

This activity is based on Megan and Richard's Squeaky Clean Cars. You are interested in buying one of their franchises. Before you feel you can commit yourself to this venture you have decided to conduct some serious market research.

The first question you need to consider is - who are your potential customers? Consider the area you live in and write down exactly who you could target with your questionnaire. Justify your answers. How big is your potential population?

## ACTIVITY

Using Table 12.1 suggest and justify the type of sampling method you are going to use to discover the type of customers that might use Squeaky Clean Cars.

Non-probability sampling involves picking the sample randomly and there is no way of knowing who will be included. Anybody could be questioned simply because they were available at the time. This method of research is often cheaper. Non-probability sampling can also be broken down further.

| TYPE | DESCRIPTION | EXAMPLE |
|---|---|---|
| Quota sampling | The interviewer will select who they want to interview by age, gender or occupation. | This method is used when the business has already decided who their product/service will be aimed at.<br><br>If a business were launching a new luxury chocolate bar they may have decided to aim it at women. Interviewers would therefore only speak to females. |
| Purpose sampling | This involves the business deliberately biasing a sample depending on the market being investigated. | The business only wants to find out the opinions of those people who already use the product/service or a similar product/service.<br><br>For example, a lot of running magazines get their readers to test clothes or running shoes. The results are biased because the product has only been used by the people who already use a similar product. |
| Cluster sampling | This involves selecting a random sample from a selected area. | A business may decide that it can only afford to trial its new product or service in a certain area of the country in order to reduce costs.<br><br>For example, a business is trying to launch a new type of soap. They have decided to trial it in Manchester due to high costs of market research. The business hopes that the results gained will be representative of the whole country. |
| Convenience sampling | This is probably the cheapest form of sampling. It involves talking to those people who were available at the time of the survey.<br><br>To improve the results of convenience sampling judgement sampling can be used. This involves the interviewer selecting respondents who are judged to be the potential purchasers of the product/service. | This method of sampling is likely to be less reliable than other sampling methods as it may only question a biased sample.<br><br>For example, if you questioned people outside the local leisure centre at 2pm on a Monday afternoon in June you are likely to only speak to mothers or fathers with young children, shift workers or people who are retired or unemployed. |

Table 12.2 *Different methods of non-probability sampling*

# Questionnaires

Before a business starts designing a questionnaire it must first consider what it hopes to find out. Does it want to know:

- who its customers are going to be?
- how much they will pay for the product/service?
- how often will they purchase the product/service?

In order to collect the correct information the questions need to be carefully planned and worded. Many a poor response has been received by interviewers because the quality of the questions was insufficient to gain the information required by the company conducting the research.

Questions can either be 'closed' or 'open'. Closed questions will generally produce quantifiable responses. A business is then able to turn their responses into statistical data. For example, if a business wanted to know how many people swim at the local leisure centre, they could simply ask 'Have you been swimming within the last two weeks?' The business would then be able to calculate what percentage of their survey had actually swum within the last two weeks.

Open questions give a business much more information and would include opinions. For example, within the leisure centre questionnaire the next question could be 'What do you think of the swimming pool?' This would encourage the respondents to pass on their own ideas and these would be more difficult to turn into statistical data. For example, six people thought the pool was often too cold. The rest of the sample did not make a comment.

## *Secondary market research*

This could include using past sales figures in order to predict the potential sales of a new product. Alternatively, the business could use statistics collected by the Government. Government statistics are freely available from the reference section of public libraries or via the Internet.

Other forms of secondary research include:

- trade journals
- periodicals
- professional associations
- national organisations
- organisations which specialise in collecting data, for example Mintel and Key Note.

## ACTIVITY

In order to find out how many people might use the services of Squeaky Clean Cars you need to design a questionnaire.

Try out your questionnaire on a few of your friends and family. Make any adjustments necessary to improve the quality of your answers.

## ACTIVITY

In order to fully establish a demand for Squeaky Clean Cars in your area you are going to look up the following statistics.

- How many people live in your local area?
- How many people are employed in your area?
- What is the average wage per month?
- How many people on average own cars?
- How much money is spent on cleaning cars or similar activities?
- When you have obtained all the above information explain how the statistics could be used to help you decide whether or not to invest in Squeaky Clean Cars.

# Advertising

Advertising is how a business makes itself known to the general public or to other businesses. It can involve many different methods from elaborate television advertisements to cards in shop windows. The purpose is always the same: to get the enterprise known. All businesses should advertise regardless of their size. The first considerations should be:

- Would it help to advertise locally?

- Would it help to advertise nationally and internationally in the trade and technical press?

- Would it help to advertise in a national or international directory?

- Could I use a website to advertise my product/service?

Advertising is an important part of the promotion element of the **marketing mix,** along with direct marketing, PR (**public relations**), exhibitions or a website. The aim of each of these is to promote your enterprise and communicate information to your target audience. Remember the summer holidays are often a slow time for businesses.

The best time to advertise to your target audience is when they are most likely to buy your product or service. If you are intending to sell to other businesses it is worth trying to work out when they will have the budget to spend.

Why advertise? Often a business will run an advertising campaign in order to boost their sales. It may also coincide with the launch of a new product or service.

## GLOSSARY

**Marketing mix:**
This consists of four main elements: product, price, place and promotion.

## CASE STUDY

### *Think Tyres – Think Black Circle*

Black Circle was started by Michael Welch in November 2001. The company, based in Scotland, links more than 700 independent tyre fitters across the UK. When contacted through its call centre or website, it locates the customer's nearest and cheapest tyre fitter.

Michael explains what he did to start his advertising. 'We needed to start advertising from day one to attract customers. I started by looking for places to advertise which I thought would reach our target market, such as car magazines like *Revs* and *Max Power*. The readers of these magazines are a captive market – as fast-car enthusiasts and owners, they need to buy tyres regularly.

I got the circulation figures and the demographics of the people that were reading these magazines. This included information such as their salary and the age and the type of car they drove. I then broke down our potential customers into similar categories and decided which magazines would target them best. With advertising, your approach should always be targeted, never random.

At the moment we spend around £25,000 to £30,000 per month on advertising and our turnover is £3 million. We manage to convert about 70 per cent of our advertising spend into sales.'

Source: Adapted from www.businesslink.gov.uk

1 Describe the niche in the market that Michael was able to target.
2 Describe how Michael segmented his target audience.
3 Describe how this benefited his advertising.
4 Explain why a business's approach to advertising should always be targeted rather than random? Justify your answer.

## Developing a brand profile

The first question we must ask ourselves is what is a **brand**? Branding gives products an identify that distinguishes them from similar products developed by rival firms.

A brand profile helps the product build up customer loyalty. It makes the product more familiar to customers, therefore encouraging more purchasing decisions at the **point of sale**. It can also mean that the product is less sensitive to changes in price. If the price increases, demand will only fall slightly. Selecting the correct brand name is therefore a very important part of an enterprise's marketing strategy.

Businesses can develop their brand image in a number of ways, including **individual** or **multiple branding** and **corporate** or **overall family branding**.

### ACTIVITY

In small groups, consider as many brand names as you can. The group that comes up with the most is the winner!

### GLOSSARY

**Point of sale:** advertising on view where the product can be purchased, e.g. a 'dumpbin' of crisps or snacks.

### GLOSSARY

**Individual** or **multiple branding**: This is where the business uses a range of brand names for a variety of products: for example, Coca Cola is one of the world's best known product names, but the company uses individual branding for its other products, e.g. Sprite.

**Corporate** or **overall family branding**: This is where all of the business's products are branded with the same name: for example, Virgin, Peugeot, Heinz. The advantage of this is that the promotion of one product within the range will also promote the other products. It can increase consumer confidence in the entire range and therefore increase sales and profits.

# Promotions and gimmicks

These are all part of the promotion part of the marketing mix and are one way that an enterprise can encourage people to buy its products and services.

Within the retail industry, especially in food, there is fierce competition. One of the methods used by supermarkets is the promotion of 'buy one get one free'.

These promotions might increase demand while the offer is current. Will customers still buy the products once the offer has been withdrawn or will they simply move on to alternative products that are on offer?

## Real business

Promotions can be extremely successful. McDonalds ran a promotional campaign about four years ago – buy one Big Mac get the next one free. It was so successful they ran out of burgers. In August 2005 they ran the campaign again but this time changed the deal each day; one day it was a Big Mac the next a Chicken Burger. This campaign not only appealed to a wider range of people, it also meant McDonalds did not run out of food.

While considering a promotional offer to get people interested in your product/service you have to consider the potential cost. Will you be selling your product for less than production costs? If so for how long can you continue to make a loss?

Gimmicks are like promotions but are often less expensive to fund. It could include a free toy with the purchase of a product. It might be the right to enter into a free draw.

All promotions and gimmicks encourage people to try out your product or service for the first time. They raise awareness and act as encouragement. However, you also need to be sure that once the customer has enjoyed the initial promotion or gimmick they will remain faithful to your business.

# Generating free publicity (PR)

Public relations is the process and methods that a business uses to enhance the success of its product or service by developing a productive relationship with the public and, hopefully, its customers.

PR generally involves trying to present the business and its products to the general public in a more favourable light. PR activities may not always be about selling more products in the immediate term but building up the image of the business. A local builder may spend a few hundred pounds sponsoring the local youth football team. This is unlikely to increase sales in the short term but will improve the image of the business in the long term.

*'Don't they look smart. Expert Double Glazing did us proud.'*

If Portsmouth Football Club were about to make an expensive new signing they would issue a press release or hold a press conference to inform the media of its plans. By presenting this news to journalists, television and radio the football club will generate a considerable amount of publicity for itself.

Small businesses may try to get articles about themselves in the local press or be interviewed on the local radio station.

All of these activities raise the profile of a business which in turn will, hopefully, generate further sales.

## Portfolio tip

*Relate the results of your own market research to each of the above categories.*

*The focus of your market research needs to be on how best to advertise your idea. You need to ask who are your potential customers? What would be the best way to reach them? Think back to the case study on 'Black Circle' (page 279). Michael targeted his advertising to the magazines that his target group read.*

*Having established the medium to reach your target audience you then need to consider how you could build up a brand identity, what promotions or gimmicks might appeal to your customers and, finally, how you could make the most of the local media in order to promote your new idea.*

# AO5 Demonstrate how to value customers and build their loyalty

It is vitally important for all enterprises to turn the first time buyer into a loyal advocate of the enterprise. To ensure that this happens the enterprise must ensure the quality of the product/ service is excellent and the service received by the customer is second to none.

It is a well-known fact it is a lot harder to attract new customers than to keep existing ones. Bearing this in mind, this part of the unit is going to examine how other businesses go about keeping their customers loyal.

## Portfolio tip

*Within the specifications the guidance for the completion of this assessment objective states candidates must conduct research and then explain, using examples, the methods used by entrepreneurs to attract customers.*

*Candidates will need to research how other organisations build loyalty with their customers. They should explain how they will try and build up this loyalty within their own enterprise, basing their evidence on their research.*

## Taking care over detail

This is the very first stage in ensuring that everything about the product or service offered is up to standard. There is nothing worse than purchasing a product, only to find when you get it home that there is a 'bit missing' or it does not perform to the standard expected or, even worse, it does not work at all! It is time-consuming and frustrating to have to keep returning goods. It is equally disappointing if you have paid to enjoy a specific service, for example a massage, and at the end of the process you are left feeling dissatisfied as it was not to the standard that you expected.

Customers are more likely to tell their family and friends about poor service and experiences than those they have fully enjoyed.

How can an enterprise make sure that they have covered all the different areas to ensure maximum customer satisfaction? There are a number of ways that this can be done. The entrepreneur could visit a similar business to experience its customer service and think of the different ways they could better the service. The second method is to consider the whole customer's experience from start to finish. The entrepreneur will then be able to come up with ideas about where improvements can be made. Once an enterprise has been running for a period of time and has established a few regular customers, it could talk to its customers to see how they view the service and what improvements they consider could be made.

## Enabling customers to build association with a brand

Earlier in this unit we looked at the advantages of creating a brand image. It will enhance the recognition of a product and can often reassure customers that the product will be of a high quality. Products/services will become less price sensitive as the brand becomes established.

## CASE STUDY

### T-Hair Takes Care

Earlier on in the unit we met the hair salon T-Hair. One of Tanya's main aims was to ensure that customer service was first class. In order to do this she put in place the following systems.

- The reception area is kept neat and tidy, fitted out with comfortable sofas and a vase of fresh flowers.
- Somebody is always on reception so no client is kept waiting.
- As soon as a client is booked in they were offered a seat and informed how long they will have to wait. If a customer is particularly early for an appointment they would be offered magazines and a drink.
- Whilst being dealt with the client is again offered a drink.

- If the client is waiting for a treatment to finish they are offered reading material and a drink.
- Stylists are highly trained and as part of the service must discuss with the client in detail what their requirements are. Advice must be offered and this must be unbiased and factual.
- Customer records are all kept on a computer so that the stylists know exactly what treatment the customer has had in the past.

1 How do you think the following systems help Tanya maintain loyal customers?
2 Suggest and justify any improvements you think Tanya could make to her current customer service provision.

Having recognised the advantages of brand association many businesses spend thousands of pounds trying to establish their own brand identify. However, this can often be easier said than done.

Establishing a brand is about getting people to remember your product or service. It is about customers

remembering the enjoyment of the experience and wanting to purchase it again. It is the ability to build up the story/experience of the brand which will keep it in your customers' minds. One of the advantages of all well-known brands is that they have a heritage. Customers have had time to buy and use the brand, time to make the brand part of their lives and passed this experience on through the generations. It is going to take time for any new enterprise to establish this kind of status for their product or service.

### Real business

Chanel's brand story is that of a sensual, strong and independent woman who is seeking romance, spiritual love, and the experience of ecstasy.

### Real business

Nike's brand story is one of maximum performance, of challenging oneself to strive for their very best and calling that achievement perfection.

# Exceeding the expectations of customers, guaranteeing 100 per cent satisfaction and becoming a trusted adviser

In order to remain one step ahead of its competitors an enterprise does not just need an excellent product which will establish itself as a brand in its own right. It needs to ensure that it exceeds its customers' expectations by supplying them with 100 per cent satisfaction every time they purchase the product or service.

In a rush to develop brand identity an enterprise can forget that the largest and most important part of delivering a service is the interaction the customer has with the enterprise. First-hand experience will strongly influence consumers' repurchase decisions.

Banking customers are more likely to return by a ratio of 10 to 20 times if the business has outstanding employees.

Pizza Hut is totally focused on meeting and exceeding the expectations of their customers in order to maintain their market share of the semi-fast food market. In order to do this they bought in the Champs Check List. This is an extremely detailed check list that looks at every aspect of customer service. The check list is used daily to ensure that the standards of customer service are continually maintained throughout all of their stores within the

UK. A mystery shopper is employed to check how each restaurant is doing. The mystery shopper reports back to the manager, clearly outlining the improvements that need to be made in order to meet the requirements of the organisation. This is done in order to ensure that the customer experience is 100 per cent and consumers will become loyal and regular customers of Pizza Hut.

The main key to achieving 100 per cent customer service is to ensure that your staff are trained how to deal with customers to a very high standard. However, this training needs to be geared towards the type of enterprise that you are choosing to run. Customers do not hold one idea of service in their minds; the public is not generic when it comes to the services they require. They will come into the enterprise with personal, specific and unique expectations about the service/product they are about to purchase. It is the ability of the staff to meet these specific needs that will enable the business to establish a brand awareness and also retain and gain customers.

Customers expect to be able to trust any enterprise that they deal with. They will expect honesty and integrity throughout their dealings with the enterprise. If a customer cannot trust the people they are dealing with they are unlikely to return. How can you ensure that your customers trust your enterprise? You need to make sure that any promises you make are met. If you say you will deliver a product or service on a set date, make sure you do. If your advertisements state that you do something, make sure that you actually can do it – do not make false statements that you are unable to follow through on. An enterprise's ability to deliver what it declares is fundamental to its reputation.

Building the brand is part of this process as it is ultimately trust based: we promise, we deliver. When this is not done, customer relationships are more likely to be short term, immediate and transactional – and will contribute little to building brand trust and ultimately repeat customers.

## Acting on complaints, ideas and suggestions

A customer who has their complaint dealt with to their satisfaction will remain as loyal as the customer who has never made a complaint. Having an efficient and effective complaints system in place is paramount to retaining customer loyalty.

Complaints are also a good way of getting to know your customers and what they expect from your business. A lot of businesses spend time analysing their complaints to ensure that they improve the customer service that they are able to offer their customers.

*The customer is always right*

## CASE STUDY

*Corby Borough Council Launches Complaints Handling System on Thursday 29th July 2004*

Corby Borough Council is launching its new complaints and comments handling system as part of the Council's 'One Corby Approach' to respond to customers and improve services, which is outlined in a new leaflet for residents called 'If Things Go Wrong'.

The leaflet contains information on:

- how to complain
- who to complain to
- a quick route system where customers can contact the service area to whom they are making the complaint
- guidance for both customers and staff on how to deal with complaints
- what to expect when you complain.

Each complaint received will be given a unique number, which will enable the progress of the complaint to be tracked, and the Council is committed to responding to all complaints and comments within 28 working days.

The Council is also introducing an electronic system to monitor and evaluate how they deal with complaints and comments, which will be regularly reported to senior officers and councillors.

Leader of Corby Borough Council, Councillor Willie Smith, said: 'The aim of this scheme is to have a user-friendly, easy to understand system to ensure the Council responds positively to customer complaints and comments with a consistent timescale. We hope this will enable the Council to provide an improved service for the people of the Borough.'

Source: www.corby.gov.uk

1 Explain why you think Corby Borough Council felt it was important to improve their complaints procedures.
2 Describe how you think this new system will assist the residents of Corby.
3 Describe how you think this new system will assist Corby Borough Council.

### Real business

Asda has suggestion boxes in all its stores. Customers are able to write down suggestions and each is reviewed by the management. If the store receives a number of suggestions about the same thing, the manager will often look into implementing the idea.

Customers often have very good ideas and suggestions about how a business could develop its products or services or improve its provision of customer service. It is always useful to allow people to offer their ideas.

## Promoting employee 'buy-in'

The most important ambassadors of any business are the employees. They are the people on the 'cliff edge'. They deal with the public on a one-to-one basis. If employees are lethargic and lack interest it will not encourage customers to purchase your product or service or to return in the future.

By offering employees fair wages and good working conditions a business is more likely to encourage their employees to become enthusiastic about the business they work for.

Training to provide employees with the appropriate skills to do their job is also vital if they are to become efficient. Customer service training ensures that employees are aware of how to deal with the many different varieties of customers that they are likely to meet – we all have very different expectations when we go shopping.

## AO6 Evaluate your personal potential as an entrepreneur and recommend how these skills could be developed

In this part of the unit you need to think very carefully about your own skills. Do you think you have what it takes to become an entrepreneur?

In AO1 we looked at the attributes that were considered necessary to become a successful entrepreneur. Throughout the following four assessment objectives you were having to demonstrate your ability to obtain finance, attract customers and keep them loyal to your enterprise. Having completed these tasks you should now have some idea of whether you think you have what it takes to be an entrepreneur.

## Evaluation

In AO1 the personal qualities of entrepreneurs were outlined as:

- being able to take risks
- having a positive attitude
- being able to solve problems
- being flexible and adaptable
- being creative
- having intuition
- having a drive to succeed.

*How did I do?*

The list above does not exhaust all the qualities you will need in order to become a successful entrepreneur.

The following three qualities are equally as important:

- being totally focused
- having commitment – being able to stay the course
- having the ability to lead and motivate other people.

In order to become an entrepreneur it takes an amazing amount of energy and commitment. When you leave work as an employee that is usually the end of your working day. If you are an entrepreneur then office hours do not exist. You are only ever as good as your last contract/sale. In order to establish yourself you need to be prepared to work long and unsocial hours. Being focused is the key to being able to keep on going when others would have given up. Weekends and holidays may fade into the distance as a mere memory. However, the ultimate reward of being successful is enormous and can be worth the struggle that it took to get there.

If you are going to run a successful enterprise you will need to have the ability to lead other people. You will need to stimulate, motivate and encourage your employees to be as enthusiastic as you are about the enterprise. As we saw earlier, employees are vital in gaining and retaining loyal customers.

One American study identified the following fifteen attributes of leadership:

- judgement
- integrity
- energy
- decisiveness
- dependability
- fairness
- dedication
- cooperation
- initiative
- foresight
- drive
- people relations skills
- emotional stability
- ambition
- objectivity.

**Did you know?**

*Charles Handy is widely recognised as Europe's best known and most influential management thinker, noted for studies of organisations and his ideas on future work and business structures. He is the author of several acclaimed business books, including* The Hungry Spirit.

Charles Handy also suggested that good leaders also possess a helicopter factor – an ability to overview things from above rather than become bogged down in detail.

This list is not very different from all the skills that we have identified an entrepreneur would need in order to be successful.

It is now your turn to consider whether you actually have what it takes to become a successful entrepreneur.

Work through the questions in Table 12.3 to draw together your ideas and feelings about how successful you have already been. Remember, everything in life is a learning curve. Do not be too negative or hard on yourself. Look at how your experiences could be built upon in the future.

## Portfolio tip

*In order to fully meet the needs of the assessment objective you may:*

- *need to enlarge the table*
- *write the evidence in more detail in order to achieve the higher grades and to improve the overall depth of your evaluation.*

*The first column identifies the skill, quality or characteristic being displayed. The second column asks you when you demonstrate this skill. The third column asks where else in your life you have demonstrated this skill. For example, you may be part of a sports team and demonstrate some of these skills in this way. The final column asks you to identify a particular strength/weakness.*

| Skills, qualities and characteristics | How did I display this within this unit? | What other evidence do I have of this skill – i.e. what else do I do? | What was a particular strength/ weakness? |
|---|---|---|---|
| Am I prepared to take risks? | | | |
| Do I have a positive attitude | | | |
| Can I solve problems? | | | |
| Am I flexible and adaptable? | | | |
| Do I have intuition? | | | |
| Do I have drive to succeed? | | | |
| Am I committed to what I do? | | | |
| Can I be totally focused? | | | |
| Can I be a leader of other people? | | | |
| Can I motivate people? | | | |

**Table 12.3** *Analysis of entrepreneurial skills*

## Analysis of own entrepreneurial skills

### Highlighting particular strengths and weaknesses

By using Table 12.3 you will have been able to identify the areas where you felt you coped very well. You will also be able to recognise the times when you found things difficult. Using the information from the table, produce a summary which clearly outlines your own strengths and weaknesses.

## Development of own entrepreneurial skills

You should now be aware of what your own personal strengths and weaknesses are. It is now time to consider how the weaknesses can be turned into strengths.

### Sources of advice

There are many different sources of advice that a new entrepreneur can tap into. All of the banks offer help and guidance to new business start-ups. Barclays have their own website for the new entrepreneur. One of the facilities within the website is to order a free starter pack which will clearly identify all the help that a new entrepreneur can receive from the bank. This will include expert advice on legal, marketing and accounting for the business. Barclays will also offer up to 18 month's free banking.

There are a number of government websites that will give help and guidance to the new entrepreneur. One of these is www.businesslink.gov.uk. This site offers help ranging from starting up, grants, how to help your business grow and health and safety.

Local councils also have people available to help local businesses, as will the tax office who will give help and guidance on financial matters.

As a young entrepreneur the following organisations all offer help, guidance, support and training.

- **Shell Livewire** helps 16-30 year olds start and develop their own business and hosts a national competition for new business start-ups. The range of business publications and training packs covers all the topics budding entrepreneurs need to know, from managing people to marketing and human resources. There are over 100 co-ordinators nationwide who can provide one-to-one advice on starting up.

- **The Prince's Youth Trust** helps young people by offering them low-cost finance and mentoring. The services are available for 18-30 year olds who wish to start up their own business.

- **Young Enterprise** is a national education charity which seeks to inspire and equip young people to learn and succeed through enterprise.

- **Youngbusiness.net** is a website where young entrepreneurs across Europe, and those agencies supporting them, can interact and access information to help create successful businesses.

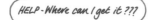

HELP - Where can I get it ???

## Real business

The York Enterprise scheme was set up to help entrepreneurs start up in the Yorkshire area. It offers a wide variety of advice and training to would-be entrepreneurs. These organisations range from The Young Business Project to the Business Link North Yorkshire. It might be worth trying to find out if there are similar schemes available in your own area.

- **The Big Small Business Initiative** is a non-profit-making partnership and offers small businesses in the UK advice, support and information from a variety of different sources, including the HM Revenue & Customs and the Patent Office.

- **Business Link** is a government agency managed by the Small Business Service and was created to support the cause of small businesses. It consists of a national network of agencies which offer advice, information and resources to help entrepreneurs.

- **Launch Pad** is a London-based enterprise group which offers free support and counselling to young people. Its aim is to help young people discover and develop their enterprising talents and holds free workshops and events. The service is available to anyone aged 14-30, whether they have already got a business idea or not.

The Internet has also opened up many new ways to tap into advice and guidance when starting out as an entrepreneur. You may the find the following sites useful.

- **Starting a New Venture (Imperial College)** provides guidance and free downloads for writing a business plan – www.imperial.ac.uk

- **Small Business Information** provides everything you need to write a business plan. It includes templates, downloads, reviews, help and advice – www.sbinformation.about.com

- **National Business Angels Network (NBAN)** looks to bring together companies seeking investment with investors looking for the right opportunity – www.bestmatch.co.uk

## Sources of training and development

There are no specific organisations that will provide training for young entrepreneurs in general terms. However, many of the organisations mentioned above will also offer/suggest training that is currently available.

When you have decided which skills you need to develop you will then be able to seek out specific training courses. You may feel that you lack the skills necessary to monitor your finances effectively. This could be resolved by taking a part-time course in book-keeping at your local college.

Local colleges are always a good starting point when thinking about updating and expanding upon the skills that you have.

Trade associations will also be able to offer specific training which is industry specific.

## Personal coaching and mentoring

The best way to learn is to have one-to-one tuition. It is often extremely beneficial to be able to learn 'on the job' as it is a 'real' experience which often has more relevance and meaning to the trainee.

Personal coaching involves being trained on a one-to-one basis. This might be available if you had an excellent idea but needed to involve someone with more business experience to ensure that the idea turns into a business success.

Mentoring involves being supported by somebody who has greater experience than yourself. You might be able to achieve this when starting out by making contact with a successful entrepreneur in your local area. They might be prepared to pass on their knowledge and experience to help you avoid the pitfalls they made in their early years of development. It is unlikely that you will persuade someone producing the same product or service as yourself to give you the 'tips of the trade'; after all you are about to become the competition!

## Networks

Networking allows small businesses to share experiences and ideas and to improve their overall knowledge. It can provide a lifeline of support and guidance for a start-up business. Businesses can network with educational establishments, trade organisations or other businesses. Networks allow businesses to:

- meet in organised or informal forums
- receive news bulletins and invitations to events of general interest, e.g. exhibitions, lectures, participate in debates on topics relevant to their business
- participate or contribute to surveys or research in the relevant business field.

Networks are able to share ideas and keep up to date with what is going on in their field or industry. This could include topics such as:

- training and recruitment
- new products and markets
- industry developments
- industry laws and regulation.

When a small business becomes involved in networking it enables the business to raise its profile. The entrepreneur is getting their 'face known', making other businesses aware of what they are trying to achieve. It might offer contacts that will enable the business to expand.

## Enterprise clubs

**Enterprise clubs** are often offered through universities with the aim of providing help and guidance to graduates who wish to start up their own businesses upon leaving university.

**Real business**

One of the services the North London Enterprise Club runs is a series of training seminars, aimed at helping the unemployed over 45 years old to run their own business successfully.

**Real business**

Bromley Borough Chamber of Commerce Enterprise Club provides advice, guidance and assistance to people who want to start their own business.

## Real business

The White Rose Centre for Enterprise is run through the universities of Leeds, Sheffield and York. The centre was formed in 1999. The key aims of the White Rose Centre for Enterprise are to increase the entrepreneurial skills and competency of graduates, postgraduates and research staff, and to give encouragement and support. One of their focuses is help in the formation of new companies. The centre offers a range of services which include conferences, competitions and sponsorship.

## Did you know?

*Bournemouth University has just set up its own enterprise club. Its aim is to support staff working or wishing to work with business. The university is also running a scheme called START whose aim is to help people who want to start up their own business or become a successful entrepreneur.*

*The training programme will cover:*

- *practical business advice*
- *business mentorship*
- *business start-up development framework*
- *comprehensive online resources.*

*The course is available to all staff and students throughout Bournemouth University.*

## SKILLS CHECK

**1** Identify the skills you think are necessary to become a successful entrepreneur.

**2** Explain what you think are the main stages involved in the development of new ideas. Justify your answer.

**3** Identify and explain four different methods by which a new business start-up could obtain finance.

**4** Explain the difference between primary and secondary market research.

**5** Describe the contents of a business plan.

**6** Describe a recent 'promotion' or 'gimmick' that has encouraged you to buy a particular product or service.

**7** Think about an occasion when you returned an item to a shop. What was the complaints procedure? Did you find the staff helpful?

**8** Describe one occasion when you have received excellent customer service. Did this experience encourage you to remain a loyal customer?

**9** Describe one occasion when you have received very poor customer service. Did you complain? If you complained did you get a satisfactory result?

**10** Using your answers from 8 and 9 above compile two lists. The first should outline what you think makes good customer service, and the second what you consider constitutes poor customer service.

# Recruitment and selection

## Getting started

Most of us at some stage or other will have to go through the recruitment and selection process. You may already have had an interview for a part-time job or for your work experience placement. If you become self-employed you may be involved in the interviewing process.

By the time we reply to an advertisement, the business offering the position has already been through four or five stages. It is vital for both the business and the potential **employee** that the recruitment process is accurate and fair. Recruiting the wrong person can be extremely expensive, not just in terms of financial expense but also the **opportunity cost** of the exercise.

Another point to remember is that a business is only ever as good as its employees and therefore all businesses want to employ the best people to ensure their continuing success. Being successful at interviews makes our choice of job much larger. It also means that when we apply for 'the job we really want' we will have a much better chance of being successful.

Throughout this unit you will develop the knowledge, understanding and skills of the recruitment procedures and the practical recruitment and selection activities carried out by businesses.

### This unit will cover

- AO1 Describe the main features of the recruitment process.
- AO2 Explain, using examples, the impact of legal and ethical constraints on the design and operation of a recruitment process.

- AO3 Produce a complete recruitment pack for a selected job vacancy in a real business organisation.
- AO4 Use the recruitment pack to conduct a selection exercise and interview for a single applicant, and evaluate its suitability.
- AO5 Evaluate the recruitment methods used by a selected business organisation.

## Overview of recruitment and selection

There are a variety of reasons a business may need to recruit more employees. These include:

- an employee moves to another business
- an employee retires
- an employee leaves due to ill-health
- the business has expanded.

When an employee chooses to leave a business it will have to decide if it wants to replace the employee. It might be possible to share the departing

| STAGE | DESCRIPTION |
|-------|-------------|
| What job? | Is there a possible job vacancy? What duties will this new employee undertake? This information is identified in the job analysis. |
| What duties? | Having decided on the position that is required the business designs the job description. This outlines exactly what the new member of staff will be required to do. |
| What kind of person? | Having identified the position, what skills and attributes will this new employee require? This is outlined in the person specification. |
| How can we attract applicants? | The next stage is to design the advertisement and then decide where the advertisement is to be placed. |
| How will potential applicants apply? | Having placed the advertisement the business has to decide how they want the applicants to apply for the position. Do they want them to write a letter of application, complete an application form or send a curriculum vitae? Could potential applicants apply online? |
| Who shall we interview? | Having received all your potential applicants the business has to devise a system whereby they can select those they wish to interview. This is known as shortlisting. |
| How to select the right person | The shortlist has been drawn up. How will the business actually interview the potential employees? Will the interview be formal or informal? Will they have to undertake practical tests, role plays? These activities will all form part of the interview process and help the business select the right candidate. |
| Review and evaluation | It is important that a business continually reviews its recruitment and selection procedures to ensure they continue to be effective. |

Table **17.1** *Features of the recruitment process*

employee's responsibilities out amongst existing members of staff. The business may decide to train another member of staff to take over the vacant position.

Having decided that there is a position to fill, let us consider the features of the recruitment process. By looking at the whole picture you will have a better understanding of how the process is interlinked and also the importance of getting every stage right in order to employ 'the best person for the job'.

## AO1  Describe the main features of the recruitment process

Recruitment is the process of attracting sufficient people to apply for vacancies within the business. A business's human resource plan will be linked to the strategic business plan to ensure that all the aims and objectives of the business can be met by ensuring sufficient staff are recruited, trained and used effectively within the business.

The process of selection is about selecting the right candidate from those who have been attracted by the recruitment process.

When a business is faced with an employee leaving the business, for whatever reason, it must decide if it wants to replace the member of staff who is leaving. As stated above, staff are not always replaced as the business may want to reduce its workforce in order to reduce costs. This process is known as '**natural wastage**'. If the business does not decide to replace the employee it may re-organise the workforce, sharing out the tasks and duties of the departing employee. If the business decides to appoint a new employee, it may take tasks away from existing employees to ease their workload and make those tasks part of the new employee's job description.

### GLOSSARY

**Natural wastage**:
This is the term used when a member of staff leaves and it is decided not to replace them.

The duties of the leaving staff member will be shared out among remaining staff.

It is a way of reducing the workforce without making redundancies.

## *Scenario*

Most of the activities throughout this unit will be related to the duties of a new school receptionist within the human resource department of your school/college.

Worked examples of recruitment and selection documents will be based on a business called The Warehouse. This business is an Internet sales company dealing with items that other businesses no longer have a use for. This can range from household items to vehicles.

*The Warehouse business full of items*

## Job analysis

This is the first stage in the recruitment process and is defined as the process of examining a job in order to identify its main features, such as:

● the main duties of the job

● the performance indicators the job holder is expected to achieve

● the tasks that the job holder undertakes

● the job's relationship with other jobs in the organisation.

The most effective way to obtain this information is to talk to the departing member of staff to ascertain exactly how they view their job and the duties that have been undertaken on a daily, weekly and monthly basis. It also gives management an opportunity to discuss with other members of staff the responsibilities of the new employee and if any changes should be made to the job role. It may give the business an excellent opportunity to reorganise roles and responsibilities within the business. Existing employees may be able to take on new duties which would make their own job role more demanding and interesting. It may also give employees a chance to hand over responsibilities that they do not like or find difficult. Spending time on this process can be beneficial to the business and existing employees and could create a happier and more efficient workforce.

## *The new receptionist*

You have just started work as an assistant within the human resource department of your school/ college. One of the school receptionists, Elizabeth, has just handed in her notice. The receptionist is due to leave her position at the end of the month.

You have been asked to spend some time talking to Elizabeth to find out exactly what her current duties are. You have also been asked to talk to other members of the team to find out exactly what their current job roles are and how they feel about their jobs. Would any of them like to take on the duties that Elizabeth currently has?

## ACTIVITY

Using the above information and your own understanding of what a school/college receptionist does, draw up a job analysis for the new position.

# Job description

The job analysis will feed directly into the job description. Having found out exactly what the new employee will be required to do the next stage is to transfer this information into the job description.

The purpose of the job description is to inform potential employees what their duties and responsibilities will be within the business. It should contain the following information:

- the job title
- where the job will be situated
- who will the job holder be responsible for
- what the main duties of the job holder will be
- who the job holder will be working with
- what the terms and conditions of the job are, such as: hours, overtime, shifts, pay.

Figure 17.1 shows the job description of Receptionist/Data Input Clerk based at The Warehouse.

**ACTIVITY**

Write a job description for the school receptionist. This must be based on the job analysis that you undertook in the previous activity.

---

### THE WAREHOUSE
#### Job Description

| | |
|---|---|
| **Post:** | Receptionist/Data Input Clerk |
| **Accountable to:** | Regional Manager |
| **Location:** | Warehouse offices reception area |
| **Job Summary:** | General reception duties, greeting and dealing with customers, answering telephones and data input of warehouse commodities |
| **Hours of work:** | 8.30 am–5 pm (total 1 hour break per day) |
| **Salary range:** | £12,000–£14,000 depending on experience |

**Principal Responsibilities**

(1) Undertakes general clerical duties, filing of dispatch notes, keying in load dispatch notes and ensuring computer systems are kept up to date.

(2) Booking in of customers, ensuring customers receive the health and safety briefing, issuing of coloured high visibility vests, ensuring customers are escorted to relevant sales managers.

(3) Answering telephone queries, directing telephone calls as required throughout the organisation.

(4) Input of inventory data and filing of data input sheets.

(5) Undertakes any other duties which may be allocated from time to time.

---

**Figure 17.1** *Job description for a Receptionist/Data Input Clerk*

# Person specification

The person specification is an extremely important feature of the recruitment and selection process as its sets out the attributes that the business is looking for in potential candidates and provides the criteria by which candidates will be judged. A person specification will generally state the educational qualifications, experience and knowledge and skills the potential applicant is required to have in order to complete the job.

There are various methods of completing a person specification. One of the most commonly used is the seven-point plan, designed by Alec Rodger in 1952 and recommended by the National Institute of Industrial Psychology.

## *Rodger's seven-point plan*

1. **Physical make up** – What is required in terms of health, strength and energy? Does the job require physical strength? Is it tiring, heavy manual work? Does the job require contact with the general public?
2. **Attainments** – What level of education and qualifications is required to undertake the job? What occupational training and occupational experience is the potential candidate required to have?
3. **General intelligence** – What does the job involve in terms of quick thinking and mental effort?
4. **Special aptitudes** – What kinds of skills will the potential applicant need in order to do the job? Will the applicant need mechanical skills, be able to work with numbers or have excellent oral skills?
5. **Interests** – What personal interests could be relevant to the job? Would experience of working with other people, working outdoors, for example, be helpful?
6. **Disposition** – What kind of personality would enable the person to perform to a high standard? Does the job require leadership skills?
7. **Circumstances** – Are there any special circumstances that the job requires of the candidates? Would the potential applicant be required to work at different times of the day, weekends, be on 24-hour call out?

## ACTIVITY

In order to complete the activity you will need to work in small groups. Taking each of the seven points in the Rodger plan, individually think of a job that would be applicable. For example, point seven might be applicable to an airline pilot who will be required to be away from home for long periods of time. When your group has decided a range of different positions for each of the seven points, discuss your ideas with the rest of the class. Were all the lists similar?

---

## THE WAREHOUSE
### Person Specification

**Post:** Receptionist and Data Input Clerk

**Education/Qualifications**

Essential: GCSE English
IT qualification
Ability to communicate effectively both verbally and in writing

Desirable: GCSE Maths
Ability to use SAGE accounts

**Experience**

Essential: Previous customer service experience
Proven experience in clerical work, including data processing

Desirable: Previous experience of reception duties

**Skills/Ability/Knowledge**

Essential: Keyboarding and communication skills
Local area knowledge

Desirable: Ability to maintain computerised database systems

**Other Requirements**

Must have a pleasant personality, good sense of humour and be prepared to work flexible hours. The ability to work as a team member and assist in a variety of jobs.

---

Figure 17.2 *Example of a person specification*

**ACTIVITY**

Compare the above person specification with the seven-point plan designed by Alec Rodger. How closely does it follow this model? Are there any improvements that you would make to it? Justify your answer.

# Attracting applicants

Once a business has decided what the potential employee will be required to do and the type of person that is required to fill the position, it has to decide how to attract the right kind of applicants.

## *Job advertisement*

Under this section there are two aspects to consider. The first is the design and content of the advertisement and the second is where to place the advertisement. The two decisions are closely linked. Where the advertisement is placed may affect the layout and design. Can you use colour and images? How much is it going to cost? It is therefore a good idea to decide where to advertise before designing the content of the advertisement.

A job advertisement is very similar to any other advertising the business undertakes. The advertisement needs to attract:

● Attention – potential applicants will stop and look at the advertisement.

- Interest – the advertisement is sufficiently informative to raise interest.
- Desire – the job is clearly explained and therefore the potential applicant will make further enquiries.
- Action – the advertisement explains how the potential candidate is to apply.

However, there is obviously one main difference – the business does not want everybody applying for the position regardless of their suitability. The advertisement must therefore be informative, clearly stating what the job entails and the type of person required to do the job. This information will be derived from the job description and the prepared personal specification.

## ACTIVITY

Look at the two different advertisements in Figures 17.3 and 17.4.

1 Analyse the two job advertisements. State what you think are their good and bad points.
2 Based on this analysis create your own job advertisement for the position of receptionist at your school/college.

---

### Head of Planning and Control – Financial Services

*London Based – salary and benefits negotiable depending on experience*

You will be working for a globally renowned organisation, led by some of the brightest minds in the industry. The business is developing its central team to ensure the organisation is properly aligned to deliver its key objectives and plans. This role will be critical to its success.

**Responsibilities include:**
- Ensure the business is tightly managed without harming the culture of the organisation.
- Develop a short to medium term robust business planning process across the organisation.
- Work with the business to develop the reporting packs for the Executive Committee which cover all the financial and operational performance information.

**The Candidate:**
- Graduate calibre with at least 8 years' financial experience which has been gained within a blue chip environment.
- Commercial experience which has been developed within a dynamic business illustrating the ability to work across the senior management levels.
- Motivated, enthusiastic with strong leadership skills.
- High levels of communication and people skills and the ability to work under stress and think on their feet.

Please apply with full career details and current salary.

---

**Figure 17.3** *Job advertisement for Head of Planning and Control – Financial Services*

---

**Credit Control Officer/Cashier**

# WEST SIDE UNIVERSITY CAMPUS

The college is looking for an experienced credit controller to join a busy finance department.

The successful applicant will be responsible for the collection of students' university fees.

Applicants will be expected to demonstrate excellent record-keeping, the ability to prioritise their workload and organisational skills. A full understanding of the credit control process is required. The role requires the use of MS Office and the university's existing student records and financial systems. The role is deadline driven and applicants will be expected to work irregular hours.

Potential applicants are expected to be educated to GCSE equivalent level and have 2 years' direct experience of credit control in a medium to large organisation.

The university offers a competitive salary structure, generous leave, pension scheme, training and development.

*Please note CVs in isolation will not be accepted*
*Please apply on line on http://www.westuniversity.ac.uk*

---

**Figure 17.4** *Job advertisement for Credit Control Officer/Cashier*

Where to advertise will be driven by two aspects: the type of position being advertised and the budget the business has available. Some businesses may decide to advertise positions internally before seeking external candidates. This might involve placing a notice on the staff notice board, including the advertisement within the staff magazine, or placing the advertisement on the business intranet. Recruiting an existing member of staff can have benefits as they are already familiar with the business and its practices. However, an external candidate may need to be recruited to replace the internally promoted candidate.

There are various methods a business can use to advertise for an external candidate and these include:

- national newspapers
- local newspapers
- specialist newspapers
- local radio
- job centres
- recruitment agencies (dealt with separately)
- advertisements in shop windows
- the Internet.

The first decision a business has to make is whether the potential employee could be recruited from the local area or whether they need to be recruited from a different area of the country due to **skill shortages.**

*Advertising for external candidates*

If the position requires a specialist or is for a higher management position it is likely that the post will be advertised nationally. Lower position jobs are often only advertised locally. Another consideration is the cost of the different types of medium. It costs approximately £5,000 to place a half page advertisement in a newspaper such as the *Guardian* or *Independent*. The local newspaper might be a lot cheaper. If a business has its own website and has an excellent reputation, placing advertisements on its website may be an inexpensive way of attracting potential candidates. This method of advertising will only work for popular businesses where the general public has become aware of vacancies via the Internet.

## ACTIVITY

Working in small groups, from the list above each take one or two places where jobs can be advertised and investigate the type of positions advertised by each. This will help you decide where to place your own advertisement. Try and find out how much each medium would cost to use. This information will be useful when you start preparing your own recruitment pack.

## Recruitment agencies

Recruitment agencies have two roles. Their first is to provide staff for businesses that have a short-term need for extra employees. This could be due to holidays, sickness or sudden surges in demand.

Their second is to undertake the recruitment process for the business and to filter out unsuitable candidates in order to save the business time and money. This can be achieved in a variety of ways:

*A high street recruitment agency*

- by filtering the **CVs** received to the most suitable five and sending these to the business for interview
- by holding some of the interviews and making recommendations to the business of the most suitable candidates
- by providing a temporary member of staff to the business for a number of weeks/months. If they are suitable, can do the job and fit into the team the business may offer them a permanent contract.

# Application methods

Having decided where to place the advertisement, a business must then decide how potential applicants will apply for the job being offered. There are a variety of different methods that could be used. The business must decide which would be the most appropriate for the type of applicants that they expect to apply for the post. The other consideration is to decide what they need to know about potential applicants.

## Letter

Letters of application can be used in three ways. The advertisement might require the applicant to write and request an application form. A letter might be the only document required to apply for the position. Finally, the applicant might be requested to send a letter of application in support of their application form.

A letter will illustrate to a potential **employer** a candidate's ability to use formal documentation correctly, their ability to spell and use punctuation. It will also reflect the time spent on the application. The amount of effort and time can reflect how keen a potential candidate is to work for the business.

If you are ever required to apply for a position using a letter, it is vitally important that you spend time considering its content, layout and spelling.

## ACTIVITY

Figure 17.5 shows a letter of application for a position as a part time cashier within a local building society.

Study the letter.

1   Identify all the errors in the letter.
2   Do you think this letter would get the applicant an interview? Justify your answers.
3   Rewrite the letter.

Hythe House
West Street
Blackpool
Lancashire
LS48 9IO

Dear Sir

I would like to apply for the position of part-time cashier as advertised in the Blackpool Gazette.

I have been currently working as a cashier in Lloyds TSB Bank but I don't like the hours that I currently have to work – they do not fit in with the children.

I have always worked in Banks as a cashier ever since leaving school. Before having my children I worked full time and was a supervisor. I don't want a supervisors position now as I only want to work part time in order to look after my family.

I look forward to hearing from you in the near future.

Yours Sincerely

Kathy Wood (Mrs)

**Figure 17.5** *Letter of application*

## Application forms

If you are currently studying at college you probably had to complete an application form in order to be offered a place within the college. An application form is a document that has been specifically designed for the purpose of finding out information about applicants for a position. They are usually 3–4 pages long and contain a variety of sections which include:

- personal details – name, address, date of birth
- qualifications
- current employment
- past employment record
- health declaration
- hobbies and interests
- two **referees** to provide **references.**

Within application forms a business may include another form which requests information about ethnic background and disabilities. This is to help the business monitor the variety of people that apply for jobs and to ensure that it does not breach any equal opportunity legislation.

Often application forms will be accompanied by instructions on how to complete them. The complexity of the application form will depend on the level of employment being sought and some businesses will have a variety of application forms. If you are required to complete an application form and want to be called for interview, follow the simple instructions below:

- Read all the instructions first – make sure you follow them!
- Gather all the relevant information together – e.g. dates of employment, when you left school, the dates you achieved your qualifications etc.
- If possible, photocopy the application form so that you can have a rough copy.
- If you are unable to photocopy the application form, write each section in rough on a separate sheet of paper prior to completing the actual form.
- Use black ink. Most application forms stipulate this as it makes the forms easier to photocopy.

The advantage of an application form is that all applicants are asked the same questions, which supply the business with the information they require rather than information supplied by the applicant.

A lot of businesses now make their application forms available on line. If you are required to complete an online application form you may need to draft out each individual section before proceeding to the next stage of the application process. You are able to print out the application forms and could produce a draft copy before completing the final version online.

### Did you know?

*Hampshire County Council and London Underground are examples of businesses that conduct most of their recruitment through the use of their website.*

### Portfolio tip

*You may need to design an application form for your recruitment pack. Make sure that you do not breach any of the equal opportunities legislation with the questions that you ask within it. These will be covered in greater depth in AO2.*

---

Curriculum Vitae

### SEBASTIAN WOODWARD

| | |
|---|---|
| **Address:** | 124 Green Lane Road, Taunton, Somerset SO4 5HY |
| **Telephone:** | 07778 745 234 |
| **Date of Birth:** | 15th March 1986 |
| **Education and Training:** | Green Park School, Taunton<br>September 1998–July 2004 |
| **Qualifications (GCSEs)** | Mathematics (A)<br>English Literature (A)<br>English Language (B)<br>Double Science (CC)<br>French (C)<br>Geography (A)<br>Technology (B)<br>Business Studies (A) |
| **Interests and activities** | Captain of the school hockey team, house captain and prefect (2002–2004). Venture Scout, Bronze award Duke of Edinburgh. |
| **Work Experience** | May 2004 to present<br>General Assistant at Asda superstore in Taunton. Responsibilities include stock replenishment, cashier and working on the customer service desk. |
| **Referees** | Mr J Pyke        Mrs G Keane<br>Head of Year     Supervisor<br>6th Form College   Asda<br>Wide Lane       Fifth Road<br>Taunton         Taunton<br>Somerset       Somerset<br>SO23 7YH      SO82 9PL |

---

**Figure 17.6** *Example of a CV*

## Curriculum vitae

This is a document that is designed by the applicant containing their personal details, educational qualifications, current employment, past employment record and the names of two referees.

There are many different ways that this document can be laid out. Professional people consider that a good CV should be no longer than two pages.

If a business requests the CV method of application for a position it can save money as no application forms have to be sent in the post. However, the disadvantage is that the business will not receive the same information from all applicants. This could make the short-listing process more complex, as the human resources department will be looking through a wide variety of documents. The business may also be persuaded by a very professional looking CV which actually hides the fact that the applicant may not be as well qualified as other applicants.

## ACTIVITY

Working in pairs, obtain copies of different application forms. Photocopy the forms so that you each have a copy. You might be able to print some from the Internet. Complete at least one application form each. Look at each others' completed application forms and make comments on the presentation and information. If you had received this application form, would you have called the applicant for an interview? Justify your answer.

## Selection methods

Once a business has placed its advertisement it has to decide how to choose from all the applications received.

### Shortlisting

It would be extremely expensive for a business to interview every applicant (assuming their advertisement has been successful and attracted a good number of applicants). The business, therefore, has to develop a system whereby it can filter through the job applications and select suitable candidates. This is known as shortlisting. The system has to be rigorous and ensure that it does not call for interview candidates who are unsuitable but, at the same time, does not reject those who may make excellent employees.

The person specification now plays a major part in the process. All applicants are matched against the requirements of the person specification and those that meet the requirements are placed on the shortlist.

A business must be very careful to ensure that during the shortlisting process prejudice does not influence its decisions. For example, one member of the panel who is undertaking the shortlisting process may prefer a woman to have the job. This may lead to favouritism towards female applicants and male applicants may be judged more harshly. One way to avoid this is to photocopy all the applications, blanking out names, gender and age. This process will ensure that all candidates are judged equally.

Using the person specification created for the Receptionist/Data Input Clerk for The Warehouse, the shortlisting document could be designed as shown in Figure 17.7.

Shortlist for Receptionist/Data Input Clerk – The Warehouse

| Essential Qualities | Candidate One | Candidate Two | Candidate Three |
|---|---|---|---|
| GCSE English<br><br>IT qualification | | | |
| Ability to communicate effectively both verbally and in writing | | | |
| Previous customer service experience | | | |
| Clerical, keyboarding and data input experience | | | |
| Local area knowledge | | | |
| **Desirable Qualities** | | | |
| GCSE Maths<br><br>Ability to use SAGE accounts | | | |
| Previous experience of reception duties | | | |
| Ability to maintain computerised databases | | | |
| Ability to work as part of a team | | | |

**Figure 17.7** *Person shortlist for Receptionist/Data Input Clerk – The Warehouse*

## *Means of assessing shortlisted applicants*

Having decided who to call for interview, the next decision the business has to make is what methods to use to interview the candidates. Remember an interview is a two-way process. The business wants to find out if the potential applicant is suitable for the job, has the right skills and competencies and will fit into the **culture** of the business. The potential applicant wants to find out if they want to work for the business. Both aspects are equally important if the process is going to be successful.

**GLOSSARY**

**Culture:** the term used to describe the way the business is run and what it is like to work there. For example, are people required to dress formally and call each other 'Mr', 'Mrs'?

## Interviews

The most common way to select a single candidate is to run interviews. This is where shortlisted candidates visit the organisation and are interviewed by a member of the human resources department. For managerial positions, it is very common for applicants to be interviewed by a panel of people rather than just one person.

A selection interview aims to:

- produce a suitable candidate for the job
- provide the candidates with information
- treat all candidates fairly and well.

The most successful interviews are those that have been carefully planned. The following list outlines the aspects a business should consider prior to conducting the interviews.

- Has the room been booked?
- Who will be conducting the interviews? Are they available and aware of the time and place for the interviews?
- Is the room free from distractions and possible interruptions?
- Has the room been arranged correctly – tables, chairs, refreshments?
- Has reception been informed of the names of candidates and the procedure to deal with them?
- Does the waiting room look comfortable and relaxing, and is there some company literature available for the candidates to read?
- Have all members of the interview panel studied the candidates' application forms thoroughly?

> ### Portfolio tip
>
> *In order to achieve this unit you will be required to participate in a set of interviews as an interviewer. Make sure you make use of this checklist to ensure that the interview(s) you are required to carry out run go as smoothly as possible.*

*An interview panel must prepare*

- Are all the members of the interview panel aware of the part they will play in the interview and the questions they will be asking?

## Selection day exercise

It is quite common for a business to set an exercise or task at the interview so they can judge the capabilities of the candidates. Exercises and tasks can take many forms depending on the nature of the job. Using the example of a Receptionist/Data Input Clerk (The Warehouse), the candidates may be asked to input information into the computer. The business can check the candidate's computer skills, the speed they can input data and also their accuracy.

When applying for a teaching position candidates are often required to teach a lesson. This enables the school/college to see how the lesson is delivered and how the candidate interacts with the students. For more senior positions a presentation may also be required.

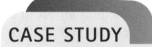

## CASE STUDY

### Two different methods

When the Office of National Statistics first started to undertake the Labour Force Survey using telephone interviews it required 100 members of staff to work a variety of shift patterns.

The organisation placed an advertisement in two local papers. Potential applicants were required to telephone in. When applicants telephoned they were given a day and time to attend an hour-long intelligence test. After the test, applicants left and were informed by telephone if they had reached the second stage. The second stage was an interview which included a telephone test. If successful in the telephone role play, applicants were asked to stay for a one-to-one interview. If successful at the final interview stage the applicant was offered the position.

Some Pizza Hut restaurants have a very high turnover of staff and are finding it increasingly difficult in certain areas of the country to find

people of the correct calibre. To overcome this, one Pizza Hut manager interviews potential employees on a one-to-one basis and then offers them a 12-week contract. This means that if the applicant is unsuitable for the position the manager does not have to renew their contract at the end of 12 weeks.

1 Describe the three stages the Office of National Statistics went through prior to offering a potential candidate the position of a telephone interviewer.

2 Suggest and justify reasons why you think the Office of National Statistics went through the three different stages prior to offering potential applicants the position.

3 Explain why you think the Pizza Hut manager uses the methods of interview as described above.

4 Suggest and justify improvements to both systems outlined above.

## Interview role plays

Interview tasks may include a role play, for example a job in customer service might require a role play scenario involving a difficult customer. The reasoning behind this type of interview technique is to see how applicants interact with people and how they react in stressful situations.

These techniques are very useful in assessing candidates' suitability, however the interview panel should remember that candidates often find interview situations very stressful and therefore may not perform to their highest standards due to nerves. If the applicant is put at ease and the scenarios set out correctly then the interview panel should be able to gain useful information from a competency-based exercise.

## *Recording applicant performance*

During the interview process the interview panel should make notes that can be referred to at the end of the process. If you were a member of an interview panel and had to interview six applicants in one day, it is very unlikely that you would remember, in detail, each candidate's responses by the end of the day. It is therefore vital that an accurate method of recording responses and performance is designed prior to the interviews taking place.

In order to design this document, you need first to consider the criteria on which you will be judging the candidates. You need to ask the following questions.

- Will you make judgements on how the candidate is dressed?
- Will you make judgements on how well the candidate presents him or herself?
- Will you make judgements on how well the candidate responded to questions?

Once the criteria are established, you can then base your pro-forma on the competencies outlined in the person specification. The candidate's answers should elaborate on the information that has already been supplied within the application form.

# Offer of employment and feedback

Having undertaken the interview process, the interview panel must agree on who to offer the position to.

## *Format of employment offer and contract*

Prior to the interview the panel has to decide how it will inform the successful candidate. There are a variety of ways of doing this.

- Candidates all wait until the end of the process and then they are informed verbally of who has got the position. This method is quite commonly used in teaching.

- The successful applicant will be telephoned after the interview process has finished. Once they have verbally accepted the position they will be sent a formal letter offering the position.

- The successful applicant is notified in writing that they have been appointed to the position.

Having accepted the position the applicant is entitled, under the Employment Rights Act of 1996, to receive a written contract of employment within two months of commencement of employment. The contract of employment will state the employee's terms and conditions of work.

## Means of candidate's acceptance

If the candidate has been offered the position on the telephone, the offer of employment will be confirmed in a letter which will also outline the terms and conditions of the job. The successful candidate will be required to sign the letter of formal acceptance. This is the official agreement that they will start work for the business on a set date and have accepted the terms and conditions being offered.

## Feedback to unsuccessful candidates

As soon as the successful candidate has formally accepted the offer of employment, the unsuccessful candidates will be notified. This can either be done by a telephone call or a formal letter.

All unsuccessful candidates are entitled to feedback on their interview performance. The purpose of this process is to help unsuccessful candidates improve their interview technique and understand why they were unsuccessful on this occasion. Feedback should be constructive and supportive, clearly stating at what points the candidate performed particularly well and where improvements could be made.

## AO2 Explain, using examples, the impact of legal and ethical constraints on the design and operation of a recruitment process

The recruitment and selection process used by any business, regardless of the size, must be fair to all candidates. There must be no discrimination. To ensure this happens, there is a variety of equal opportunity legislation that must be adhered to throughout the recruitment and selection process. There are also ethical considerations that need to be taken into account to ensure the business does in fact employ the correct person for the job.

# Data Protection Act

The Data Protection Act 1998 protects employees against the misuse of personal data, and now covers both manual and electronic records.

The Act requires that any personal data held should be:

- processed fairly and lawfully
- obtained and processed only for specific and lawful purposes
- adequate and relevant and not excessive
- accurate and kept up to date
- Held securely and for no longer than is necessary
- Not transferred to a company outside the European Economic Area unless there is an adequate level of data protection in that country.

A business is allowed to collect personal data for the purpose of recruitment and selection. It is generally accepted that personal data would fall within the following categories:

- personal details including name, address, age, status and qualifications. Where specific monitoring systems are in place, ethnic origin and nationality will also be deemed as relevant
- references and CVs
- emergency contact details
- notes on discussions between applicants and management
- health information
- bank and building society details.

Potential employees of a business must be advised of the personal data that has been obtained and retained and the source. They must also be informed why the information was obtained and to whom it will be disclosed.

To ensure compliance with the Act disclosure of the information is governed by the following conditions:

- personal data must only be used for the purposes specified
- provided that the identification of individual employees is not disclosed, aggregate or statistical information may be used to respond to any legitimate internal or external requests for data (e.g. surveys, staffing level figures)
- personal data must not be disclosed either within or outside the business to any unauthorised recipient.

Applicants for positions now have the right to access personal data held about them.

# How does this affect the recruitment and selection process?

## The application form

This form is specifically designed to gather personal information about the potential applicant. The business must consider what information is needed from the applicant, and who will have access to this information. The business must then pass this information on to the applicant. If you look at the bottom of most application forms, or within the accompanying instructions, this information will be clearly stated.

If the business wishes to collect information on race or ethnic origin, a separate form will be included that the applicant is not obliged to complete. This form will be separated from the main application form and will not form part of the shortlisting process.

## Recording applicant performance form

At the end of the selection process the applicant is entitled to have access to any notes that have been made about them during the interview process. A business must ensure that the records kept throughout the process are accurate and do not breach any of the equal opportunities legislation. If they do, the applicant may have a case of discrimination against the business.

## References

If the business has requested references from past employers, the applicant has a right to see these as they will have informed the selection process.

## ACTIVITY

As a class, collect as many different application forms as you can and then compare them. Do they all ask for similar information? Do they all comply with the Data Protection Act of 1998? Identify the different ways that potential applicants have been informed of how the business intends to use the information collected.

## Portfolio tip

*Keep all of the application forms that the class has collected. These will help when designing your own application form in order to achieve AO3.*

## Equal opportunities legislation

Equal opportunities is supported by a suite of Acts which must be recognised and adhered to. These Acts were brought into force to ensure that everybody is treated fairly throughout the recruitment and selection process and during employment. Equal oppportunities legislation is covered by:

- Disability Discrimination Act 1995
- Rehabilitation of Offenders Act 1973
- Sex Discrimination Act 1975
- Race Relations Act 1976
- Equal Pay Act 1970.

The Equal Opportunities Commission (EOC) is the leading agency working to eliminate discrimination. The Commission aims to:

- run high-profile campaigns to change public opinion as well as the law, e.g. on equal pay, the rights of pregnant women at work and the rights to flexible working

- publish research about women and men in the UK today, to show clearly where changes are still needed

- use unique legal powers of enforcement to investigate organisations or areas of life where sex discrimination is persistent or happens frequently

- take landmark cases under the Sex Discrimination Act and the Equal Pay Act to improve the situation for women and men in the future. The Commission's cases set legal precedents to secure equal treatment for women and men in areas as diverse as pay, recruitment, pensions, education and sport.

## Facts and figures

**Equal pay?** A woman and a man both work full time. On average, he earns £14.08 per hour, but she only earns on average £11.67 per hour.

**Equal choices?** In 2002, 75 per cent of working women were in the five lowest paid sectors. In engineering and construction 97 per cent of modern apprentices are men, who earn about £115 a week. In social care, 89 per cent of apprentices are women, earning about £60 a week.

**Equal power?** Women hold less than one in ten of the top positions in the top 100 companies, the police, the judiciary and trade unions.

Women's representation at Westminster is among the lowest in the world: only 18 per cent of MPs are women.

Source: www.eoc.org.uk

*Equality – I think not!*

**ACTIVITY**

Looking at the facts and figures, do you think there is still a need for equal opportunity legislation?

## Disability Discrimination Act

The Disability Discrimination Act 1995 (Section 4) made it unlawful for an employer with more that 15 employees to discriminate against a disabled person. However, from 1st October 2004, the Disability Discrimination Act was updated to include employers with fewer than 15 employees.

This Act means that employers must not discriminate against disabled employees or job applicants because of their disability. The employer may have to make reasonable adjustments to the workplace if they already have a disabled employee or a disabled person applies for the job.

## How does this affect the recruitment and selection process?

It is quite common now for businesses to request information about disability on their application forms. They will ask if a person is registered disabled and for details concerning their disability. Some businesses state that they will offer an interview to all disabled people who are able to do the job.

Reasonable adjustments to the way an employer recruits staff could include:

- making application forms available in large print or Braille
- allowing applications to be made in formats other than in writing, e.g. audio tape
- providing a sign language interpreter for interviews
- holding the interviews in a venue accessible to all.

A business must consider reasonable adjustments to the workplace under this legislation. They could include:

- rearranging furniture to provide better access
- reallocating some duties of a job to another member of staff
- allowing someone to work more flexible hours
- allowing someone time off for rehabilitation or treatment
- providing information in an accessible format such as large print, Braille or on audio tape
- providing a piece of specialist equipment such as a textphone for a hearing impaired person or a screen reader for a visually impaired person
- moving a disabled person to another available vacancy or to a more accessible site.

*Holding the interviews in a venue accessible to all*

## Rehabilitation of Offenders Act

The Rehabilitation of Offenders Act 1974 enables some criminal convictions to become 'spent', or ignored, after a 'rehabilitation period'. A rehabilitation period is a set length of time from the date of conviction. After this period, with certain exceptions, an ex-offender is not normally obliged to mention the conviction when applying for a job.

If an applicant has a spent conviction they do not have to declare it on the application form as long as the position is not exempt under the Act. A spent conviction is not considered proper grounds for rejecting applicants. However, if the applicant fails to disclose unspent convictions when asked to do so they could be dismissed on the grounds of deception.

Due to the sensitive nature of some employment there are some exceptions to the Act. These include:

- appointment to any post providing accommodation, care, leisure and recreational facilities, schooling, social services, supervision or training to people aged under 18, e.g. teachers, school caretakers, youth and social workers, child minders

- employment providing social services to elderly people, mentally or physically disabled people, alcohol or drug misusers or the chronically sick

- appointment to any office or employment involving the administration of justice, including police officers, probation officers, traffic wardens

- appointment to jobs where national security may be at risk, e.g. certain posts in the civil service, defence contractors.

## How does this affect the recruitment and selection process?

Businesses will first have to decide if the position they are offering fits into one of the categories that is considered to be exempt. If this is the case, they will have to state this on their job advertisement.

The application form will need a section which requests information on past criminal convictions. It is usual to find that application forms have a section that declares if the post being applied for is exempt from the legislation. This information must be made very clear to the applicant.

## Sex Discrimination Act

The Sex Discrimination Act 1975 makes it illegal to discriminate against anybody on grounds of their gender or marital status. Discrimination can be direct or indirect. Direct is where a position could be advertised as 'salesmen' or it could be indirect such as a job advertisement requiring an employee who can lift 25 kg. This could exclude women from applying for the job.

## CASE STUDY

### Discrimination against Offenders

Within its application form Parcels on the Move, a delivery business, uses the following statement to find out if an applicant has any previous convictions.

*Have you ever been convicted or found guilty by a Court of an offence (including ALL motoring offences) or have you been put on probation or conditionally discharged or bound over after being charged with any offence or received an official police caution or is there any action pending against you?*

*If you fail to disclose your past history or withhold any information in order to gain employment you will be guilty of an offence under STATUTE and the company will instigate prosecution in such instances.*

A large London-based transport business includes the following section in their application form.

*Apart from spent convictions, as defined under the Rehabilitation of Offenders Act 1974, have you been convicted of a criminal offence, or are there any criminal charges outstanding against you? (answer Yes or No)*

*If you are invited to interview you will be asked to give details of your criminal convictions (and outstanding charges). Unless the nature of work demands it, you will not be asked to disclose convictions which are 'spent' under the Rehabilitation of Offenders Act 1974. Criminal records will be taken into account for recruitment purposes only when the conviction is relevant. Having an 'unspent' conviction will not necessarily bar you from employment. This will depend on the circumstances and background to your offence(s).*

1  Explain why you think Parcels on the Move asks applicants to declare all motoring offences?
2  Suggest and justify ways that Parcels on the Move could improve its statement, including clear references to the Rehabilitation of Offenders Act 1974.
3  The large London transport business makes a very detailed statement. Describe how you think this would help potential applicants.

There are some instances where a job is allowed to be advertised for a specific sex. This would be due to the nature of job, for example a housemaster to be responsible for the care of young men, or a housemistress to care for young women.

## How does this affect the recruitment and selection process?

The whole recruitment and selection process is affected by this legislation. While completing the job description and person specification, a business must make sure that it does not contain any sexist language. Has the business in any way discriminated against one of the sexes?

The application form must be designed so that it does not ask any leading questions which would indirectly discriminate against men or women.

During the selection stage, gender must not influence which candidates are selected to attend for interview. The shortlist must be based on the applicant's ability and suitability to do the job. During the interview all members of the interview team must ensure that all candidates are asked the same questions and they do not allow bias into the selection process.

## CASE STUDY

### Sex Discrimination

On the 10th August 2005 a part-time payroll worker for Cornelia Care Homes was awarded £29,294 in damages by a Southampton employment tribunal. The tribunal found that her employer, Cornelia Care Homes, was wholly unwilling to discuss the issues that gave rise to this claim in refusing to consider flexible working options and adopting a position that was unreasonable and sticking to it. The decision stated: 'We have no doubt that the imposition of those criteria, whether taken singly or in combination, were indirectly discriminatory against the claimant on the grounds of sex.'

The story starts in June 2004 when the claimant was hired as a part-time payroll clerk on a 16 hours per week contract by Cornelia Care Homes, a Hampshire-based company that runs care homes. As a single parent with a two-year-old son, the claimant took on the part-time position in order to meet her caring responsibilities. However, in January 2005 her employer demanded that she should start working full-time in order to cope with the rapid growth of the company.

The claimant presented her employer with several reasonable flexible work options, including sharing her job with another part-time payroll worker on a similar 16-hour week contract – bringing her hours close to that of a full-time position. She also offered to work the additional hours from home. Her employer refused, demanding that she work a minimum of 25 hours per week in the office. This left her with no other option but to resign.

1 Describe the ways that you consider the employer breached equal opportunities legislation.
2 Explain whether you think the outcome of the tribunal was fair.

Source: www.eoc.org.uk

## Race Relations Act

The Race Relations Act 1976 states that it is illegal to discriminate against anybody due to their race. The Act is enforced by the Commission for Racial Equality which can give employers advice on how to ensure they are not inadvertently discriminating against different ethnic minorities in their recruitment and selection processes.

# How does this affect the recruitment and selection process?

While compiling the job description and person specification, businesses must make sure that they do not, in any way, prohibit people from different cultural backgrounds from applying.

The application form must be designed in such a way that it would encourage applicants from a wide variety of cultural backgrounds.

During the interview process the interview team must make sure that they do not directly or indirectly discriminate against people from different cultural backgrounds.

## CASE STUDY

### Race Discrimination

A West Indian sailor won his tribunal against Wightlink (a ferry operating company) for Race Discrimination. The claimant, a 34-year-old bachelor, worked as a temporary deckhand on the Portsmouth-Fishbourne route. The tribunal found in the claimant's favour a case of racial discrimination because an application for a permanent job was rejected despite more than a year's service with the firm. At the time the claimant was turned down a number of other people who had not worked previously for the company were employed.

The chairman stated 'There was discrimination here with regard to the failure to give him a full consideration for the job'.

Source: Adapted from *The News* (Portsmouth) Friday February 27 2004

**Suggest and recommend a policy that Wightlink could use in order to ensure they do not breach the Race Relations Act in the future when undertaking recruitment and selection exercises.**

## Equal Pay Act

The Equal Pay Act 1970 gives an individual the right to the same rate of pay/salary and benefits as a person of the opposite sex in the same employment, where the man and woman are doing:

- like work or
- work rated at the same grade under an analytical job evaluation or study
- work that is proved to be of equal value.

The employer will not be required to provide the same benefits or the same pay if it can be proved that the difference in pay or benefits is genuinely due to a reason other than one related to sex.

If an employee feels that they are being discriminated against they are able to take their case to an employment tribunal. Claims may be brought at any time during employment and within six months of leaving employment. If a claim is successful, the complainant will be entitled to:

- the same level of pay or benefits as his or her comparator for the future (if the complainant is still in the same job) and

- back pay representing the difference in pay (subject to a limit) with interest.

## How does this affect the recruitment and selection process?

Once a business has decided that a vacancy does exist it will start the job analysis. At this stage the rate of pay must be carefully matched against the pay received by other employees who are doing the same or comparable work.

The Equal Opportunities Commission does offer help and advice to employers concerning all equal opportunities matters. They hope to avoid any breach of the legislation in place and ensure that equality is maintained throughout the workforce.

## Ethical constraints

In our highly competitive world many businesses consider complying with legislation a minimum requirement. They also set themselves ethical guidelines to ensure their employees remain happy and motivated within the workplace. These ethical guidelines apply to all parts of the business, including the recruitment and selection process.

When setting up interviews one of the most important considerations is the type of questions the business will ask the potential candidates. The purpose of questioning is to find out as much as possible about the candidates. The aim is not to try and trick them. Questions have to be sufficiently demanding to discover if the candidate is 'up to the job', but also non-threatening.

There are two types of questions that could be used – open or closed. An open question allows the applicant to give a fully expanded answer. A closed question will only receive a 'yes or no' answer. A highly skilled interviewer will be able to encourage and probe the most nervous of **interviewees**, helping to maximise their chances of acquiring the position.

# Unbiased interview questions and fairness to all candidates

It takes skill to write a full set of interview questions. The first stage is to consider exactly what information about the candidate is required. The second stage is to decide the best way to obtain this information through questioning.

Let us first consider what biased means. It means to have an opinion that would favour one type of person or group of people. If you were part of an interview team and really wanted the new employee to be a young man, you might design questions that would favour young male candidates. It is therefore vitally important that any questions that are asked at interview are general and can be answered equally by all candidates.

Interviews often follow a common theme. The candidate is settled into the interview with a simple question about their journey or how they heard about the job. They will then often be asked a general set of questions that would be the same for all applicants. However, some of these might be based on information stated on their application forms. Some questions might relate to past employment history and how this could assist with the vacancy they are applying for. The questions will also be linked to the skills and personal qualities that the business is looking for. There will then be a set of questions that link directly to the candidate's application form, which could be focused on hobbies, ability to work in teams or past experiences.

# Feedback to unsuccessful candidates

All candidates who have participated in the interview process are entitled to have feedback concerning their performance. The purpose of this is to assist unsuccessful candidates improve their own performance, helping them to secure employment in the future.

Feedback must be constructive not destructive. A candidate may be disappointed they failed to get the job and therefore do not need their confidence further damaged by harsh and maybe unfair feedback.

When giving feedback the interviewer must remember to:

- start the conversation discussing the areas in which the applicant interviewed well
- then move on to areas where improvements could be made
- make suggestions as to how the candidate could improve their performance in the future
- ask the candidate if they have any questions.

## AO3  Produce a complete recruitment pack for a selected job vacancy in a real business organisation

In order to achieve this assessment objective you need to use all the knowledge, understanding and skills that you have achieved working through AO1 and AO2.

This section requires you to design your own recruitment pack. Remember it must be:

- **attractive** – will potential applicants apply to your advertisement?

- **informative** – does your job description and personal specification contain sufficient information for potential applicants?

- **accurate** – do your selection documents, shortlist pro-forma and interview recording sheets provide sufficient information to make an informed decision?

- **fair** – is your interview and selection day exercise fair? Will it give all applicants the same opportunity for success?

- **unbiased** – have all the documents completed allowed the interview panel to make an unbiased, non-discriminatory and informed decision. Do the procedures you have put in place enable you to choose the best candidate for the job?

### Portfolio tip

*This section gives you the opportunity to put into practice all the theory covered within AO1 and AO2. You need to look back at the purpose and layout of all the documents. As you design your documents, ask yourself 'do they breach any equal opportunities legislation'? Compare your documents with those produced by other businesses.*

## Elements of the recruitment pack

In order to achieve this assessment objective you are required to design and complete all the documents outlined below. Remember, as you design the forms, you must consider all the equal opportunities legislation and ethical constraints that were outlined in AO2.

### Materials for the applicant

This is probably the largest section and requires you to start the recruitment process. The documents you need to design/complete are outlined below:

- **Job analysis** - records the tasks and duties that the new employee must undertake.

- **Job description** – tasks, duties and responsibilities that will make up the position.

- **Person specification** – the qualifications, skills and experience that the employee should have in order to fulfil the position.

- **Advertisement** – will inform potential applicants of the vacancy. Must inform applicants how to apply for the position – will they apply by letter, CV or application form or a mixture?

- **Application form** – if you want your applicants to use an application form, you will have to design a suitable one.

## Materials for recruiting personnel to receive applications and shortlist

You should devise a form which will enable you to shortlist your applicants in order to only select those who are most suitable for the job being advertised. If you refer back to page 309 you will see an example of a shortlist pro-forma.

---

Highland Holiday Homes
Black Ridge Farm
Oban
Scotland
OB19 7HY

Telephone: 0245 871298
Fax: 0245 871299
Email – www.highlandhols@ntl.co

15 September 2005

Miss J Hooper
23 Burns Avenue
Oban
Scotland
OB91 2WM

Dear Miss Hooper

Further to your application for the position of Receptionist at Highland Holiday Homes I would like to invite you to attend an interview on Tuesday 20 September 2005 at 10 am.

The interviews will be held at the Holiday Homes site, Black Ridge Farm. The interview will take about 2 hours and will consist of a tour of the holiday site, telephone role play and a formal interview. You are required to bring with you a copy of your birth certificate or passport and certificates for qualifications stated in your application form.

Would you please telephone me on the above number to confirm your attendance at the interview. I have enclosed a map and directions to the site and look forward to seeing you on the 20 September.

Yours sincerely

Margaret Drinkwater
Human Resources Manager

Enc

---

**Figure 17.8** *Example of letter inviting candidate for interview*

## Standard letters

In order to complete this section you are required to design and complete three standard letters:

- invite candidates to interview (see Figure 17.8)
- offer the job to the successful candidate
- post-interview rejection letters. These could include some feedback on each candidate's interview performance.

In order to make your recruitment pack look professional you will need to design headed paper for your selected business. Remember to include the following information in your header.

- name and address
- telephone and fax number
- website address.

You will also need to follow these conventions:

- date the letter – 20 May 2005
- use open punctuation in the address, date and salutation – Mr Smith, Dear Mr Smith ... Yours sincerely, Dear Madam ... Yours faithfully
- 5 line spaces between Yours faithfully/sincerely ... the signature block
- if you have enclosed information – Enc (2 line spaces after the signature).

## Selection day exercise

A formal interview which solely consists of questions and answers does not always fully indicate to a potential employer the abilities of a candidate.

One way to find out the capabilities of a candidate is to set an exercise or task for them to complete as part of the interview process.

If the position is task-based, the candidate could be asked to perform a simple task, for example:

- undertake data input
- a role play to demonstrate customer service
- a telephone role play.

All these tasks will enable the candidate to demonstrate their abilities and suitability for the position.

If the position is for a higher grade the applicant may be asked to give a presentation on a set subject. A presentation will show the interview panel how well a potential employee organises his or her thoughts and ideas, ability to talk to an audience and answer questions.

When devising your selection day exercise make sure it is related to the position that you are advertising. First of all, consider what the candidates will actually be required to do within this position and how this could be tested through a simple exercise. Remember that your applicants will be nervous so do not make it too difficult. You must also record how long the exercise takes to ensure that your candidates are given sufficient time to complete the exercise.

## Interview materials

Having organised the interview as outlined in AO1, you need to consider the type and variety of questions you will use within the process. Remember equal opportunities here – make sure your questions are not biased and are appropriate for a wide variety of applicants.

In order to adhere to equal opportunities legislation, candidates should all be asked similar, if not identical, questions. A range of headings to consider when planning your own interview are given below.

- **Welcome introduction to the business** – Did you have a good journey? How did you hear about the job?

- **Tell 'me' about yourself** – questions based on the applicant's application form, e.g. hobbies, interests, involvement in charity work, personal achievements

- **Qualifications** – discussion about what the qualifications entailed

- **Current and past employment experiences** – questions based on previous and current employment status

- **What qualities could you bring to this position** – Why do you think we should appoint you?

- **Questions from candidate** – invite the candidate to ask any questions.

> **Real business**
>
> Asking where a candidate heard about the position enables the business to ascertain how well it placed its advertisements.

## Interview record sheet

Having decided who to interview and what format the interview will take, the interview team will need a method of recording the responses of the candidate. This will then feed into the final selection decision. Making notes throughout an interview is very useful as it allows interviewers to look back and evaluate all the positives and negatives of each candidate. At the end of a long day of interviews it is very difficult to remember exactly what the first candidate's response was to a particular question!

An interview record sheet can take a number of formats. It may allow the interview panel to make general comments or it may be directly linked to the questions being asked and the candidate's responses. Figure 17.9 shows an example of an interview record sheet that assesses the general performance of the candidate.

You may wish to follow this format or you may choose to link your interview record sheet more directly to the structure of your interview.

## INTERVIEW RECORD SHEET

Position applied for: ................................................   Name of Applicant: ................................................

| | 1 | 2 | 3 | 4 | 5 |
|---|---|---|---|---|---|
| **Appearance**: Suitability of dress, personal grooming | | | | | |
| **Appearance - comments** | | | | | |
| **Manner**: Confident, natural, mature | | | | | |
| **Manner – comments** | | | | | |
| **Verbal skills**: Ability to explain and develop ideas and arguments | | | | | |
| **Verbal skills – comments** | | | | | |
| **Disposition**: Positive, friendly, flexible in attitude | | | | | |
| **Disposition – comments** | | | | | |
| **Intelligence**: ability to reason, solve problems and analyse | | | | | |
| **Intelligence – comments** | | | | | |
| **Academic background**: recent examinations taken – reasons for chosen courses | | | | | |
| **Academic – comments** | | | | | |
| **Interests and experiences**: hobbies, interests and personal achievements | | | | | |
| **Interests – comments** | | | | | |
| **Past employment**: skills qualities gained, relevance to position | | | | | |
| **Past employment – comments** | | | | | |
| **Leadership experience**: evidence of past leadership, team player | | | | | |
| **Leadership experience – comments** | | | | | |

*Key: – 1 – Outstanding 2 – Above average standard 3 – Average standard 4 – Below Average  5 – Poor*

**Overall grade of candidate**

**General Comments**

Signed: ................................................   Date: ................................

Figure 17.9 *Interview record sheet*

## Offer letter and typical contract terms

The interview process is complete and the panel has selected the person for the job. Now is the time to let the successful candidate know. In order to speed up the process it is quite common for the business to contact the successful candidate by telephone to offer the position. The candidate will be required to state verbally (after an agreed period for consideration) whether they are prepared to accept the terms and conditions of the job. If

---

**Highland Holiday Homes**
**Black Ridge Farm**
**Oban**
**Scotland**
**OB19 7HY**

Telephone: 0245 871298
Fax: 0245 871299
Email – www.highlandhols@ntl.co

21 September 2005

Miss J Hooper
23 Burns Avenue
Oban
Scotland
OB91 2WM

Dear Miss Hooper

Further to your interview for the position of Receptionist I am very pleased to confirm our offer of employment, together with the relevant documentation.

In accepting this appointment, under the terms and conditions of the contract will you please sign one copy of the Statement (enclosed) and return to me as soon as possible.

As agreed at the interview your first day will be Monday 3rd October 2005 starting at 9am. Would you please report to reception and ask for Diane who will be responsible for your induction to the business.

We all look forward to seeing you on the 3rd. If you have any queries please do not hesitate to contact me.

Yours sincerely

Margaret Drinkwater
Human Resources Manager

Enc

---

**Figure 17.10** *Example of letter offering the successful candidate the job*

both parties agree, then the business will send the formal job offer which will contain the written terms and conditions of the post (see Figure 17.10). The candidate will be required to sign both copies of the document, return one copy to the business and keep a copy for their own records. The official offer may include the contract of employment.

Under the **Employment Rights Act 1996** all employees are entitled to receive a contract of employment provided their work lasts for more than one month (see Figure 17.11). This must be received no later than two months after commencement of employment. The contract of employment must contain the following information:

- the name of the employer and employee
- the date when the employment began
- remuneration (pay) and the intervals at which it is to be paid
- hours of work
- holiday entitlement
- entitlement to sick leave and sick pay
- pensions and pension schemes
- notice of termination required by employer and employee
- job title or a brief job description
- where the job is not permanent, the period for which the employment is expected to continue or, if it is for a fixed term, the date when it is to end
- the place of work
- details of any relevant collective agreements with trade unions or staff associations which directly affect the terms and conditions of the employee's employment.

---

### Contents of a contract of employment

**Job title:** This is the title of the position an employee is being appointed to do. For example: Clerical Assistant Grade 2.

**Hours of Work**

The Working Time Regulations state that no employee can be made to work more than 48 hours per week unless they choose to do so. This section will outline the hours the employee is required to work. The hours could be described as outlined below.

Monday – Friday 9.00 am – 5.30 pm with one hour for lunch. Or simply 37.5 hours per week.

Shift patterns could be described, for example 6.00 am – 2.00 pm, 2.00 pm – 10.00 pm and 10.00 pm – 6.00 am.

---

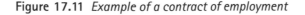

Figure 17.11 *Example of a contract of employment*

The **Employment Act 2002** supports the Government's commitment to create highly productive, modern and successful workplaces through fairness and partnership at work. The main provisions of the Act aim to:

- help working mothers – increase in maternity leave to 26 weeks paid and 26 weeks unpaid

- recognise the role of fathers and adoptive parents – 2 weeks paid paternity leave for working fathers

- facilitate flexible working – mothers and fathers of children under 6 or disabled children under 18 are able to request flexible working arrangements

- dispute resolution – the Act aims to develop constructive employment relations and void the need for litigation through better communication in the workplace and improved conciliation.

Flexitime may be in operation and the contract will explain how this system works within the business. Flexitime is where the employee is required to work a set number of hours per week but can choose when to do these hours between set core times. For example, the employee is required to work 37.5 hours per week. The business is open from 7 am to 7 pm, but the core time the employee must be in work is 10 am-12 pm and 2 pm–4 pm. The remainder of the hours can be fitted in around the opening times of the business.

Hours of work could also include arrangements for overtime.

## Rate and method of payment
As from October 2005 the national minimum wage will be as follows:

- Main (adult) rate for workers aged 22 and over – £5.05 per hour increasing to £5.35 in October 2006.

- Development rate for workers aged 18–21 inclusive – £4.25 per hour increasing to £4.45 in October 2006.

- New Young Workers rate for 16- and 17-year-olds will remain at £3.00 per hour.

- 16–17-year-old apprentices will be exempt from the New Young Workers rate.

This section outlines how much the employee will be paid. This could be an hourly rate or an annual salary. If an employee is paid hourly it may include overtime rates as applicable. Salaried employees are not often paid overtime. Their salary reflects the hours they are required to work in order to complete their work load.

The method of payment will state how and when the employee will receive payment for the work undertaken. Employees can be paid weekly or monthly.

Employees will also need to know how they will receive their wages. This could be by cheque in a pay packet or payment via their bank account.

*Holidays are an important part of working life*

## Holiday arrangements

Under the Working Time Directive every worker, whether full-time or part-time, is entitled to four weeks' paid holiday a year. The leave entitlement is not additional to bank holidays. There is no statutory right to take bank holidays off.

A week's leave should allow workers to be away from work for one week. It should be the same amount of time as the normal working week. For example, if an employee works a 5-day week, he or she is entitled to 20 days' paid holiday. If an employee works a 3-day week, he or she is entitled to 12 days' paid leave.

In this section the employee will be informed of leave entitlement. It may also state when leave can be taken and how much advanced notice the employer requires before leave can be taken.

## Notice requirements

This section will inform the employee how much notice is required by either party in order to terminate employment with the business.

If an employee is paid weekly, the notice period required is usually one week. If an employee is paid monthly then often a month's notice is required on either side.

## Pension arrangements

A lot of businesses offer their employees a company pension. This section will outline what percentage of the employee's pay will be deducted each week/month to go towards their pension fund. It will also state the amount the business will contribute to the employee's pension.

## Trade union rights

This will outline any collective agreements that the company has with trade unions. The employee can choose whether to join a trade union or not.

## Disciplinary procedures

From October 2004 **all** businesses must have a written disciplinary and grievance procedure in place. This must cover:

- the disciplinary rules which apply to the employee
- the job title or name of the person to whom the employee can apply, and the way in which the application can be made if the employee is dissatisfied with any disciplinary decision
- any further steps which follow from the making of such an application.

## AO4   Use the recruitment pack to conduct a selection exercise and interview for a single applicant, and evaluate its suitability

This assessment objective revolves around the practical activity of running the interview using the recruitment pack you created in AO3. You can undertake this activity individually or as part of a group where you will be one member of the interview panel.

Being involved in an exercise such as this is extremely beneficial. It enables you to have an insight into what it is like to conduct an interview. You will also learn skills that will prove extremely useful when applying for employment or even interviews as part of university applications. However, in order to gain the most from the exercise, you have to take the whole process seriously.

In order to complete the unit you may have to take on the role of interviewee for another group. You must also take this role seriously. In order to achieve the assessment objective. You will not be judged on your how well you did as an interviewee. However, your assessor might give you some feedback on your performance which could help you improve your overall performance when attending external interviews.

There are two distinct stages to this assessment objective. The first is to actually plan and run the whole recruitment and selection process. The second stage is to evaluate the suitability of the pack that you have created.

Throughout this unit we have been looking at all the documents and paperwork you will need to prepare in order to conduct an interview. Throughout AO3 you have prepared these documents. Now you must evaluate how successful they were. In order to do this, let us first think about what evaluate actually means. In this context it requires you to make judgements about how successfully your recruitment pack worked. You will need to consider what went particularly well and why, what was not so successful and why and, finally, what improvements you could make to the documents and processes used.

## Portfolio tip

*As you use your recruitment pack make notes of any parts that do not work well or that work particularly well. These points will help you complete your evaluation at the end of this assessment objective.*

# Selection

The first part of your evaluation requires you to evaluate the selection process. This includes all the documents that you used in order to attract your applicants, select them and request they attend an interview.

The criteria you need to consider for your evaluation are outlined in the following sections.

## Suitability for the role

When looking at suitability you need to consider whether each of the documents produced gave the required and expected results.

Ask yourself the following questions:

- Did your advertisement attract the people who were suitable for the position?

- Was the job description adequate? Did it fully describe the tasks to be undertaken by the employee? Were these tasks suitable for the job title, level of pay being offered? Was the job description too complex with too many tasks? Did it contain too few tasks?

- Was the person specification accurate? Were these the correct skills required to carry out the tasks? Did the position require a more highly-skilled or less highly-skilled person? Did the personal specification deter suitable candidates?

- Did the application form collect the data required to assess applicants' ability to perform the task being advertised?

- Did the shortlisting system work? Were the correct applicants shortlisted? Were more suitable applicants rejected? Was the procedure too rigid, too flexible?

## Level of difficulty

There is an overlap here with suitability. If part of the process was considered too difficult for applicants, it would also have been unsuitable. When trying to evaluate level of difficulty the evaluation must focus on the language used within the documentation. Was the language appropriate for the level of position being offered? Had the applicants completed the application form with the information that the panel was expecting? If not, were some of the questions ambiguous? How could the application form be made more accessible to all applicants?

A major consideration here should be the selection day activity that you prepared for your applicants. You will need to consider:

- How well did the majority of the applicants complete the set task?

- Did the applicants understand the instructions or did they need to seek further clarification?

- Was the time allowed sufficient for the task to be completed by the majority of the applicants?
- Was the task suitable for the level of position being offered?

## Access

This area requires you to evaluate whether your documents met all of the legal considerations discussed in AO2. A good way to tackle this is to take each of the documents that you created and identify how they meet equal opportunities legislation, where there might be a slight problem and how they could be improved to ensure full access for all candidates.

You will also have to consider your selection day task. Did this create problems for any specific group of candidates? Were all the candidates able to complete it without problems?

### Portfolio tip

*You could annotate (add your comments to) your documents and then provide a written paragraph as a summary of your findings.*

# Interview

The second part of this assessment objective is to evaluate the actual interview. The list of criteria to complete this section are outlined in the following sections.

## Conduct

When evaluating this section you need to consider it from two angles:

- How effective was the conduct of the panel?
- How well did the interview flow. Did it proceed in a logical manner? Did the sequencing need to be changed?

The conduct of the panel must reflect how you and the other members of the panel worked together. Consider the following questions:

- Did everybody take their role seriously?
- Did nerves affect the way that you or other members of the panel conducted the interview?
- Were the interview panel dressed appropriately?
- Did the panel present a professional image?
- Did the panel manage to relax the interviewees?
- What improvements could you make?

When evaluating how you actually conducted the interview consider the following points:

- Did you and the panel greet the interviewees and put them at ease?
- Did you clearly introduce yourselves?
- Did the order of events work?

- Did the selection day exercise come at the right point in the interview?
- . Did you ask questions in the correct sequence?

## Environment

The next part of the evaluation requires you to think about the environment in which the interviews were conducted. In order to achieve this section you could consider the following points:

- Could the layout of the chairs and tables have been improved? Did the chosen layout keep the interview formal/informal? What was your intention?
- Was the room quiet and free from interruptions?
- Was the sun shining directly into the candidate's eyes?
- Where did the candidate have to undertake the selection day exercise? Was this suitable? Did they have access to a computer if required? Was anybody available to help the candidate with the technology if required?

## Suitability of questions

The purpose of questioning is to find out as much as possible about each candidate in a short space of time. You designed the questions in order to find out if the applicant could do the job advertised and would fit into the culture of the business. You now need to go back and consider the responses that you received for each of your questions and consider the following points:

- Did the candidates give the type of answers that you were expecting?
- Did you get all the information you needed in order to appoint the most suitable candidate?
- Did the candidates understand all the questions – were there any obvious ambiguous questions.
- Was the time allowed for questioning during the interview too short? Or was the time allocated too long?
- Did you have to probe your candidate to get the depth of answer that you required? If so, how could questions have been rephrased in order to avoid this?
- Did all questions meet equal opportunities legislation?

If you work your way through all of the above sections, using the bullet points as reminders, you will have produced a detailed evaluation of your selection and recruitment exercise. Do not forget to suggest and justify improvements to the process as you work through each section.

## AO5  Evaluate the recruitment methods used by a selected business organisation

In order to achieve this unit you will need to investigate how a real business recruits its new members of staff. You will need to apply all the theory covered in AO1–AO3 to evaluate the procedures that the business uses to recruit and select their staff.

In order to develop the depth of your evaluation you could compare your selected business with another business you are familiar with or the recruitment and selection package that you developed in order to achieve AO4.

You will need to base your evaluation on the following criteria:

- fitness for purpose
- cost to the organisation
- impact on the applicants
- compliance with legal and ethical constraints.

Having completed your evaluation you will be required to recommend any changes you consider would improve the recruitment and selection processes used by the business.

In order to help you with your evaluations we will base this part of the unit on four scenarios which are outlined below. Each scenario explains the recruitment and selection process used by different businesses for different levels of staff.

### Scenario One

Earlier in the unit we met The Warehouse as a business and will now return to investigate this business again.

In order to recruit clerical and warehouse staff, The Warehouse uses a recruitment agency. New employees join the business as temporary employees. If the candidate likes the business and their work is up to standard, they are offered a permanent contract. This process would take approximately three months.

### Scenario Two

When The Warehouse needs to employ a member of the management team it uses a more traditional method of recruitment. It advertises the job nationally, and then runs two-day interviews. The first day evaluates how well the potential employees work together as a team, how well they perform under pressure and their ability to make decisions. The second day is spent giving a formal presentation and then an interview which is conducted by the senior management team.

This method of recruitment and selection is appropriate for this type of position for the following reasons.

The position is advertised nationally so that it will reach a wide audience in order to attract candidates with the correct level of skills and experience. It is unlikely that employees of management calibre would be seeking work through an employment agency and they are unlikely to be prepared to work on a temporary contract. The two-day interviews allow management to get to know the candidates in more depth and also allows candidates to familiarise themselves with the business. This will also help them to decide if this is the correct job for them. It can be a very stressful and expensive process to move into a new area to take up a new position. Therefore candidates must be sure that they make the correct decision.

The activities undertaken on the first day allow management to see how candidates mix with other people, their communication skills and if they have the ability to lead a team. The purpose of a formal presentation is to witness the communication skills of the candidate and to see how confident they are presenting to an audience. It will also show how well the candidate can cope with questions. The formal interviews give the management team a chance to talk in depth to each candidate to find out about their past experiences, interests, expectations and ambitions. All of this information will give the management team a good idea of the qualities of the candidates being interviewed. This information will allow The Warehouse to appoint the correct person who will be able to perform their duties to the required standard and who will also enjoy working for the business.

One of the measures that a business can use to assess how well their recruitment and selection methods are working is to look at their labour retention rate. This indicates how many people leave the business over a set period of time. If the labour turnover is high this could indicate that the business in not recruiting the right people or there are fundamental problems within the business. Management will have to investigate the reasons behind the labour turnover. If the reason links to the recruitment and selection process then the business will have to think about how it could improve its recruitment and selection processes in order to meet the requirement of 'fitness for purpose'.

## Scenario Three

A fast food restaurant was suffering from two problems. The first was a very high turnover of staff. The second was that staff that had been employed were proving to be unsuitable and, once employed on a full-time contract, were very difficult to 'sack'. The main reason for the high turnover was the unsociable and long hours that employees were being asked to work. The nature of the work and the unsociable hours meant the vacancies were attracting students who often left when their courses finished.

The manager decided that one way round the recruitment problem was to only offer new employees a temporary contract which would last for 12 weeks. If the employee had proved themselves over the first 12 weeks they would be offered a permanent contract. This allowed the manager to see how reliable the employee was, how they interacted within the team and also the level of their customer service skills. The employee could also establish if this was the correct position for them. The action solved the first problem, ensuring that all staff employed were suitable. The turnover of staff did decrease, but only slightly as some employees did leave after the initial 12-week trial period. However, those members of staff who gained a permanent contract were still with the business one year later, resulting in a more stable working environment. Working conditions have also improved through better employee and employer relations. Managers are now able to establish good working relationships with their staff because they actually stay with the company for a longer period of time.

## Scenario Four

The local doctors' surgery advertises clerical positions locally. This would include a notice within the surgery and advertisements in the local free press and local newspapers. The skills required for the position can be found in the local area and therefore a national advertising campaign is not required. Due to the size of the business, potential applicants are asked to send a letter of application and a recent CV. The surgery has to cover a wide range of opening hours and so the majority of the clerical positions are part-time, enabling the surgery to cover unsociable hours. There is a plentiful supply of well-qualified personnel who would be willing and able to undertake the duties required.

## Fitness for purpose

This concept considers whether the recruitment and selection processes used by the business produced the required end result. Did the business manage to recruit staff that proved to be efficient and dedicated, or did the process produce an employee who lacked motivation and only performed to a mediocre standard?

The first thing to consider is what position the business recruiting for. This will then give you a basis to decide if the systems in place are actually 'fit for purpose'. You may need to consider the following points:

- Where does the business place its advertisements – will these attract applicants with the required qualifications and skills?

- Are the recruitment and selection documents that the business uses suitable for the level of job being recruited for? Will all applicants understand the questions? Are the questions suitable for all applicants?

## ACTIVITY

Using scenario one, evaluate how the recruitment and selection processes used meet the concept of 'fitness for purpose'.

● Did the interview obtain the information required to judge the candidate's ability to perform the job being interviewed for?

**Figure 17.12** *Assessing 'fitness for purpose'*

## Cost to the organisation

The whole process of recruitment and selection is expensive. It involves many different costs. One of the major costs is labour. Personnel need to get together to discuss the job analysis, construct the job description, person specification and the advertisement. They will then be required to spend time reviewing the applicants and preparing the shortlist. The next stage is to plan the interview, who will be involved, how long the process will last. The final stage is getting the interview panel together to actually run the interviews.

Other costs would include placing the advertisement. It can be extremely expensive to place advertisements in newspapers and trade journals. However, this may be a necessary expense in order to recruit the most suitably experienced and qualified personnel. There are also costs involved in producing application forms, job descriptions and person specifications. Postage costs will also have to be considered. This is one reason why businesses often include in their advertisements the note that if an applicant has not heard from the business within 14 days, they should assume they have been unsuccessful. This saves the business time and money replying to all applicants.

# Impact on the applicants

The recruitment and selection process should have a positive impact on the applicants. Applicants should feel that they have enjoyed and benefited from the process, rather than coming away de-motivated and lacking in confidence.

A business must consider how it can make their recruitment and selection processes accessible to all who apply.

As soon as the recruitment and selection process begins it will have an impact on potential candidates.

The advertisement is designed to have the impact of attracting potential applicants. It must be informative and truthful.

The person specification and job description must be written in such a way that it is easy to understand and truthful.

The application form must be clearly laid out, only containing questions that are relevant to the position being applied for. If a generic application form is being used, inappropriate questions should be crossed through. Some businesses may use the same application form for all members of staff. It might well contain questions that would be seen as inappropriate for lower-skilled employees. If the applicant is applying for a lower-skilled position these might deter them as they feel under-qualified or that they do not have the ability to undertake the job. Some businesses now have two separate application forms – one for lower-skilled employees and another more complex application form for higher-skilled positions. This would reduce the possible negative impact of an over-complex application form.

## ACTIVITY

Using all the scenarios listed above, consider the impact of the different recruitment and selection methods used by the different businesses.

# Compliance with legal and ethical constraints

As you learnt in AO3, there are stringent legal and ethical constraints that must be adhered to throughout the recruitment and selection processes.

You will need to look over all the recruitment and selection material produced by your selected business and evaluate whether it complies with all the legal and ethical constraints as outlined in AO3.

# Recommend changes to procedures

The final part of this section involves your making recommendations for possible improvements the business could make to its recruitment and selection processes.

You should base these recommendations on the evaluation you have conducted on the four criteria. Any weak points could be developed in order to form the basis of your evaluation. In order to gain the higher grades you will need to justify why you think the business should adopt your recommendations. This requires you to state why you think your suggestions will help the business improve its overall recruitment and selection process.

## ACTIVITY

Using the four scenarios above, recommend changes that each business could make to their recruitment and selection procedures. Remember to justify your recommendations.

## SKILLS CHECK

**1** Explain the purpose of the following documentation:
(a) job analysis
(b) job description
(c) person specification.

**2** Design a job advertisement for a checkout assistant at your local supermarket.

**3** Outline the main criteria of the Data Protection Act.

**4** Design five questions that a potential employer could ask applicants for the job of a checkout assistant.

**5** Design a letter that could be used to invite a potential candidate to an interview for the position of checkout assistant.

**6** Design a letter that could be used to inform the successful candidate that they have achieved the position of checkout assistant.

**7** Explain what the term 'fitness for purpose' means in the context of recruitment and selection documentation.

**8** Identify all the legal constraints that affect the recruitment and selection process.

**9** Describe one of the legal constraints that you have identified in (8) above.

# Practical administration

## Getting started

You may be interested in working as an administrator or in some other role within an office environment. This unit will give you the knowledge and understanding of how businesses plan and operate their administration systems, the layout,

resources and systems within those offices, and the role computers play.

You will consider the human resources required for a selected office and the health and safety risks, and identify realistic and practicable measures to reduce those risks.

Finally, you will demonstrate a range of practical skills and will clearly identify sources of help and advice for office administration. To complete this unit successfully, you will need to produce evidence to meet the seven assessment objectives that are contained in the specification. To achieve AO2, AO4, AO5 and AO6 you must produce evidence based on work experience in a 'real (active) office'.

### This unit will cover

- AO1 Explain the importance of establishing effective office administration teams and practices.

- AO2 Investigate an 'active office' and analyse the layout, resources and associated administration systems in operation.

- AO3 Describe the use and purpose of office computer hardware and software, and explain the key issues involved in administration using computers.

- AO4 Explain human resource considerations for a selected office environment.

- AO5 Investigate a selected office environment and propose measures to reduce the health and safety risks and improve the general working environment.
- AO6 Demonstrate a range of practical administration skills.
- AO7 Identify sources of help and advice for a range of office administration functions.

# AO1 Explain the importance of establishing effective office administration teams and practices

To complete this assessment objective successfully, you may produce evidence based on work experience in an 'active office' or you may use offices in a range of businesses, using supporting examples.

Good planning is essential in almost everything you do. For example, you and your friends may decide to organise a day out at a theme park. The first thing you will probably do is to sit down together and rough out a plan. This is likely to look something like the one in Figure 21.1.

With a plan such as this, your day out is likely to be successful and enjoyed by everyone. However, without planning the day may not take place at all. There would have been no vital decisions on where to go and how to get there.

Businesses also need to plan carefully. Administration systems, which are well thought out and tried and tested, are more likely to be successful than those that have not been adequately considered.

In offices, people need systems so that they know exactly what is expected of them. They will want to know what their duties and responsibilities are and the resources that are available to them in order to do their work.

An administration system could be something fairly straightforward such as a holiday rota. Staff would need a system to ensure that everyone is able to book their holiday to suit their circumstances but, at the same time, taking into account that the business could not operate if everyone were to take holiday at the same time.

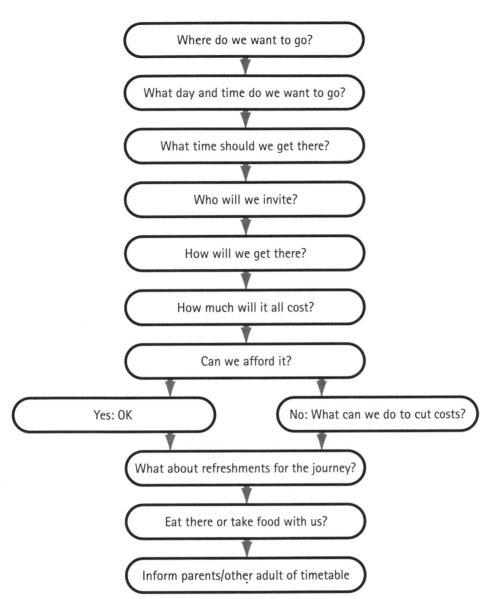

**Figure 21.1** *Plan for day out*

## Development of specialist administration

There are many specialist administrators and these range from those who work in farms, in the legal and medical professions, to those who work in the Houses of Parliament. However, specialist administration can also relate to those people who specialise in a particular role within administration. For example, an employee may have expertise in the production of specific documentation, such as disciplinary or grievance cases, or may be a specialist in using particular equipment or in devising and maintaining procedures such as dealing with incoming and outgoing mail.

Employees are often extensively trained in the use of specific equipment such as photocopiers, computers and software development, and many other specialisms.

Companies often combine people with specialist knowledge into teams. For example, a team of workers may carry out all the document production needs of a business. They work together in order to ensure that all the work is accurate and meets deadlines. They will help each other, offering support and guidance where appropriate to ensure that the work of the team is always carried out in a professional manner so that they will become trusted and can be relied upon.

In your portfolio, you will need to look at specialist administration roles and how these may be developed. You may do this in one office or a number of offices. It may be possible for your tutor to organise a visit, preferably to a variety of offices where you will be able to see at first hand what specialist administration is carried out in those offices and by whom, how they carry out their tasks and the training that they received in order for them to do their jobs.

## CASE STUDY

### Ronald Perkins

Ronald has worked for the same company for over 25 years. Some years ago he undertook specialist training so that he could operate and maintain the company's photocopying machines. Since that time, Ronald has learned not only how to use the more advanced features of the photocopiers but also how to deal with breakdowns such as paper jamming. He receives regular update training and is now the 'expert' on photocopiers in his company. His colleagues rely on him and often ask him for help when they have a problem or cannot work out how to photocopy a document.

Ronald is now a supervisor and also has responsibility for training new staff in the use of the various photocopiers the company uses. He begins with new employees using the basic machines efficiently before showing them how to use the more complicated photocopiers that can produce multi-page, double-sided photocopies and also collate and staple the pages at the end of the photocopying process.

1 How does his company ensure that Ronald can properly operate and maintain up-to-date photocopiers?

2 Outline the system Ronald uses to train new members of staff.

3 In an office that you are familiar with, investigate what specialisms people have. Produce a report for your tutor outlining your findings.

# Personnel

The people who work in a business are an important asset to that organisation. They are also vital in establishing effective office administration systems. People working in offices are likely to be multi-skilled; that is, they have many skills that they put to good use in their jobs. For example, an administrator may have responsibility for document production, organising meetings and maintaining electronic diaries.

The administrative roles that people undertake in a working day will depend very much on the size and type of business in which they are employed. For example, a small building company may employ just one person to carry out all the administrative duties required. On the other hand, a very large multinational company may employ hundreds of people to do this work. They may work in teams so that their particular skills and expertise may be easily utilised.

## *Financial*

In a small business, one person may carry out all the financial affairs of the business. In a larger organisation, however, there is likely to be a finance office with a manager in charge. The work of a finance office is likely to include:

- preparing and checking invoices and sending out statements

- receiving and recording payments from customers

- monitoring expenditure against budgets set by senior management

- banking money received, which may be cheques, credit card vouchers and cash

- overseeing all documentation regarding purchases

- paying suppliers

- keeping records of all transactions

- paying wages and salaries of employees

- dealing with employee expense forms.

## *Document production*

This relates to the production of the different documents that a business needs in order to survive and succeed. In a small office, one person will probably produce all the documentation required. In a larger office, a team of people are likely to be responsible for document production. All documents must go through various stages:

1. The initial stage, where documents are either handwritten or marked-up typescript, or the required documents may be dictated to someone using a system of shorthand, note-taking or an audio transcriber, or the documents may be produced using computer voice recognition software.

**ACTIVITY**

Explain the role of personnel who work in the finance office, or who have responsibility for the financial affairs of a selected business.

2. The processing stage, where the documents are produced accurately and displayed professionally, using a word processor.
3. The final stage, where the document is printed, using either a laser or inkjet printer.

People with specialist expertise in particular documents, such as complicated documents requiring a high level of presentation, would be given responsibility for these, while others would work on more basic documents.

### QUESTIONS

1  Give a definition of the term 'document production'.
2  What type of documents would you expect a trainee to produce?
3  Give examples of the types of documents that would be produced in a small office that has one administrator only.

## Phone handling

All administrators need to be proficient at receiving and making telephone calls. These may be from customers, colleagues, managers or potential customers. Good telephone technique is vital and some companies arrange special training courses for employees to learn the important skills related to use of the telephone. Junior administrators, in particular, may need special help as they may be nervous. Most companies have procedures to help employees when dealing with incoming calls and when making calls.

## ACTIVITY

1  Compile a procedure suitable for employees working in an office to follow when making a telephone call to a client.
2  Working in groups, discuss the procedures that each of you have compiled.
3  Produce a final procedure upon which you are all agreed.

## Fax handling

### GLOSSARY

**Fax cover**:
a sheet of paper that accompanies a fax and contains details of the sender and recipient, such as name, company, fax number.

Some small fax machines are simple and basic and therefore fairly easy to use. Others can be quite complicated to use. Most companies arrange for new members of staff to be shown how to use the fax machines and to complete **fax covers** competently, so that they are able to send and receive faxes with confidence. For example, people using a fax machine for the first time need to follow company procedures carefully, as if the documents to be transmitted are not loaded correctly, it is possible for the machine to scan the wrong side of the document, so sending nothing.

## ACTIVITY

A trainee has asked you for help when sending a two-page fax.

1 Produce a procedure, listing the steps that the trainee should follow in order to send a two-page fax.
2 Make sure that you 'test' your procedure before handing it to the trainee.
3 When the trainee (or a colleague acting as a trainee) has sent the fax, ask him or her for feedback on the procedure you compiled.

# Clarity of roles and allocation of responsibility

Everyone employed in an office will have precise roles. With those roles come specific responsibilities.

All employees receive job descriptions and these will give detailed information about their job, including the hours, the place of work and the duties that are involved. For example, a human resource administrator would expect to carry out duties involving the recruitment and training of employees. A receptionist would work at the reception desk, greeting visitors and answering the telephone.

All the people who work in an administrative role will know who does what jobs and who to go to for help on specific issues. All the roles of these people will be clear. Some firms produce a list of employees, with their duties clearly and simply stated, and give their extension numbers so that communication between employees is easy and straightforward. Enquiries and complaints can also be handled much more easily because all employees will know to whom these should be referred.

# Effective use of resources

Once an administrator knows his or her duties, the next important step would be to know what resources they can use in order to carry out those duties. There are many resources in an office and these may include:

- time – having the time to do the job properly
- people – having the people who have the expertise to do the work efficiently and to deadlines
- equipment – having everything needed to ensure the work is produced accurately and on time
- finance – having the money to buy the resources that are needed and those that may be identified as necessary, as well as sufficient funds to pay the staff for the work they do.

## ACTIVITY

1 Give reasons why time is included as an important resource.
2 Working in groups, discuss the reasons that have been given by individuals.
3 Produce a final list of the reasons given by all the members of the group.

# Management efficiency

A small business may have just one owner who manages his or her company single-handed. In this type of organisation, the owner will have a variety of skills that will ensure the business is successful.

In larger organisations, however, the business is more likely to be managed by a team of people who use their individual skills and expertise. A team of managers will also be able to work closely together, so that each person brings his or her own point of view to a situation.

A management team that works well together will contribute to the overall success of the business, but one that does not work well could lead to the failure of that business. A management team also works well where people work on more than one site within the same company.

The skills required by a management team include sales and marketing, production, finance and administration. However, this list may vary depending on the type and size of the business.

To be efficient, management needs to have clear roles and responsibilities and good communication structures. These may include more formal structures such as regular management meetings, reports on progress made, briefings, or may include informal structures such as team meetings, discussions.

Many companies now use an **appraisal system** to determine what progress has been made over a given timescale, to identify any gaps in an employee's skills and to identify any training that may be required to fill those gaps to ensure improvement in the future.

For efficient management, performance measurement is often put in place. To measure performance, a number of factors can be introduced such as key performance indicators (KPIs). These will identify and measure targets (those areas the business is aiming for) and budgets (resources available to deliver the targets). KPIs can include sales and profit levels (increased or reduced), customer satisfaction, staff turnover and levels of staff sickness absence.

> ### GLOSSARY
>
> **Appraisal system**: used by many businesses to determine the progress of employees and identify skills gaps and training needs.

*Manager and business team working together*

## Communication benefits

Communication with people you work with is easy; effective communication is not so straightforward. Communication can be:

- verbal
- written
- non-verbal.

To be effective, communication needs to:

- have clear aims
- be completely clear and unambiguous
- be easily understood by all parties.

Verbal communication may be face to face (discussions, meetings) or by telephone.

Face-to-face discussions are useful to ensure employees have opportunities to share problems and so help each other to resolve them, to highlight resources that may be needed or simply to talk through shared procedures. You may find it useful to revise this topic by referring back to Unit 3.

Telephone discussions may be used if people are located on different sites or in different geographical regions of the world. They enable people to get an instant response and to have a dialogue to clear up any problems or misunderstandings. They also save people from having to find a colleague in a building.

The use of mobile phones can be of great benefit to a company as they allow people to stay in touch wherever they are and, when contact is not possible, messages can be left via answering machines, voice mail or text message.

Written communication in business includes letters, memos, reports and other items such as notices, information leaflets, etc. Look back at Unit 3 for more details concerning written communications.

Email is another form of communication. Many people working in an office communicate almost exclusively by email, even though the person with whom they are communicating can be seated at the desk next to them.

The use of non-verbal communication, more commonly known as body language, can help people to gauge how a colleague is feeling. For example, someone who is unwilling to maintain eye contact may not be feeling confident in what they are saying.

**Portfolio tip**

*In order to provide the evidence required in your portfolio for this assessment objective, you will need to provide a comprehensive explanation of the importance of establishing effective office administration teams and practices, together with a wide range of supporting examples.*

**QUESTIONS**

1 Give three instances when face-to-face communication would be advantageous in an office.
2 What benefits are there in using a telephone to communicate – with clients and colleagues?
3 What body language would you expect a colleague to display if they were upset about something?

# AO2 Investigate an 'active office' and analyse the layout, resources and associated administration systems in operation

To complete this assessment objective successfully, you will need to produce evidence based on work experience in an 'active office'. You will analyse the office layout, resources and associated administration systems in operation within your chosen office.

## Office layout

Offices may use traditional or open plan layouts. This is often determined by the age of the building in which the office is situated.

### Traditional layout

This provides individual offices or units where one to three people may work together. For example, the traditional layout often provides accommodation in a single room for a manager or other senior staff member and next door in another individual room may be his or her PA, secretary or administrator.

### Open plan layout

Offices situated in newer buildings are often large, open plan areas where several people work together. They have small cubicles or work areas which may be open or screened. The screens are thought to offer some degree of soundproofing.

Some open plan offices have colour-coordinated furnishings, carpets, window blinds and décor. The offices may be air conditioned, and have good amounts of natural daylight. Some companies try to ensure that all employees' workstations are positioned near a source of natural daylight.

# Workstations/seating

Most businesses now minimise the risks to employees using computers and there is legislation such as the Health and Safety (Display Screen Equipment) Regulations with which they must comply. Arranging workstations and equipment to suit employees is very important. For example, a left-handed employee or someone who is very tall may need different settings to someone who is right-handed or quite short. The incidence of **repetitive strain injury** (RSI) is well documented but the number of employees who suffer from upper limb disorders, such as pains in their neck or back, is increasing. These disorders may become persistent or even disabling if not treated promptly.

## *Workstations*

Workstations come in all shapes and sizes. Most businesses will ensure that the workstations they provide for their staff are spacious enough for them to carry out the diverse tasks that will be required in a working day.

Where an employee is using a standalone computer system, such as in Figure 21.2, the desk should be large enough to adequately accommodate all the equipment required. For example, there should be enough space for the monitor, the top of which should be level with the user's eyes. The keyboard may be placed on the desktop or may be stored away in a sliding drawer in the centre of the desk. However, there must be adequate space for the user's legs and the drawer must not rest on his or her legs. The mouse should be close enough for the user to use it with a relaxed arm and a straight wrist. The central processor unit may be accommodated on the floor or may be tucked away in a drawer or cupboard within the desk. It is not usually stored on the desktop. Drawers should be provided so that the user can store stationery that is used regularly, such as letterheads.

All items that a user may require in a normal working day should be within easy reach. This relates to such items as writing and telephone message pads, pens, pencils, rulers, etc.

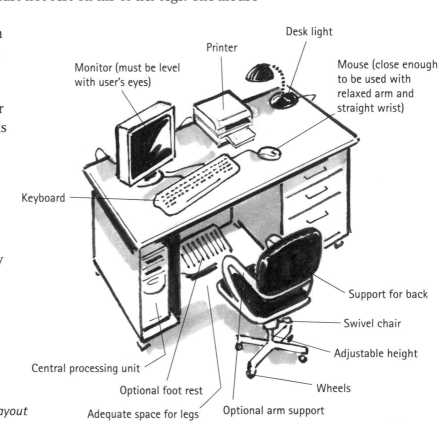

Monitor (must be level with user's eyes)

Printer

Desk light

Mouse (close enough to be used with relaxed arm and straight wrist)

Keyboard

Support for back

Swivel chair

Adjustable height

Central processing unit

Wheels

Optional foot rest

Optional arm support

Adequate space for legs

**Figure 21.2** *Workstation layout*

## *Seating*

Computer users should use chairs that are stable and be able to adjust the height and tilt to ensure that they are working in a comfortable position. Arm supports are preferred by some users, but some prefer their arms to have free movement. The back rest of a chair must provide support for the user's back, particularly the lumbar region, in all sitting positions. Some people, especially those whose feet cannot reach the ground, like to use a foot rest, but others prefer to have their feet flat on the floor.

### ACTIVITY

Using the Internet, office furniture catalogues or brochures that contain items of office furniture, research: (a) a workstation suitable for a standalone computer user, (b) a chair suitable for a computer user.

1   Write a report to your tutor including your findings, together with at least one photograph or picture of each of the above.
2   Highlight in your report those areas where special attention needs to be paid, e.g. height of the chair.

## Filing

A few years ago it was thought that the use of computers would lead to a paperless office. This has not materialised as businesses still prefer to have hard copies that can be referred to in the future.

There are two types of filing – hard copy and electronic.

## *Hard copies*

Every office needs some form of system in which to store hard copies of documents and to ensure easy retrieval. There are many storage systems that may be used and these include:

- vertical filing cabinets – comprising two to six drawers, with suspension pockets into which document folders can be easily placed
- horizontal filing cabinets – normally used for filing very large documents such as architect plans or drawings
- lateral filing cabinets – these resemble a large open cupboard with a solid, lockable door to keep the area secure and clean.

## *Electronic*

One of the most obvious forms of electronic filing is to keep a copy of a file you have created using a word processor. Another form of electronic filing is to use computer software called a database. Although you may have also taken a hard copy of a document, for example a letter that was sent to a

*Electronic filing*

customer, you will also retain the file copy on one of the computer's drives. Most companies using computer networks will have a system of folders where specific documents can be stored and accessed by any employee. This system will work well when a relatively small amount of information needs to be stored. However, when a document is very large, perhaps containing a number of images or graphics, the space required would be much greater. In these instances, other forms of storage would be used such as CDs, CD-RWs or USB flash sticks or pens. Magnetic tape is still used by some companies but is used rarely, as disks and CDs have become much more popular. Holography may offer an exciting new form of electronic filing and this would enable large amounts of storage on a disk the size of a CD.

Optical disks are also commonly used to store large quantities of information. These are digital devices, such as WORM (Write Once Read Many) and CD-ROMs, that are ideal for storing graphics, such as clipart, and which utilise laser technology.

EDMS (electronic document management system) is another electronic filing system and is automated, being used to support the creation, use and maintenance of electronically created documents.

> **GLOSSARY**
>
> **Write Once Read Many (WORM):** This device uses data storage technology to write information to a disk on one occasion but prevents the user from erasing any of the data.

### QUESTIONS

1 Name the two types of filing used in an office.
2 Give two advantages of filing hard copies.
3 Identify and explain four systems of electronic filing.

## Meeting areas

Those administrators who work in small individual offices may have a small area, with comfortable chairs, away from their workstation where meetings can take place. These offices tend to be quiet and more peaceful than large open plan offices and it is therefore an easy matter for meetings to be held.

A large open plan office tends to be noisy and offers little privacy, but space can be made available in a quieter area of the office for meetings to be held. If this is not possible, companies will make available special rooms

### ACTIVITY

Explain why it is necessary for meeting areas to be set aside for the use of office staff.

within a building for meetings to be held in privacy and in a quiet area away from the hubbub of normal office life. These are then booked through the company's electronic diary system to ensure no double booking.

## Access/routes through the office

Open plan offices will have through routes that people will be using constantly during the working day. It is important that these access routes are kept clear at all times. Potential hazards such as frayed carpets should be reported to management. Trips and falls in offices are quite common and risk assessment to try to avoid these would be carried out to ensure staff safety at all times.

The correct positioning of computer workstations and equipment such as filing cabinets is vital, but it may be necessary to move any that could cause someone to walk into them, or trip over. Filing cabinets should always be closed properly after use and boxes, bags or other items should not be left in a position that someone could fall over them.

## ACTIVITY

1   In your selected office, carry out an inspection of all access routes.
2   Produce a report for your superior listing the problems you have identified during your inspection and give recommendations to alleviate these problems.

## Organisation of teams

Many businesses use teams of employees. There are various reasons for this but the major one is that it enables an employer to use the specific skills that an individual brings to a team, ensuring that the team works well and productively.

### Location/resources

In a traditional individual office, a team may be grouped together, usually in small offices in the same area of a building. Some may work together in one office where space permits.

In a large open plan office, teams are often located so that they sit close together. The work of a team could be to file and retrieve documents, another may produce all the company's documents and a third may carry out all the **reprographics**. Some companies use a business service administration support system where all documentation, filing and photocopying is carried out in one area by a team of expert administrators.

Other teams may work together to carry out specific tasks or projects. For example, a firm of solicitors may have administrative teams with specific specialisms such as the production of documents concerning **conveyancing**, **matrimonial affairs**, criminal cases or those concerning children.

### GLOSSARY

**Reprographics**: different methods of copying, such as photocopying, printing etc.

**Conveyancing**: a legal process necessary to transfer ownership of a property from a seller to a buyer.

**Matrimonial affairs**: legal processess concerned with marriage, divorce and the care of children.

# Resources

Resources include the equipment, facilities and other items that are needed for an office to operate effectively and efficiently.

## Individual resources

These are the resources that individual employees will need to be able to do their work and include such things as computers, telephones, etc. They may also include the space that is needed in order to work and an area that is clean and tidy. Individuals not only need equipment but also need to have it to hand. For example, individuals need to have all the stationery required and that this is stored in an easy to access place.

## Shared resources

These resources are those items that are shared between employees, including printers, photocopiers, computer supplies, stationery, and materials such as files, catalogues, price lists and email address books.

A computer network will enable printers to be shared which will save money. Four or five computers may be easily connected to one high-specification printer which will produce high-quality printouts.

Software can also be shared. Central automatic back-ups can take place regularly and data can be shared across the network, for example allowing employees working on a project or pilot scheme to use a database at the same time.

People working in a small traditional office can also share resources, such as printers, but this is not popular and often not cost-effective as much time can be wasted when users have to go to another office or work area to collect printouts and possibly also have to wait in a queue of other staff waiting for their work to be printed.

## ACTIVITY

Give two advantages and two disadvantages of office administrators using shared printers.

**Portfolio tip**

*In order to provide the evidence required in your portfolio for this assessment objective, you will need to produce a comprehensive analysis of the office layout, resources and systems operating within an actual office environment.*

# Systems

We all have systems in our lives to help us cope with everything that we need to deal with. For example, you may have a procedure that you follow to help you prepare for the working day – you set your alarm clock for a specific time, get up, shower, put on your clothes, make a drink, perhaps have breakfast, gather together all the things you will need and then leave your home, ready to start your day. In much the same way, businesses need systems to ensure that they can work efficiently.

In this section you will investigate and analyse the administration systems that operate within your chosen office. You will look into the reasons why particular systems are required. You will then consider the step-by-step procedures that are needed in order to ensure that these administration systems operate correctly. Procedures may be available in the form of manuals or checklists or, in some circumstances, may be given verbally.

You may find it helpful to discuss with your mentor, supervisor or tutor the particular administration system that you could investigate. You will then produce a comprehensive analysis resulting from the findings of your investigation.

Examples of administration systems that you could investigate are given below. During your investigation of a specific administration system, ensure you keep thorough and complete notes that will help you to produce a comprehensive analysis of that system.

## Information storage and retrieval

Your office will have systems for storing information. There may be a central filing system or filing may be done in individual offices. You should investigate the types of filing that are used and the system and the procedures that are used for the filing and retrieval of documents. You may find it helpful to refer to the notes on pages 354–355.

## Communications (e.g. written, verbal, electronic)

As you have already seen, there are many different methods of communication. The methods used are likely to vary depending on the type and size of the business. Generally, the bigger the company, the more sophisticated the communication methods that are used. In your investigation, you should find out the communication systems that are used by staff in your office, such as written, verbal and electronic, and why these particular ones are used. There will be procedures in place to ensure employees use the correct communication method for different situations. Refer to Unit 3 for more information on communications.

## Staff roles and responsibilities

Everyone in every organisation has a job role. This is normally formalised by production of a job description that lays down what is expected of each employee. You should investigate the staff roles in your chosen office. There may be an organisation chart that identifies all the staff and their roles within the organisation that might be helpful.

You will then investigate the responsibilities that different members of the staff have. For example, the person in charge of health and safety; the trained first aiders; where staff work flexitime, someone will be responsible for keeping rotas to ensure that the office is properly staffed during all opening hours.

## Resource planning (personnel and equipment)

This is a vital system in every organisation. Resource planning is crucial for the organisation's success in meeting its aims and objectives. In your chosen office investigate the administration system and procedures that exist for this. You may be able to investigate a specific aspect of resource planning. For example, you may choose to investigate the way in which visitors to your building are dealt with and whether there is sufficient personnel and equipment to ensure that visitors are always greeted warmly and dealt with in a courteous, efficient manner.

## Holiday planning

This may seem a small area of concern for an organisation, but if an administration system is not put in place for this, the consequences can be catastrophic. Procedures for planning staff holidays will vary. For example, a small business can easily plan the holidays for its entire staff accurately by using a wall planner. A large multinational organisation, however, would be more likely to use some form of e-management or other electronic system of planning for staff holidays to ensure that particular members of staff do not take holidays at the same time and that staff are able to plan the holidays they want, when they want them. Most companies see proper staff holiday planning as vital to maintaining staff morale.

In your investigation, therefore, you would look at the system for planning staff holidays in your chosen office. For example, one person may have responsibility for this or there may be an electronic system in place. Find out how the system works and whether the staff cooperate to ensure it is efficient.

## Sickness recording

Many companies have administration systems for recording staff sick leave for a number of different reasons. A good system of recording levels of staff sickness enables management to see, for example, whether there may be stress levels among the staff. It would also enable managers to see if there is a pattern of staff absence, such as people who take sick leave at particular times of the year that may be stressful, such as at stocktaking. Investigate the system that is used to record staff absence due to sickness and how it works.

## Administration support for other functional areas

Some companies operate a central administration support department which services all the other functional areas of that organisation. Other companies have small units which operate independently and have their own administration support staff attached to each one. Investigate how administration support is provided to other functional areas in your chosen business.

## Training and development

In a large organisation, training and development is likely to be handled by the human resource department. However, in a small business one person may have responsibility for all the training and development needs of its staff. The administration systems for dealing with training and development of staff will, therefore, differ from one organisation to another. You should investigate the systems and procedures operating in your chosen business for staff training and development, including appraisal and any other evaluation process that may highlight a need for staff training.

### Portfolio tip

*In order to provide the evidence required in your portfolio for this assessment objective, you will need to investigate the office layout, resources and systems operating within an actual office environment and to produce a comprehensive analysis resulting from the findings of your investigation.*

### ACTIVITY

1 Choose one administration system from the list given below:
   - information storage and retrieval
   - communications (e.g. written, verbal, electronic)
   - staff roles and responsibilities
   - resource planning (personnel and equipment)
   - holiday planning
   - sickness recording
   - administration support for other functional areas
   - training and development.

2 Investigate your chosen system in an 'active office', which may be a training or administration office in your centre, or one where you are working, or on work experience placement. Investigate the procedures that are included in that system. Produce a comprehensive analysis of the administration system from the findings of your investigation.

## AO3 Describe the use and purpose of office computer hardware and software, and explain the key issues involved in administration using computers

To complete this assessment objective successfully, you may produce evidence based on work experience in an 'active office' or you may use a range of businesses and provide supporting examples. You do **not** need to describe *how* computer systems work.

# Use and purpose of computer hardware, peripherals, components, networks

Computers are used by the large majority of businesses and many companies now provide a computer for each office employee.

## *Use and purpose of computer hardware*

**Figure 21.3** *Computer hardware*

Computer hardware is a term used to describe all those items of computer equipment that you could pick up and carry, such as the monitor, keyboard, central processing unit (CPU) and printer. Many businesses use computer hardware to cut costs through the automation of routine tasks and to help employees work more efficiently, so that the profit earned by the company will increase.

Most employees use desktop computers, but those who work away from the office, e.g. sales personnel, will use laptops; these may also be used by employees who regularly carry out some of their duties at home.

## Monitors

There are many types of monitors, ranging from an inexpensive small normal screen to a flat screen costing a great deal more. Most monitors these days are colour screens. They should be flicker-free and kept clean so that the users can work with them safely. Sizes of screens vary from 10″ to 19″ but most companies tend to purchase 17″ screens as it has been proven that this size is advantageous for health and safety reasons.

## Keyboards

There is a huge variety of keyboards available, ranging from ones that are small and compact to ergonomic and wire-free keyboards. All the keyboards have the same alpha and numeric keys but the function keys, such as F1, tend to be in different places, depending on the type of keyboard. Many modern keyboards also now have special buttons for easy access to emails and the Internet, as well as volume control, calculator, etc.

*An ergonomic keyboard*

## Central processing unit

A central processing unit is where all the instructions are carried out – it is the computer's brain. It includes the control unit, which controls the timing of operations and movement of data inside the computer and between the computer and peripherals. Central processing units are also known as processors and these days tend to be 'towers' that are placed on the floor alongside the computer user.

## Printers

The type of printer used in a business depends on how it will be used and for what purpose. Laser printers are commonly used because they have a high quality of print and relatively low running costs. They are now quite small and can easily be positioned on a workstation. Inkjet printers can produce good quality prints, including colour, but they are slower and running costs tend to be higher than lasers.

## Scanners

These are able to scan text and send them to a computer. The data that has been scanned can then be manipulated and printed. There are two types of scanners – hand-held and flat bed; the flat bed tends to be more expensive. Many companies also now use multi-function printers that are able to print, scan and photocopy.

## *Peripherals*

Peripherals are those products that are needed in order to use a computer efficiently, such as floppy disks, USB flash pens, zip drives, CDs, DVDs, graphics digitisers and pens, mice, tracker balls, scanners, speakers and USB cables. Also included are other items such as ink cartridges, paper and many other miscellaneous items that would be required by a computer user.

## ACTIVITY

1 Explain what is meant by the term computer hardware and give four examples of items of computer hardware.
2 What is an ergonomic keyboard? Use the Internet to find a photograph of an ergonomic keyboard, take a printout and include this in your portfolio.
3 What is the function of a central processing unit?
4 Compare a laser printer with an inkjet printer.
5 Give reasons why a company may purchase a multi-function printer.

Floppy disks, USB flash pens, zip drives, CDs and DVDs (see page 367) are used when the storage of files, images, photographs and pictures is required on secure, safe removable media. A mouse usually has two buttons and often a small wheel positioned in the centre of the mouse for quick and easy movement. The mouse is used as a pointing device and to move the cursor around the screen. A tracker ball is like an upside down mouse – the user rotates the ball but the mouse does not move. Graphics digitisers (or tablets) are alternatives to using a mouse, tracker ball or other pointing device. The tablet is a flat surface for drawing with a cursor, pen or stylus. The cursor traces over a technical drawing that can then be manipulated on screen. USB cables are required to connect various items of equipment to the computer, such as printers and scanners.

## Components

The hardware components of a computer include:

- memory – this enables a computer to store data and programs

- mass storage device – allows a computer to permanently retain large amounts of data; common mass storage devices include disk drives

- input device – this is the means by which data and instructions are entered into a computer; examples are a keyboard and a mouse

- output device – a display screen (monitor) or printer that lets you see what has been processed by the computer

- central processing unit (CPU) – the heart of the computer; this is where all instructions are carried out.

## Networks

The use of computers continues to grow and networks enable users to share the cost of peripherals such as printers and scanners and provide access to shared data.

Those businesses that operate in a single building only will often make use of a local area network (LAN). These enable two or more computers to be connected directly, allowing the users to share peripherals as well as files or programs. Many companies now build their own internal networks, known as **intranets**, which store information on a central system at a private Internet address. Intranets are similar to the Internet, in that they have pages of information, but they can be accessed only via the LAN as there is no phone link necessary. Email messages can also be sent to colleagues via the LAN.

Another type of network is a wide area network (WAN), which is used by companies with offices in different locations. The WAN can connect different local area networks together into a more complicated network, using a telecommunications network, satellite and/or microwaves.

# Use and purpose of range of computer software, operating systems, applications programs, file management systems, Internet and email

Computer software relates to those things that you cannot pick up and carry. It is a general term that describes all the programs that are run on computer hardware. Software includes operating systems and applications programs.

## Operating systems

These systems tell the computer how to function. Commonly used operating systems include LINUX, UNIX and Windows. The user instructs the computer what he or she wishes to do and the operating system provides those routines needed to enable the hardware to interact with applications programs, such as word processing software.

## Applications programs

These programs are used for specific purposes such as word processing, databases, spreadsheets, graphics and charts, presentations, desktop publishing and payroll and accounts. Some applications programs have to be used with a particular operating system.

Word processing software includes MS Word, WordPerfect and Lotus. This software is used to produce documents such as letters, memos and reports. It enables people to amend text, to incorporate images such as clipart, and to import data from a database or spreadsheet. Individual personalised letters can be produced using a word processor's mailmerge facility.

Database software includes Access, dBase, Paradox and Oracle. This software is an electronic filing system that enables data to be sorted, and searches to be carried out for particular data. Reports can then be produced containing specific information such as that found during a search.

Spreadsheet software includes MS Excel and Lotus 1-2-3 and is used for financial analysis and to produce graphs and charts. Calculations can be done automatically or by using formulae.

Presentation software includes Corel Presentations and MS PowerPoint. This software enables a speaker to produce a slide show, with high-quality colour slides to enhance a presentation. A projector is used to display the slide show on a large screen.

Desktop publishing software includes MS Publisher, PageMaker, Ventura and Quark Xpress. It allows the user to produce text and graphics that is then organised into pages that can be published.

Payroll and accounts software includes Sage and Quicken. It enables records of all sales and purchases to be entered in relevant accounts and invoices and for statements to be produced automatically. Other financial documents that may be required, such as VAT returns, bank analysis and trial balance, can also be produced using this software.

## ACTIVITY

1 Organise yourselves into four groups. Two of the groups should make a list of computer hardware and its functions and the other two groups should make a list of computer software and its functions.
2 Each of the two groups should then combine to discuss their lists.
3 The two groups, still working together, should then prepare, produce and deliver a ten-minute presentation to the whole class, including the information used in their lists of hardware/software and the functions of that hardware/software.
4 The class should then discuss each group's presentation.

## *File management systems*

Computer users will use a system of files and folders when saving and storing their work. This is known as file management. A folder is a name given to a number of files that you want to store together in one place. This may be a particular topic or project name, or a customer's name. To save a file in a folder, it is necessary to ensure that that particular folder has been selected, otherwise files will be saved elsewhere and it may be difficult to find them again.

Whether a user has a standalone computer or is part of a network, they need to be able to find files easily and quickly, so the careful use of files, folders and filenames is necessary. Many companies give guidance to their employees on how files should be stored, and also give the names of the files and folders to be used.

It is important that folders are checked regularly and unwanted files deleted. If a folder is no longer required for any reason, then it too can be deleted. However, users working on a network may not be permitted to delete any files, or may need special permission to delete them.

## Internet

The Internet provides a network for people to access the World Wide Web to search for information on a wide variety of topics. Many companies restrict the use of the Internet to only those employees whose jobs require them to use the Internet. Some companies restrict their employees to use of the company's intranet only and denies them access to the Internet itself. More details on the use of the Internet can be found on pages 105 onward.

## Email

Most companies now enable their employees to use email (electronic mail) to send messages directly from one computer to another. Email provides instant communication and sometimes almost instant response. Some employees set up their email system to provide them with a receipt each time they send an email to a colleague or client, giving proof that the email had been sent and received.

Emails have replaced face-to-face communication in many ways and some employers have decided to restrict their employees' use of email. Not only were they concerned that people did not talk to each other any more, but they felt that too much time was being taken up reading unnecessary email messages, time that could be used more appropriately.

# Data Protection Act

The Data Protection Act 1998 requires companies who use a computerised data system to register as data users. They must state:

- what information is being held on a computer
- why it is stored in such a way
- how and from where they have obtained the information
- to whom it will be disclosed.

A company's customers and employees have a right of access to all computerised information held about them. Look back at the notes concerning data protection in Unit 2.

# Data security and safety measures

These are vital to ensure businesses can continue working efficiently. If the computer system were to be disabled, there would be serious consequences.

Some of the data that is input into a computer may be highly confidential, so security of that data is essential.

## *Data security measures*

Loss of data can be a problem in areas of the country where loss of power occurs on a regular basis. Data can also be lost because a computer user is inexperienced and not fully familiar with a particular applications program.

Many users make back-up copies of files, especially those that are particularly important. Back-ups can be made on any type of removable media such as CDs, floppy disks, flash pens or zip drives. However, floppy disks have relatively small capacity and will not be capable of holding large files that contain images, etc. It is necessary, therefore, to select the appropriate method of storage carefully. Then if there are power cuts, or system failures, or the computer is stolen, the back-ups can be used.

Back-up copies must be kept well away from the computer, otherwise a person intent on stealing a computer may search the desk drawers and remove the disks as well. Back-ups of very important data, such as customer databases, should also be kept off-site, in case of fire or theft.

Files containing confidential or sensitive data can be protected by **encryption**. This software is very useful, especially with the use of laptops as it ensures that, the information on the hard drive cannot be accessed, even if the laptop is stolen.

Employees using computer networks will be given IDs and passwords that must be used in order to gain access to the computer system. These IDs and passwords will usually be made of alphanumeric or numeric characters to make it more difficult for an unauthorised person to guess them.

To ensure the security of data, companies use anti-virus software such as Norton and McAfee. This software can detect and disable viruses that may be transmitted by email (especially through email attachments) before they can do any damage to a computer.

## ACTIVITY

Mario is a trainee whose team leader has asked him to save a document to a floppy disk so that she can take it home to work on an important file. Mario is not sure what to do, as he has never used a floppy disk before. Produce a memo, explaining to Mario how he should use and care for floppy disks.

*Protect your confidential data*

## ACTIVITY

1   Working in groups, discuss what you think is happening in the above picture.
2   Give advice to the office worker on how confidential information on a computer screen could be protected.

## Safety measures

Many companies ensure that their computers are protected from hazards such as fire and theft.

Most offices are fitted with smoke detectors and have doors that are especially designed to stop fires from spreading. Sprinkler systems are installed in many offices to try to put out, or douse, a fire before it takes hold. Removable media, such as flash pens, should be locked away in fireproof containers.

The safety of employees and those who may be visiting a company's offices for any reason is paramount. Companies carry out risk assessments regularly to ensure that computers are being used in a safe manner. During the assessments, issues such as wires that are trailing or frayed, computer equipment that is not correctly positioned on desktops, will be dealt with.

## AO4 Explain human resource considerations for a selected office environment

To complete this assessment objective successfully, you will need to produce evidence based on work experience in an 'active office'.

In this section, you will look at the human resource considerations included in recruitment planning and the employment policies and procedures used. You will consider the methods used to supervise trainees, the levels of stress in the workplace, their causes and possible remedies. Finally, you will look at the human resource considerations for teamworking.

## Recruitment planning

The purpose of recruitment is to ensure that a company employs people with the skills, experience and qualifications required in order to meet the organisation's staffing needs.

Recruitment planning varies from company to company. A large company employing hundreds of people may use a plan that involves carrying out an **audit** of current staff to highlight those employees who may soon be retiring, those who may be happy and willing to take on new challenges, for example if a new line of work is to be undertaken, and those who may be promoted within the business. Other considerations will include the possibility of increased workload, perhaps because of new business or the development of new technology, that may require more people or those experienced in the use a particular piece of equipment.

Recruitment is expensive. As well as the costs of advertising it also includes all the administration costs involved in dealing with applicants, management time spent in shortlisting candidates and costs incurred in the interview process. For this reason, some companies may decide to reorganise their workforce in order to fill any vacancies. For example, increased flexibility may be needed and the use of part-time employees or staff who wish to job-share may be appropriate.

If a need for a new employee is highlighted, either part-time or full-time, then the company's next step will normally be to design a job description. This will include all the details about the job and the exact responsibilities involved. A person specification will then be compiled that will include full details of the person who would be ideal to fill this vacancy (see Unit 17).

It is at this point that companies are then able to decide whether to appoint a current employee or whether to advertise for someone from outside the company.

The company's recruitment process will then be implemented. This will start with advertising the post in an appropriate medium, for example a local newspaper (and some companies advertise vacancies on their company website), and will end with interviewing candidates and appointing the most suitable.

The use of temporary staff in an office is quite usual these days. Temps, as they are commonly known, are not normally employed by the company they work for, but are employed by a recruitment agency. The company is usually in control of the temps, but they are paid by the agency. Temps may help to fill temporary skills gaps or to cover staff absences such as **maternity leave**.

## ACTIVITY

1  In your selected office, find out what recruitment planning your company undertakes.
2  Produce a list clearly showing your company's recruitment planning.
3  What differences would there be in the recruitment planning in small and large companies?

## Employment policies and procedures

Employment policies and procedures set out the rules and procedures that all the staff need to know. Policies help both employers and their employees to understand what standards are expected and how the range of activities required in a business should be carried out.

### Employment policies

The policies that are implemented will depend very much on the size of the business and what that organisation actually does. For example, where the operation of machinery is required, a company might consider the implementation of a policy on the use of alcohol or drugs by employees.

Having clear policies that are easily understood by everyone can help ensure good employer–employee relations and few disciplinary or grievance cases as a result. A good relationship between all parties within an organisation can also lead to a good public image, better productivity, good staff motivation and morale, and may also help to attract new staff.

Employment policies may include various legal requirements such as maternity and paternity leave, equal opportunities, health and safety, but may also include areas such as holiday entitlement, sick pay arrangements, hours of work, rest breaks that may be taken, whether overtime is required and if this is paid in addition to salary. Some companies also try to encourage a healthy work–life balance; for example, to enable parents to take special leave when a child is ill.

Other employment policies may cover the conduct of employees and include such things as discipline, harassment, bullying, as well as disputes that could lead to industrial action. Some companies operate a dress code and this would be included in the company's employment policies. Other considerations would include personal use of emails, the Internet and telephone. Most of these factors would be included in a staff handbook and companies would ensure that all employees were given a personal copy.

There have been some recent cases where employees have raised concerns about an organisation in the national press. These people are often called 'whistleblowers'. Many companies now include a policy to deal with these employees internally. This has helped to ensure that problems highlighted by these employees are not publicised externally, thus retaining the company's public image.

## Supervision of office trainees

The supervision of office trainees will vary depending mainly on whether the business is a small company employing one person to be responsible for all administration, or a large company that has many office staff.

In a small company, a trainee is likely to work closely with a PA, secretary or administrator, who will act as a **mentor**. The trainee will receive advice, guidance and close supervision and will be able to watch and learn.

In a larger company, a trainee will often join a team, whose team leader will supervise the work of the trainee. Some large companies also operate a 'mentor' system in much the same way as smaller companies and this enables trainees to quickly gain experience and, in many cases, rapid promotion. Trainees are often given opportunities to work for short periods in different areas within the business – to gain experience in different functions of a business, such as sales, human resources, finance. The supervision of the trainee is then carried out by nominated people in those departments, usually a senior administrator or team leader.

## Stress and workload

Workplace stress is becoming a problem in many offices and the numbers of employees affected are rising. Unacceptably high levels of stress are causing concern among business owners, managers, trade unions and workers.

There are many reasons people feel stressed and some of these are not directly connected with work, such as financial or domestic problems and bereavement. Those that are connected with the workplace usually include the employees' workload. This can be seen as too demanding, or even impossible to accomplish in the given timescale.

Symptoms of stress can include:

- a high level of sickness absence – physical illness could be a signal because the body's natural resistance to illness can be lowered as a result of stress

**ACTIVITY**

Identify the employment policies and procedures that apply in your selected office.

**GLOSSARY**

**Mentor:**
A mentor is a person who provides guidance and help to a junior member of staff and can recommend courses of action that should be taken.

*Excessive workload can lead to stress*

- other absences for no apparent reason – lack of motivation can be a major factor and going to work is simply too much for a person to cope with when levels of stress are high

- reduced productivity – work may not be carried out efficiently, although the employee had previously been reliable and trustworthy

- high turnover of labour – can be an indicator of stress among the workforce

- ineffective working – an employee who suddenly fails to meet deadlines, or whose work is so poor that it necessitates the work being redone

- poor interpersonal relations – an employee may alienate colleagues, cause disputes, refuse to take management instructions or offend a client.

Some companies offer counselling and training to help people deal with their stress levels. Unfortunately, some people are so badly affected by stress that it causes them to leave their job and find work elsewhere.

## Teamworking

A large office may have different teams that do different things in a variety of ways. Research has shown that people who work in a team that works well together can be more productive, a major consideration for many businesses. A team consists of individual employees who have different skills and experience. When this is pooled, it can lead to an efficient team that produces work of a high, professional quality and does so to strict timescales.

### ACTIVITY

In your 'selected office', investigate the levels of staff absenteeism. You should:

1 Calculate the percentage of absenteeism and suggest reasons for it.
2 Find out if the company has taken any steps to *prevent* workplace stress.
3 Where stress has been highlighted, find out what the company has done to *relieve* the causes of stress.

Many teams are paid a bonus for meeting their targets, while others are given incentives such as extra holiday leave.

When recruited, applicants are often asked if they are a 'team player'. People who work well together and can offer help and support to each other will often make good team players. Those who prefer to work on their own and do not form good relationships within a team usually work better on their own. These issues are considered when companies are recruiting staff to ensure that the right people are employed for an environment that is appropriate to each of them.

> **Portfolio tip**
>
> *In order to provide the evidence required in your portfolio for this assessment objective, you will give a comprehensive explanation of the human resource considerations for the selected office environment.*

## AO5 Investigate a selected office environment and propose measures to reduce the health and safety risks and improve the general working environment

To complete this assessment objective successfully, you will need to investigate a 'selected office'. You should describe the working environment and identify any health and safety risks within that environment. Once this has been completed, you will propose measures to reduce the health and safety risks you identified in an effort to improve the general working environment in your selected office.

## Health and safety risks

These exist in every work environment. You would expect to see health and safety risks in a job such as a welder or an engineer and may believe that office work is safe as people work indoors, in a warm and safe environment.

All employees should be familiar with health and safety legislation and their responsibilities with regard to risks and the reduction of those risks.

In this assessment objective, you should look at the various health and safety risks that may be found in an office environment.

> **Portfolio tip**
>
> *Once you have identified health and safety risks in your chosen office, you should then propose ways of reducing these risks.*

### Fire

In an office, fires could be caused by faulty electrics, such as badly worn or frayed wiring or overloaded electrical sockets. Occasionally, fires are started deliberately, by outsiders or people who work inside an office. There may be risks caused by the use of flammable materials that are left out, instead of being stored away safely. Most offices do not allow smoking but this could be a danger if employees are permitted to smoke in their workplace.

Smoke detectors and sprinkler systems have been installed in many offices and these will help prevent fires spreading. Special fire doors can also stop fires taking hold quickly.

Most fire alarms are loud bells or sirens. New employees are told what to expect in the case of fire and make themselves familiar with the company's procedure, usually given in the staff handbook. Companies hold regular practice drills so that all employees know what the fire alarm sounds like and practise what they need to do, for example where their nearest exit is located and the position of their assembly point.

## ACTIVITY

1   In your selected office, carry out an inspection, taking into account the following:
   - Look at the fire exits and escape routes – do you consider that these are suitable for all employees?
   - Are all the corridors and fire exit routes free from obstruction?
   - Do the exits and emergency routes lead directly to a safe area, e.g. assembly points well away from the building?
   - Is there adequate fire-fighting equipment available to deal with a fire and is it clearly identified? Are extinguishers sited near to specific hazards and close to exit doors or escape routes? Is the equipment regularly inspected, tested and monitored?
   - Are there signs in the building informing people what to do in the event of a fire and are these large enough to be seen easily?
   - Is there a clear policy detailing what action should be taken with regard to visitors who may be in the building?
   - Are those people who may be disabled taken into consideration? For example, a person who is hard of hearing may not be able to hear the alarm; someone whose mobility is poor may not be able to escape the building.
2   Produce a report including all your findings and propose remedies to any problems you may have found.

## Electricity

All electrical equipment should be installed correctly and safely by a certified, authorised electrician. It should be positioned in a safe area, so that it cannot easily be knocked over. Companies will produce procedures for the operation of electrical equipment such as photocopiers, fax machines, computers, and a safety officer may be employed to carry out regular checks on the equipment and to ensure staff are using it correctly.

A safety officer (or similar person) will also regularly check that electrical wiring is safe and that no wires are trailing. A check on electrical sockets will also be carried out and on the number of plugs being used in one socket.

Companies will also ensure that equipment is maintained regularly and employees are given a procedure to report any faults. This is very often done by emailing or sending a memo to the maintenance team.

## Manual handling

There are regulations covering manual handling and companies will ensure these are incorporated into health and safety procedures. Even office staff may be required to lift objects, so it is important that they know how to do this safely. Companies often now provide trolleys with wheels for easy transportation of internal and external mail. Heavy boxes should not be lifted – a forklift truck (or similar) should be used instead.

## Waste disposal

Many offices have procedures to deal with waste. All companies are required by law to store, handle, manage and transport all their waste safely.

Hazardous waste, such as solvent-based inks, fluorescent light tubes and chemicals, must be disposed of safely and must not be discarded along with other waste. Specialist companies will then be called in to take away the hazardous waste and dispose of it in a safe manner.

Many companies are now considering ways in which waste can be minimised, reused or recycled. Many offices have two waste sacks, one for normal paper and cardboard and another, often labelled red, for confidential material. Cardboard boxes that may have contained items of stationery can be recycled, as can paper. Any confidential material can be shredded – even paper that has been shredded can be recycled.

> **GLOSSARY**
>
> **Waste:** Any material that a company wishes to dispose of.

## Use of computers

Users of computers must ensure that they make their environment as safe as possible. A risk assessment can be undertaken for any employee with specific needs, such as a disability which requires special seating or other equipment such as wrist and foot rests.

Users must be sure to use good posture at all times. A comfortable chair that is adjustable is essential and should allow the user to keep his or her feet flat on the floor if possible; if not, a foot rest should be provided. The monitor, keyboard and mouse must all be positioned correctly so that there

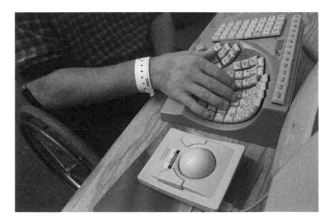

*Employee with special needs*

is no strain involved when using the equipment. Employees who work continuously on computers should be given regular breaks away from their computers. By ensuring a comfortable and safe working environment, health problems such as repetitive strain injury (RSI), back pain, eye strain and headaches should be avoided.

## Access

Most large open plan offices will have through access routes. These should be kept clear at all times.

### Trip hazards

These hazards include polished floors, poorly laid flooring, such as carpets, and those that have become badly worn and may be frayed at the edges. Other hazards that may result in trips are filing cabinets that have not been closed properly after use, so that people fall over an open drawer, and bags or boxes that have been left in gangways.

### Reaching high objects

There will always be occasions when someone needs to reach something that has been placed on a high shelf or on top of a cupboard. Care must be taken to use the correct stepladder to do this and not a computer user's chair or other swivel chair. Falling off a chair can result in nasty injuries, including back strain, possibly needing hospitalisation, and could lead to an employee being off work for some weeks.

## The working environment

The design of offices will usually ensure that they are safe places in which to work.

## Communication

Those who have difficulty in hearing may require special equipment, such as an induction loop to help them communicate by telephone, and may need signers to help interpret what has been said face to face. Many companies now provide training for employees to learn how to use sign language. Others with a disability may find it easier if signs were replaced with pictures or other images. Those who are partially sighted, or who may be blind, will also have special needs and offices can now accommodate guide dogs and will provide other aids, such as Braille signing along corridors, to help people find their way around a building.

## *Décor and layout*

There are regulations laid down by government covering lighting, temperature and ventilation, and doors, windows and lifts must also be safe and regularly maintained.

New offices are more likely to be people-friendly than those in older buildings. Modern offices will probably have colour-coordinated furnishings, carpets and curtains, which make for a tasteful, comfortable environment, which is pleasing to the eye and in which people want to work. Research has shown that plants in various positions in an office can improve the working environment. Colour can also be useful. For example, warm, neutral colours are more relaxing than bright colours.

Many offices are now air-conditioned. However, there have been some instances recorded of 'office rage' caused by disagreements about how cold the office should be.

## *Ergonomics*

In an office, ergonomics is particularly important for those employees who use computers. Workstations should be designed correctly so that the desk, chair and document holder are all correctly positioned. The workstation should also be positioned so that you can sit comfortably, but should allow some flexibility to enable you to reach for items on the desktop. A good quality computer chair that is adjustable to allow good posture is absolutely vital and should offer support so that back pain and tiredness are reduced. Keyboards are now available that have been designed with ergonomics in mind (see page 362). For good ergonomics, all the parts involved in using a computer should be adjustable to the fit the user's physical size and particular needs.

> ### GLOSSARY
>
> **Ergonomics**:
> The application of scientific information concerning humans to the design of objects, systems and environment for human use.

## *Access*

People must be able to gain access to all parts of their working area. These may include cupboards whose access is difficult, stairways that must be kept clear at all times and should have non-slip surfaces, and lifts that work properly and are maintained regularly by a specialist company. Access to buildings by people who may be disabled is also an important consideration. Newer offices may have been constructed with wide doors, good access for wheelchair users and others with mobility problems, such as ramps and handles and non-slip floor surfaces, but older buildings can be adjusted, although this may be expensive.

## ACTIVITY

*Safety at work*

1   Organise yourselves into four groups. Each group should take one of the above pictures.
2   Each group should identify any health and safety hazards that appear in their picture and discuss these within their group.
3   Each group should then make a list on a flipchart of the hazards that have been identified.
4   Each group should then present its findings to the whole class.
5   The class should discuss the health and safety hazards each group has identified and then highlight any other hazards that could exist.
6   Everyone should discuss the measures that could be taken to reduce these health and safety hazards.

## Portfolio tip

*In order to provide the evidence required in your portfolio for this assessment objective, you should identify and comprehensively describe the health and safety risks in your selected office. You should then propose a range of realistic measures to reduce the health and safety risks you have identified. Drawings, illustrations and photographs may be used to enhance your evidence.*

# AO6 Demonstrate a range of practical administration skills

To complete this section successfully, you will need to produce evidence in your portfolio that you have demonstrated a range of practical administrative skills including:

- telephone call and fax handling
- printing and photocopying
- resource planning
- information storage and retrieval
- data input
- document production.

You will also need to submit witness statements from your tutor verifying that you have successfully demonstrated all these skills.

**Figure 21.4** *Administrative skills*

# Telephone call and fax handling

You need to show that you can make and receive telephone calls and can handle faxes. You may do this as part of your work experience, or by using simulated exercises in the classroom.

## *Telephone calls*

You should demonstrate that you communicate with colleagues or customers by telephone. You should demonstrate that you are able to listen effectively, to clarify issues, for example by checking that you have understood what has been said to you, and by dealing with potential problem areas such as complaints.

You should ensure that you address customers and colleagues with correct language and appropriate tone, and be polite and helpful. You may need to record information and this must be accurate. A record of what has been said may need to be filed, particularly in the case of a customer complaint, and you may need to show that you can refer the call to a more senior member of staff, where appropriate.

## ACTIVITY

As part of your work experience or using role play:

1 Demonstrate receiving at least two telephone calls from people who may be colleagues or customers (or acting as colleagues or customers).
2 Record the calls in an appropriate manner and, if necessary, refer the calls to a senior member of staff.
3 Produce a brief summary of the calls you received.
4 Then demonstrate making at least two calls to either colleagues or customers. You will need to prepare for these calls thoroughly, e.g. identify the aim of each call, what you will say and any questions you may need to ask.
5 Produce a brief summary of the calls that you made.
6 Ask your tutor to complete a witness statement.

## *Fax handling*

You need to show that you can send and receive faxes. You may use any fax machine or computer in order to do this. You should receive faxes, log them and then distribute them. When sending faxes, you should complete cover sheets, transmit the faxes, which should be of one to three pages in length, check confirmation reports, and carry out basic maintenance such as replacing paper in the fax machine.

## ACTIVITY

1  Receive at least two faxes, log them in an appropriate record, file or book and distribute them as appropriate.
2  Send at least two faxes, one of which should be at least three pages, complete cover sheets accurately, transmit the faxes correctly and check confirmation reports.
3  Replace the paper in the fax machine if possible.
4  Ask your tutor to complete a witness statement.

# Printing and photocopying

You should demonstrate that you can print a document from a computer, using a mixture of laser and inkjet printers, if possible, and undertake photocopying of various documents. As part of your demonstration, you should be able to show that you understand the need to minimise waste by handling paper correctly and checking quality before running multiple copies.

## ACTIVITY

1  Print at least two documents that you have produced on a word processor, using both laser and inkjet printers, if possible.
2  Demonstrate photocopying skills:
    - copy and assemble documents, including single, multiple and duplex (back-to-back) pages, reduce and enlarge, and use different paper sizes
    - collate and fasten pages
    - replace the paper supply, if possible
    - keep appropriate records, if appropriate
    - report problems with photocopier, if appropriate.
3  Ask your tutor to complete a witness statement.

# Resource planning

You should demonstrate the planning of resources; this may be resources that are required for a particular project or task, which may include equipment required to carry out that project or task.

## ACTIVITY

1 Consider a project or task that you could undertake in order to demonstrate the skills required when planning resources. Ask your tutor for guidance on the project or task that you could undertake in order to provide the evidence required for your portfolio. For example, the task may be to produce a holiday rota for staff, or to arrange a small meeting.
2 Produce a plan of the resources that you would require in order to complete the task or project.
3 Ask your tutor to complete a witness statement.

# Information storage and retrieval

To show evidence of storage and retrieval of information, you should store different documents or files and retrieve pieces of information from lateral and vertical filing cabinets, if possible.

## ACTIVITY

1 You should carry out good filing practice such as sorting documents prior to filing them.
2 You should file at least one document in each of the three classifications – alphabetical, numerical and chronological. If possible, you should use a variety of filing systems, such as lateral and vertical.
3 Create at least two new files and correctly store documents within those files.
4 Retrieve at least three files, from different sources if possible.
5 During your filing activities, you should follow safe practices with the use of equipment, such as staplers, staple removers, use of cabinets, opening and closing drawers.
6 Ask your tutor to complete a witness statement.

## GLOSSARY

**Data:**
Text, figures and so on that are entered into and processed by a computer.

## ACTIVITY

Enter some data into a word processor, database or spreadsheet. Ensure your tutor is able to witness that you have carried out this inputting of data.

# Data input

To evidence data input, you should enter some **data** into a computer system. This may be text into a word processor, or data into a database or spreadsheet. Your tutor should witness that you can enter data into a computer in a safe and correct manner.

# Document production

This relates to the production of documents, which may be reports, letters, memos, notices, information leaflets, or advertisements. You may be able to use documents that you have produced for this unit or other units for the Level 3 qualification.

## ACTIVITY

1   Search through your portfolios that you have produced for this and other units for documents that you have already produced. You need to provide evidence of a mixture of documents that you have produced and these should be accurate and professionally displayed.
2   If you have insufficient examples that you can use for your portfolio, you may be able to retrieve stored documents that you can edit so that they are suitable as evidence.
3   Ask your tutor for help if you are not sure.

## AO7   Identify sources of help and advice for a range of office administration functions

In this section, you will look at some of the sources of help and advice that are available to people who work in office administration or who need to use office administration in the running of their business. These include:

- the Council for Administration (CfA)
- reference books and library services
- small business advisory services
- Internet sites for businesses
- Government institutions.

## The Council for Administration

The Council for Administration (CfA) is responsible for defining and promoting excellence in business and administration skills and practice across all industry sectors. The Council has recently set up an online learner resource which is a free service and is available to anyone who is involved in any type of office administration.

The Council is an independent charity and works with government and its agencies to ensure that national standards, qualifications and training frameworks promote excellence to all administrators and to those using administration skills alongside other technical skills. It also works with employers and employees to conduct research into current and future skills needs.

## ACTIVITY

Using the Internet, visit the Council for Administration website (www.cfa.uk.com) and peruse the various pages available on the website. This will give you a good insight into the work of the CfA and the resources it provides.

# Reference books and library services

Reference and lending libraries are very useful sources of information. Most companies would find it impossible to house every reference book that might be needed in their offices. Libraries are very useful because they enable businesses to access a wide range of services, including reference books. However, most libraries will not allow reference books to be taken outside the building; they must be used inside the library. Reference facilities that may be of help to office staff may include telephone directories for all parts of the UK and Yellow Pages, specialist dictionaries, encyclopedias, thesauruses, street plans, listings of local hotels, information on recent legislation concerned with the workplace, and government services. Other resources that are available in libraries include:

- magazines and journals
- various leaflets, brochures, catalogues (including CD-ROMs)
- CD-ROMs on various subjects, including technical information that may be required
- other reference materials such as timetables, road maps, etc.
- current and back copies of national and local newspapers, which may include articles of particular interest or include detailed information concerning business and administration.

Another very useful service that libraries offer is to be able to search for and locate any book that may be required for a particular project or to help with some research.

# Small business advisory services

There are a number of small business advisory services – some of these will be available in your area. Most offer free and confidential advice to people wishing to start up a small business, and some of these services also offer help to people who are running small businesses. The range of help available is vast and includes:

- enquiry services – enabling businesses to ask for help on a specific problem
- discussion groups – enabling people to communicate with and help each other
- help and advice on
  - finance, grants, taxes, PAYE, VAT, and payroll
  - employing people
  - health and safety
  - ICT and e-commerce.

## ACTIVITY

Visit your local library, look at all the facilities it has to offer and identify sources of help and advice. Look for the reference section and make a list of the type of resources it has to offer. Compare this with the above list. You may wish to ask the librarians for help and advice. If you explain what it is you require, and why, they will be happy to help you.

## ACTIVITY

Using the Internet and any other resources you have available, such as reference and lending libraries, research the help and advice that is available to local small businesses in your area. Produce a brief description of your findings.

# Internet sites for businesses

There are many Internet sites that businesses can visit to get help and advice on a range of topics (see Table 21.1). Some of them are aimed at all businesses, large and small, while others are directed at helping businesses with particular problems such as administration queries, how to be more organised etc.

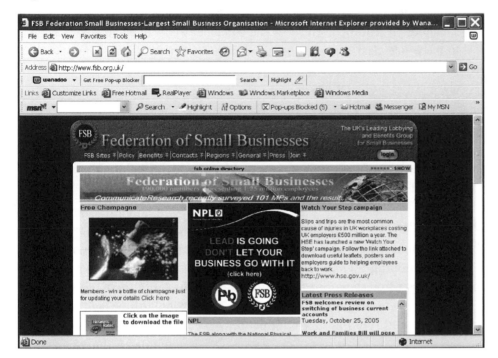

**Figure 21.5** *Website with information on business*

| WEBSITES FOR BUSINESSES | |
|---|---|
| **WEBSITE** | **DESCRIPTION** |
| www.ask-the-boss.co.uk | help with administration |
| www.yourlearnedfriend.co.uk | help with legal queries |
| www.ruralindex.net | help and advice on rural affairs |
| www.fsb.org.uk | Federation of Small Businesses |
| www.smallbiz.uk.com | help with website design |
| www.hmrc.gov.uk | HM Revenue and Customs |
| www.dti.gov.uk | Department of Trade and Industry |
| www.defra.gov.uk | Department for Rural Affairs |

**Table 21.1** *Some websites for businesses*

## ACTIVITY

1 Use the Internet sites given above and visit some of the websites listed.
2 Use search engines to find more websites giving advice and help to businesses if desired.
3 Find out what advice and help each website offers to businesses.
4 Organise yourselves into pairs and prepare, produce and deliver a 5-minute presentation, which should combine each pair's findings, to the whole class.
5 The class should compile a final list of websites from the information given in the presentations.

# Government institutions

There is a variety of government institutions that offer help and advice to businesses. These include:

## Department for Education and Skills (DfES)

The department offers advice and help to businesses concerning young people – equipping them with life and work skills and providing opportunities through work to encourage adults to reach their full potential.

The department also offers advice to companies regarding the employment and training of young people and adults.

## Department of Environment, Food & Rural Affairs (DEFRA)

This department offers advice and guidance to businesses on rural affairs, including farmers and those involved in agriculture and horticulture.

## Home Office

The Home Office provides help and advice on various legal matters such as employing people who need work permits and on legislation that may affect businesses.

## Department of Trade and Industry (DTI)

The DTI helps businesses to become more productive by promoting enterprise, innovation and creativity.

## HM Revenue and Customs (HMRC)

This department consists of the former HM Customs and Excise and the Inland Revenue; these have now been combined into one department. It is responsible for collecting tax revenue. It manages many sections of relevance to businesses, including:

- income, corporation, capital gains, insurance premium, stamp, land and petroleum revenue taxes
- vat
- environmental taxes, including aggregates levies and landfill taxes
- customs duties
- excise duties
- national insurance
- enforcement of the national minimum wage.

## Department for Transport (DfT)

The Department for Transport is responsible for overseeing the delivery of a reliable, safe and secure transport system in the United Kingdom. It works with industry and other businesses to try to ensure that the transport system is efficient and at the same time ensures that it safeguards the environment.

## Department for Work and Pensions (DWP)

This department works with businesses to help people into work, it aims to improve the rights and opportunities for disabled people, and to help people plan for retirement.

## Portfolio tip

*In order to provide the evidence required in your portfolio for this assessment objective, your explanations of each source of help and advice for a range of office administration functions should be comprehensive.*

## CASE STUDY

### S & A Interior Design

Serena and Anneka would like to set up a painting and decorating business. They think they have found a niche in the market and want to aim their business particularly at the elderly, single women and one-parent families.

They offer a comprehensive decorating service and have become specialists in using paint effects such as stippling, stencilling, sponging and rag rolling.

They have just commenced a course on interior design at the local college and hope to expand the business as soon as they feel confident enough to also offer an interior design service, which they hope will be of interest to companies and organisations in their area.

1 Serena and Anneka have no experience of administration and want some idea of what will be required before seeking professional advice.
2 They have asked you for advice. They have been told that there is a lot of information that will help them but they don't know how to find it.
3 Using the notes given above, and by searching the Internet, produce a list of organisations, with website addresses where possible, that would help Serena and Anneka.

## SKILLS CHECK

1. Explain what is meant by administration systems.

2. Give two different examples of specialist administration.

3. What does the term multi-skilled mean in relation to office administration?

4. Give four different functions of a finance office.

5. Explain the process of document production.

6. Produce a procedure for a junior for receiving a telephone call.

7. List the steps that should be followed when receiving a fax.

8. Explain what action could be taken if the need for a particular item of office equipment was highlighted.

9. Give one likely outcome if management was not efficient.

10. What are KPIs? Give at least two examples.

11. What do you understand by body language? Give three examples of body language signals that you would expect to see in an office environment.

12. Give two advantages and one disadvantage of traditional individual offices.

13. Describe a workstation and chair suitable for a computer user.

14. Name three classifications and four systems of filing.

15. Give reasons why companies use shared resources in an office.

16. What is file management?

17. Explain what is meant by a back-up copy. Describe one way in which a back-up copy could be made.

18. Name and explain four items that would be found in employment policies and procedures.

19. List four symptoms of workplace stress.

20. Produce a procedure for office staff to follow when the fire alarm sounds.

21. Explain how a heavy box should be lifted.

22. List the steps that should be followed when preparing to make a telephone call.

23. Explain the procedure that should be followed when opening post.

24. Briefly describe the role of HMRC.

# Glossary

**above the line promotion** involves using what are called *independent media* to promote the firm's products or services. Popular examples of this type of promotion include television, national and local press and radio advertisements.

**ACORN classification** the ACORN (A Classification of Residential Neighbourhoods) system is a data base based on postcodes which assumes that people living in similar neighbourhoods will tend to have similar purchasing and lifestyle habits.

**agenda** details of items that will be discussed at a meeting

**appraisal system** a system to determine employees' progress

**ATM** automated teller machine

**backdata** information such as past sales figures and customer records which the business already has and can use to analyse sales patterns and market trends

**balance sheet** a statement compiled on a set date which shows all the assets and liabilities of a business

**bank loan** an amount of money lent to a person for a fixed period of time. They will be charged interest on the amount borrowed. Regular repayments will be required.

**bank mortgage** a long term loan used to purchase buildings issued by banks or other financial institutions

**bank overdraft** when you have spent more money than you actually have in your account

**below the line promotion** involves the promotional activities that businesses use such as trade promotions, sponsorships, discounts, prize draws, money off coupons etc. It can be distinguished from above the line promotion which covers TV, radio and press advertising.

**board of directors** the group of senior managers who make all the key decisions in a limited liability company

**bookmarking** storing a link to a particular website so that you can easily return to it (sometimes known as 'Favorites')

**brand** branding gives a product an identity that distinguishes it from similar products developed by rival firms

**call centre** a telephone-based service that is used by business for customer service operations, as well as banking and insurance

**capital** the money the owner invests in the business to get it started

**cartel** occurs where several businesses agree to act together to fix prices or engage in other activities to restrict competition. Cartels are illegal in the UK.

**cash cows** products which, according to the Boston matrix, have a large market share in a low growth market. These products tend to be in the mature phase of their life cycle.

**cash flow forecast** illustrates the expected income and expenditure of a business

**CD-R** a compact disk that be read only. No information may be stored on the disk.

**CD-RW** a compact disk that can be written, erased and rewritten

**chain of command** is the channel by which instructions and orders pass down the organisation through the different levels of hierarchy

**chairperson's agenda** a document used by the chairperson of a meeting to ensure the meeting is held in an orderly and proper manner

**closing stock** stock that has not been sold at the end of the financial year becomes the opening stock of the following financial year

**competitor audit** a detailed analysis of the other rival businesses competing in the market

**conveyancing** a legal process necessary to transfer ownership of property from a seller to a buyer

**cost of sales** opening stock + purchases – closing stock

**cost plus pricing** a pricing strategy based upon the firm's cost of production. Average cost + profit margin = selling price

**creditors** people who the business owes money to for goods or services received on credit

**culture** the way a business is run and what it is like to work there

**current assets** items that can be quickly turned into cash. Includes stock, debtors, money in the bank and cash

**current liabilities** money a business owes to other people for goods and services received. These debts will require payment within one year and will include creditors, bank overdraft, dividends due to shareholders and tax due to the Inland Revenue

**customer centred** a business which puts its customers' requirements at the very centre of its organisation

**customer profile** identifies the main characteristics of customers who buy a particular product or service. If a business has an accurate picture of who buys the product then it can then create an appropriate marketing mix.

**CV** curriculum vitae

**data** information entered into a computer

**debenture** loans that are offered for sale

**debtors** people who owe the business money for goods or services received on credit

**deed of partnership** another name for a partnership agreement which outlines, among other things, how much capital each partner has contributed and how profits and losses are to be shared

**delayering** involves removing layers of management from an organisation to create a flatter structure and reduce wage costs

**demutualisation** a building society floats its business on the stock exchange by selling shares

**depreciation** the amount a fixed asset devalues due to wear and tear

**direct debit** the customer agrees that a business can draw money out of the customer's account at set times

**distribution channel** describes the route by which the product gets from the producer to the final customer

**dividend** is the share of profits that is paid out to shareholders in a limited liability company

**dogs** according to the Boston matrix, products which have a low market share in a low growth market

**e-commerce** the buying and selling of goods or services via computers

**employee's grievance** a complaint made by an employee against management or one or more employees. It may concern a breach of contract.

**enterprise clubs** mainly run by universities to support graduates when leaving university. They help young people start up their own business.

**entrepreneur** a person who takes all the risks involved in developing a business idea

**entrepreneur** another name for a person who sets up and runs their own business

**ergonomics** the application of information concerning humans to the design of objects and systems for human use

**ethical stance** following a set of values or beliefs

**ethics** a set of values or beliefs about what is right and wrong

**expenditure** general expenses that the business has to pay in order to operate – wages, heat, light, telephone

**extension strategy** a method for prolonging the life of a product. This may involve making changes to the product or packaging or running special promotions.

**fax cover** a sheet of paper that accompanies a fax and contains contact details

**fixed asset** an item that has been purchased to be used within the business. It will have a life expectancy of longer than one year. Examples include machinery, cars, equipment and computers.

**flash stick/pen** a removable storage device

**flat structure** describes an organisation that has few layers of hierarchy and large spans of control

**franchise** a business that has the legal right to sell a company's goods in a certain areas, for example McDonalds

**franchisee** the person who buys the licence which enables them to trade under the same name

**franchisor** the person/business that sells the licence for another person to trade under the same name

**grants** money that has been given to a business in order to help them start up. They do not usually require repayment.

**gross profit** sales revenue – cost of sales (opening stock + purchases – closing stock)

**hierarchy** describes an organisation that has many different layers of management. This provides a promotion ladder for staff and everyone knows their place in the organisation. However, decision-making and communication may be quite slow.

**holography** a scientific term related to three-dimensional optical recording

**hot spot** a link on a website that will connect with further pages of information concerning a product or service

**industrial inertia** describes a situation where a business remains in its current location even if the original reasons for choosing the location no longer exist

**inflation** the increase in prices measured by the retail price index

**interest** is charged on money that has been borrowed from external sources

**intranet** an internal network

**intuitiveness** being able to react to instinct – to know what will work without knowing why

**ISP** a company that provides connections to the Internet

**leasing** a fixed asset is leased to the business in exchange for regular payments. the business does not have automatic right to buy at the end of the lease agreement.

**limited liability** a legal concept which means that shareholders in a limited liability company (Ltd or plc) only risk the money that they have invested in the business. Their own personal assets are not at risk.

**liquidity** the amount of money a business has to pay its immediate debts

**lobbying** a technique which involves individuals or businesses bringing pressure to bear on opinion formers and government policy-makers to bring about change in the law to promote or protect their interests

**market centred business** a business which devotes considerable resources to finding out what type of products and services its customers want

**market leader** the biggest selling company, product or brand in the market. For example, Tesco has the largest share of the UK grocery market.

**market penetration** – this refers to how successful the product or service is in its market. Market share is a useful measure of well the business is performing in its market.

**market research** investigating peoples' opinions on products or services, looking into trends

**market segmentation** describes the way in which markets can often be broken down into smaller sub-markets called **segments** using a number of important characteristics such as age, gender and income

**market share** the proportion of total market sales that are made by one company or product: $\dfrac{\text{sales of brand X}}{\text{total market sales}} \times 100 = \%$ market share

**marketing mix** made up of four elements, sometimes referred to as 'the 4 Ps': product, price, place and promotion. Each of these elements must be considered when marketing a product.

**mass market product** a product that is sold in very large quantities such as soap powder, toothpaste or fizzy drinks

**maternity leave** the right that employees have to take time off work to take care of their newborn or newly adopted child

**matrimonial affairs** legal processes concerned with marriage, divorce and the care of children

**matrix management** involves organising staff into multi-skilled teams that work on particular projects rather than organising staff into departments based upon the job they do, e.g. finance or marketing

**mentor** person who provides guidance to junior members of staff

**merger** when two or more businesses voluntarily agree to join together to form a bigger and stronger business

**mission statement** a statement of the key aims, and sometimes values, of the business

**monopolistic competition** a market structure where many businesses compete supplying similar products and branding plays an important role as businesses attempt to differentiate their products from those of rival firms

**monopoly** a monopoly exists where there is only one supplier in the market. UK competition law defines a monopoly as a business which has a market share of 25% or more.

**mystery shopper** a popular method used in retail to establish the customer service offered by a business. A person unknown to the staff comes into the store as a normal shopper and makes notes on the service that they receive as a customer.

**natural wastage** the term used when a member of staff leaves and it is decided not to replace them. Their duties will be shared out among remaining staff. It is a way of reducing the workforce without making redundancies.

**net book value** the value of a fixed asset at a certain moment in time

**net profit** sales revenue – all expenses

**networks** allow businesses to share experiences and ideas and to improve their overall knowledge and allow people to meet up and discuss problems

**non-price competition** refers to the various methods of competing other than through price. Businesses may use techniques such as a unique selling point (USP), advertising campaigns or free gifts.

**notice of meeting** a written communication announcing a meeting is to take place (often accompanied by the agenda)

**oligopoly** a market dominated by a small number of large companies. This is quite a common type of market in the UK, e.g. supermarkets and petrol companies.

**opening stock** stock that is left over from the last financial year

**opportunity cost** you can only spend money once. The opportunity cost is what else you could have bought with your money. For example, if you buy a car the opportunity cost might be a holiday.

**outsourcing** when a business decides to buy in materials from an outside source rather than making them itself, usually to reduce costs. Many businesses also buy in services such as catering and cleaning rather employing their own staff to perform these functions.

**penetration pricing** this approach to pricing a new product involves initially setting a low price so that the product can become established in the market. The price can later be raised once the product is established in the market.

**perfect competition** a market with a large number of small businesses each supplying virtually identical products and unable to influence the market price

**PEST analysis** a tool for analysing some of the external forces that act upon a business. PEST stands for political, economic, social and technological factors all of which can have an impact upon the success of a business.

**plc** public limited company

**point of sale** advertising on view where the product can be purchased

**population** the total number of people involved in research

**portal website** often acts as a starting point for a visit to a company's website

**positive attitude** the ability to believe in oneself and what you are trying to do, being able to make things happen

**premium pricing** involves charging a higher than normal price to promote an image of quality or exclusivity. For example, Nescafé Gold Blend sells for a higher price than standard Nescafé coffee.

**pressure group** a group that represents the views and interests of a particular group of people or organisations and campaigns to raise awareness of issues and bring about changes in public opinion and the law

**price discrimination** involves charging different prices for the same product or service in different market segments. For example, a standard rail return fare to London will cost more than the same journey taken during an off-peak period.

**price elasticity of demand (PED)** measures how sensitive customers are to price changes. If small changes in price lead to significant changes in the amount of the product sold demand is said to be price elastic. It can be calculated by:

$$\frac{\% \text{ change in demand}}{\% \text{ change in price}}$$

**primary industry** is the first stage in the productive process. Primary industries include agriculture, fishing and mining. They obtain resources from the natural world and industries such as mining, quarrying and drilling for oil are known as *extractive industries*.

**primary research** market research carried out by a business in order to find out what their customers think of its products or services. It involves collecting information about customer behaviour and market trends first hand using methods such as questionnaires and interviews, focus groups or observation.

**problem child** see **question mark**

**product placement** means that a business pays a film or programme maker to have its product shown prominently in a programme or film. In recent years, James Bond films have often shown well-known branded products.

**product portfolio** the range of products or services that a particular business sells

**profit** the aim of private sector businesses. A firm makes a profit if the revenue from sales exceeds the firm's costs.

**profit and loss statement** summarises the sales and expenditure of a business over a set period of time, usually 12 months

**pro-forma** a standard document or form

**public relations** the process and methods that a business uses to enhance the success of its products or services by developing a relationship with the public and press

**qualitative performance indicators** non-numeric indicators

**quantitative performance indicators** numeric indicators

**question mark** according to the Boston matrix, a product which has a small market share in a high growth market (also known a **problem child**)

**ratio analysis** a tool used to analyse the financial health of a business. Allows comparisons between financial years and similar businesses.

**recession** a downturn (slump) in the economy leading to rising unemployment and falling consumer spending

**repetitive strain injury (RSI)** pain caused by overuse of hands and wrists

**reprographics** different methods of copying

**residual value** the value of a fixed asset at the end of its useful life

**restrictive practices** business practices which tend to reduce competition within the market and lead to higher prices and a poorer standard of service to the consumer

**risk** the possibility of incurring loss. In this sense it would be a financial loss.

**sales revenue** total amount of money taken for sale of products or services

**sampling** the method used to select the people you will talk to while conducting market research

**secondary industries** take materials and produce finished or semi-finished goods. They include manufacturing industries such as brewing and steel making and the construction industry.

**secondary research** is data that is already available in published form. It includes government statistics, industry surveys, reports by pressure groups and press articles as well as the firm's own records which will provide useful information about the market.

**share capital** the value of all the shares that have been issued by the business

**shareholders** the legal owners of a limited liability company (Ltd or plc). They all enjoy limited liability and usually have voting rights.

**skills shortage** where skills required for a job are in short supply in local area

**skimming** involves initially setting a high price for a new, innovative product to 'skim' the market and recoup development costs. However, as rivals firms develop their own products, the price will then tend to fall.

**SMART** stands for specific, measurable, attainable (agreed), realistic and timed

**socio-economic** group a way of categorising consumers by their occupation and income

**sole proprietor** a business owned by only one person

**span of control** describes the number of subordinates (workers) that a manager has direct control over

**stakeholders** are individuals or groups who have an interest in a business or who are affected by its activities. Stakeholders may be *internal* such as employees and managers or *external* such as local residents.

**standing order** a customer mandate stating that the bank pays a person/ business the same amount of money on set dates

**star** according to the Boston Matrix, a product or brand which has a high market share in a high growth market, e.g. iPod

**SWOT analysis** a useful business tool for analysing how well a product, brand or company is performing in its market. SWOT stands for strengths, weaknesses, opportunities and threats.

**takeover** this occurs when one business gains control of another. Buying over 50% of the ordinary shares in a business gives effective control over it.

**target audience** those people you think will buy your product or service

**tertiary industry** is the service sector of the economy and includes businesses such as banks, retailers, advertising agencies and transport companies

**unique selling point (USP)** some unique or special feature that distinguishes one product or brand from the competition

**unlimited liability** a legal concept which means that the owner of the business is personally liable for the debts of the business. This is a significant drawback of operating as a sole trader or partnership.

**venture capitalists** people who lend money to a business and are prepared to take a higher risk than the bank. The loan will usually carry higher interest charges and the investor may want a share of the business.

**virus** a program that invades programs or disks and causes severe disruption to them

**waste** material to be disposed of

**workers' co-operative** a business which is owned and managed by the workers

**working capital** current assets – current liabilities represents the liquidity of the business

**worm** information that can be written to a disk but cannot be erased

# Index